Saint Athanasius

Select treatises of St. Athanasius in controversy with the Arians

Saint Athanasius

Select treatises of St. Athanasius in controversy with the Arians

ISBN/EAN: 9783337276218

Printed in Europe, USA, Canada, Australia, Japan

Cover: Foto ©Andreas Hilbeck / pixelio.de

More available books at **www.hansebooks.com**

SELECT TREATISES

OF

ST. ATHANASIUS

IN CONTROVERSY WITH THE ARIANS.

FREELY TRANSLATED

BY

JOHN HENRY CARDINAL NEWMAN.

VOL. II.

BEING AN APPENDIX OF ILLUSTRATIONS.

SECOND EDITION.

London:

PICKERING AND CO.

1881.

APPENDIX.

INDEX OF ANNOTATIONS ALPHABETICALLY ARRANGED.

A 2

NOTE.

THE words from Boethius (infr. p. 325), there translated "in Him which They are," are in the original, (p. 273 Ed. Lugd. and p. 1122 Ed. Basil.) "in eo quod ipsæ sunt," that is, rather, "in That which They are."

ANNOTATIONS

ILLUSTRATIVE OF THE FOREGOING TREATISES

ALPHABETICALLY ARRANGED.

ANNOTATIONS

ADAM.

THOUGH the Fathers, in accordance with Scripture, hold that Adam was created sinless, they also hold that he could not have persevered in his state of innocence and uprightness without a special grace, which he lost upon his fall, and which is regained for us, (and that in far greater measure,) by our Lord's sufferings and merits.

¶ The Catholic doctrine is, that Adam innocent was mortal, yet in fact would not have died; that he had no principle of eternal life within his body naturally, but was sustained continually by divine power till such time as immortality should have been given him. Vid. Incarn. 4. "If God accorded to the garments and shoes of the Israelites," says S. Augustine, "that they should not wear out during so many years, how is it strange that to man obedient by His power should be accorded, that, whereas his body was animal and mortal, it was so constituted as to become aged without decay, and at such time as God willed might pass without the intervention of death from mortality to immortality? For as the flesh itself, which we now bear, is not therefore invulnerable, because it may be preserved from wounding, so Adam's was not therefore not mortal, because he was not bound to die. Such a habit even of their present animal and mortal body I suppose was granted also to them who have been translated hence without death; for Enoch and Elias too have through so long a time been preserved from the decay of age." De Pecc. Mer. i. 3. Adam's body, he says elsewhere, was "mortale quia poterat mori, immortale quia poterat non mori;" and he goes on to say that immortality was given him "de ligno vitæ, non de constitutione naturæ." Gen. ad Lit. vi. 36. This doctrine came into the controversy with Baius, and Pope S. Pius V. condemned the assertion, "Immortalitas primi hominis non erat gratiæ beneficium, sed naturalis conditio."

Then, as to his soul, S. Augustine says, "An aid was [given to the first Adam], but a more powerful grace is given to the Second. The first is that by which a man has justice if he will; the second does more, for by it he also wills, and wills so strongly, and loves so ardently, as to overcome the will of the flesh lusting contrariwise to the will of the spirit," &c. De Corr. et Grat. 31. And S. Cyril, "Our forefather Adam seems to have gained wisdom, not in time, as we, but appears perfect in understanding from the very first moment of his formation, preserving in himself the illumination, given him by nature from God, as yet untroubled and pure, and leaving the dignity of his nature unpractised on," &c. In Joan. p. 75.

ALEXANDER'S ENCYCLICAL.

Vid. supr. vol. i. p. 1, *Prefatory Notice.*

I HERE set down the internal evidence in favour of this Letter having been written by Athanasius.

A long letter on Arius and his tenets, addressed by Alexander to his namesake at Constantinople, has been preserved for us by Theodoret, and we can compare the Encyclical on the one hand with this Letter, and with the acknowledged writings of Athanasius on the other, and thereby determine for ourselves whether the Encyclical does not resemble in style what Athanasius has written, and is not unlike the style of Theodoret's Alexander. Athanasius is a great writer, simple in his diction, clear, unstudied, direct, vigorous, elastic, and above all characteristic ; but Alexander writes with an effort, and is elaborate and exquisite in his vocabulary and structure of sentences.

Thus, the Encyclical before us, after S. Athanasius's manner in treating of sacred subjects, has hardly one scientific term ; its words, when not Arius's own, are for the most part from Scripture, such as λόγος, σοφία, μονογενὴς, εἰκών, ἀπαύγασμα, just as they are found in Athanasius's controversial Treatises ; whereas, in Alexander's letter in Theodoret, phrases are found, certainly not from Scripture, perhaps of Alexandrian theology, perhaps peculiar to the writer, for instance, ἀχώριστα πράγματα δύο· ὁ υἱὸς τὴν κατὰ πάντα ὁμοιότητα αὐτοῦ ἐκ φύσεως ἀπομαξόμενος· δι' ἐσόπτρου ἀκηλιδώτου καὶ ἐμψύχου θείας εἰκόνος· μεσιτεύουσα φύσις μονογενής· τὰς τῇ ὑποστάσει δύο φύσεις. And, instead of the οὐσία of the Father, of the Son, of the Word, which is one of the few, as well as familiar, scientific terms of Athanasius (Orat. i. § 45, ii. 7, 9, 11, 12, 13, 18, 22, 47, 56), and which the Encyclical uses too, we read in the Letter of Alexander, preserved by Theodoret, ὑπόστασις, and that again and again ; e.g., τὴν ἰδιότροπον αὐτοῦ ὑπόστασιν· τῆς ὑποστάσεως αὐτοῦ ἀπεριεργαστοῦ· νεωτέραν τῆς ὑποστάσεως γένεσιν· ἡ τοῦ μονογενοῦς ἀνεκδιήγητος ὑπόστασις· τὴν τοῦ λόγου ὑπόστασιν, phrases quite out of keeping with the style of the Encyclical. Nor is it only in the expression of theological ideas that the style of the Letter in Theodoret differs from the style of the Encyclical ; thus, when the latter speaks of φθορέας τῶν ψυχῶν, the former uses the compound φθοροποιός. Such, too, are ἡ φίλαρχος καὶ φιλάργυρος πρόθεσις· χριστεμπορίαν· φρενοβλαβοῦς· ἰδιότροπον· ὁμοστοίχοις συλλαβαῖς· θεηγόρους ἀποστόλους· ἀντιδιαστολὴν· τῆς πατρικῆς μαιεύσεως· φιλόθεος σαφήνεια· ἀνοσιουργίας· φληνάφων μύθων. It is very difficult to suppose that the same man wrote this Letter to the Bishop of Constantinople and the Encyclical which is the subject of this note.

On the other hand, that Athanasius wrote the latter becomes almost certain when, in addition to what has been observed above, in the Prefatory Notice, the following coincidence of words and phrases is considered, on comparing the Encyclical with Athanasius's acknowledged writings:—

Encyclical, ap Socr. Hist. i. § 6. (Oxf. Ed. 1844.)	Athan. Opp. (Ed. Benedict. Paris.)
1. p. 6, l. 2, *ἐξῆλθον*, 1 John ii. 19.	1. *αἵρεσις νῦν ἐξελθοῦσα*, Orat. i. § 1.
2. *ibid. ἄνδρες παράνομοι.*	2. *παράνομοι*, &c. Orat. iii. § 2; Ep. Æg. 16; Hist. Ar. 71, 75, 79.
3. *ibid.* l. 4, *ἐξῆλθον διδάσκοντες ἀποστασίαν,πρόδρομον τοῦ 'Αντιχρίστου.*	3. *νῦν ἐξελθοῦσα, πρόδρομος τοῦ 'Αντιχρίστου*, Orat. i. § 7.
4. *ibid. καὶ ἐβουλόμην μὲν σιωπῇ . . . ἐπειδὴ δὲ*, &c.	4. This form of apology, introductory to the treatment of a subject, is usual with Athan., e.g. Orat. i. § 23, *init.*, ii. 1, *init.*, iii. 1, *init.*; Apol. c. Ar. 1, *init.*; Decr. § 5; Serap. i. 1 and 16, ii. 1, *init.*, iii. 1, *init.*, iv. 8; Mon. 2; Epict. 3 fin.; Max. 1; Apoll. i. 1, *init.*
5. *ibid.* l. 6, *ῥυπώσῃ.*	5. Orat. i. § 10; Decr. § 2; Hist. Ar. 3; Ep. Æg. 11.
6. *ibid. τὰς ἀκοάς.*	6. Orat. i. § 7 and 35; Hist. Ar. 56; Ep. Æg. 13.
7. *ibid. ἀκεραίων.*	7. Orat. i. § 8, ii. 34, iii. 16; Syn. § 20, 32, and 45; Ap. c. Ar. 1; Ep. Æg. 18; Epict. 1; Adelph. 2.
8. *ibid.* l. 14, *ῥημάτια.*	8. Orat. i. § 10; Decr. § 8 and 18; Sent. Dion. 23.
9. *ibid.* l.15, *κακόνοιαν.*	9. Decr. § 1; Hist. Ar. § 75.
10. *ibid.* l. 22, &c. The enumeration of Arius's tenets	10. runs with Orat. i. § 5; Decr. § 6; Ep. Æg. 12, more closely than with the Letter to Constantinople.
11. p. 7, l. 1, *ἀναισχυντοῦντες.*	11. Decr. § 20.
12. *ibid.* l. 7, *τίς γὰρ ἤκουσε*, &c.	12. Vid. similar form in Orat. i. § 8; Ep. Æg. 7; Epict. 2; Ap. c. Ar. 85; Hist. Ar. 46, 73, 74, &c.
13. *ibid.* l. 8, *ξενίζεται.*	13. Orat. i. § 35 and 42, ii. 34, 73, and 80, iii. 30, 48; Decr. § 22.

Encyclical, ap. Socr. Hist. i. § 6. (Oxf. Ed. 1844.)	Athan. Opp. (Ed. Benedict. Paris.)
14. p. 8, l. 27. The apology here made for the use of Mal. iii. 6, is	14. almost *verbatim* with that found in Orat. i. § 36.
15. p. 8, l. 12. The text 1 Tim. iv. 1 in this place, is	15. applied to Arians by Athan. also Orat. i. § 8. By whom besides?

ANGELS.

ANGELS were actually worshipped, in the proper sense
of the word, by Gnostics and other heretics, who even
ascribed to them a creative power; and certainly, to
consider them the source of any good to man, and
the acceptable channel intrinsically of approaching
God, in derogation of our Lord's sole mediation, is
idolatry. However, their presence in and about the
Church, and with all of us individually, is an inestim-
able blessing, never to be slighted or forgotten; for, as
by our prayers and our kind deeds we can serve each
other, so Angels, but in a far higher way, serve us, and
are channels of grace to us, as the Sacraments are. All
this would doubtless have been maintained by Athanasius had there been occasion for saying it. For
instance, in commenting on Psalm 49, *Deus Deorum*,
he says so in substance :—

" 'He shall summon the heaven from above.' When
the Saviour manifested Himself, He kindled in us the
light of true religious knowledge; He converted that
which had wandered; He bound up that which was
ailing; as being the Good Shepherd, He chased away
the wild beasts from the sheepfold; He gave His people
sanctification of the Spirit, and the protection of Angelic
Powers, and He set those over them through the whole
world who should be holy mystagogues. 'He will

summon,' He says, 'the Angels who are in heaven and
the men on earth chosen for the Apostolate, to judge
His people.' . . . That with those mystagogues and their
disciples Angels co-operate, Paul makes clear when he
says, Heb. i. 14," &c., &c.

¶ If it be asked why, such being his substantial teaching, his language in particular passages of his Orations
tends to discourage such *cultus Angelorum* as the Church
has since his time sanctioned, I answer first that he is
led by his subject to contrast the Angelic creation with
our Lord the Creator; and thus, while extolling Him as
Supreme, he comes to speak with disparagement of
those who were no more than works of His hands. And
secondly, the idolatrous honour paid to Angels by the
heretical bodies at that time made unadvisable, or
created a prepossession against, what in itself was
allowable. Moreover, the Church, as divinely guided,
has not formulated her doctrines all at once, but has
taken in hand, first one, and then another. As to S.
Athanasius, if he seemingly disparages the Angels, it
is in order to exalt our Lord. He is arguing against
the Arians somewhat in this manner : " You yourselves
allow that the Son is the Creator, and, as such, the
object of worship ; but, if He be the Creator, how can
He be a creature? how can He be only a higher kind
of Angel, if it was He who created Angels? If so, He
must have created Himself. Why, it is the very
enormity of the Gnostics, that they ascribe creative
power and pay divine honours to Angels; now are you
not as bad as they ? " Athanasius does not touch the
question whether, as Angels and Saints according to

him are (*improprie*) gods, (vid. next paragraph), so in a corresponding sense worship may (*improprie*) be paid to them.

¶ "The sacred writer, with us in view, says, 'O God, who is like unto Thee?' and though he calls those creatures who are partakers (μετόχους) of the Word gods, still those who partake are not the same as, or like, Him who is partaken. For works are made, and make nothing," ad Afros 7. "Not one of things which come-to-be is an efficient cause," ποιητικὸν αἴτιον, Orat. ii. § 21; *ibid.* § 2, iii. 14, and contr. Gent. 9 init. "Our reason rejects the idea that the Creator should be a creature, for creation is by the Creator." Hil. Trin. xii. 5. πῶς δύναται τὸ κτιζόμενον κτίζειν; ἢ πῶς ὁ κτίζων κτίζεται; Athan. ad Afros, 4 fin. Vid. also Serap. i. 24, 6, iii. 4.

¶ As to Angels, vid. August. de Civ. Dei xii. 24; de Trin. iii. 13—18; Damasc. F. O. ii. 3; Cyril in Julian. ii. p. 62. "For neither would the Angels," says Athan., Orat. ii. § 21, "since they too are creatures, be able to frame, though Valentinus, and Marcion, and Basilides think so, and you are their copyists; nor will the sun, as being a creature, ever make what is not into what is; nor will man fashion man, nor stone devise stone, nor wood give growth to wood." The Gnostics who attributed creation to Angels are alluded to in Orat. iii. 12; Epiph. Hær. 52, 53, 62, &c.; Theodor. Hær. i. 1 and 3. They considered the Angels consubstantial with our Lord, as the Manichees after them, seemingly from holding the doctrine of emanation. Vid. Bull. D. F. N. ii. 1, § 2, and

Beausobre, Manich. iii. 8. "If, from S. Paul saying
better than the Angels, they should therefore insist
that his language is that of comparison, and that
comparison in consequence implies oneness of kind, so
that the Son is of the nature of Angels, they will in the
first place incur the disgrace of rivalling and repeat-
ing what Valentinus held, and Carpocrates, and those
other heretics, of whom the former said that the Angels
were one in kind with the Christ, and Carpocrates that
Angels are framers of the world." Orat. i. § 56.

¶ As to the sins incident to created natures, all
creatures, says Athanasius, depend for their abidance
in good upon the Word, and without Him have no
stay. Thus, ad Afros 7, after, as in Orat. i. § 49,
speaking of ἀγγέλων μὲν παραβάντων, τοῦ δὲ Ἀδὰμ
παρακούσαντος, he says, "no one would deny that
things which are made are open to change (Cyril. in
Joan. v. 2), and since the Angels and Adam trans-
gressed, and all showed their need of the grace of the
Word, what is thus mutable cannot be like to the immutable God, nor the creature to the Creator." On the
subject of the sins of Angels, vid. Huet. Origen. ii. 5;
Petav. Dogm. t. iii. p. 73; Dissert. Bened. in Cyr.
Hier. iii. 5; Nat. Alex. Hist. Æv. i. Dissert. 7.

¶ So far Athanasius says nothing which the Church
has not taught up to this day; but he goes further.

"No one," he says, Orat. iii. § 12, "would pray
to receive aught from 'God and the Angels,' or from
any other creature, nor would he say 'May God and
the Angel give thee.'" Vid. Basil de Sp. S. c. 13
(t. ii. p. 585). "There were men," says Chrysostom

on Col. ii., "who said, We ought not to have access
to God through Christ, but through Angels, for the
former is beyond our power. Hence the Apostle
everywhere insists on his teaching concerning Christ,
'through the blood of the Cross,'" &c. And Theodoret on Col. iii. 17, says: "Following this rule, the
Synod of Laodicea, with a view to cure this ancient
disorder, passed a decree against the praying to
Angels, and leaving our Lord Jesus Christ." "All
supplication, prayer, intercession, and thanksgiving
is to be addressed to the Supreme God, through the
High Priest who is above all Angels, the Living Word
and God. . . . But Angels we may not fitly call upon,
since we have not obtained a knowledge of them more
than human." Origen contr. Cels. v. 4, 5. Vid. also
for similar statements Voss. de Idolatr. i. 9. These
extracts are here made in illustration of the particular
passage of Athan. to which they are appended, not as if
they contain the whole doctrine of Origen, Theodoret,
or S. Chrysostom, on the *cultus Angelorum*. Of course
they are not inconsistent with such texts as 1 Tim. v. 21.

¶ Elsewhere Athan. says that "the Angel who delivered Jacob from all evil," from whom he asked a
blessing, was not a created Angel, but the Angel of
great Counsel, the Word of God Himself, Orat. iii. § 12 ;
but he says shortly afterwards that the Angel that
appeared to Moses in the Bush "was not the God of
Abraham, but what was seen was an Angel, and in the
Angel God spoke," § 14 ; vid. Bened. edit. Monitum in
Hilar. Trin. lib. iv. Thus Athan. does not differ from
Augustine, as noted infr. Art. *Scripture Passages*, No. i.

¶ As to the word " worship," as denoting the *cultus Angelorum*, worship is a very wide term, and has obviously more senses than one. Thus we read in one passage of Scripture that "all the congregation . . . worshipped the Lord, and *the king*" [David]. S. Augustine, as S. Athanasius, Orat. ii. § 23, makes the characteristic of divine worship to consist in sacrifice. " No one would venture to say that sacrifice was due to any but God. Many are the things taken from divine worship and transferred to human honours, either through excessive humility, or mischievous adulation ; yet without giving us the notion that those to whom they were transferred were not men. And these are said to be honoured and venerated ; or were worshipped, if much is heaped upon them ; but who ever thought that sacrifice was to be offered, except to Him whom the sacrificer knew or thought or pretended to be God ? " August. de Civ. Dei, x. 4. " Whereas you have called so many dead men gods, why are ye indignant with us, who do but honour, not deify the martyrs, as being God's martyrs and loving servants ? . . . That they even offered libations to the dead, ye certainly know, who venture on the use of them by night contrary to the laws. . . . But we, O men, assign neither sacrifices nor even libations to the martyrs, but we honour them as men divine and divinely beloved." Theodor. contr. Gent. viii. pp. 908—910. It is observable that incense was burnt before the Imperial Statues, vid. art. *Imperial Titles*. Nebuchadnezzar offered an oblation to Daniel, after the interpretation of his dream.

ANTICHRIST.   13

ANTICHRIST.

As the early Christians, in obedience to our Lord's
words, were ever looking out for His second coming,
and for the signs of it, they associated it with every
prominent disturbance, external or internal, which
interfered with the peace of the Church; with every
successive persecution, heretical outbreak, or schism
which befell it.   In this, too, they were only following
the guidance of our Lord and His Apostles, who told
them that "great tribulation," "false prophets," dis-
union, and "apostasy," and at length "Antichrist,"
should be His forerunners.   Also, they recollected
S. John's words, "Omnis Spiritus qui solvit Jesum,
ex Deo non est, et hic est Antichristus de quo audistis,
quoniam venit," &c.   Hence "forerunner of Antichrist"
was the received epithet employed by them to designate
the successive calamities and threatenings of evil, which
one after another spread over the face of the *orbis
terrarum.*

¶ Thus we have found S. Athanasius calling Arianism
"the forerunner of Antichrist," Syn. § 5, πρόδρομος,
præcursor; vid. also Orat. i. §§ 1 and 7; Ap. c. Ar. fin.;
Hist. Ar. 77; Cyr. Cat. xv. 9; Basil. Ep. 264; Hilar.
Aux. 5, no distinction being carefully drawn between
the apostasy and the Antichrist.   Constantius is called
Antichrist by Athan. Hist. Arian. 67; his acts are the
προοίμιον καὶ παρασκευὴ of Antichrist, Hist. Arian. 70,

fin., 71 and 80. Constantius is the image, εἰκὼν, of
Antichrist, 74 and 80, and shows the likeness, ὁμοίωμα,
of the malignity of Antichrist, 75. Vid. also 77.
"Let Christ be expected, for Antichrist is in possession." Hilar. contr. Const. init., also 5. Speaking of
Auxentius, the Arian Bishop of Milan, he says, "Of
one thing I warn you, beware of Antichrist; it is ill
that . . . your veneration for God's Church lies in
houses and edifices. . . . Is there any doubt that Antichrist is to sit in these? Mountains, and woods, and
lakes, and prisons, and pits are to me more safe," &c.
Contr. Auxent. 12. Lucifer calls Constantius "præcursor
Antichristi," p. 89; possessed with the spirit of Antichrist,
p. 219; friend of Antichrist, p. 259. Vid. also Basil, Ep.
264. Again, S. Jerome, writing against Jovinian,
says that he who teaches that there are no differences
of rewards is Antichrist, ii. 21. S. Leo, alluding to
1 John iv. 10, calls Nestorius and Eutyches, "Antichristi
præcursores," Ep. 75, p. 1022; again, Antichrist is who-
ever withstood what the Church has once settled, with
an allusion to opposition to the see of S. Peter, Ep.
156, c. 2. Anastasius speaks of the ten horns of Mo-
nophysitism, Hodeg. 8 and 24; and calls Severus
Antichrist, for usurping the judicial powers of the
Church, ibid. p. 92. Vid. also Greg. I. Ep. vii. 33.

¶ The great passage of S. Paul about the ἀποστασία,
1 Tim. iv. 1, 2, is taken to apply to the Arians in Orat.
i. § 8, cf. ad Ægypt. § 20, 21; but the Fathers more
commonly refer it to the Oriental sects of the early
centuries, who fulfilled one or other of those conditions which it specifies. It is predicated of the

Marcionists by Clement, Strom. iii. 6. Of the Valentinians, Epiph. Hær. 31. 34. Of the Montanists and others, ibid. 48. 8. Of the Saturnilians (according to Huet), Origen in Matt. xiv. 16. Of apostolic heretics, Cyril. Cat. iv. 27. Of Marcionites, Valentinians, and Manichees, Chrysost. de Virg. 5. Of Gnostics and Manichees, Theod. Hær. ii. præf. Of Encratites, ibid. v. fin. Of Eutyches, Ep. Anon. 190 (apud Garner. Diss. v. Theod. p. 901). Pseudo-Justin seems to consider it fulfilled in the Catholics of the fifth century, as being Anti-pelagians. Quæst. 22; vid. Bened. note in loc. Besides Athanasius, no early author by whom it is referred to the Arians, occurs to the writer of this, except S. Alexander's Letter ap. Socr. i. 6; and, if he may hazard the conjecture, there is much in that letter like Athan.'s own writing. Vid. supr. art. *Alexander*.

APOSTLE.

"THE Apostle" is the usual title of S. Paul in antiquity, as "the Philosopher" at a later date is appropriated to Aristotle. " When 'the Apostle' is mentioned," says S. Augustine, " if it is not specified which, Paul only is understood, because he is more celebrated from the number of his Epistles, and laboured more abundantly than all the rest," ad Bonifac. iii. 3. E.g. "And this is what *Peter* has said, ' that ye may be partakers in a divine nature ; ' as says also *the Apostle*, ' know ye not that ye are the Temple of God,' " &c. Orat. i. § 16. Vid. also Eno. supr. vol. i. p. 7 (t. i. p. 315, ed Ben. § 3); Decr. §§ 15 and 17. "The Apostle himself, the Doctor of the Gentiles," Syn. § 28 and 39. " John saying and the Apostle," Orat. i. § 47.

However, S. Peter also is called the Apostle, Orat. i. § 47.

ARIUS.

It is very difficult to gain a clear idea of the character of Arius. Athanasius speaks as if his theological song, or Thalia, was but a token of his personal laxity; and certainly the mere fact of his having written it seems incompatible with any remarkable seriousness and strictness. "He drew up his heresy on paper," Athan. says, "and imitating, as if on a festive occasion (ὡς ἐν θαλίᾳ) no grave writer, but the Egyptian Sotades, in the character of his music, he writes at great length," &c. De Syn. § 15 (*Arim. n.* 19). Again, Orat. i. §§ 2—5 (*Disc. n.* 2—5), he calls him the Sotadean Arius; and speaks of the " dissolute manners," and " the effeminate tone," and the "jests" of the Thalia; a poem which, he says shortly before, " is not even found among the more respectable Greeks, but among those only who sing songs over their wine, with noise and revel." Vid. also de Sent. D. 6. Constantine also, after the Ἄρες Ἄρειε, proceeds, ἐπισχέτω δέ σε ἡ γοῦν Ἀφροδίτης ὁμιλία. Epiph. Hær. 69. 9 fin. Socrates too says that "the character of the book was gross and dissolute." Hist. i. 9. The Arian Philostorgius tells us that "Arius wrote songs for the sea, and for the mill, and for the road, and set them to suitable music," Hist. ii. 2. It is remarkable that Athanasius should say the *Egyptian* Sotades, as again in Sent. D. 6. There were two Poets of the

name; one a writer of the Middle Comedy, Athen.
Deipn. vii. 11; but the other, who is here spoken of,
was a native of Maronea in Crete, according to Suidas
(in voc.), under the successors of Alexander, Athen.
xiv. 4. He wrote in Ionic metre, which was of infamous
name from the subjects to which he and others applied
it. Vid. Suid. ibid. Some read " Sotadicos " for "So-
craticos," Juv. Satir. ii. 10. Vid. also Martial,
Ep. ii. 86. The characteristic of the metre was the
recurrence of the same cadence, which virtually
destroyed the division into verses, Turneb. in Quinct.
i. 8, and thus gave the composition that lax and
slovenly air to which Athanasius alludes. Horace's
Ode, " Miserarum est neque amori," &c., is a specimen of
this metre, and some have called it Sotadic; but Bentley
shows in loc. that Sotades wrote in the Ionic à majore,
and that his verse had somewhat more of system than
is found in the Ode of Horace. Athenæus implies that
all Ionic metres were called Sotadic, or that Sotades
wrote in various Ionic metres. The Church adopted
the Doric music, and forbade the Ionic and Lydian.
The name " Thalia " commonly belonged to convivial
songs; Martial contrasts the " lasciva Thalia " with
" carmina sanctiora," Epigr. vii. 17. Vid. Thaliarchus,
" the master of the feast," Horat. Od. i. 9. This would
be the more offensive among Christians in Athan.'s day,
in proportion to the keener sensibilities of the South,
and the more definite ideas which music seems to have
conveyed to their minds; and more especially in a case
where the metre Arius employed had obtained so
shocking a reputation, and was associated in the minds

of Christians with the deeds of darkness, in the midst
of which in those heathen times the Church lived and
bore her witness.

Such is Athan.'s report, but Constantine and Epiphanius speak of Arius in very different terms, yet each in
his own way, as the following extracts show. It is possible that Constantine is only declaiming, for his whole
invective is like a school exercise or fancy composition.
Constantine too had not seen Arius at the time of this
invective, which was prior to the Nicene Council, and
his account of him is inconsistent with itself, for he
also uses the very strong and broad language about
Arius quoted above. "Look then," he says, "look all
men, what words of lament he is now professing, being
held with the bite of the serpent; how his veins and
flesh are possessed with poison, and are in a ferment of
severe pain; how his whole body is wasted, and is all
withered and sad and pale and shaking, and fearfully
emaciated. How hateful to see, how filthy is his mass
of hair, how he is half dead all over, with failing eyes,
and bloodless countenance, and woe-begone! so that
all these things combining in him at once, frenzy,
madness, and folly, for the continuance of the complaint, have made thee wild and savage. But not
having any sense what bad plight he is in, he cries
out, 'I am transported with delight, and I leap and
skip for joy, and I fly:' and again, with boyish im-
petuosity, 'Be it so,' he says, 'we are lost.'" Harduin.
Conc. t. i. p. 457. Perhaps this strange account may
be taken to illustrate the words "mania" and "Ariomaniacs." S. Alexander too speaks of Arius's melan-

c 2

cholic temperament, μελαγχολικοῖς ἡρμοσμένης δόξης
κενῆς. Theod. Hist. i. 3, p. 741. S. Basil also speaks
of the Eunomians as εἰς λαμπρὰν μελαγχολίαν παρε-
νεχθέντας. Contr. Eun. ii. 24. Elsewhere he speaks of
the Pneumatomachists as worse than μελαγχολῶντες.
De Sp. S. 41.

Epiphanius's account of Arius is as follows:—"From
elation of mind the old man swerved from the mark.
He was in stature very tall, downcast in visage, with
manners like a wily serpent, captivating to every guileless
heart by that same crafty bearing. For ever habited
in cloak and vest, he was pleasant of address, ever
persuading souls and flattering; wherefore what was
his very first work but to withdraw from the Church in
one body as many as seven hundred women who professed virginity?" Hær. 69. 3. Arius is here said to
have been tall; Athanasius, on the other hand, would
appear to have been short, if we may so interpret
Julian's indignant description of him, μηδὲ ἀνὴρ, ἀλλ'
ἀνθρωπίσκος εὐτελὴς, "not even a man, but a common
little fellow." Ep. 51. Yet S. Gregory Nazianzen
speaks of him as "high in prowess and humble in
spirit, mild, meek, full of sympathy, pleasant in speech,
more pleasant in manners, *angelical in person*, more
angelical in mind, serene in his rebukes, instructive in
his praises," &c. &c. Orat. 21. 9. There is no proof
that S. Gregory had ever seen him.

THE ARIANS.

1. *Their Ethical Characteristics.*

WHEN we consider how grave and reverent was the temper of the Ante-Nicene Church, how it concealed its sacred mysteries from the world at large, how writers such as Tertullian make the absence of such a strict discipline the very mark of heresy, and that a vulgar ostentation and profaneness was the prominent charge brought against the heretic Paul of Samosata, Bishop of Antioch, we need not a more ready evidence or note against the Arian party than our finding that the ethical character, which is in history so intimately associated with Paul and the heretics generally of the first three centuries, is the badge of Arianism also.

1. Athan. in various passages of his Theological Treatises refers to it, and it is one of the reasons why he speaks so familiarly of their " madness." " What pressed on us so much," he says of the Councils of Seleucia and Ariminum, "was that the whole world should be thrown into confusion, and those who then bore the profession of ecclesiastics should run about far and near, seeking forsooth how best to learn to believe in our Lord Jesus Christ. Certainly, if they were believers already, they would not have been seeking, as though they were not. And to the catechumens, this was no small scandal; but to the heathen, it was

something more than common, and even furnished
broad merriment, that Christians, as if waking out of
sleep at this time of day, should be making out how
they were to believe concerning Christ, while their
professed clergy, though claiming deference from their
flocks, as teachers, were unbelievers on their own showing, in that they were seeking what they had not."
Syn. § 2.

The heathen Ammianus supports this complaint in
the well-known passage which tells of "the troops of
Bishops hurrying to and fro at the public expense,"
and "the Synods, in their efforts to bring over the
religion everywhere to their side, being the ruin of the
posting establishments." Hist. xxi. 16. Again, "The
spectacle proceeded to that pitch of indecency," says
Eusebius, "that at length, in the very midst of the
theatres of the unbelievers, the solemn matters of
divine teaching were subjected to the basest mockery."
In Vit. Const. ii. 61.

Also Athan., after speaking of the Arian tenet that
our Lord was once on His trial and might have fallen,
says, "This is what they do not shrink from conversing
about in full market." Orat. i. § 37. And again, "When
they commenced this heresy, they used to go about with
dishonest crafty phrases which they had got together;
nay, up to this time some of them, when they fall in
with boys in the market-place, question them, not out
of divine Scripture, but thus, as if bursting out with
the abundance of their heart:—'He who is, did He,
from Him who is, make him who was not, or him who
was?'" Orat. i. § 22.

Alexander speaks of the interference, even by legal process, in its behalf against himself, of disobedient women, δι' ἐντυχίας γυναικαρίων ἀτάκτων ἃ ἠπάτησαν, and of the busy and indecent gadding about of the younger, ἐκ τοῦ περιτροχάζειν πᾶσαν ἀγυιὰν ἀσμένως. Ap. Theod. Hist. i. 3, p. 730 ; also p. 747; also of the men's buffoon conversation, p. 731. Socrates says that "in the Imperial Court the officers of the bedchamber held disputes with the women, and in the city in every house there was a war of dialectics." Hist. ii. 2. This mania raged especially in Constantinople ; and S. Gregory Nazienzen speaks of these women as "Jezebels in as thick a crop as hemlock in a field." Orat. 35. 3. He speaks of the heretics as "aiming at one thing only, how to make good or refute points of argument," making "every market-place resound with their words, and spoiling every entertainment with their trifling and offensive talk." Orat. 27. 2. The most remarkable testimony of the kind, though not concerning Constantinople, is given by S. Gregory Nyssen, and often quoted, "Men of yesterday and the day before, mere mechanics, off-hand dogmatists in theology, servants too and slaves that have been flogged, runaways from servile work, are solemn with us and philosophical about things incomprehensible. . . . With such the whole city is full; its smaller gates, forums, squares, thoroughfares; the clothes-venders, the money-lenders, the victuallers. Ask about pence, and he will discuss the Generate and Ingenerate ; inquire the price of bread, he answers, Greater is the Father, and the Son is subject; say that a bath would suit you, and he

defines that the Son is out of nothing." t. 2, p. 898.
(de Deitate Fil. &c.)

Arius set the example of all this in his Thalia;
Leontius, Eudoxius, and Aetius, in various ways, followed
it faithfully.

2. Another characteristic of the Arian party was
their changeableness, insincerity, and want of principle (vid. *Chameleons*). This was owing to their fear
of the Emperor and of the Christian populations, which
hindered them speaking out; also, to the difficulty of
keeping their body together in opinion, and the necessity they were in to deceive one party and to please
another, if they were to maintain their hold upon the
Church. Athanasius observes on their reluctance to
speak out, challenging them to present "the heresy
naked," de Sent. Dionys. 2, *init.* "No one," he says
elsewhere, "puts a light under a bushel; let them show
the world their heresy naked." Ad Ep. Æg. 18. Vid.
ibid. 10. In like manner, Basil says that though
Arius was, in faith, really like Eunomius (contr. Eunom.
i. 4), Aetius his master was the first to teach openly
(φανερῶς) that the Father's substance was unlike,
ἀνόμοιος, the Son's. Ibid. i. 1. Epiphanius too, Hær.
76, p. 949, seems to say that the elder Arians held
the divine generation in a sense in which Aetius did
not; that is, they were not boldly consistent and definite
as he was. Athan. de Decret. § 7, enumerates some of
the attempts of the Arians to find some theory short of
orthodoxy, yet short of that extreme heresy, on the
other hand, which they felt ashamed to avow.

The Treatise *De Synodis*, above translated, supplies

abundant proof of their artifices and shuffling. (Vid. art. *Hypocrites.*)

3. Cruelty, as in the instance of George of Cappadocia and Macedonius of Constantinople, is another charge which falls heavily on both Arians and Semi-Arians.

"In no long time," Athan. says, anticipating their known practice, de Decret. § 2, "they will be turning to outrage." As to the Council of Tyre, A.D. 335, he asks, Apol. contr. Arian. § 8, "How venture they to call that a Council in which a Count presided, and an executioner was present, and a registrar [or jailer] introduced us instead of the deacons of the Church?" Vid. also § 10 and 45; Orat. ii. § 43; Ep. Encycl. § 5. Against employing violence in religious matters, vid. Hist. Arian. § 33, 67. (Hil. ad Const. i. 2.) On the other hand, he observes, that at Nicæa, "it was not necessity which drove the judges to" their decision, " but all vindicated the Truth from deliberate purpose." Ad Ep. Æg. 13.

4. They who did not scruple to use force were consistent in their use of bribes also. S. Athanasius speaks of them as δωρόδοκοι, and of the κέρδος τῆς φιλοχρηματίας which influenced them, and of the προστασίας φίλων. Orat. i. §§ 8, 10, and 53; also ii. § 43.

And so S. Hilary speaks of the exemptions from taxes which Constantius granted the Clergy as a bribe to Arianize: " You concede taxes as Cæsar, thereby to invite Christians to a denial; you remit what is your own, that we may lose what is God's," contr. Const. 10. Again, he speaks of Constantius as " hostem blandientem, qui non dorsa cædit, sed ventrem palpat, non proscribit ad vitam, sed ditat in mortem, non caput gladio desecat, sed animam auro occidit." Ibid. 5. Vid. Coustant. in loc. Liberius says the same, Theod. Hist. ii. 13. And S. Gregory Naz. speaks of φιλο-χρύσους μᾶλλον ἢ φιλοχρίστους. Orat. 21. 21. It is true that, Ep. Æg. 22, Athan. contrasts the Arians with the Meletians in this respect, as if, unlike the latter, the Arians were not influenced by secular views. But there were, as was natural, two classes of men in the heretical party;—the fanatical class who began the heresy and were its real life, such as Arius, and afterwards the Anomœans, in whom misbelief was a "mania;" and the Eusebians, who cared little for a theory of doctrine or consistency of profession, com-pared with their own aggrandizement. With these must be included numbers who conformed to Arianism lest they should suffer temporal loss.

Athan. says, that after Eusebius (Nicomed.) had taken up the patronage of the heresy, "he made no progress till he had gained the Court," Hist. Arian. 66, showing that it was an act of external power by which Arianism grew, not an inward movement in the Church, which indeed loudly protested against the Emperor's proceed-ing, &c. (Vid. *Catholic Church.*)

2. *The Arian Leaders.*

Arius himself refers his heresy to the teaching of Lucian, a presbyter of Antioch (Theod. Hist. i. 4 and

5), who seems to have been the head of a theological party, and a friend of Paulus the heretical Bishop, and out of communion during the time of three Bishops who followed. Eusebius of Nicomedia, who seems to have held the Arian tenets to their full extent, is claimed by Arius as his "fellow-Lucianist." Pronounced Arians also were the Lucianists Leontius and Eudoxius. Asterius, another of his pupils, did not go further than Semi-Arianism, without perhaps perfect consistency; nor did Lucian himself, if the Creed of the Dedication (A.D. 341) comes from him, as many critics have held. He died a martyr's death. (Vid. supr. vol. i. p. 96, Syn. § 23, and notes.)

Asterius is the foremost writer on the Arian side, on its start. He was by profession a sophist; he lapsed and sacrificed, as Athan. tells us, in the persecution of Maximian. His work in defence of the heresy was answered by Marcellus of Ancyra, to whom Eusebius of Cæsarea in turn replied. Athan. quotes or refers to it frequently in the treatises translated supr. Vid. Decr. § 8, 20; Syn. § 18—20; Orat. i. § 30, 31; ii. § 24. fin., 28, 37, 40; iii. § 2, 60, (according to Bened. Ed., and according to this translation; *Nicen.* 13, 28; *Arim.* 23 and 24; *Disc.* 47, 58, 60, 135, 139, 151, 155, 226.) He and Eusebius of Cæsarea seem to be Semi-Arians of the same level.

We must be on our guard against confusing the one Eusebius with the other. He of Nicomedia was an Arian, a man of the world, the head of the Arian party; he of Cæsarea was the historian, to whom we are so much indebted, learned, moderate, liberal, the private friend of Constantine, a Semi-Arian. (Vid. infr., art. *Semi-Arianism*, and *Eusebius*.)

The leading Arians at the time of the Nicene Council, besides Eusebius Nicom., were Narcissus, Patrophilus, Maris, Paulinus, Theodotus, Athanasius of Nazarba, and George (Syn. § 17).

Most of these original Arians were attacked in the work of Marcellus which Eusebius (Cæsar.) answers. " Now he replies to Asterius," says Eusebius, "now to the great Eusebius," [of Nicomedia,] "and then he turns upon that man of God, that indeed thrice blessed person, Paulinus (of Tyre). Then he goes to war with Origen. . . Next he marches out against Narcissus, and pursues the other Eusebius," i. e. himself. "In a word, he counts for nothing all the Ecclesiastical Fathers, being satisfied with no one but himself." Contr. Marc. i. 4. Vid. art. *Marcellus*. There is little to be said of Maris and Theodotus. Nazarba is more commonly called Anazarbus, and is in Cilicia.

As is observed elsewhere, there were three parties among the Arians from the first :—the Arians proper, afterwards called Anomœans ; the Semi-Arian reaction from them; and the Court party, called Eusebians or Acacians, from their leaders, Eusebius of Nicomedia and Acacius of Cæsarea, which sometimes sided with the Semi-Arians, sometimes with the Arians proper, sometimes attempted a compromise of Scripture terms. The six named by Athanasius as the chief movers in the Bipartite Council of Seleucia and Ariminum, were Ursacius, Valens, Germinius, Acacius, Eudoxius, and Patrophilus. He numbers also among the Bishops at

Ariminum, Auxentius, Demophilus, and Caius. And at Seleucia, Uranius, Leontius, Theodotus, Evagrius, and George. Eusebius of Nicomedia was a kinsman of the Imperial family and tutor to Julian. He was, as has been already said, a fellow-disciple with Arius of Lucian. He was Bishop, first of Berytus, then of Nicomedia, and at length of Constantinople. He received Arius with open arms, on his expulsion from the Alexandrian Church, put himself at the head of his followers, corrected their polemical language, and used his great influence with Constantine and Constantius to secure the triumph of the heresy. He died about the year 343, and was succeeded in the political leadership of the Eusebians by Acacius and Valens.

George, whom Athanasius, Gregory Naz., and Socrates, call a Cappadocian, was born, according to Ammianus, in Epiphania of Cilicia, at a fuller's mill. He was appointed pork-contractor to the army, Syn. § 12, Hist. Arian. 75, Naz. Orat. 21, 16, and, being detected in defrauding the government, he fled to Egypt. Naz. Orat. 21. 16. How he became acquainted with the Eusebian party does not appear. Sozomen says he recommended himself to the see of Alexandria instead of Athan. by his zeal for Arianism and his τὸ δραστήριον; and Gregory calls him the hand of the heresy as Acacius (?) was the tongue. Orat. 21. 21. He made himself so obnoxious to the Alexandrians, that in the reign of Julian he was torn to pieces in a rising of the heathen populace. He had laid capital informations against many persons of the place, and he tried to persuade Constantius that, as the successor of Alexander its founder, he was proprietor of the soil and had a claim upon the houses built on it. Ammian. xxii. 11. Epiphanius tells us, Hær. 76. 1, that he made a monopoly of the nitre of Egypt, farmed the beds of papyrus, and the salt lakes, and even contrived a profit from the undertakers. His atrocious cruelties to the Catholics are well known. Yet he seems to have collected a choice library of philosophers and poets and Christian writers, which Julian seized on. Vid. Pithæus in loc. Ammian.; also Gibbon, ch. 23.

Acacius was a pupil of Eusebius of Cæsarea, and succeeded him in the see of Cæsarea in Palestine. He inherited his library, and is ranked by S. Jerome among the most learned commentators on Scripture. Both Sozomen and Philostorgius speak, though in different ways, of his great talents. He seems to have taken up, as his weapon in controversy, the objection that the ὁμοούσιον was not a word of Scripture, which is indirectly suggested by Eusebius Cæs. in his letter to his people, § 8, supr. His formula was the vague ὅμοιον (like), as the Anomœan was ἀνόμοιον (unlike), the Semi-Arian ὁμοιούσιον (like in substance), and the orthodox ὁμοούσιον (one in substance). However, like most of his party, his changes of opinion were considerable. At one time, after professing the κατὰ πάντα ὅμοιον, and even the τῆς αὐτῆς οὐσίας, Soz. iv. 22, he at length avowed the Anomœan doctrine. Ultimately, after Constantius's death, he subscribed the Nicene formula. Vid. "Arians of the Fourth Century," p. 275, 4th ed.

Valens, Bishop of Mursa, and Ursacius, Bishop of

Singidon, are generally mentioned together. They were pupils of Arius, and, as such, are called young by Athan. ad Episc. Æg. 7; and in Apol. contr. Arian, § 13, "young in years and mind;" by Hilary ad Const. i. 5, "imperitis et improbis duobus *adolescentibus*;" and by the Council of Sardica, ap. Hilar. Fragm. ii. 12. They first appear at the Council of Tyre, A. D. 335. The Council of Sardica deposed them; in 349 they publicly retracted their charges against Athanasius, who has preserved their letters. Apol. contr. Arian. 58. Valens was the more prominent of the two; he was a favourite Bishop of Constantius, an extreme Arian in his opinions, and the chief agent at Ariminum in effecting the lapse of the Latin Fathers.

Germinius was made Bishop of Sirmium by the Eusebians in 351, instead of Photinus, whom they deposed for a kind of Sabellianism. However, in spite of his Arianism, he was obliged in 358 to sign the Semi-Arian formula of Ancyra; yet he was an active Eusebian again at Ariminum. At a later date he approached very nearly to Catholicism.

Eudoxius is said to have been a pupil of Lucian, Arius's master, though the dates scarcely admit of it. Eustathius, Catholic Bishop, of Antioch, whom the Eusebians subsequently deposed, refused to admit him into orders. Afterwards he was made Bishop of Germanicia in Syria, by his party. He was present at the Council of Antioch in 341, the Dedication, vid. not. supr. vol. i. p. 94, and he carried into the West, in 345, the fifth Confession, called the Long, μακρόστιχος, Syn. § 26. He afterwards passed in succession to the sees of Antioch and Constantinople, and baptized the Emperor Valens into the Arian profession.

Patrophilus was one of the original Arian party, and took share in all their principal acts, but there is nothing very distinctive in his history. Sozomen assigns to the above six Bishops, of whom he was one, the scheme of dividing the Council into two, Hist. iv. 16; Valens undertaking to manage the Latins, Acacius the Greeks.

There were two Arian Bishops of Milan of the name of Auxentius, but little is known of them besides. S. Hilary wrote against the elder; the other came into collision with S. Ambrose. Demophilus, Bishop of Berea, was one of those who carried the long Confession into the West, though Athan. only mentions Eudoxius, Martyrius, and Macedonius, Syn. § 26. He was afterwards claimed by Aetius, as agreeing with him. Of Caius, an Illyrian Bishop, nothing is known except that he sided throughout with the Arian party.

Euzoius was one of the Arian Bishops of Antioch, and baptized Constantius before his death. He had been excommunicated with Arius in Egypt and at Nicæa, and was restored with him to the Church at the Council of Jerusalem. He succeeded at Antioch S. Meletius. who, on being placed in that see by the Arians, professed orthodoxy, and was forthwith banished by them.

The Leaders of the Semi-Arians, if they are on the rise of the heresy to be called a party, were in the first instance Asterius and Eusebius of Cæsarea, of whom I have already spoken, and shall speak again. Semi-

Arianism was at first a shelter and evasion for pure Arianism, or at a later date it was a reaction from the Anomœan enormities. The leading Semi-Arians of the later date were Basil, Mark, Eustathius, Eleusius, Meletius, and Macedonius. Basil, who is considered their head, wrote against Marcellus, and was placed by the Arians in his see ; he has little place in history till the date of the Council of Sardica, which deposed him. Constantius, however, stood his friend till the beginning of the year 360, when Acacius supplanted him in the Imperial favour, and he was banished into Illyricum. This was a month or two later than the date at which Athan. wrote his first draught or edition of his *De Syno-dis*. He was condemned upon charges of tyranny and the like, but Theodoret speaks highly of his correctness of life, and Sozomen of his learning and eloquence. Vid. Theod. Hist. ii. 20 ; Soz. ii. 33. A very little conscientiousness, or even decency of manners, would put a man in strong relief with the great Arian party which surrounded the Court, and a very great deal would not have been enough to secure him against their unscrupulous slanders. Athan. reckons him among those who "are not far from accepting even the phrase, 'One in substance,' in what he has written concerning the faith," vid. Syn. § 41. A favourable account of him will be found in "The Arians," &c., ed. 4, p. 300, &c., which vid. also for a notice of the others. Of Macedonius little is known except his cruelties. "The Arians," p. 311.

The Anomœans, with whose history this work is scarcely concerned, had for their leaders Actius and

Eunomius. Of these Aetius was the first to carry out
Arianism in its pure logical form, as Eunomius was
its principal apologist. He was born in humble life,
and was at first a practitioner in medicine. After a
time he became a pupil of the Arian Paulinus; then
the guest of Athanasius of Nazarba; then the pupil of
Leontius of Antioch, who ordained him deacon, and
afterwards deposed him. This was in 350. In 351 he
seems to have held a dispute with Basil of Ancyra, at
Sirmium, as did Photinus; in the beginning of 360 he
was formally condemned in that Council of Constantinople which confirmed the Creed of Ariminum, and
just before Eudoxius had been obliged to anathematize
his confession of faith. This was at the time Athan.
wrote the *De Syn.*

3. *Arian Tenets and Reasonings.*

¶ The Arians refused to our Lord the name of God,
except in the sense in which they called Him Word
and Wisdom, not as denoting His nature and essence,
but as epithets really belonging to God alone or to His
attributes, though out of grace or by privilege transferred by Him in an improper sense to the creature.
In this sense the Son could claim to be called God,
but in no other.

¶ The main argument of the Arians was that our Lord
was a Son, and *therefore* was not eternal, but of a
substance which had a beginning. With this Arius
started in his dispute with Alexander. "Arius, a man
not without dialectic skill, thinking that the Bishop

was introducing the doctrine of Sabellius the Libyan, out of contention fell off into the opinion diametrically opposite, ... and he says, '*If* the Father begot the Son, he that was begotten had a beginning of existence; and from this it is plain that once the Son was not; and it follows of necessity that He had His subsistence out of nothing.'" Socr. i. 5. Accordingly, Athanasius says (in substance) early in his Decr., "Having argued with them as to the meaning of their own selected term, 'Son,' let us go on to others, which on their very face make for us, such as Word, Wisdom, &c."

¶ In what sense then was "Son" to be predicated of the Divine Nature? The Catholics said that the essential meaning of the word was consubstantiality with the Father, whereas the point of posteriority to the Father depended on a condition, *time*, which could not exist in the instance of God.

¶ But the Arians persisted, maintaining that a son has his origin of existence from his father; what has an origin, has a beginning; what has a beginning is not from eternity; what is not from eternity is not God; forgetting, first that origination and beginning are not convertible terms, and that the idea of a beginning is not bound up with the idea of an origin; and secondly, that a son not only has his origin of existence from his father, but also his nature, and all that is proper to his nature.

¶ The Arians went on to maintain that to suppose a true Son, was to think of God irreverently, as implying division, change, &c. The Catholics replied that the notion of materiality was quite as foreign from

the Divine Essence as time, and as a Divine Sonship
could be eternal, in like manner it implied neither
composition nor development, συμβεβηκὸς, περιβολὴ or
προβολή.

¶ The Arians, moreover, argued in behalf of their
characteristic tenet from the inferiority necessarily
involved in the very idea of a Son. But since He was
distinct from His Father, and inferior, He was not God ;
and, if not God, then created, even though a Son. Sonship was a mere quality or characteristic bestowed upon
a creature. The Catholics, in answer, denied that a son
was in his *nature* inferior to his father ; just the reverse ;
and the question here simply was about our Lord's
nature, whether it was divine, whether He was of one,
of the same, nature with the Father.

¶ Though the Arians would not allow to Catholics
that our Lord was Son *by nature*, and maintained that the
word implied *a beginning of existence*, they were unwilling
to say that He was Son merely in the sense in which we
are sons, though, as Athan. contends, they necessarily
tended to this conclusion, as soon as they receded from
the Catholic view. Thus Arius said that He was a
creature, "but not as one of the creatures." Orat.
ii. § 19. Valens at Ariminum said the same. Jerom.
adv. Lucifer. 18. Hilary says, that, not daring directly
to deny that He was God, the Arians merely asked
"whether He was a Son." De Trin. viii. 3.

¶ If once they could be allowed to deny our Lord's
proper divinity, they cared not what high titles they
heaped upon Him in order to cloke over their heresy,
and to calm the indignation and alarm which it roused ;

nay, in the case of many of the Semi-Arians, to hide
the logical consequences of their misbelief from themselves. · They did not like to call our Lord ·barely a
creature ; certainly the political party did not, who
had to carry the Emperor with them, and, if possible,
the laity. Any how, in their preaching He was the
first of creatures ; more than a creature, because a son,
though they could not say what was meant by a son,
as distinct from a creature : and so far they did in fact
confess a mystery ; that is, the Semi-Arians, such as
Eusebius, as shown in a passage quoted in art. *Son ;*
though Arius and Arians proper, and the Anomœans,
who spoke out, and had no fear of the Imperial Court,
avowed their belief that our Lord, like other creatures,
was capable of falling. However, as represented by
their Councils and Creeds, they readily called Him "a
creature not as other creatures, an offspring not as other
offsprings," the primeval and sole work of God, the
Creator, and created in order to create, the one Mediator,
the one Priest, God of the world, Image of the Most
Perfect, the Mystical Word and Wisdom of the
Highest, and, as expressive of all this, the Only
begotten.

¶ " What use is it," says Athan., " to pretend that He
is a creature and not a creature ? for though ye shall say,
Not as ' one of the creatures,' I will prove this sophism
of yours to be a poor one. For still ye pronounce Him
to be one of the creatures ; and whatever a man might
say of the other creatures, such ye hold concerning the
Son. For is any one of the creatures just what another
is, that ye should predicate this of the Son as some

prerogative ?" Orat. ii. § 19. And so S. Ambrose, " Quæ enim creatura non sicut alia creatura non est ? Homo non ut Angelus, terra non ut cœlum." De Fid. i. n. 130 ; and a similar passage in Nyss. contr. Eun. iii. p. 132, 3.

¶ The question between Catholics and Arians was whether our Lord was a true Son, or only *called* Son. "Since they whisper something about Word and Wisdom as only *names* of the Son, &c." ὀνόματα μόνον, Decr. § 16. "The title of Image too is not a token of a similar substance, but His *name* only," Orat. i. § 21 ; and so ii. § 38, where τοῖς ὀνόμασι is synonymous with κατ ἐπίνοιαν, as Sent. D. 22, vid. also ibid. § 39; Orat. iii. § 11, 18; "not named Son, but ever Son," iv. § 24, fin.; Ep. Æg. 16. "We call Him so, and mean truly what we say ; they say it, but do not confess it." Chrysost. in Act. Hom. 33. 4. Vid. also νόθοις ὥσπερ ὀνόμασι, Cyril. de Trin. ii. p. 418. "Non hæc nuda nomina," Ambros. de Fid. i. 17. Yet, though the Arians denied the reality of the Sonship, so it was that since Sabellianism went beyond them, as denying the divine Sonship in any sense, Orat. iv. 2, they were able to profess that they believed that our Lord was "true Son." E.g., this is professed by Arius, Syn. § 16; by Euseb. in Marc. pp. 19, 35, 161 ; by Asterius, Orat. ii. § 37; by Palladius and Secundianus in the Council of Aquileia ap. Ambros. Opp. t. 2, p. 791 (ed. Bened.) ; by Maximinus ap. August. contr. Max. i. 6. As to their sense of "real," it was no more than the sense in which Athan. uses the word of us, when he says υἱοποιούμεθα ἀληθῶς.

¶ When the Nicene controversialists maintained, on

the contrary, that He was "true God" because He was "of true God," as the Creed speaks (vid. art. *Son*); of one nature with God as the offspring of man is of one nature with man, and of one essence as well as of one nature, because God is numerically one, the Arians in answer denied that He was true God by reason of His being true Son. They said that in order to be a true Son it was sufficient to *partake* of the Father's nature, that is, to have a certain *portion* of divinity, μετουσία; this all holy beings had, and without it they could not be holy; of this S. Peter speaks; but, as this participation of the divine nature does not make holy beings who possess it God, neither is the Son God, though He be Son κυρίως καὶ ἀληθῶς. And it must be granted that the words κυρίως and ἀληθῶς are applied by the Fathers themselves to the sonship conveyed in the gifts of regeneration and sanctification. (Arts. *Father* and *Grace*.)

¶ The Catholics would reply that it was not a question of the use of terms: any how, to have a μετουσία of divinity, as creatures have, is not to have the divine οὐσία, as our Lord has. No μετουσία is a proper *gennesis*. "When God is *wholly* partaken, this," says Athanasius, and we may add, this only, "is equivalent to saying He begets." In this sense Augustine says, " 'As the Father has life in Himself, so hath He given also to the Son to have life in Himself,' *not by participating*, but *in* Himself. For we men have not life in ourselves, but in our God. But that Father, who has life in Himself, begat a Son such, as to have life in Himself, not to become partaker of life, but *to be*

Himself life; and of that life to make us partakers."
Serm. 127, de Verb. Evang. 9. It was plain, then, that,
though the Arians professed to accept the word " Son "
in its first and true sense, they did not understand it in
its literal fulness, but in only a portion or aspect of its
true sense, that is, figuratively.

¶ Hence it stands in the Nicene Creed, " from the
Father, *that is*, from the substance of the Father." Vid.
Eusebius's Letter (Decr. App.). According to the received
doctrine of the Church, all rational beings, and in one
sense all beings whatever, are " from God," over and
above the fact of their creation ; and of this truth the
Eusebians made use to deny our Lord's proper divinity.
Athan. lays down elsewhere that nothing continues in
consistence and life, except from a participation of
the Word, which is to be considered a gift from Him,
additional to that of creation, and separable in idea from
it. Vid. art. *Grace.* Thus he says that "the all-powerful
and all-perfect, Holy Word of the Father, pervading
all things, and developing everywhere His power, and
illuminating all things visible and invisible, gathers
them within Himself and knits them in one, leaving
nothing destitute of His power, but quickening and
preserving all things and through all, and each by
itself, and the whole altogether." Contr. Gent. 42.
Again, " God *not only* made us of nothing, *but also*
vouchsafed to us a life according to God, *by the grace of
the Word.* But men, turning from things eternal to the
things of corruption at the devil's counsel, have brought
on themselves the corruption of death, who were, as I
said, *by nature corrupted,* but by *the grace of the parti-*

THE ARIANS.												41

cipation (μετουσίας) *of the Word*, would have escaped
their natural state, had they remained good." Incarn.
5. Man thus considered is, in his first estate, a son of
God and born of God, or, to use the term which occurs
so frequently in the Arian controversy, in the number,
not only of the creatures, but of *things generate, γενητά.*
This was the sense in which the Arians said that our
Lord was Son of God; whereas, as Athan. says, "things
generate, *being works* (δημιουργήματα,) cannot be called
generate, except so far as, *after* their making, they partake of the begotten Son, and are therefore *said* to have
been generated also; not at all in their own *nature*, but
because of their participation of the Son in the Spirit."
Orat. i. 56. The question then was, as to the *distinction*
of the Son's divine generation over that of holy men;
and the Catholics answered that He was ἐξ οὐσίας, from
the substance of God; not by participation of grace,
not by resemblance, not in any limited sense, but really
and simply from Him, and therefore by an internal
divine act. Vid. Decr. § 22.

¶ The Arians availed themselves of certain texts as
objections, argued keenly and plausibly from them, and
would not be driven from them. Orat. ii. § 18;
Epiph. Hær. 69. 15. Or rather they took some words
of Scripture, and made their own deductions from
them; viz. "Son," "made," "exalted," &c. "Making
their private impiety as if a rule, they misinterpret
all the divine oracles by it." Orat. i. § 52. Vid.
also Epiph. Hær. 76. 5, fin. Hence we hear so much
of their θρυλληταὶ φωναί, λέξεις, ἔπη, ῥητά, sayings
in general circulation, which were commonly founded

on some particular text; e. g. Orat. i. § 22, "amply
providing themselves with words of craft, they used to
go about, &c." περιήρχοντο. Vid. vol. i. p. 29, note.
Also ἄνω καὶ κάτω περιφέροντες, De Decr. § 13;
τῷ ῥητῷ τεθρυλλήκασι τὰ πανταχοῦ, Orat. ii. § 18;
τὸ πολυθρύλλητον σόφισμα, Basil. contr. Eunom. ii.
14; τὴν πολυθρύλλητον διαλεκτικήν, Nyssen contr.
Eun. iii. p. 125; τὴν θρυλλουμένην ἀπορροήν, Cyril.
Dial. iv. p. 505; τὴν πολυθρυλλητὸν φωνήν, Socr. ii. 43.

¶ Eusebius's letter to Euphration, mentioned Syn.
§ 17, illustrates their sharp and shallow logic—"If they
coexist, how shall the Father be Father and the Son
Son? or how the One first, the Other second? and the
One ingenerate and the Other generate?" Acta Conc.
7, p. 1015, Ed. Ven. 1729. Hence Arius, in his Letter
to Eusebius Nic., complains that Alexander says, ἀεὶ ὁ
θεός, ἀεὶ ὁ υἱός· ἅμα πατήρ, ἅμα υἱός. Theod. Hist.
i. 4. " 'Then their profaneness goes farther,' says
Athan; Orat. i. § 14. 'If there never was, when
the Son was not,' say they, ' but He is eternal, and co-
exists with the Father, call Him no more the Father's
Son, but brother.' " As the Arians here object that the
First and Second Persons of the Holy Trinity are ἀδελφοὶ,
so did they say the same in the course of the controversy
of the Second and Third. Vid. Athan. Serap. i. 15; iv. 2.

¶ "They contend that the Son and the Father are not
in such wise One or Like as the Church preaches, but
. . . since what the Father wills, the Son wills also,
in all respects concordant, . . . therefore it is that He
and the Father are one." Orat. iii. § 10.

¶ "The Arians reply, 'So are the Son and the Father

One, and so is the Father in the Son, and the Son in the Father, as we too may become one in Him.' " Orat. iii § 17.

¶ In the Arian Creed of Potamius, Bishop of Lisbon, our Lord is said "hominem suscepisse per quem *compassus* est," which seems to imply that He had no soul distinct from His Divinity. "Non passibilis Deus Spiritus," answers Phœbadius, "licet in homine suo passus." The Sardican confession also seems to impute this heresy to the Arians. Vid. supr. vol. i. note, p. 116, and infr. art. *Eusebius*, fin.

¶ They did not admit into their theology the notion of mystery. In vain might Catholics urge the *ne sutor ultra crepidam*. It was useless to urge upon them that they were reasoning about matters upon which they had no experimental knowledge ; that we had no means of determining whether or how a spiritual being, really trine, could be numerically one, and therefore can only reason by means of our conceptions, and as if nothing were a fact which was inconceivable. It is a matter of faith that Father and Son are one, and reason does not therefore contradict it, because experience does not show us how to conceive of it. To us, poor creatures of a day, —who are but just now born out of nothing, and have everything to learn even as regards human knowledge, —that such truths are incomprehensible to us, is no wonder.

¶ The Anomœan Arians, who arose latest and went farthest, had no scruple in answering this considera- tion by denying that God was incomprehensible. Arius indeed says in his Thalia that the Son cannot know

the Father by comprehension, κατὰ κατάληψιν: "for
that which has origin, to conceive how the Unoriginate
is, is impossible." Syn. § 15 ; but on the other hand the
doctrine of the Anomœans, who in most points agreed
with Arius, was, that all men could know God as He
knows Himself; according to Socrates, who says, "Not
to seem to be slandering, listen to Eunomius himself,
what words he dares to use in sophistry concerning God ;
they run thus :—'God knows not of His own substance
more than we do; nor is it known to Him more, to us
less ; but whatsoever we may know of it, that He too
knows ; and what again He, that you will find without
any difference in us.' "   Hist. iv. 7.

¶ Κατάληψις was originally a Stoical word, and even
when the act was perfect, it was considered attribu-
table only to an imperfect being.   For it is used in
contrast to the Platonic doctrine of ἰδέαι, to express the
hold of things obtained by the mind through the senses ;
it being a Stoical maxim, "nihil esse in intellectu quod
non fuerit prius in sensu."   In this sense it is also used
by the Fathers, to mean real and certain knowledge
after inquiry, though it is also ascribed to Almighty
God.   As to the position of Arius, since we are told in
Scripture that none "knoweth the things of a man
save the spirit of man which is in him," if κατάληψις
be an exact and complete knowledge of the object of
contemplation, to deny that the Son comprehended the
Father, was to deny that He was in the Father, that is,
to deny the doctrine of the περιχώρησις,—vid. in the
Thalia, Syn. § 15, the word ἀνεπίμικτοι ; or to maintain
that He was a distinct, and therefore a created, being.

On the other hand, Scripture asserts that, as the Holy
Spirit which is in God "searcheth all things, yea, the
deep things" of God, so the Son, as being "in the
bosom of the Father," alone "hath declared Him."
Vid. Clement. Strom. v. 12. And thus Athan., speaking
of Mark 13, 32, "If the Son is in the Father, and the
Father in the Son, and the Father knows the day
and the hour, it is plain that the Son too, being in the
Father, and knowing the things in the Father, Himself
also knows the day and the hour." Orat. iii. 44, vid.
also Matt. xi. 27.

4. Historical Course of Arianism.

There seems to have been a remarkable anticipation
of this heresy in the century before its rise, as is recorded by its condemnation by Pope Dionysius. Vid.
supr. vol. i. pp. 45—47. It seems then to have arisen, and
to have incurred his vigilant protest, as the issue of
a dangerous opinion, which was looked at with favour
in some Catholic quarters, founded apparently upon the
Stoic doctrine of the λόγος ἐνδιάθετος and προφορικὸς,
viz., that the Divine, Eternal, Personal Word, was born
into Sonship for, and not until, the creation of the universe
(vid. Orat. 4, and "Theological Tracts"). The advocates
of this opinion doubtless held the eternity à parte ante
of the One Word and Son, since they held that He
belonged to, and was an offspring of the Divine Nature;
that is, was consubstantial with the Eternal God; but, by
saying that our Lord existed from everlasting, as the
Word, not as the Son, they raised the question of the

identity of the Word and the Son, which, if answered
negatively, as it was in certain heretical sects, led to
the further question whether personality did not more
naturally attach to the idea of a Son than to the idea
of a Word.   And thus we are brought to Arianism.

¶ When this conclusion was reached by a number of
men sufficient in position and influence to constitute a
party, the first Ecumenical Council was held in A.D. 325
at Nicæa for its condemnation.

The Nicene Fathers, in the first place, defined the
proper divinity of the Son of God, introducing into
their creed the formulas ἐξ οὐσίας and ὁμοούσιος, as
tests of orthodoxy, and next they anathematized the
heretical propositions : and this with the ready adhesion
of Constantine.   He died in 337.

¶ During his later years he had softened towards the
Arians, and on his death they gained his son Constantius, who tyrannized over Christendom, persecuting the
orthodox Bishops, and especially Athanasius, till his
immature death in 361.

¶ The Arians regained political power on the accession of Valens, in 364, who renewed the persecutions
of Constantius.

¶ They came to an end, as far as regards any
influence on the State, upon the accession of Theo-
dosius and the Second Ecumenical Council, 381.

In the controversies and troubles they occasioned,
while the orthodox *formulas* were, as has been said, the
ἐξ οὐσίας and the ὁμοούσιος, viz. that our Lord was
from and in the Divine Essence, the Semi-Arians
maintained the ὁμοιούσιον, or that He was like the

Divine Essence; the political and worldly party of
Eusebius, Acacius, and Eudoxius, professed vaguely the
ὅμοιον κατὰ πάντα, or that our Lord was like God in
all things; and the fanatical Anomœans gained their
name because they denied any likeness in Him to God
at all.

ASTERIUS.

THIS writer, already noticed in art. *Arian Leaders,* seems according to Athan. to have been hired to write upon the Arian side, and argued on the hypothesis of Semi-Arianism. He agrees very much in doctrine with Eusebius, and in moderation of language, judging by the extracts which Athan. has preserved. (Vid. also Epiph. Hær. 72, 6.)

¶ Like Eusebius, he held (Orat. ii. § 24) that the God of all created His Son as an instrument or organ, or ὑπουργὸς of creation, by reason of the necessary incapacity in the creature, as such, to endure the force and immediate presence of a Divine Hand (vid. art. ἄκρατος), which, while It created, would have annihilated. (Euseb. Demonstr. iv. 4; Eccl. Th. i. 8, 13; Præp. vii. 15; Sabell. p. 9.)

¶ But, says Athanasius, it is contrary to all our notions of religion to suppose God is not sufficient for Himself, and cannot create, enlighten, address, and unite Himself to His creatures immediately. "The Word has with His Father the oneness individual of God-head. Else, why does the Father through Him create, and in Him reveal Himself to whom He will, &c. . . . If they say that the Father is not all-sufficient, their answer is impious." Orat. ii. § 41. And such an answer seems to be implied in saying that the Son was created for creation, illumination, &c., &c.; vid. art. *Mediation*.

¶ He considered that our Lord was taught to create, and without teaching could not by His mere nature have acquired the skill. "Though He is a creature, and has been brought into being," Asterius writes, "yet as from Master and Artificer has He learned to frame things, and thus has ministered to God who taught Him," Orat. ii. § 28, vid. art. *Eusebius*, who speaks of the Word in the poetical tone of Platonism.

¶ Also he distinguishes, after the manner of the Semi-Arians, between the γεννητικὴ and the δημιουργικὴ δύναμις. Again, the illustration of the Sun (Syn. § 19) is another point of agreement with Eusebius; vid. Demonstr. iv. 5.

¶ And he, like Eusebius, is convicted of Arianism beyond mistake, in whatever words he might cloke his heresy, by his rejection of the doctrine of the περιχώρησις. "He is in the Father," he says, "and the Father again in Him, because neither the word on which He is discoursing is His own but the Father's, nor the works, but the Father's who gave Him the power." Orat. iii. § 2.

He defined the ἀγέννητος, or "Ingenerate, to mean that which never came into being, but was always" (Orat. i. § 30); and then he would argue, that God being ἀγέννητος, and a Son γεννητὸς, our Lord could not be God.

While, with the other Arians, he introduced philosophical terms into theology, he with them explained away Scripture. They were accustomed to interpret

our Lord's titles, " Son," " Word," " Power," by the
secondary senses of such terms, as they belong to us,
God's children by adoption ; and so Asterius, perhaps
flippantly, answered such arguments, as " Christ God's
Power and Wisdom," by objecting that the locust was
called by the prophet " God's great power." Syn. § 19.

He argues, in behalf of our Lord's *gennesis* following
upon an act of Divine counsel and will, that we must
determine the point by inquiring whether it is more
worthy of God to act with deliberation or not.   Now
the Creator acted with such counsel and will in the
work of creation ; therefore so to act is most worthy
of Him ; it follows that will should precede the *gennesis*
also.   But in that case the Son is posterior to the Father.

ATHANASIUS.

THIS renowned Father is in ecclesiastical history the special doctor of the sacred truth which Arius denied, bringing it out into shape and system so fully and luminously that he may be said to have exhausted his subject, as far as it lies open to the human intellect. But, besides this, writing as a controversialist, not primarily as a priest and teacher, he accompanies his exposition of doctrine with manifestations of character which are of great interest and value. Here some of the more prominent of these traits shall be set down, as they are seen in various of his Treatises.

1. The fundamental idea with which he starts in the controversy is a deep sense of the authority of Tradition, which he considers to have a definitive jurisdiction even in the interpretation of Scripture, though at the same time he seems to consider that Scripture, thus interpreted, is a document of final appeal in inquiry and in disputation. Hence, in his view of religion, is the magnitude of the evil which he is combating, and which exists prior to that extreme aggravation of it (about which no Catholic can doubt) involved in the characteristic tenet of Arianism itself. According to him, opposition to the witness of the Church, separation from its communion, private judgment overbearing the authorized catechetical teaching, the fact of a deno-

mination, as men now speak, this is a self-condemnation ; and the heretical tenet, whatever it may happen to be, which is its formal life, is a spiritual poison and nothing else ; the sowing of the evil one upon the good seed, in whatever age and place it is found ; and he applies to all separatists the Apostle's words, "They went out from us, for they were not of us." Accordingly, speaking of one Rhetorius, an Egyptian, who, as S. Austin tells us, taught that "all heresies were in the right path and spoke truth," he says that "the impiety of such doctrine is frightful to mention." Apoll. i. § 6.

This is the explanation of the fierceness of his language, when speaking of the Arians ; they were simply, as Elymas, "full of all guile and of all deceit, children of the devil, enemies of all justice," θεομάχοι,— by court influence, by violent persecution, by sophistry, seducing, unsettling, perverting, the people of God.

2. It was not his way to be fierce, as a matter of course, with those who opposed him ; his treatment of the Semi-Arians is a proof of this. Eusebius of Cæsarea indeed he did not favour, for he discerned in that eminent man what, alas, was genuine Arianism ; and Eusebius's conduct towards him, and his partisan-ship with the heretics, and his antagonism to the Nicene Council, confirmed his judgment ; but with the Semi-Arian body, who rose up against the pure Arians, he was very gentle, considering them, or at least many of them, of good promise, as the event proved them to be. He calls some of them "brethren" and ἀγαπητοί (Syn. §§ 41, 43), as Hilary calls them "Sanctissimi viri," (Syn. 80, vid. art. *Semi-Arianism* infr.) Nor is there

any violence in his treatment of Marcellus, Apollinaris, Hosius, or Liberius. Vid. art. 'Αληθεία.

And so in the account he has left us of the death of Arius (de Mort. Ar.), which he considers, and truly, as an awful judgment of God, there is no triumph in his tone, though he held him in holy horror; not those fierce expressions, which certainly are to be found in the Orations. "I was not at Constantinople," he says, "when he died, but Macarius the Presbyter was, and I heard the account of it from him. Arius had been summoned by the Emperor Constantine, through the interest of the Eusebians, and, when he entered the presence, the Emperor inquired of him, whether he held the faith of the Catholic Church, and he declared upon oath that he held the right faith. . . The Emperor dismissed him saying, 'If thy faith be right, thou hast done well to swear; but if thy faith be impious, and thou hast sworn, God judge thee according to thy oath.' When he thus came from the presence of the Emperor, the Eusebians, with their accustomed violence, desired to bring him into the Church; but Alexander the Bishop . . . . was greatly distressed, and, entering into the Church, he stretched forth his hands to God, and bewailed himself; and, casting himself upon his face in the chancel, he prayed upon the pavement. Macarius also was present and prayed with him, and heard his words. And he sought these two things, saying, 'If Arius is brought to communion to-morrow, let me Thy servant depart, ... but, if Thou wilt spare Thy Church . . . take off Arius, lest the heresy may seem to enter with him'. . . . A wonderful and extraordinary circumstance took place. While the Eusebians threatened, the Bishop prayed; but Arius, who had great confidence in the Eusebians, and talked very wildly, seized by indisposition withdrew, and suddenly, in the language of Scripture, *falling headlong, burst asunder in the midst,* and immediately expired as he lay, and was deprived both of communion and of his life together." Then he adds, "Such was the end of Arius; and the Eusebians, overwhelmed with shame, buried their accomplice, while the blessed Alexander, amid the rejoicing of the Church, celebrated the Synaxis with piety and orthodoxy, praying with all the brethren and greatly glorifying God, not as exulting in his death (God forbid), for *it is appointed unto* all men once to die, but . . . that the Lord Himself judged between the threats of the Eusebians and the prayer of Alexander, and condemned the Arian heresy."

4. His language, in speaking of Constantius, gives opportunity for more words. Up to the year 356, Athanasius had treated Constantius as a member of the Church; but at that date the Eusebian or Court party abandoned the Semi-Arians for the Anomœans. George of Cappadocia was placed as Bishop in Alexandria, Athanasius was driven into the desert, S. Hilary and other Western Bishops were sent into banishment. Hosius was persecuted into signing an Arian confession, and Pope Liberius into communicating with the Arians. Upon this Athanasius changed his tone and considered that he had to deal with an Antichrist. In his Apol. contr. Arian. init. (A.D. 350), ad Ep. Æg. 5 (356), and his Apol. ad Constant. passim. (356), he calls the

Emperor most pious, religious, &c. At the end of the last-mentioned work, § 27, the news comes to him, while in exile, of the persecution of the Western Bishops and the measures against himself. He still in the peroration calls Constantius "blessed and divinely favoured Augustus," and urges on him that he is a "Christian Emperor, φιλόχριστος." In the works which follow, Apol. de fuga, § 26 (357), he calls him an heretic; and Hist. Arian. § 45, &c. (358), speaking with indignation of the treatment of Hosius, &c., he calls him "Ahab," "Belshazzar," "Saul," "Antichrist." The passage at the end of the Apol. contr. Arian., in which he speaks of the "much violence and tyrannical power of Constantius," is an addition of Athan.'s at a later date. Vid. Montfaucon's note on § 88, fin. This is worth mentioning, as it shows the unfairness of the following passage from Gibbon, ch. xxi. note 116. "As Athanasius dispersed secret invectives against Constantius, see the Epistle to the monks" [i. e. Hist. Arian. ad Monach. A.D. 358], "at the same time that he assured him of his profound respect, we might distrust the professions of the Archbishop, tom. i. p. 677" [i. e. apparently Apol. ad Const. A.D. 356]. Again, in a later part of the chapter. "In his public Apologies, which he addressed to the Emperor himself, he sometimes affected the praise of moderation; whilst at the same time in secret and vehement invectives he exposed Constantius as a weak and wicked prince, the executioner of his family, the tyrant of the republic, and the Antichrist of the Church." He offers no proof of this assertion. It may be added that S. Greg. Naz.

praises Constantius, but it is in contrast to Julian. Orat. 4. 3, and 5. 6. And S. Ambrose, but it is for his enmity to paganism. Ep. i. 18, n. 32.

5. It is the same prudent, temperate spirit and practical good sense, which leads Athanasius, though the prime champion of the Nicene Homoüsion, to be so loth to use that formula, much less abruptly to force it upon his adversaries in the first instance, and to content himself with urging and inculcating our Lord's Divinity in other language and by casual explanations, when prejudice or party-spirit made it difficult to get a hearing for the terms which the Church had determined. Hence in his Three Orations he hardly names the Homoüsion, though the doctrine which it upholds is never out of his thoughts. He accepted the Semi-Arian Homœüsion, though he is so often represented by the shallow ignorance of modern times to have waged war with other theologians whose views did not differ from his own except by a single letter. "Those," he says, "who accept everything else that was determined at Nicæa, and quarrel only with the Homoüsion, must not be received as enemies, nor do we here attack them as Ariomaniacs, nor as opposers of the Fathers, but we discuss the matter with them, as brothers with brothers, who mean what we mean, and dispute only about the word." Syn. § 41. (*Arim. n.* 47.) Vid. arts. ὅμοιος, *Semi-Arians,* &c.

¶ 6. It arises from the same temper of mind that he is so self-distrustful and subdued in his comments on Scripture and his controversial answers; he, the foremost doctor of the Divine Sonship, being the most modest as

well as the most authoritative of teachers. Thus,
" They had best have been silent," i.e. in so sacred a
matter, he says, " but since it is otherwise, after
many prayers that God would be gracious to us, thus
we might ask them in turn," &c., Orat. i. § 25. (*Disc.*
n. 39.) " Against their profaneness I wish to urge a
further question, bold indeed, but with a religious
intent,—be propitious, O Lord ! " Orat. iii. § 63. (*Disc.*
n. 50.) " The unwearied habits of the religious man
is to worship the All (τὸ πᾶν) in silence, and to hymn
God his benefactor with thankful cries . . . . but
since &c., Apoll. i. init.

¶ And especially in his letter to the Monks, " I
thought it needful to represent to your piety what
pains the writing of these things has cost me, in order
that you may understand thereby how truly the Blessed
Apostle has said, *O, the depth,* &c., and may kindly bear
with a weak man, such as I am by nature. For the
more I desired to write and endeavoured to force myself
to understand the Divinity of the Word, so much the
more did the knowledge thereof withdraw itself from
me, and in proportion as I thought that I apprehended
it, in so much I perceived myself to fail of doing so.
Moreover, I was also unable to express in writing even
what I seemed to myself to understand, and that which
I wrote was unequal to the imperfect shadow of the
truth which existed in my conceptions," ad Monach. i.
Vid. also Serap. i. 15—17, 20 ; ii. init., iv. 8, 14 ; Epict.
12 fin. ; Max. init. ; Ep. Æg. 11 fin. Once more : " It
is not safe for the writings of an individual to be published, especially if they relate to the highest and chief

doctrines, lest what is imperfectly expressed, through infirmity or the obscurity of language, do hurt to the reader," &c.   Mort. Ar. § 5.

¶ He set the example of modesty to others. Vid. Basil. in Eunom. ii. 17; Didym. Trin. iii. 3, p. 341; Ephr. Syr. adv. Hær. Serm. 55 init. (t. 2, p. 557); Facund. Tr. Cap. iii. 3 init.

¶ 7. And his repetitions of statements in these Treatises are not without a place in the evidences of his religious caution.   Often indeed they must be accounted purely accidental, arising from forgetfulness, as he wandered or travelled about, what it was that he had written the day before; often, too, they may have subserved the purpose of catechetical instruction; but sometimes they would seem to be owing to his anxiety to confine himself to words which had stood the test of time or of readers, or at least were existing forms which he could improve upon or at least reconsider and appeal to, as after his time is instanced in S. Leo.

¶ 8. As to his acquirements, they were considerable. Gregory only says that he had a knowledge τῶν ἐγκυκλίων, but Sulpitius speaks of him as a jurisconsult (vid. *philosophy* and οὐσία).   His earliest works, written when perhaps he was not more than twenty-one, give abundant evidence of a liberal education.   He had a knowledge of Homer and Plato, and his early style, though it admits of pruning, is graceful and artistic.   I cannot, with Gibbon, talk of its "rude eloquence," though it has not the refined and elaborate elegance of Basil. And Gibbon grants that his writings are " clear, forcible, and persuasive."   Erasmus seems to prefer him, as a writer, to all the Fathers, and certainly, in my own judgment, no one comes near him but Chrysostom and Jerome. " Habebat," says Erasmus, "vere dotem illam, quam Paulus in Episcopo putat esse præcipuam, τὸ διδακτικόν ; adeo dilucidus est, acutus, sobrius, adtentus, breviter omnibus modis ad docendum appositus. Nihil habet durum, quod offendit in Tertulliano, nihil ἐπιδεικ-τικὸν, quod vidimus in Hieronymo, nihil operosum, quod in Hilario, nihil laciniosum, quod est in Augustino, atque etiam Chrysostomo, nihil Isocraticos numeros aut Lysiæ compositionem redolens, quod est in Gregorio Nazianzeno, sed totus est in explicandâ re." ap. Mont-faucon, t. 1. p. xxi. ed. Patav.

Photius's praise of Athan.'s style and matter is quoted supr. in the Notice prefixed to the Orations.

THE VICARIOUS ATONEMENT.

¶ "Formerly the world, as guilty, was under judgment from the Law; but now the Word has taken on Himself the judgment, and, having suffered in the body for all, has bestowed salvation on all." Orat. i. § 60.

¶ "When the Father willed that ransom should be paid for all, and to all grace should be given, then truly the Word . . . did take earthly flesh . . . that, as a high priest . . . He might offer Himself to the Father and cleanse us all from sins in His own blood." Orat. ii. § 7.

¶ The perfect Word of God puts around Him an imperfect body, and is said to be created for the creatures, that, paying the debt in our stead (ἀνθ' ἡμῶν τὴν ὀφειλὴν ἀποδιδούς), He might by Himself perfect what was wanting in man. Now immortality was wanting to him, and the way to paradise." Orat. ii. § 66.

¶ "How, were the Word a creature, had He power to undo God's sentence, and to remit sin?" Orat. ii. § 67. Our Lord's death is λύτρον πάντων, Incarn. V. D. 25, et passim; λύτρον καθάρσιον, Naz. Orat. 30, 20 fin.

¶ "Therefore was He made man, that what was as though given to Him, might be transferred to us; for a mere man had not merited this, nor had the Word

Himself needed it. He was united therefore to us, &c."
Orat. iv. § 6. Vid. also iii. § 33 init. and *In Illud
Omnia*, § 2 fin.

¶ "There was need He should be both man and God;
for unless He were man, He could not be killed; unless
He were God, He would have been thought, not, unwilling to be what He could, but unable to do what He
would." August. Trin. xiii. 18. " Since Israel could
become sold under sin, he could not redeem himself
from iniquities. He only could redeem, who could not
sell Himself, who did no sin; He is the redeemer from
sin." Id. in Psalm. 129, n. 12. "In this common
overthrow of all mankind, there was but one remedy,
the birth of some son of Adam, a stranger to the
original prevarication and innocent, to profit the rest
both by his pattern and his merit. Since natural
generation hindered this, . . the Lord of David became
his Son." Leon. Serm. 28, n. 3. " Seek neither a
' brother ' for thy redemption, but one who surpasses
thy nature; nor a mere 'man,' but a man who is God,
Jesus Christ, who alone is able to make propitiation for
us all . . . One thing has been found sufficient for all
men at once, which was given as the price of ransom of
our soul, the holy and most precious blood of our Lord
Jesus Christ, which He poured out for us all." Basil. in
Psalm 48, n. 4. " One had not been sufficient instead
of all, had it been simply a man; but if He be understood as God made man, and suffering in His own
flesh, the whole creation together is small compared to
Him, and the death of one flesh is enough for the
ransom of all that is under heaven." Cyril. de rect.

fid. p. 132. Vid. also Theod. Eran. iii. pp. 196—8, &c.
Procl. Orat. i. p. 63 (ed. 1630); Vigil. contr. Eutych.
v. 9 fin. § 15, &c.; Greg. Moral. xxiv. init; Job. ap.
Phot. 222, p. 583.

¶ Pardon, however, could have been bestowed without an Atonement such as our Lord made, though not
renovation of nature.　Vid. art. *Incarnation.*

CATECHISING.

ATHANASIUS lays much stress on this practice, as in fact supplying the evidence of Tradition as to the doctrine which Arius blasphemed.

E.g. " Let them tell us, by what teacher or by what tradition they have derived these notions concerning the Saviour? " de Decr. § 13 init.

" For who was ever yet a hearer of such a doctrine? or whence or from whom did the abettors and hirelings of the heresy gain it? who thus expounded to them when they were at school? who told them, ' Abandon the worship of the creation, and then draw near and worship a creature and a work?' But if they themselves own that they have heard it now for the first time, how can they deny that this heresy is foreign, and not from our fathers? But what is not from our fathers, but has come to light in this day, how can it be but that of which the blessed Paul has foretold, that *in the latter times some shall depart from the sound faith*," &c.? Orat. i. § 8.

" Who is there, who when he heard, upon his first catechisings, that God had a Son, and had made all things in His proper Word, did not so understand it in that sense which we now intend? who, when the vile Arian heresy began, but at once, on hearing its teachers, was startled, as if they taught strange things ?" Orat. ii. § 34.

¶ Hence too Athan.'s phrases μαθὼν ἐδίδασκεν, de Decr. § 7, Orat. iii. 9, ἐρωτῶντες ἐμάνθανον, Orat. ii. § 1, after S. Paul, 1 Cor. xv. 3. And so "What Moses taught, that Abraham observed, that Noe and Enoch acknowledged, &c.," de Decr. § 5. Vid. art. *Rule of Faith.*

CATHOLIC: THE NAME AND THE CLAIM.

FOR the adoption into Christianity, and the sense and force, of the word "Catholic," not a very obvious word, we must refer to the Creed. The Articles of the Creed are brief enunciations and specimens of some, and of the chief, of the great mercies vouchsafed to man in the Gospel. They are truths of pregnant significance, and of direct practical bearing on Christian life and conduct. Such, for instance, obviously is "one Baptism for the remission of sins," and " the resurrection of the body." Such then must be our profession of "catholicity." And, thus considered, the two, " the Catholic Church " and "the Communion of Saints," certainly suggest an explanation of each other; the one introducing us to our associates and patrons in heaven, and the other pointing out to us where to find the true teaching and the means of grace on earth. Indeed, what else can be the meaning of insisting on the "*One* Holy Catholic Apostolic Church? does it not imply a contrast to other so-called Churches? Now this plain sense of the Article, this its obvious or rather its only sense, is abundantly confirmed by such passages of the Fathers as the following, taken in connexion and illustration of each other.

Thus, to begin with the title "Christian." Orat. i. § 2, 3. "Though the blessed Apostles have become our teachers, and have ministered the Saviour's Gospel, yet not from

VOL. II.   F them have we our *title*, but from Christ we are and are *named* Christians. But for those who derive the faith which they profess from others, good reason is it they should bear their *name*, whose property they have become." Also, "Let us become His disciples and learn to live according to Christianity; for whoso is called by other name beside this, is not of God." Ignat. ad Magn. 10. Hegesippus speaks of "Menandrians, and Marcionites, and Carpocratians, and Valentinians, and Basilidians, and Saturnilians," who "each in his own way and that a different one brought in his own doctrine." Euseb. Hist. iv. 22. "There are, and there have been, my friends, many who have taught atheistic and blasphemous words and deeds, coming in the Name of Jesus; and they are called by us from the appellation of the men, whence each doctrine and opinion began. . . . . Some are called Marcians, others Valentinians, others Basilidians, others Saturnilians," &c. Justin. Tryph. 35. "They have a name from the author of that most impious opinion, Simon, being called Simonians." Iren. Hær. i. 23. "When men are called Phrygians, or Novatians, or Valentinians, or Marcionites, or Anthropians, or by any other name, they cease to be Christians; for they have lost Christ's *name*, and clothe themselves in human and foreign titles." Lact. Inst. iv. 30. "*A.* How are you a Christian, to whom it is not even granted to bear the *name* of Christian? for you are not called Christian, but Marcionite. *M.* And you are called of the Catholic Church; therefore ye are not Christians either. *A.* Did we profess man's name, you would have spoken

to the point, but, if we are so called for being all over
the world, what is there bad in this?" Adamant.
Dial. § 1, p. 809. "We never heard of Petrines, or
Paulines, or Bartholomeans, or Thaddeans, but from
the first there was one preaching of all the Apostles,
not preaching themselves, but Christ Jesus the Lord.
Wherefore also they all gave one *name* to the Church,
not their own, but that of their Lord Jesus Christ,
since they began to be called Christians first at
Antioch ; which is the *sole* Catholic Church, having
nought else but Christ's, being a Church of Christians,
not of Christs, but of Christians; He being one, they
from that one being called Christians. After this
Church and her preachers, all others are no longer of
the same character, making show by their own
epithets, Manichæans, and Simonians, and Valentinians,
and Ebionites." Epiph. Hær. 42, p. 366. "This is
the fearful thing, that they change the *name* of
Christians of the Holy Church, which hath no epithet
but the name of Christ alone, and of Christians, to. be
called by the name of Audius," &c. Ibid. 70, 15. Vid.
also Hær. 75, 6 fin.

¶ Having thus laid down the principle that the
name, given to a religious body, is a providential
or divine token, they go on to instance it in
the word "Catholic." "Since one might properly and truly say that there is a 'Church of
evil doers,' I mean the meetings of the heretics, the Marcionists, and Manichees, and the rest,
the faith hath delivered to thee by way of security
the Article, 'And in *One* Holy Catholic Church,' that

thou mayest avoid their wretched meetings ; and ever abide with the Holy Church Catholic, in which thou wast regenerated.   And if ever thou art sojourning in any city, inquire not simply where the Lord's House is, (for the sects of the profane also make an attempt to call their own dens houses of the Lord,) nor merely where the Church is, but where is the *Catholic* Church. For this is the *peculiar name* of this Holy Body," &c. Cyril Cat. xviii. 26.   "Were I by chance to enter a populous city, I should in this day find Marcionites, Apollinarians, Cataphrygians, Novatians, and other such, who called themselves Christian ; by what *surname* should I recognize the congregation of my own people, were it not called Catholic ? . . . . Certainly that word ' Catholic' is not borrowed from man, which has survived through so many ages, nor as the sound of Marcion or Apelles or Montanus, nor takes heretics for its authors . . Christian is my *name,* Catholic my *surname."*   Pacian. Ep. 1.   "If you ever hear those who are called Christians, *named,* not from the Lord Jesus Christ, but from some one else, say Marcionites, Valentinians, Mountaineers, Campestrians, know that it is not Christ's Church, but the synagogue of Antichrist." Jerom. adv. Lucif. fin.

¶ Athan. seems to allude, Orat. i. § 2, to Catholics being called Athanasians ; supr., vol. i. p. 155, fin. Two distinctions are drawn between such a title as applied to Catholics, and again to heretics, when they are taken by Catholics as a *note* against them.   S. Augustine says, *" Arians* call Catholics Athanasians or Homoüsians, *not other heretics call them so.*   But ye not only by Catholics *but also by heretics*, those who agree with you and those who disagree, are called Pelagians; as *even by heresies* are Arians called Arians. But ye, and ye only, call us Traducianists, as Arians call us Homoüsians, as Donatists Macarians, as Manichees Pharisees, and as the other heretics use various titles." Op. imp. i. 75. It may be added that the heretical name *adheres*, the Catholic dies away. S. Chrysostom draws a second distinction, " Are we divided from the Church ? have we heresiarchs? are we called from man ? is there any leader to us, as to one there is Marcion, to another Manichæus, to another Arius, to another some other author of heresy ? for if we too have the name of any, still it is not those who began a heresy, but our superiors and governors of the Church. We have not 'teachers upon earth,'" &c. in Act. Ap. Hom. 33 fin.

¶ Athan. says, that after Eusebius had taken up the patronage of the heresy, he made no progress till he had gained the Court, Hist. Arian. 66, showing that it was an act of external power by which Arianism grew, not an inward movement in the Church, which indeed loudly protested against the Emperor's proceeding. " If Bishops are to judge," he says, § 52 supr., " what has the Emperor to do with this matter ? if the Emperor is to threaten, what need of men styled Bishops ? where in the world was such a thing heard of ? where had the Church's judgment its force from the Emperor, or his sentence was at all recognized ? " Vid. art. *Heretics*.

"Many Councils have been before this, many judgments of the Church, but neither the Fathers ever argued

with the Emperor about them, nor the Emperor meddled
with the concerns of the Church.   Paul the Apostle had
friends of Cæsar's household, and in his Epistle he saluted
the Philippians in their name; but he took them not to
him as partners in his judgments.   But now a new
spectacle, and this the discovery of the Arian heresy,"
&c. § 52.   Again, "In what then is he behind Antichrist? what more will he do when he comes? or
rather, on his coming will he not find the way prepared for him by Constantius unto his deceiving
without effort? for he is claiming to transfer causes to
the court instead of the Churches, and presides at them
in person." Hist. Arian. § 76.   And so also Hosius to
Constantius, "Cease, I charge thee, and remember that
thou art a mortal man.   Fear the day of judgment;
keep thyself clear against it.   Interfere not with
things ecclesiastical, nor be the man to charge us in
a matter of the kind; rather learn thou thyself from
us.   God has put into thy hand the kingdom; to us
He hath entrusted the things of the Church,—and as
he who is traitorous to thy rule speaks against God
who has thus ordained, so fear thou, lest drawing to
thyself the things of the Church, thou fallest beneath
a great accusation." ap. Athan. ibid. 44.

CHAMELEONS.

The Arians were ever shifting their ground or changing their professions, in order to gain either the favour of the State, or of local bishops, or of populations, or to perplex their opponents. Hence Athan. calls them chameleons, as varying their colours according to their company, Decr. § 1, and Alexander, Socr. i. 6. Cyril, however, compares them to " the leopard which cannot change his spots." Dial. ii. init. ; vid. also Naz. Orat. 28, 2. Athan. says, " When confuted, they are confused, and when questioned, they hesitate ; and then they lose shame and betake themselves to evasions." Decr. § 1. "What wonder that they fight against their fathers, when they fight against themselves ? " Syn. § 37. " They have collisions with their own principles, and conflict with each other, at one time saying that there are many wisdoms, at another maintaining one," &c. Orat. ii. § 40. He says, Æg. Ep. 6, that they treated creeds as yearly covenants, and as State Edicts, Syn. § 3, 4. He calls also the Meletians chameleons, Hist. Ar. § 79; indeed the Church alone and her children are secure from change.

THE COINHERENCE,

περιχώρησις, circumincessio or coinherence of the Divine Three with each other, is the test at once against Arianism and Tritheism. Arius denies it in his Thalia, ἀνεπίμικτοι ἐαυτοῖς αἱ ὑποστάσεις. It is the point of doctrine in which Eusebius so seriously fails. Vid. art. *Eusebius.* When Gibbon called this doctrine "perhaps the deepest and darkest corner of the whole theological abyss," he made as irrelevant and feeble a remark as could fall from an able man, as if any Catholic pretended that it was on any side of it comprehensible, and as if this was not the very enunciation in which the in-comprehensibility lies; as we profess in the Creed, "neque confundentes personas, neque substantiam separantes." This doctrine is not the deepest part of the whole, but it is the whole, other statements being in fact this in other shapes. Each of the Three who speak to us from heaven is simply, and in the full sense of the word, God, yet there is but one God; this truth, as a statement, is stated most intelligibly when we say the Father, Son, and Holy Ghost are in each other, which is the doctrine of the περιχώρησις.

¶ "They next proceed," says Athanasius, "to dis-parage our Lord's words, *I in the Father and the Father in Me,* saying, 'How can the One be contained in the

Other and the Other in the One?' &c.; and this state
of mind is consistent with their perverseness, who
think God to be material, and understand not what
is True Father and True Son. . . When it is said, *I in
the Father and the Father in Me,* They are not therefore, as these suppose, discharged into Each Other,
filling the One the Other, as in the case of empty
vessels, so that the Son fills the emptiness of the
Father and the Father that of the Son, and Each of
Them by Himself is not complete and perfect, (for
this is proper to bodies, and therefore the mere assertion of it is full of impiety,) for the Father is full and
perfect, and the Son is the Fulness of Godhead. Nor
again, as God, by coming into the Saints, strengthens
them, is He also thus in the Son. For He is Himself
the Father's Power and Wisdom, and by partaking
($\mu\epsilon\tau o\chi\hat{\eta}$) of Him things generate are sanctified in the
Spirit; but the Son Himself is not Son by participa-
tion ($\mu\epsilon\tau ov\sigma ia$, vid. art. *Arian Tenets*), but is the Father's
proper Offspring. Nor again is the Son in the Father,
in the sense of the passage, *In Him we live and move
and have our being;* for He, as being from the Fount of
the Father, is the Life, in which all things are both
quickened and consist; for the Life does not live in Life,
else it would not be Life, but rather He gives life to
all things." Orat. iii. § 1. And again : "The Father is
in the Son, since the Son is what is from the Father and
proper to Him, as in the radiance the sun, and in the
word the thought, and in the stream the fountain : for
whoso thus contemplates the Son, contemplates what
belongs to the Father's Substance, and knows that the

Father is in the Son. For whereas the Nature (εἶδος) and Godhead of the Father is the Being of the Son, it follows that the Son is in the Father and the Father in the Son." ibid. § 3.

¶ In accordance with the above, Thomassin observes that by the mutual coinherence or indwelling of the Three Blessed Persons is meant "not a commingling as of material liquids, nor as of soul with body, nor as the union of our Lord's Godhead and humanity, but it is such that the whole power, life, substance, wisdom, essence, of the Father, should be the very essence, substance, wisdom, life, and power of the Son." de Trin. 28, 1. S. Cyril adopts Athan.'s language to express this doctrine. "The Son in one place says, that He is in the Father and has the Father again in Him; for what is simply proper (ἴδιον) to the Father's substance, by nature coming to the Son, shows the Father in Him." in Joan. p. 105. "One is contemplated in the other, and is truly, according to the connatural and consubstantial." de Trin. vi. p. 621. "He has in Him the Son, and again is in the Son, because of the identity of substance." in Joan. p. 168. Vid. art. *Trinity in Unity.*

¶ The περιχώρησις is the test of orthodoxy, as regards the Holy Trinity, against Arianism. This is seen clearly in the case of Eusebius, whose language approaches to Catholic more nearly than that of Arians in general. After all his strong assertions, the question recurs, is our Lord a distinct being from God, as we are, or not? he answers in the affirmative, vid. infra, art. *Eusebius*, whereas we believe that He is literally and numerically one with the Father, and therefore His Person dwells in the Father's Person by an ineffable unity. And hence the strong language of Pope Dionysius, supr. vol. i. p. 45, " the Holy Ghost must repose and dwell in God," ἐμφιλοχωρεῖν τῷ θεῷ καὶ ἐνδιαιτᾶσθαι. And hence the strong figure of S. Jerome (in which he is followed by S. Cyril, Thesaur. p. 51), " Filius locus est Patris, sicut et Pater locus est Filii." in Ezek. 3, 12. Hence Athan. contrasts creatures, who are ἐν μεμερισμένοις τόποις, with the Son. vid. Serap. iii. 4. Accordingly, one of the first symptoms of reviving orthodoxy in the second school of Semi-Arians is the use in the Macrostich Creed, of language of this character, viz. " All the Father embosoming the Son," they say, " and all the Son hanging and adhering to the Father, and alone resting on the Father's breast continually." supr. vol. i. p. 107.

¶ St. Jerome's figure above might seem inconsistent with S. Athanasius's disclaimer of material images; but Athan. only means that such illustrations cannot be taken literally, as if spoken of natural subjects. The Father is the τόπος or locus of the Son, because when we contemplate the Son in His fulness as ὅλος θεὸς, we do but view the Father as that Person in whom God the Son is; our mind abstracts His Substance which is the Son for the moment from Him, and regards Him merely as Father. Thus Athan. τὴν θείαν οὐσίαν τοῦ λογοῦ ἡνωμένην φύσει τῷ ἑαυτοῦ πατρί. in illud Omn. 4. It is, however, but a mode of speaking in theology, and not a real emptying of Godhead from the Father, if such words may be used. Father and Son are both the same God, though really and eternally distinct from each other; and Each is full of the Other, that is, their Substance is one and the same. This is insisted on by S. Cyril, " We must not conceive that the Father is held in the Son as body in body, or vessel in vessel; . . . for the One is in the Other. ὡς ἐν ταὐτότητι τῆς οὐσίας ἀπαραλλάκτῳ, καὶ τῇ κατὰ φύσιν ἑνότητί τε καὶ ὁμοιότητι. in Joan. p. 28. And by S. Hilary: " Material natures do not admit of being mutually in each other, of having a perfect unity of a nature which subsists, of the abiding nativity of the Only-begotten being inseparable from the verity of the Father's Godhead. To God the Only-begotten alone is this proper, and this faith attaches to the mystery of a true nativity, and this is the work of a spiritual power, that to be, and to be in, differ nothing; to be in, yet not to be one in another as body in body, but so to be and to subsist, as to be in the subsisting, and so to be in, as also to subsist," &c. Trin. vii. fin.; vid. also iii. 23. The following quotation from S. Anselm is made by Petavius, de Trin. iv. 16 fin.: " Though there be not many eternities, yet if we say eternity in eternity, there is but one eternity. . . And so whatever is said of God's Essence, if repeated in itself, does not increase quantity, nor admit number. . . Since there is nothing out of God, when God is born of God. . . He will not be born out of God, but remains in God."

¶ " There is but one Face (εἶδος, nature) of God, which is also in the Word, and One God, the Father, existing by Himself and according as He is above all, and appearing in the Son according as He pervades all things, and in the Spirit according as in Him He acts in all things through the Word. And thus we confess God to be One through the Trinity." Orat. iii. § 15. And so : " The Word is in the Father, and the Spirit is given from the Word." iii. § 25. "That Spirit is in us which is in the Word which is in the Father." ibid. "The Father in the Son taketh the oversight of all." § 36 fin.; vid. art. *the Father Almighty*, 2. "The sanctification which takes place from Father through Son in Holy Ghost." Serap. i. § 20.; vid. also ibid. 28, 30, 31, iii. 1, 5 init. et fin., also Hil. Trin. vii. 31. Eulogius says, " The Holy Ghost, proceeding from the Father, having the Father as an Origin, and proceeding through the Son unto the creation." ap. Phot. cod. p. 865. Damascene speaks of the Holy Spirit as δύναμιν τοῦ πατρὸς προερχομένην καὶ ἐν τῷ λόγῳ ἀναπαυομένην, F. O. i. 7; and in the beginning of the ch. he says that "the Word must have Its Breath (Spirit) as our word is not without breath, though in our case the breath is distinct from our substance." "The way to knowledge of God is from One Spirit through the One Son to the One Father." Basil. de Sp. S. 47. " We preach One God by One Son with the Holy Ghost." Cyr. Cat. xvi. 4. " The Father through the Son with the Holy Ghost bestows all things." ibid. 24. " All things have been made from Father through the Son in Holy Ghost." Pseudo-Dion. de Div. Nom. i. p. 403. " Through Son and in Spirit God made all things consist, and contains and preserves them." Pseudo-Athan. c. Sab. Greg. 10.

¶ Since the Father and the Son are the numerically
One God, it is but expressing this in other words to
say that the Father is in the Son, and the Son in the
Father, for all They have and all They are is common
to Each, excepting Their being Father and Son. A
περιχώρησις of Persons is implied in the Unity of
Substance. This is the connexion of the two texts so
often quoted: "the Son is in the Father and the
Father in the Son," because " the Son and Father are
one." And the cause of this unity and περιχώρησις is
the Divine γέννησις. Thus S. Hilary: " The perfect
Son of a perfect Father, and of the Ingenerate God
the Only-generate Offspring, who from Him who hath
all hath received all, God from God, Spirit from Spirit,
Light from Light, says confidently, 'The Father in
Me and I in the Father,' for as the Father is Spirit so
is the Son, as the Father God so is the Son, as the
Father Light so is the Son. From those things therefore which are in the Father, are those in which is the
Son; that is, of the whole Father is born the whole
Son; not from other, &c. . . . not in part, for in the
Son is the fulness of Godhead. What is in the Father,
that too is in the Son; One from the Other and Both
One (unum); not Two One Person ('unus,' vid. however, the language of the Athan. Creed, which expresses
itself differently after S. Austin) but Either in Other,
because not Other in Either. The Father in the Son,
because from Him the Son . . . the Only-begotten in
the Ingenerate, because from the Ingenerate the Only-
generate," &c. Trin. iii. 4.

¶ And so ἐργαζομένου τοῦ πατρὸς, ἐργάζεσθαι καὶ τὸν

υἱόν. in illud Omn. 1. "Cum luce nobis prodeat, In Patre totus Filius, et totus in Verbo Pater." Hymn. Brev. in fer. 2. Ath. argues from this oneness of operation the oneness of substance. And thus S. Chrysostom on the text under review argues that if the Father and Son are one κατὰ τὴν δύναμιν, They are one also in οὐσία. in Joan. Hom. 61, 2. Tertullian in Prax. 22, and S. Epiphanius, Hær. 57, p. 488, seem to say the same on the same text. Vid. Lampe, Joan. x. 35. And so S. Athan. τριὰς ἀδιαίρετος τῇ φύσει, καὶ μια ταύτης ἡ ἐνέργεια. Serap. i. 28; ἒν θέλημα πατρὸς καὶ υἱοῦ καὶ βούλημα, ἐπεὶ καὶ ἡ φύσις μία. in illud Omn. 5. Various passages of the Fathers to the same effect, (e. g. of S. Ambrose, "si unius voluntatis et operationis, unius est essentiæ," de Sp. ii. 12 fin., and of S. Basil, ὧν μία ἐνέργεια, τούτων καὶ οὐσία μία, of Greg. Nyss. and Cyril. Alex.) are brought together in the Lateran Council. Concil. Hard. t. 3, p. 859, &c. The subject is treated at length by Petavius, Trin. iv. 15, § 3.

As to the very word περιχώρησις, Petavius observes, de Trin. iv. 16, § 4, that its first use in ecclesiastical writers was one which Arianism would admit of; its use to express the Catholic doctrine was later.

CURSUS PUBLICUS.

ON the Cursus Publicus, vid. Gothofred, in Cod. Theod. viii. tit. 5. It was provided for the journeys of the Emperor, for parties whom he summoned, for magistrates, ambassadors, and such private persons as the Emperor indulged in the use of it. The use was granted by Constantine to the Bishops summoned to Nicæa, as far as it went. Euseb. Constant. iii. v. 6. The Cursus Publicus brought the Bishops to the Council of Tyre, ibid. iv. 43. In the conference between Liberius and Constantius, Theod. Hist. ii. 13, it is objected that the Cursus Publicus is not sufficient to convey Bishops to the Council which Liberius contemplates. Constantius answers that the Churches are rich enough to convey their Bishops as far as the sea. Thus St. Hilary was compelled ("datâ evectionis copiâ," Sulp. Hist. ii. 57) to attend at Seleucia, and Athan. at Tyre. Julian complains of the abuse of the Cursus Publicus, perhaps with an allusion to these Councils of Constantius, vid. Cod. Theod. viii. 5, § 12, where Gothofred quotes Libanius's Epitaph in Julian. t. i. p. 569, ed. Reize. Vid. the passage in Ammianus, who speaks of the Councils being the ruin of the *res vehicularia*, Hist. xxi. 16. The Eusebians at Philippopolis say the same thing. Hil. fragm. iii. 25. The Emperor provided board and perhaps lodging for the Bishops at

Ariminum, which the Bishops of Aquitaine, Gaul, and Britain declined, excepting three British by reason of poverty, Sulp. ii. 56. Hunneric in Africa, after assembling 466 Bishops at Carthage, dismissed them without conveyances, provision, or baggage. Vict. Ut. iv. fin. In the Emperor's letter before the sixth Ecumenical Council, A.D. 678 (Hard. Conc. t. 3, p. 1048 fin.), he says he has given orders for the conveyance and maintenance of its members. Pope John VIII. (A.D. 876) reminds Ursus, Duke of Venice, of the same duty of providing for the members of a Council, "secundum pios principes, qui in talibus munificè semper erant intenti." Colet. Concil. t. xi. p. 14, Venet. 1730.

Gibbon says that by the Government conveyances "it was easy to travel 100 miles in a day," ch. ii.; but the stages were of different lengths, sometimes a day's journey, Coust. in Hilar. Psalm. 118, Lit. 5, 2 (as over the Delta to Pelusium, and then coasting all the way to Antioch), sometimes half a day's journey, Herman. ibid. Vid. also Ambros. in Psalm. 118, Serm. 5, 5. The halts were called μοναὶ or mansiones, and properly meant the building where soldiers or other public officials rested at night; hence applied to monastic houses, a statement which, if correct, disconnects the word from μόνος. Such buildings included granaries, stabling, &c. Vid. Cod. Theod. t. 1, p. 47, t. 2, p. 507; Ducange, Gloss. t. 1, p. 426, col. 2.

DEFINITIONS.

FROM the first the Church had the power, by its divinely appointed representatives, to declare the truth upon such matters in the revealed message or gospel tidings as from time to time came into controversy, for, unless it had this power, how could it be the " columna et firmamentum veritatis "?); and these representatives, of course, were the Rulers of the Christian people, who received, as a legacy, the depositum of doctrine from the Apostles, and by means of it, as need arose, exercised their office of teaching. Each Bishop was in his own place the Doctor Ecclesiæ for his people; there was an appeal, of course, from his decision to higher courts; to the Bishops of a province, of a nation, of a patriarchate, to the Roman Church, to the Holy See, as the case might be; and thus at length a final determination was arrived at, which in consequence was the formal teaching of the Church, and, as far as it was direct and categorical, was, from the reason of the case, the Word of God. And being such, was certain, irreversible, obligatory on the inward belief and reception of all subjects of the Church, or what is called *de fide*.

All this could not be otherwise if Christianity was to teach divine truth in contrast to the vague opinions and unstable conjectures of human philosophers and moralists, and if, as a plain consequence, it must have authoritative organs of teaching, and if true doctrines never can be false, but what is once true is always true. What the Church proclaims as true never can be put aside or altered, and therefore such truths are called ὁρισθέντα or ὅροι, *definitions,* as being boundaries or landmarks. Vid. Athan. Decret. § 2.

¶ Decrees or definitions of Councils come to us as formal notices or memoranda setting forth in writing what has ever been held orally or implicitly in the Church. Hence the frequent use of such phrases as ἐγγραφῶς ἐξετέθη with reference to them. Thus Damasus, Theod. Hist. v. 10, speaks of that "apostolical faith, which was *set forth in writing* by the Fathers in Nicæa." On the other hand, Ephrem of Antioch speaks of the doctrine of our Lord's perfect humanity being "inculcated by our Holy Fathers, but not as yet [i.e. till the Council of Chalcedon] being *confirmed* by the decree of an Ecumenical Council." Phot. 229, p. 801. (ἐγγραφῶς, however, sometimes relates to the act of the Bishops in subscribing, Phot. *ibid.,* or to Scripture, Clement. Strom. i. init. p. 321.) Hence Athan. says, ad Afros 1 and 2, that "the Word of the Lord, which was given through the Ecumenical Council in Nicæa *remaineth for ever;*" and uses against its opposers the texts, "Remove not the ancient landmark which thy fathers have set " (vid. also Dionysius in Eus. Hist. vii. 7), and "He that curseth his father or his mother shall surely be put to death." Prov. 22, 28, Ex. 21, 17; vid. also Athan. ad Epict. 1. And the Council of Chalcedon professes to "drive away the doctrines of

error by a common decree, and *renew* the unswerving
faith of the fathers," Act. v. p. 452, "according as,"
they proceed, "from of old the prophets spoke of
Christ, and He Himself instructed us, and the creed of
the Fathers has delivered to us," whereas "other faith
it is not lawful for any to bring forth, or to write, or
to draw up, or to hold, or to teach," p. 456.

¶ And so S. Leo *passim* concerning the Council of
Chalcedon, " Concord will be easily established, if the
hearts of all concur in that faith, which, &c., *no discussion* being allowed whatever with a view to retractation." Ep. 94. He calls such an act a " magnum
sacrilegium." Ep. 157, c. 3. " To be seeking for what
has been perfected, to tear up what has been laid down
(definita), what is this but to be unthankful for what
we gained ? " Ep. 162, vid. the whole of it. He says
that the attempt is "no mark of a peacemaker but a
rebel." Ep. 164, c. 1 fin. ; vid. also Epp. 145 and 156,
where he says, none can assail what is once determined,
but " aut antichristus aut diabolus," c. 2.

¶ At Seleucia Acacius said, " If the Nicene faith has
been altered once and many times since, no reason why
we should not dictate another faith now." Eleusius
the Semi-Arian answered, "This Council is convoked,
not to learn what it does not know, not to receive a
faith which it does not possess, but walking in the
faith of the Fathers," (meaning the Semi-Arian Council
of the Dedication, A.D. 341, vid. Syn. § 22), "it swerves
not from it in life or death." On this Socrates (Hist.
ii. 40) observes, " How call you those who met at
Antioch Fathers, O Eleusius, you who deny *their*

Fathers? for those who met at Nicæa, and unani-
mously professed the Consubstantial, might more
properly receive the name, &c. But if the Bishops at
Antioch set at nought their own fathers, those who
come after are blindly following parricides; and how
did they receive a valid ordination from them, whose
faith they set at nought as reprobate? But if those
had not the Holy Ghost, which cometh through laying
on of hands, neither did these receive the priesthood;
for did they receive from those who have not where-
with to give?"

¶ This reconsideration of points once settled Athan.
all through his works strenuously resists, and with
more consistency than the Semi-Arians at Seleucia.
And so in their Letter the Fathers at Ariminum observe that the Emperor had commanded them "to treat
of the faith," to which ambiguous phrase they reply that
they mean rather to "adhere" to the faith, and to reject
all novelties. And so at Sardica the Council writes
to Pope Julius, that the Emperors Constantius and
Constans had proposed three subjects for its consideration; first, "that all points in discussion should be
debated afresh (de integro), and above all concerning
the holy faith and the integrity of the truth which
[the Arians] had violated." Hil. Fragm. ii. 11.
Enemies of the Arians seem to have wished this as
well as themselves; and the Council got into difficulty
in consequence. Hosius the president and Protogenes
Bishop of the place wrote to the Pope to explain,
"from fear," says Sozomen, "lest some might think
that there was any innovation upon the Nicene de-

crees." iii. 12. From his way of stating the matter, Sozomen seems to have himself believed that the Council did publish a creed. And, in fact, a remarkable confession, and a confession attributed to the Council, does exist. Accordingly Athanasius, Eusebius of Vercellæ, and the Council of Alexandria, A.D. 362, protest against the idea of a treatment *de integro.* "It is true," they say, "that certain persons wished to add to the Nicene Council as if there was something wanting, but the Holy Council was displeased," &c. Tom. ad Antioch. § 5. However, Vigilius of Thapsus repeats the report. contr. Eutych. v. init.

¶ This, however, did not interfere with their *adding* without *undoing.* "For," says Vigilius, "if it were unlawful to receive aught further after the Nicene statutes, on what authority venture we to assert that the Holy Ghost is of one substance with the Father, which it is notorious was there omitted?" contr. Eutych. v. init.; he gives other instances, some in point, others not; vid. also Eulogius, apud Phot. Cod. 23, pp. 829, 853. Yet to add to the *confession* of the Church is not to add to the *faith,* since nothing can be added to the faith. Leo, Ep. 124, p. 1237. Nay, Athan. says that the Nicene faith is sufficient to refute every heresy, ad Max. 5 fin. also Leo. Ep. 54, p. 956, and Naz. Ep. 102 init., *excepting, however,* the doctrine of the Holy Spirit; which explains his meaning. The Henoticon of Zeno says the same, but with the intention of dealing a blow at the Council of Chalcedon. Evagr. iii. 14, p. 345. Actius at Chalcedon says that at Ephesus and Chalcedon the Fathers did not profess to draw up an exposition of faith, and that Cyril and Leo did but *interpret the Creed."* Conc. t. 2, p. 428. Leo even says that the Apostles' Creed is sufficient against all heresies, and that Eutyches erred on a point " of which our Lord wished no one of either sex in the Church to be ignorant," and he wishes Eutyches to take the plentitude of the Creed " puro et simplici corde." Ep. 31, p. 857, 8.

DEIFICATION.

The titles which belong to the Divine Word by nature, are by grace given to us, a wonderful privilege, of which the Arians showed their sense, not by teaching the elevation of the creature to the Son of God, but by lowering the Son to the level of the creature. The means by which these titles become ours are our real participation (μετοχὴ) of the Son by His presence within us, a participation so intimate that in one sense He can be worshipped in us as being His temple or shrine. Vid. art. μετουσία.

Athanasius insists on this doctrine again and again.

¶ "The Word was made flesh in order to offer up this body for all, and that we, partaking of His Spirit, might be made gods." Decr. § 14.

¶ "While all things which are made, have by participation (ἐκ μετουσίας) the grace of God, He is the Father's Wisdom and Word, of whom all things partake. It follows that He, being the deifying and enlightening power of the Father, in which all things are deified and quickened, is not alien in substance from the Father, but one in substance." Syn. § 51.

¶ "He was not man, and then became God, but He was God and then became man, and that to make us gods." Orat. i. § 39.

¶ "This is our grace and high exaltation, that even

when He became man, the Son of God is worshipped,
and the heavenly powers are not startled at all of us,
who are one body with Him, being introduced into
their realms." ibid. § 42.

¶ "Because of our relationship to His body, we
too have become God's Temple, and in consequence
are made God's Sons, so that even in us the Lord
is now worshipped, and beholders report, as the
Apostle says, that 'God is in them of a truth.'"
ibid. § 43.

¶ "God created Him for our sakes, because of us
preparing for Him that created body, that in Him we
might be capable of being renewed and made gods."
Orat. ii. § 47.

¶ "Therefore did He assume the body generate and
human, that, having renewed it as its framer, He
might make it god. . . . For man had not been made
god, if joined to a creature, . . . the union was of this
kind, . . . that his salvation and deification might be
sure." ibid. § 70.

"Although there be but one Son by nature, True and
Only-begotten, we too become sons, . . . and, though
we are men from the earth, we are yet called gods . . .
as has pleased God who has given us that grace." Orat.
iii. § 19.

¶ "As we are sons and gods, because of the Word in
us, so shall we be in the Son and in the Father,
because the Spirit is in us." ibid. § 25.

¶ "We men are made gods by the Word, as being
joined to Him through His flesh," ibid. § 34.

¶ "That He might redeem mankind . . . that He

might hallow them and make them gods, the Word became flesh." ibid. § 39.

¶ "What is this advance but the deifying and grace imparted from Wisdom to men?" ibid. § 53.

Vid. also Adelph. 4; Serap. i. 24; Cyr. in Joann. p. 74; Theod. Hist. p. 846 init.

ECONOMICAL LANGUAGE.

¶ By " Economical," I mean language relating to matters beyond the direct apprehension of those to whom it is addressed, and which, in order to have a chance of conveying to them any idea, however faint, of the fact, must be more or less of an analogous or figurative character, as viewed relatively to the truths which it professes to report, instead of a direct and literal statement of the things which have to be conveyed. Thus a child's idea of a king is that of a man richly dressed with a crown and sceptre, sitting on a throne; thus an attempt might be made to convey to a blind man the character of scarlet contrasted with other colours by telling him that it is like the sound of a trumpet; thus, since none of us can imagine to ourselves a spirit and its properties, it is a received economy to represent Angels as bright beings with wings. Hence, again, it is an economy to speak of our Lord as sitting on the right hand of God, as if right and left were possible in Him; and, indeed, Scripture is necessarily full of economies, when speaking of heavenly things, because there is no other way of introducing into our minds even a rude idea, even any idea at all, of matters so utterly out of our experience. About such economies in the revealed statement of religious truths, two rules must be observed.

First, while aware of their imperfection as informations, still we must keep strictly to what is told us in them, because we cannot know more exactly what is told us in them than they tell us. Thus we read, "God is a consuming fire;" now fire is a material substance, and cannot literally belong to the Divine Nature; but it is the only, or at least the truest, mode in which His nature, in a certain relation to us, can be brought home to us, and we must accept it and believe it as a substantial truth, in spite of its not being the whole truth or the exact impress of the truth. Secondly, it must be recollected that we cannot argue and deduce freely from economical language as if it were adequate and complete, and that in revealed matters we may fall into serious error, if we argue and deduce except under the *magisterium* of the Church. Thus it is that some Calvinists have argued against freewill from St. Peter's words in his first Epistle ("Ye, as living *stones*, are built up a spiritual house,") thus, "This is giving freewill a stab under the fifth rib, for can stones build themselves?" Copleston *on Predestinat.* p. 129. And thus it was, that Arius argued, from the economical word Son, given us as the nearest approximation in human language to the ineffable truth itself, that our Lord was not the everlasting God, because human sons have a beginning of existence.

Hence it is that mystery is the necessary note of divine revelation, that is, mystery subjectively to the human mind : because, when the mind goes on freely to reason from language which only partially corresponds to eternal truths, which cannot be adequately expressed in human words, it draws from one revealed information what is inconsistent with what it draws from another, and instead of saying, "This collision of deductions arises from the imperfection of our knowledge of premisses," it refuses to believe what it cannot understand, acting like a man who, having learned some geometrical truths by means of arithmetic or algebra, and having found that by multiplying a quantity into itself, and again into itself, he could reach a number which in its properties corresponded to a geometrical cube, he should go on to multiply once more, and then should consider that he had been brought to the absurdity of a fourth dimension in space, and in consequence should withdraw his faith from algebraical deductions altogether. Vid. art. *Trinity*, also *Illustrations*, and others.

¶ "Such illustrations and such images," says Athanasius, "has Scripture proposed, that, considering the inability of human nature to comprehend God, we might be able to form ideas even from these, however poorly and dimly, as far as is attainable." Orat. ii. 32, ἀμυδρῶς, vid. also ἀμυδρὰ; ii. 17.

¶ Elsewhere, after adducing the illustration of the sun and its light, he adds, "From things familiar and ordinary we may use some poor illustration, and represent intellectually what is in our mind, since it were presumptuous to intrude upon the incomprehensible Nature." in Illud Omnia 3 fin. Vid. also 6; also Serap. i. 20, and Decr. § 12. And S. Austin, after an illustration from the nature of the human mind, proceeds: "Far other are these Three and that Trinity...

When a man hath discovered something in them and stated it, let him not at once suppose that he has discovered what is above them," &c. Confess. xiii. 11. And again, "Ne hanc imaginem ita comparet Trinitati, ut omni modo existimet similem." Trin. xv. 39. And S. Basil says, "Let no one urge against what I say, that the illustrations do not in all respects answer to the matters in question. For it is not possible to apply with exactness what is little and low to things divine and eternal, except so far as to refute," &c. contr. Eunom. ii. 17.

¶ Scripture is full of mysteries, but they are mysteries of *fact*, not of words. Its dark sayings or ænigmata are such, because in the nature of things they cannot be expressed clearly. Hence contrariwise, Orat. ii. § 77 fin. he calls Prov. 8, 22 an enigma, with an allusion to Prov. 1, 6, Sept. In like manner S. Ambrose says, "Mare est scriptura divina, habens in se sensus profundos, et altitudinem propheticorum *ænigmatum*, &c." Ep. ii. 3. What is commonly called " explaining away" Scripture, is the transference of this obscurity from the subject to the words used.

¶ Nothing is more common in theology than comparisons which are only parallel to a certain point as regards the matter in hand, especially since many doctrines do not admit of exact illustrations. Our Lord's real manhood and imputed sinfulness were alike adjuncts to His Divine Person, which was of an Eternal and Infinite Nature ; and therefore His Manhood may be compared to an Attribute, or to an accident, without meaning that it really was either. The Athan. Creed compares the Hypostatic Union to that of soul and body in one man, which, as taken literally by the Monophysites, became their heresy. Again S. Cyril says, " As the Bread of the Eucharist, after the invocation of the Holy Ghost, is mere bread no longer, but the Body of Christ, so also this holy ointment is no more simple ointment," &c. Catech. xxi. 3, Oxf. Tr. ; but no one contends that S. Cyril held either a change in the chrism, or no change in the bread. Hence again we find the Arians arguing from John xvii. 11, that our union with the Holy Trinity is *as* that of the Adorable Persons with Each Other; vid. Euseb. Eccl. Theol. iii. 19, and Athanasius replying to the argument, Orat. iii. 17–25. And so " *As* we receiving the Spirit, do not lose our own proper substance, *so* the Lord, when made man for us and bearing a body, was no less God," Decr. § 14; yet He was God made man, and we are but the temple of God. And again Athanasius compares the Incarnation to our Lord's presence in the world of nature. Incarn. 41–42.

ECUMENICAL.

THIS name was given from the first to Councils of the whole Church, whose definitions could not be altered, vid. art. *Definitions.* Athan. twice in his Decr. calls the Nicene by this name, viz. § 4 and § 27. "Are they not committing a crime to gainsay so great and ecumenical a Council?" § 4, and "the devil alone persuades you to slander the ecumenical Council," § 27; vid. also Orat. i. § 7; ad Afros 2 twice; Apol. contr. Arian. 7; ad Ep. Æg. 5; Epiph. Hær. 70, 9; Euseb. Vit. Const. iii. 6. The second General Council, A.D. 381, took the name of ecumenical, vid. Can. 6 fin.; but incidentally. The Council of Ephesus so styles itself in the opening of its Synodical Letter.

EUSEBIUS.

VID. arts. *Semi-Arianism* and *Asterius* for a notice of the symbol of the ὁμοιούσιον, in opposition to the orthodox ὁμοούσιον and ἐξ οὐσίας on the one hand, and to ἀνόμοιον on the other. Eusebius is one of the special supporters of this form of heresy. Asterius is another (vid. art. *Arian Leaders*); the statements set down here and under the title "Asterius" are mainly taken from what we find in their controversial works.

¶ In his Letter to his people, supr. vol. i. p. 55, &c. Eusebius scarcely commits himself to any positive sense in which the formula "of the substance" (ἐξ οὐσίας), is to be interpreted, but only says what it does not mean. His comment on it is "of the Father, but not as a part;" where, what is not negative, instead of being an explanation, is but a recurrence to the original words of Scripture, "of the Father," of which ἐξ οὐσίας itself is the explanation; a curious inversion. Indeed it is very doubtful whether he admitted the ἐξ οὐσίας at all. He says, that the Son is not like the radiance of light so far as this, that the radiance is an inseparable accident of substance, whereas the Son is by the Father's will, κατὰ γνώμην καὶ προαίρεσιν. Dem. Ev. iv. 3. (vid. art. Βούλησις). And though he insists on our Lord being *alone* ἐκ θεοῦ, yet he

means in the sense which Athan. refutes, Decr. § 7, viz.
that He alone was created immediately from God.   It
is true that he plainly condemns with the Nicene Creed
the ἐξ οὐκ ὄντων of the Arians, " the Son was out of
nothing," but an evasion was at hand here also; for
he not only adds, according to Arian custom, " not as
others," but he has a theory that no being whatever
is out of nothing, for non-existence cannot be the
cause of existence.   God, he says, "proposed His own
will and power as *a sort of matter and substance* of the
production and constitution of the universe, so that it
is not reasonably said, that anything is out of nothing.
For what is from nothing cannot be at all.   How
indeed can nothing be to anything a cause of being ?
but all that is, takes its being *from One* who only
is and was, who also said, ' I am that I am.' " Dem.
Ev. iv. 1.   Again, speaking of our Lord, " He who
was from nothing would not truly be Son of God, *as
neither is any other of things generate.*" Eccl. Theol.
i. 9 fin.

¶ He distinctly asserts, Dem. Ev. iv. 2, that our Lord
is a creature.   "This offspring," he says, " did He
first produce Himself from Himself as a foundation of
those things which should succeed; the perfect handy-
work, δημιούργημα, of the Perfect, and the wise structure
ἀρχιτεκτόνημα, of the Wise," &c.   It is true in his Lett.
§ 6, he grants that "He was not a work resembling the
things which through Him came to be ;" but this again
is only the ordinary Arian evasion of "an offspring, not
as the offsprings."   E.g. "It is not without peril to
say recklessly that the Son is generate out of nothing

similarly to the other generates." Dem. Ev. v. 1 ; vid.
also Eccl. Theol. i. 9, iii. 2. And he considers our Lord
the only Son by a divine provision similar to that by
which there is only one sun in the firmament, as a
centre of light and heat. " Such an Only-begotten
Son, the excellent artificer of His will and operator,
did the supreme God and Father of that operator
Himself first of all beget, through Him and in Him
giving subsistence to the operative words (ideas or
causes) of things which were to be, and casting in Him
the seeds of the constitution and governance of the
universe; . . . Therefore the Father being one, it
behoved the Son to be one also ; but should any one
object that He constituted not more, it is fitting for
such a one to complain that He constituted not more
suns, and moons, and worlds, and ten thousand other
things." Dem. Ev. iv. 5 fin.; vid. also iv. 6.

¶ He does not say that our Lord is *from the substance
of* the Father, but that He has *a substance from* the
Father "not from other substance, but from the Father."
This is the Semi-Arian doctrine, which, whether confessing the Son from the substance of the Father or
not, implied that His substance was not the Father's
substance, but a second substance. The same doctrine
is found in the Semi-Arians of Ancyra, though they
seem to have confessed, " of the substance." And
this is one object of the ὁμοούσιον, to hinder the confession " of the substance " from implying a second
substance, which was not obviated or was even
encouraged by the ὁμοιούσιον. The Council of Ancyra,
quoting the text " As the Father hath life in Himself,

so," &c., says, "since the life which is in the Father means substance, and the life of the Only-begotten which is begotten from the Father means substance, the word 'so' implies a likeness of substance to substance." Epiph. Hær. 73, 10 fin. Hence Eusebius does not scruple to speak of "two substances," and other writers of three substances. contr. Marcell. i. 4, p. 25. He calls our Lord "a second substance," Dem. Ev. vi. Præf.; Præp. Ev. vii. 12, p. 320, and the Holy Spirit a third substance, ibid. 15, p. 325. This it was that made the Latins so suspicious of three hypostases, because the Semi-Arians, as well as they, understood ὑπόστασις to mean substance. Eusebius in like manner calls our Lord "another God," "a second God," Dem. Ev. v. 4, p. 226, v. fin.; "second Lord," ibid. 3 init. 6 fin.; "second cause," Dem. Ev. v. Præf.; "not the True God." Syn. § 17, Concil. vii. art. 6. p. 409. Vid. also ἕτερον ἔχουσα τὸ κατ᾽ οὐσίαν ὑποκείμενον, Dem. Ev. v. 1, p. 215; καθ᾽ ἑαυτὸν οὐσιωμένος, ibid. iv. 3. And so ἕτερος παρὰ τὸν πατέρα, Eccl. Theol. i. 20, p. 90; and ζωὴν ἰδίαν ἔχων, ibid.; and ζῶν καὶ ὑφεστὼς καὶ τοῦ πατρὸς ὑπάρχων ἔκτος, ibid. Hence Athan. insists so much on our Lord *not* being external to the Father. Once admit that He is in the Father, and we may call the Father, the *only* God, for He is included. And so again as to the Ingenerate, the term does not exclude the Son, for He is generate in the Ingenerate. Vid. Ἀγένητος and *Marcellus*.

¶ The Semi-Arians, however, considering the Son as external to the Father, and this as a necessary truth, maintained, in order logically to escape Sabellianism,

that the ὁμοούσιον implied a separation or divulsion of
the Divine Substance into two, following the line of
argument of Samosatene, who seems to have stopped
the reception of that formula at Antioch in the third
century by arguing that it involved either Sabellianism
(vid. Hilary) or materialism (vid. Athan. and Basil).
E.g. Euseb. Demonstr. iv. 3, p. 148, p. 149, v. 1, p.
213–215 ; contr. Marcell. i. 4 ; p. 20; Eccl. Theol.
i. 12, p. 73; in laud. Const. p. 525; de Fide i. ap.
Sirmond. tom. i. p. 7; de Fide ii. p. 16; and apparently
his de Incorporali. And so the Semi-Arians at Ancyra,
Epiph. Hær. 73, 11, p. 858. And so Meletius, ibid.
p. 878 fin., and Cyril Hier. Catech. vii. 5, xi. 18.
οὐ πάθει πατὴρ γενόμενος, οὐκ ἐκ συμπλοκῆς, οὐ κατ᾽
ἄγνοιαν, οὐκ ἀπορρεύσας, οὐ μειωθεὶς, οὐκ ἀλλοιωθείς.
Vid. also Eusebius's letter to his people as given by
Athan. Cyril, however, who had friends among the
Semi-Arians and apparently took their part, could not
be stronger on this point than the Nicene Fathers.

¶ The only sense then in which the word ὁμοούσιον
could be received by such as Eusebius, would seem
to be negative, unless it should rather be taken as
a mere formula of peace; for he says, "We assented
&c. . . . without declining even the term ‘Consubstantial,’ peace being the object which we set before
us and maintenance of the orthodox view . . . ‘Consubstantial with the Father’ suggests that the Son of
God bears no resemblance to the creatures which have
been made, but that He is in every way after the
pattern of His Father alone who begat Him." Euseb.
Lett. § 7. These last words can hardly be called an

interpretation of ὁμοούσιον, for it is but saying that ὁμοούσιον means ὁμοιούσιον, whereas the two words notoriously were antagonistic to each other.

¶ It must be observed too that, though the Semi-Arian ὁμοιούσιον may be taken, as it is sometimes by Athan., as satisfying the claims of theological truth, especially when it is understood in the sense of ἀπαράλλακτος εἰκὼν, "the exact image" of the Father, (vid. Decr. § 20, Theod. Hist. i. 4,) yet it could easily be explained away. It need mean no more than a likeness of Son to Father, such as a picture to its original, while differing from it in substance. "Two men are not of like nature, but of the same nature, Tin is like silver but not of the same nature." Syn. § 47–50. Also Athan. notices that "like" applies to qualities rather than to substance. Also Basil. Ep. 8, n. 3; "while in itself," says the same Father, "it is frequently used of faint similitudes, and falling very far short of the original." Ep. 9, n. 3. But the word ὁμοούσιον implies "the same in likeness," ταὐτὸν τῇ ὁμοιώσει, that the likeness may not be considered analogical. vid. Cyril. in Joan. iii. 5, p. 302. Eusebius makes no concealment that it is in this sense that he uses the word ὁμοιούσιον, for he says, "Though our Saviour Himself teaches that the Father is the only True, still let me not be backward to confess Him also the true God, *as in an Image*, and that possessed; so that the addition of 'only' may belong to the Father alone as Archetype of the Image. . . . As supposing one king held sway, and his image was carried about into every quarter, no one in his right mind would say that those who held sway were two, but one, who was honoured through his image." de Eccl. Theol. ii. 23; vid. ibid 7, pp. 109, 111.

¶ Accordingly, instead of ἐξ οὐσίας, which was the Nicene formula, he held μετουσία, that is, "like to the Father by participation of qualities," as a creature may be; ἐξ αὐτῆς τῆς πατρικῆς [not οὐσίας, but] μετουσίας, ὥσπερ ἀπὸ πηγῆς, ἐπ' αὐτὸν προχεομένης πληρούμενον. Eccl. Theol. i. 2. Whereas Athan. says, οὐδὲ κατὰ μετουσίαν αὐτοῦ, ἀλλ' ὅλον ἴδιον αὐτοῦ γέννημα. Orat. iii. § 4. (Disc. n. 228.) "If ye speak of the Son as being merely such by participation, μετουσία, then call Him ὁμοιούσιον," Syn. 53; but no, it is for creatures to possess God μετουσία, but when God is said to beget, this is all one with enunciating the ἐξ οὐσίας, and a *whole* participation. Vid. Orat. i. § 16.

¶ Hence St. Austin says, as quoted supr. *Arian tenets,* " As the Father has life in Himself, so hath He given also to the Son to have life in Himself, *not by partici-pating,* but in Himself. For we have not life in our-selves, but in our God. But that Father, who has life in Himself, begat a Son such, as to have life in Himself, not to become partaker of life, but *to be Himself life; and of that life to make us partakers.*" Serm. 127, de Verb. Evang. 9.

¶ In Eusebius's Letter to Euphration, as quoted in the seventh Ecum. Council, he introduced the usual Arian argument against the Son's Eternity. " If They co-exist, how shall the Father be Father and the Son Son? or how the One first, and the Other second? and the

One ingenerate and the Other generate?" Vid. supr. *Arian tenets.*

¶ And further he explained away what Catholics held of the eternity of the *gennesis* by insisting that God was a Father *in posse* from eternity, not in fact. " Our religious Emperor did at the time," at Nicæa, " prove in a speech, that our Lord was in being even according to His Divine generation, which is before all ages, since even before He was generated in fact He was in virtue with the Father ingenerately, the Father being always Father, as King always and Saviour always, being all things in virtue, and having all things in the same respects and in the same way." Eus. Lett. § 10.

Theognis too, another of the Nicene Arians, says the same, according to Philostorgius; viz. " that God even before He begat the Son was a Father, as having the power, δύναμις, of being so," Hist. ii. 15, 16; and Asterius. They are answered by Catholics, on the ground that Father and Son are words of nature, but Creator, King, Saviour, are external, or what may be called accidental to Him. Thus Athanasius observes, that Father actually implies Son, but Creator only the power to create, as expressing a δύναμις; "a maker is before his works, but he who says Father, forthwith in Father implies the existence of the Son." (*Disc.* n. 231.) Orat. iii. 6. Vid. Cyril too, Dial. ii. p. 459; Pseudo-Basil. contr. Eun. iv. 1 fin. On the other hand Origen argues the reverse way, that since God is eternally a Father, therefore eternally Creator also. " As one cannot be father without a son, nor lord without possession, so neither can God be called All-powerful, without subjects of His power," Periarch. i. 2, n. 10; hence he argued for the eternity of creation, which Suarez, after St. Thomas, allows to be abstractedly possible. Vid. Theol. Tracts ii. § 11 circ. fin.

¶ Athan. distinguishes as follows: that, as it is of the *essence* of a son to be *of the nature* of the father, so is it of the *essence* of a creature to be *of nothing,* ἐξ οὐκ ὄντων; therefore, while it was *not* impossible, *from the nature of the case,* for Almighty God to be always Father, it *was* impossible for the same reason that He should be always a Creator, impossible from incapacity, not in the Infinite, but in the finite. Orat. i. 29. Vid. ibid. § 58, where he takes "They shall perish," in the Psalm, not as a fact, but as the definition of the *nature* of a creature. Also ii. § 1, where he says, "It is proper to creatures and works to have said of them, ἐξ οὐκ ὄντων and οὐκ ἦν πρὶν γεννηθῇ." Vid. Cyril. Thesaur. 9, p. 67. Dial. ii. p. 460.

It has been above shown that Eusebius held with the run of Arians that our Lord was created by the God of all in order that He might create all else. And this was because the creation could not bear the Divine Hand, as the Arians also said. Vid. a clear and eloquent passage in his Eccl. Theol. i. 8, also 13, to show that our Lord was brought into being before all creation, ἐπὶ σωτηρίᾳ τῶν ὅλων. Vid. also Demonstr. iv. 4; Præp. vii. 15; but especially his remark, " not because the Father was not able to create, did He beget the Son, but because those things which were made were not able to sustain the power of the Ingenerate, therefore

speaks He through a Mediator," contra Sabell. i.
p. 9.

There is another peculiarity of Eusebius's view of the
creative office of the Divine Word, in contrast with
the Catholic doctrine. It is that the Word does not
create from His own designs, as being Himself really
the τύπος, εἰκὼν, and ὑπόγραμμα of those things which
He is creating, but that He copies the Father's
patterns as an external minister. "The Father *designed*
(διετύπου) and prepared with consideration, *how*, and
of *what shape, measure,* and *parts.* . . . And He
watching (ἐνατενίζων) the Father's thoughts, and alone
beholding the depths in Him, went about the work,
subserving the Father's orders (νεύμασι) . . . As a
skilful painter, *taking the archetypal ideas from* the
Father's thoughts, He transferred them to the substances of the works." Eccl. Theol. iii. 3, pp. 164, 5.

In this Eusebius follows the Platonists; so he does,
when he attributes our Lord's Priesthood to His
Divine Nature, as the Word, in which case His human
sufferings have no part in it.

Moreover, it is doubtful whether he held that our
Lord, in becoming incarnate, took on Him a human soul
as well as body. In his work against Marcellus, p. 54,
he seems to grant his opponent's doctrine, when he
says, εἰ μὲν ψυχῆς δίκην (δίχα) οἰκῶν ἐν αὐτῷ τῷ σώματι;
and at p. 55 he seems to say that, if the Word retired
from the ζωοποιὸς σάρξ, the σάρξ would be left ἄλογος;
vid. also ibid. p. 91.

THE FATHER ALMIGHTY.

1. THE idea of an Almighty, All-perfect Being, in its fulness involves the belief of His being the Father of a co-equal Son, and this is the first advance which a habit of devout meditation makes towards the intellectual apprehension of the doctrine of the Holy Trinity, when once that doctrine has been received with the claim and the sanction of having been revealed.

¶ The Fathers speak as if it were nothing short of a necessary truth, involved in the nature of things, that One who is infinite in His attributes should subsist over again in an infinite perfect Image, Impress, Likeness, Word, or Son, for these names denote the same sacred truth. A redundatio in imaginem or in Verbum is synonymous with a generatio Filii. "Naturam et essentiale Deitatis," says Thomassin, "in suo Fonte assentiuntur omnes esse plenitudinem totius Esse. At hæc necesse est ut statim exundet nativâ fœcunditate suâ. Infinitum enim illud Esse non Esse tantum est sed Esse totum est; vivere id ipsum est intelligere, sapere; opulentiæ suæ, bonitatis, et sapientiæ rivulos undique spargere; nec rivulos tantum, sed et fontem et plenitudinem ipsam suam diñundere. Hæc enim demum fœcunditas Deo digna, Deo par est, ut a Fonte bonitatis non rivulus sed flumen effluat, nec extra effluat, sed in ipsomet, cùm extra nihil sit, quo illa plenitudo capi possit." de Trin. 19, 1.

Thus Athan. says, "Let them dare to say openly .. that the Fountain failed to beget Wisdom, whence it would follow that there is no longer a Fountain, but a sort of pool, as if receiving water from without, yet usurping the name of Fountain." Decr. § 15; vid. also Orat. i. § 14 and 19. And so πηγὴ ξηρὰ, Serap. ii. 2; Orat. i. § 14 fin.; also καρπογόνος ἡ οὐσία, ii. § 2, where Athanasius speaks as if those who deny that Almighty God is Father cannot really believe in Him as a Creator. "If our Lord be not a Son, let Him be called a work .. and let God be called, not Father, but Framer only and Creator, .. and not of a generative nature. But if the divine substance be not fruitful (καρπογόνος), but barren, as they say, as a light which enlightens not, and a dry fountain, are they not ashamed to maintain that He possesses the creative energy?" Vid. also πηγὴ θεότητος, Pseudo-Dion. Div. Nom. ii. 4; πηγὴ ἐκ πηγῆς, of the Son, Epiphan. Ancor. 19. And Cyril, "If thou take from God His being Father, thou wilt deny the generative power (καρπογόνον) of the divine nature, so that It no longer is *perfect*. This then is a token of its perfection, and the Son who went forth from Him apart from time, is a pledge (σφραγὶς) to the Father that He is perfect." Thesaur. p. 37. Vid. also γεννητικὸς, Orat. ii. § 2, iii. § 66, iv. § 4 fin.; ἄγονος, i. 14, 19, and Sent. Dion. 15 and 19; ἡ φυσικὴ γονιμότης, Damasc. F. O. i. 8; ἄκαρπος, Cyr. Thes. p. 45; Epiph. Hær. 65, p. 609; also the γέννησις and the κτίσις connected together, Orat. i. 29. This doctrine is briefly expressed in Orat. iv. 4, εἰ ἄγονος, καὶ ἀνενέργητος. So much at least is plain at first sight, that a divine *gennesis* is not more difficult to our imagination than a creation out of nothing.

This is the first conclusion which we are in a position to draw under the sanction given to our reasonings by the revelation of the doctrine of the Holy Trinity in Unity.

2. A second conclusion is suggested by Thomassin's words, towards the end of the above quotation, " ut effluat nec extra effluat." It is the first of truths that there is but one only Supreme Almighty Being. The Arians and others accused Catholics, in their maintenance of our Lord's Divinity, of virtually contravening this initial doctrine of all faith; as Euseb. Eccl. Theol. i. 10, p. 69; and accordingly they insisted on His being external and thereby subordinate and inferior to God. But this was in fact to admit that He was not born from God at all, but κεκολλῆσθαι τῷ πατρὶ λόγον, Orat. iv. § 3; and Marcellus, according to Eusebius, spoke of Him as ἡνωμένον τῷ θεῷ λόγον (vid. συμβεβηκὸς), Athan. protesting on the other hand against the notion " that the Fountain begat not wisdom from Itself, but acquired it from without," vid. supr. Decr. § 15, and Orat. iv. § 4, and laying down the principle οὐδὲν ἐν πρὸς τὸν πατέρα, εἰ μὴ τὸ ἐξ αὐτοῦ. Orat. iv. 17.

¶ But the Son still was *in* as well as *from* the Father, and this union of distant characteristics in the Son was signified by S. John by the word πρὸς, i. 1, whereas the Sabellians preferred to say ἐν τῷ θεῷ. Hence

Basil, ὁ ἐν ἀνθρώπῳ λόγος οὐ πρὸς αὐτὸν εἶναι λέγεται ἀλλ' ἐν αὐτῷ, c. Sabell. 1 fin., but the Divine Son was πρὸς τὸν θεόν, not ἐν τῷ θεῷ. It was in this sense and with this explanation that Catholics held and insisted on the Divine Unity; or, as they then called it, the *Monarchia*: and thence they went on to the second great doctrine associated in theology with the Eternal Father, and signified by Thomassin in the above extract in the words, " ut effluat flumen Deitatis nec extra effluat." The Infinite Father of an Infinite Son must necessarily be conterminous (so to speak) with Him. A second self (still to use inaccurate language) cannot be a second God. The *Monarchia* of the Father is not only the symbol of the Divine Unity, but of the Trinity in that Unity, for it implies the presence of Those who, though supreme, are not ἀρχαί. This was especially its purpose in the first centuries, when polytheistic errors prevailed. The Son and Spirit were then viewed relatively to the Father, and the Father as the absolute God. Even now statements remain in the Ritual of the old usage, as in the termination of Collects, and as in the Sunday Preface in the Mass: " Pater Omnipotens, qui cum Unigenito Filio tuo et Spiritu Sancto, Unus es Deus," instead of the " Pater, Filius, Spiritus Sanctus, Unus Deus " of the Psalmus *Quicunque*.

And so, " The Word," says Athan., " being the Son of the One God, is *referred* to Him *of whom* also He is." Orat. iv. § 1. εἰς αὐτὸν ἀναφέρεται. vid. also Nazianz. Orat. 20, 7 ; Damasc. F. O. i. 8, p. 140 ; Theod. Abuc. Opusc. 42 , p. 542. And so ἀνάγεται, Naz. Orat. 42, 15 ; and ἵνα ἡμᾶς ἀναπέμψῃ ἐπὶ τὴν τοῦ πατρὸς αὐθεντίαν, Euseb. Eccl. Theol. i. 20, p. 84, though in an heretical sense. (Vid. a remarkable illustration of this, under *Ignorance* in Basil on Mark xiii. 32.) This, then, is the Catholic doctrine of the Monarchia, in opposition to the Three Archical Hypostases of Plato and others. The Son and the Spirit were viewed as the Father's possession, as one with Him yet as really distinct from Him as a man's hands are one and not one with himself; but still, in spite of this, as being under the conditions of a nature at once spiritual and infinite, therefore, in spite of this analogy, not inferior, even if subordinate to the Father. The word "parts" belongs to bodies, and implies magnitude; but as the soul has powers and properties, conscience, reason, imagination, and the like, but no parts, so each Person of the Holy Trinity must either be altogether and fully God, or not God at all.

¶ By the Monarchy is meant the doctrine that the Second and Third Persons in the Ever-blessed Trinity are ever to be referred in our thoughts to the First as the Fountain of Godhead. It is one of the especial senses in which God is said to be one. " We are not introducing three origins or three Fathers, as the Marcionites and Manichees, just as our illustration is not of three suns, but of sun and its radiance." Orat. iii. § 15 ; vid. also iv. § 1. Serap. i. 28 fin. Naz. Orat. 23, 8. Bas. Hom. 24, init. Nyssen. Orat. Cat. 3, p. 481. " The Father is *unition*, ἕνωσις," says S. Greg. Naz., "from whom and unto whom are the others." Orat. 42, 15; also Orat. 20, 7,

and Epiph. Hær. 57, 5. Tertullian, and Dionysius of
Alexandria after him (Athan. Decr. § 26), uses the word
Monarchia, which Praxeas had perverted into a kind
of Unitarianism or Sabellianism, in Prax. 3. Irenæus
too wrote on the Monarchy, i. e. against the doctrine
that God is the author of evil. Eus. Hist. v. 20. And
before him was Justin's work " de Monarchiâ," where
the word is used in opposition to Polytheism. The
Marcionites, whom Dionysius also mentions, are
referred to by Athan. de Syn. § 52; vid. also Cyril.
Hier. Cat. xvi. 4. Epiphanius says that their three
origins were God, the Creator, and the evil spirit,
Hær. 42, 3. or as Augustine says, the good, the just,
and the wicked, which may be taken to mean nearly
the same thing. Hær. 22. The Apostolical Canons
denounce those who baptize into Three Unoriginate;
vid. also Athan. Tom. ad Antioch. 5; Naz. Orat. 20, 6.
Basil denies τρεῖς ἀρχικαὶ ὑποστάσεις, de Sp. S. § 38.

¶ When characteristic attributes and prerogatives
are ascribed to God, or to the Father, this is done only
to the exclusion of creatures, or of false gods, not to
the exclusion of His Son who is implied in the mention
of Himself. Thus when God is called only wise, or
the Father the only God, or God is said to be ingenerate, ἀγένητος, this is not in contrast to the Son, but to
all things which are distinct from God. vid. Athan.
Orat. iii. 8; Naz. Orat. 30, 13; Cyril. Thesaur. p. 142.
"The words 'one' and 'only' ascribed to God in
Scripture," says S. Basil, "are not used in contrast
to the Son or the Holy Spirit, but with reference to
those who are not God, and falsely called so." Ep. 8,

n. 3. On the other hand, when the Father is mentioned, the other Divine Persons are implied in Him. " The Blessed and Holy Trinity," says S. Athan., "is indivisible and one with Itself ; and when the Father is mentioned, His Word is present too (πρόσεστι), and the Spirit in the Son ; and if the Son is named, in the Son is the Father, and the Spirit is not external to the Word." ad Serap. i. 14. " I have named the Father," says S. Dionysius, "and before I mention the Son, I have already signified Him in the Father ; I have mentioned the Son, and though I had not yet named the Father, He had been fully comprehended in the Son," &c. Sent. D. 17, vid. art. *Coinherence.*

¶ Passages like these are distinct from that in which Athan. says that "Father implies Son," Orat. iii. § 6, for there the question is of words, but here of fact. That the words are correlative, even Eusebius does not scruple to admit in Sabell. i. (ap. Sirm. t. i. p. 8.) "Pater statim, **ut** dictus fuit pater, *requirit ista vox* filium, &c. ;" but in that passage no περιχώρησις is implied, which *is* the orthodox doctrine. Yet Petavius observes as to the very *word* περιχώρησις that one of its first senses in ecclesiastical writers was this which Arians would not disclaim ; its use to express the Catholic doctrine here spoken of was later. Vid. de Trin. iv. 16.

3. Thirdly, from what has been said, since God, although He is One and Only, nevertheless is Father because He is God, we are led to understand that He is Father in a sense of His own, not in a mere human sense ; for a Father, who was like other fathers,

would of course impart to a Son that which he was
himself, and thus God would have a Son who could be
a father, and, as God, would in His Son commence a
θεογονία; this was the objection of the Arians; but His
Son is His Image, not as Father, but as God; and to
be Father is not the accident of His Person, as in the
case of men, but belongs necessarily to it; and His
personality in the Godhead consists, as far as we know
it, in His being Father and in nothing else; and can only
so be defined or described; and so in a parallel way as
regards the Son. The words " Father " and " Son "
have a high archetypical sense, and human fathers
and sons have but the shadow of it.

¶ With us a son becomes a father because our
nature is ῥευστὴ, transitory and without stay, ever
shifting and passing on into new forms and relations :
but God is perfect and ever the same; what He is
once, that He continues to be; God the Father remains
Father, and God the Son remains Son. Moreover men
become fathers by detachment and transmission, and
what is received is handed on in a succession; thus Levi
before his birth was in the loins of Abraham; whereas it
is by imparting Himself wholly that the Father begets
the Son; and a perfect *gennesis* finds its termination in
itself. The Son has not a Son, because the Father has
not a Father. Thus the Father is the only true Father,
and the Son only true Son; the Father only a Father,
the Son only a Son; being really in Their Persons
what human fathers are but by function, circumstance, accident, and name. And since the Father
is unchangeable as Father, in nothing does the Son

more fulfil the idea of a perfect Image than in being unchangeable too. Thus S. Cyril. also, Thesaur. 4, pp. 22, 23; 13, p. 124, &c.

Men differ from each other as being individuals, but the characteristic difference between Father and Son is, not that they are separate individuals, but that they *are* Father and Son. In these extreme statements it must be ever borne in mind that we are contemplating divine things according to *our notions,* not in *fact:* i. e. we are speaking of the Almighty Father, *as such;* there being no real separation between His Person and His Substance.

¶ Thus Athanasius: "'If the Son is the Father's offspring and image, and is like in all things to the Father,' say the Arians, 'then it necessarily holds that as He is begotten, so He begets, and He too becomes father of a son. And again, he who is begotten from Him, begets in his turn, and so on without limit; for this is to make the Begotten like Him that begat Him.' Authors of blasphemy, . . if God be as man, let Him be also a parent as man, so that His Son should be father of another, and so in succession one from another, till the series they imagine grows into a multitude of gods. But if God be not as man, as He is not, we must not impute to Him the attributes of man. For brutes and men, after that a Creator has begun their line, are begotten by succession; and the son, having been begotten of a father who was a son, becomes accordingly in his turn a father to a son, in inheriting from his father that by which he himself has come into being. Hence in such instances there is not, properly speaking, either father or son, nor do the father and the son stay in their respective characters, for the son himself becomes a father, being son of his father, and father of his son. But it is not so in the Godhead ; for not as man is God; for the Father is not from father; therefore doth He not beget one who shall beget; nor is the Son from effluence of the Father, nor is He begotten from a father that was begotten ; therefore neither is He begotten so as to beget. Thus it belongs to the Godhead alone, that the Father is properly (κυρίως) father, and the Son properly son, and in Them, and Them only, does it hold that the Father is ever Father and the Son ever Son. Therefore he who asks why the Son has not a son, must inquire why the Father had not a father. But both suppositions are indecent and impious exceedingly. For as the Father is ever Father and never could be Son, so the Son is ever Son and never could be Father. For in this rather is He shown to be the Father's Impress and Image, remaining what He is and not changing, but thus receiving from the Father to be one and the same." Orat. i. § 21, 22. Presently he says, "For God does not *make men His pattern,* but rather, for that God *is properly* and alone truly Father of His Son, we men also are called fathers of our own children, for ' of Him is every fatherhood in heaven and on earth named.' " § 23. The Semi-Arians at Ancyra quote the same text for the same doctrine. Epiphan. Hær. 73, 5. As do Cyril. in Joan. iii. p. 24 ; Thesaur. 32, p. 281 ; and Damascene de Fid. Orth. i. 8.

Again : " As men create not as God creates, as their

being is not such as God's being, so men's generation
is in one way, and the Son is from the Father in another.
For the offspring of men are portions of their fathers,
since the very nature of bodies is not uncompounded,
but transitive, and composed of parts; and men lose
their substance in begetting, and again they gain
substance from the accession of food. And on this
account men in their time become fathers of many
children; but God, being without parts, is Father of
the Son without partition or passion; for of the Immaterial there is neither effluence nor accession from
without, as among men; and being uncompounded in
nature, He is Father of One Only Son. This is why the
Son is Only-begotten, and alone in the Father's bosom,
and alone is acknowledged by the Father to be from
Him, saying, *This is My beloved Son, in whom I am
well pleased."* de Decr. § 11. The parallel, with which
this passage begins, as existing between creation and
generation, is insisted on by Isidor. Pel. Ep. iii. 355;
Basil. contr. Eun. iv. 1, p. 280, A; Cyril. Thesaur. 6.
p. 43; Epiph. Hær. 69, 36; and Gregor. Naz. Orat. 20,
9, who observes that God creates with a *word*, Ps. 148,
5, which evidently transcends human creations. (Vid.
also supr. 1st part of this art.) Theodorus Abucara,
with the same object, draws out the parallel of life, ζωή,
as Athan. that of being, εἶναι. Opusc. iii. p. 420–422.

The word κυρίως, used in the first of these passages,
also occurs on the same subject in Serap. i. § 16.
" The Father, being one and only, is Father of a Son
one and only; and in the instance of Godhead only
have the names Father and Son stay, and are ever; for

of men if any one be called father, yet he has been son
of another; and if he be called son, yet is he called
father of another; so that in the case of men the
names father and son do not properly, κυρίως, hold."
Vid. the whole passage. Also ibid. iv. 4 fin. and 6;
vid. also κυρίως, Greg. Naz. Orat. 29, 5; ἀληθῶς,
Orat. 25, 16; ὄντως, Basil. contr. Eunom. i. 5, p.
215.

¶ 'Ο μὲν πατὴρ, πατήρ ἐστι. Orat. iii. § 11. And so,
"In the Godhead only, ὁ πατὴρ κυρίως ἐστὶ πατὴρ,
καὶ ὁ υἱὸς κυρίως υἱός." Serap. i. 16. He speaks of
"receding from things generate, casting away created
images, and ascending to the Father." Syn. § 51, and
of men "not being in nature and truth benefactors,"
Almighty God being Himself the type and pattern.
Orat. iii. § 19. And so S. Cyril, τὸ κυρίως τίκτον ἐξ ἑαυτοῦ
τὸ θεῖόν ἐστιν, ἡμεῖς δὲ κατὰ μίμησιν. Thesaur. 13, p. 133,
πατὴρ κυρίως, ὅτι μὴ καὶ υἱός· ὥσπερ καὶ υἱὸς κυρίως, ὅτι
μὴ καὶ πατήρ. Naz. Orat. 29, 5; vid. also 23, 6 fin. 25,
16; vid. also the whole of Basil. adv. Eun. ii. 23.
"One must not say," he observes, "that these names
properly and primarily, κυρίως καὶ πρώτως, belong to
men, and are given by us but by a figure καταχρησ-
τικῶς (vol. i. p. 19, note 2) to God. For our Lord Jesus
Christ, referring us back to the Origin of all and True
Cause of beings, says, 'Call no one your father upon
earth, for One is your Father, which is in heaven.'" He
adds, that if He is properly and not metaphorically the
Father even of us, much more is He the πατὴρ τοῦ κατὰ
φύσιν υἱοῦ. Vid. also Euseb. contr. Marc. i. 4, p. 22. Eccl.
Theol. i. 12 fin.; ii. 6. Marcellus, on the other hand,

contrasting Son and Word, said that our Lord was κυρίως λόγος, not κυρίως υἱός. ibid. ii. 10 fin.

S. Basil says in like manner that, though God is Father κυρίως (properly), yet it comes to the same thing though we were to say that He is τροπικῶς and ἐκ μεταφορᾶς, figuratively, Father; contr. Eun. ii. 24; for in that case we must, as in other metaphors used of Him (anger, sleep, flying), take that part of the human sense which can apply to Him. Now γέννησις implies two things—passion, and relationship, οἰκείωσις φύσεως; accordingly we must take the latter as an indication of the divine sense of the term. On the terms Son, Word, &c., being figurative, or illustrative, and how to use them, vid. also de Decr. § 12; Orat. i. § 26, 27, ii. § 32, iii. § 18, 67; Basil. contr. Eunom. ii. 17; Hil. de Trin. iv. 2. Vid. also Athan. ad Serap. i. 20, and Basil. Ep. 38, n. 5, and what is said of the office of faith in each of these.

FLESH.

WE know that our Lord took our flesh and in it by His death atoned for our sins, and by the grace communicated to us through that Flesh, renews our nature; but the question arises whether He took on Him our flesh as it was in Adam before the fall, or as it is now. To this the direct and broad answer is,—He assumed it as it is after the fall,—though of course some explanations have to be made.

¶ It was usual to say against the Apollinarians, that, unless our Lord took on Him our nature, *as it is*, He had not purified and changed it, as it is, but another nature; "The Lord came not to save Adam as free from sin, that unto him He should become like; but as, in the net of sin and now fallen, that God's mercy might raise him up with Christ." Leont. contr. Nestor. &c. ii. t. 9. p. 692, Bibl. Max. Accordingly Athan. says, "He took a servant's form, putting on that flesh, which was enslaved to sin." Orat. i. § 43. And, "Had no Sinlessness appeared *in the nature which had sinned*, how was sin condemned in the flesh?" in Apoll. ii. 6. "It was necessary for our salvation," says S. Cyril, "that the Word of God should become man, that human flesh *subject to corruption* and *sick with the lust of pleasures*, He might make His own; and, *whereas He is life and life-giving*, He might *destroy the corruption*

&c. . . . . For by this means might sin in our flesh become dead." Ep. ad Success. i. p. 138. And S. Leo, "Non alterius naturæ erat ejus caro quam nostra, nec alio illi quam cæteris hominibus anima est inspirata principio, quæ excelleret, non diversitate generis, sed sublimitate virtutis." Ep. 35 fin.; vid. also Ep. 28, 3; Ep. 31, 2; Ep. 165, 9; Serm. 22, 2, and 25, 5. It may be asked whether this doctrine does not interfere with that of the Miraculous Conception; but that miracle was wrought in order that our Lord might not be born in original sin, and does not affect, or rather we may say it includes, His taking flesh of the Blessed Virgin's substance, i. e. of a fallen nature. If indeed sin were *of the substance* of our fallen nature, as some heretics have said, then He could not have taken our nature without partaking our sinfulness; but if sin be, as it is, a fault of the *will*, then the Divine Power of the Word could sanctify the human will, and keep it from swerving in the direction of evil. Hence S. Austin says, "We say not that it was by the *felicity of a flesh* separated from sense that Christ *could not* feel the desire of sin, but that *by perfection of virtue*, and by a flesh not begotten through concupiscence of the flesh, He had not the desire of sin." Op. Imperf. iv. 48. On the other hand, S. Athanasius expressly calls it Manichean doctrine to consider τὴν φύσιν of the flesh ἁμαρτίαν, καὶ οὐ τὴν πρᾶξιν, contr. Apoll. i. 12 fin., or φυσικὴν εἶναι τὴν ἁμαρτίαν, ibid. i. 14 fin. His argument in Apoll. i. 15 is on the ground that all *natures* are from God, but God made man upright nor can be the author of evil (vid. also Vit.

Anton. 20); " not as if," he says, " the devil wrought in
man a nature, (God forbid!) for of a nature the devil
cannot be maker (δημιουργὸς), as is the impiety of the
Manichees, but he wrought a bias of nature by transgression, and 'so death reigned over all men.'
Wherefore, saith He, 'the Son of God came to
destroy the works of the devil;' what works? that
nature, which God made sinless, and the devil biassed
to the transgression of God's command and the assault
of sin which is death, did God the Word raise
again, so as to be secure from the devil's bias and the
assault of sin.   And therefore the Lord said, 'The
prince of this world cometh and findeth nothing in
Me.' " vid. also § 19.   Ibid. ii. 6, he speaks of the
devil having introduced " the *law* of sin." vid. also § 9.

¶ " As, since the flesh has become the all-quickening
Word's, it overbears the might of corruption and
death, so, I think, since the soul became His who
knew not error, it has an unchangeable condition for
all good things established in it, and far more vigorous
than the sin that of old time tyrannized over us.   For,
first and only of men on the earth, Christ did not sin,
nor was guile found in His mouth; and He is laid
down as a root and firstfruit of those who are re-
fashioned unto newness of life in the Spirit, and unto
immortality of body, and He will transmit to the whole
human race the firm security of the Godhead, as by
participation and by grace."   Cyril. de Rect. Fid.
p. 18.   Vid. art. *Specialties.*

USE OF FORCE IN RELIGION.

" In no long time," says Athan., "they will turn to
outrage ; and next they will threaten us with the band
and the captain." Vid. John xviii. 12.   Elsewhere he
speaks of tribune and governour, with an allusion to
Acts xiii. 22, 24, &c. Hist. Arian. § 66 fin. and 67 ; vid.
also § 2.   " How venture they to call that a Council,
in which a Count presided, &c." Apol. c. Ar. 8 ; vid.
also 10, 45 ; Ep. Enc. 5.   And so also doctrinally,
"Our Saviour is so gentle that He teaches thus, *If
any man wills to come after Me,* and *Whoso wills to be
My disciple;* and coming to each, He does not force
them, but knocks at the door and says, *Open unto Me,
My sister, My spouse;* and, if they open to Him, He
enters in, but if they delay and will not, He departs
from them.   For *the Truth* is not preached with swords
or with darts, nor by means of soldiers, but by per-
suasion and counsel." Ar. Hist. § 33 ; vid. also 67, and
Hilar. ad Const. i. 2.   On the other hand he observes
of the Nicene Fathers, " It was not necessity which
drove the judges " to their decision, "but all vindicated the Truth of deliberate purpose."   Ep. Æg. 13.

As to the view taken in early times of the use of
force in religion, it seems to have been that that was
a bad cause which depended upon it ; but that, when
a cause was good, there was nothing wrong in using

secular means in due subordination to argument; that it was as lawful to urge religion by such means on individuals who were incapable of higher motives, as by inducements of temporal advantage. Our Lord's kingdom was not of this world, in that it did not depend on this world; but means of this world were sometimes called for in order to lead the mind to an act of faith in that which was not of this world. The simple question was, whether a cause depended on force for its success. S. Athanasius declared, and the event proved, that Arianism was thus dependent. When Emperors ceased to persecute, Arianism ceased to be; it had no life in itself. Again, active heretics were rightly prevented by secular means from spreading the poison of their heresy. But all exercise of temporal pressure, long continued or on a large scale, was wrong, as arguing an absence of moral and rational grounds in its justification. Again, the use of secular weapons in ecclesiastical hands was a scandal, as *negotiatio* would be. And further there is an abhorrence of cruelty, just and natural to us, which may easily be elicited, unless the use of the secular arm is directed with much discretion and charity. For a list of passages from the Fathers on the subject, vid. Limborch on the Inquisition, vol. i. and ii. 2 and 5; Bellarmin. de Laicis, c. 21, 22. For authors who defend its adoption, vid. Gerhard de Magistr. Polit. p. 741. So much as to the question of principle, which even Protestants act on and have generally acted; in this day and here, State interference would so simply tell against the Catholic cause, that it would be a marvel to find any Catholic advocating it.

In that day it was a thought which readily arose in the minds of zealous men. Thus :

¶ " Who comprehends not the craft of these God-assailants ? who but would stone such madmen ? οὐκ ἂν καταλιθώσειεν." Decr. § 28. .

" If then they thus conceive of the Son, let all men throw stones at them, considering, as they do, the Word a part of this universe, and a part insufficient without the rest for the service committed to Him. But if this be manifestly impious, let them acknowledge that the Word is not in the number of things made, but the sole and proper Word of the Father, and their Framer. His words are βαλλέσθωσαν παρὰ πάντων," Orat. ii. § 28. Vid. also i. 38, and iii. 41.

¶ There is an apparent allusion in such passages to the punishment of blasphemy and idolatry under the Jewish Law. Vid. art. *Definition*, supra, Ex. xxi. 17. Thus, for instance, Nazianzen : " While I go up the mount with good heart, . . that I may become within the cloud, and may hold converse with God, for so God bids, if there be any Aaron, let him go up with me and stand near. . . And if there be any Nadab or Abiud, or any of the elders, let him go up, but stand far off, according to the measure of his purification. . . . But if any one is an evil and savage beast, and quite inca-pable of science and theology . . let him stand off still further, and depart from the mount ; *or he will be stoned* and crushed ; for the wicked shall be miserably destroyed. For *as stones for the bestial are true words and strong.* Whether he be leopard, let him die spots and all," &c. Orat. 28, 2. The stoning then was

metaphorical; the stones were strong words. In the
same way S. Dionysius speaks of the charges of heterodoxy brought against him before the Roman See.
"By two words taken out of their context, as with
stones, they sling at me from a distance." Athan. de
Sent. D. § 18.

¶ "Are they not deserving of many deaths?" Orat.
ii. § 4. "You *ought* (ὤφειλες) to have your impious
tongue cut out," the Arian Acacius says to Marcellus,
ap. Epiph. Hær. 72, 7. "If Eutyches thinks otherwise
than the decrees of the Church, he *deserves* (ἄξιος) not
only punishment, but the fire." Dioscorus ap. Concil.
Chalced. (Hard. t. 2, p. 100.) In time they advanced
from accounting to doing. The Emperor Justin
proposes to cut out the heretic Severus's tongue,
Evagr. iv. 4; and "blasphemiis lapidasti," Theodor.
ap. Concil. 6. (Labbe, t. 6, p. 88.) Afterwards
we find an advance from allegory to fact. Sometimes
it was a literalism deduced from the doctrine in dispute;
as the heretics at the Latrocinium cried, " Cut in two
those who assert two Natures." Concil. Hard. t. 2, p.
81. Palladius relates a case in which a sort of ordeal
became a punishment: Abbot Copres proposed to a
Manichee to enter a fire with him. After Copres had
come out unharmed, the populace forced the Manichee
into it, and then cast him, burnt as he was, out of the
city. Hist. Lausiac. 54. S. Gregory mentions the
case of a wizard, who had pretended to be a monk,
and had used magical arts against a nun, being subsequently burned by the Roman populace. Dial. i. 4.

FREEDOM OF OUR MORAL NATURE.

THIS, it need hardly be said, is one of the chief blessings which we have secured to us by the Incarnation. We are by nature the captives and prisoners of our inordinate and unruly passions and desires; we are not our own masters, till our Lord sets us free; and the main question is, how does He set us free, and by what instrumentality?

1. Here we answer, first, by bringing home to us the broad and living law of liberty and His own pattern which He has provided for us. "Whereas," Athan. says, "of things made the nature is alterable, . . therefore there was here need of One who was unalterable, that men might have the immutability of the righteousness of the Word as an image and type for virtue." Orat. i. § 51. (*Disc.* n. 84.)

¶ Vid. Athan. de Incarn. § 13, 14; vid. also Gent. 41 fin. "Cum justitia nulla esset in terrâ, doctorem misit, quasi vivam legem." Lactant. Instit. iv. 25. "The Only-begotten was made man like us, . . . as if lending us His own steadfastness." Cyril. in Joann. lib. v. 2, p. 473; vid. also Thesaur. 20, p. 198; August. de Corr. et Grat. 10—12; Damasc. F. O. iv. 4. And this pattern to us He is, not only through His incarnation, but as manifested in a measure by His glory, as πρωτότοκος, in the visible universe.

Vid. a beautiful passage, contr. Gent. 42, &c. Again,
"He made them [men] after His own image, imparting to them of the power of His proper Word, that,
having as it were *certain shadows of the* Word, and
becoming rational, λογικοὶ, they might be enabled to
continue in blessedness." Incarn. 3; vid. also Orat.
ii. § 78, (*Disc.* n. 215), where he speaks of Wisdom as
being infused into the world on its creation, that the
world might possess "an impress and semblance of
Its Image."

So again, "He is the Truth, but we by imitation
become virtuous and sons; . . that, as He, being the
Word, is in His own Father, so we too, taking Him as
an exemplar, might live in unanimity," &c. &c. Κατὰ
μίμησιν. Orat. iii. § 19. (*Disc.* n. 252); Clem. Alex.
τῶν εἰκόνων τὰς μὲν ἐκτρεπομένους, τὰς δὲ μιμουμένους.
Pædag. i. 3, p. 102, ed. Pott. and μιμήσει τοῦ νοὸς
ἐκείνου. Naz. Ep. 102, p. 95 (ed. Ben.). Vid. Leo
in various places, infra, p. 190, art. *Incarnation;* "ut
imitatores operum, factores sermonum, &c. Iren. Hær.
v. 1; exemplum verum et adjutorium. August.
Serm. 101, 6; mediator non solum per adjutorium,
verùm etiam per exemplum. August. Trin. xiii. 22,
also ix. 21, and Eusebius, though with an heretical
meaning, κατὰ τὴν αὐτοῦ μίμησιν. Eccl. Theol. iii. 19.

2. But of course an opportunity of imitation is not
enough : a powerful internal grace is necessary, however great the beauty of the Moral Law and its Author,
in order to set free and convert the human heart.
"Idly do ye imagine to be able to work in yourselves
newness of the principle which thinks (φρονοῦντος) and

actuates the flesh, expecting to do so by imitation . . .
for if men could have wrought for themselves newness
of that actuating principle without Christ, and if what
is actuated follows what actuates, what need was there
of Christ's coming?" Apoll. i. § 20 fin. And again:
"The Word of God," he says, "underwent a sort of
creation in the Incarnation, in order to effect thereby
our new creation. If He was not thus created for us,"
but was absolutely a creature, which is the Arian
doctrine, "it follows that we are not created in Him;
and, if not created in Him, we have Him not in ourselves, but externally, as, for instance, receiving instruction from Him as from a teacher. And, it being
so with us, sin has not lost its reign over the flesh,
being inherent and not cast out of it." Orat. ii. § 56.
(*Disc.* n. 180.) And this is necessary, he goes on to
say, "that we might have ἐλεύθερον τὸ φρόνημα."

¶ He speaks, contr. Gent., of man "having the
grace of the Giver, and his own virtue from the
Father's Word;" of the mind "seeing the Word,
and in Him the Word's Father also," § 2; of "the way
to God being, not as God Himself, above us and far
off, or external to us, but in us," 30, &c. &c.; vid. also
Basil. de Sp. S. n. 19. This is far more than mere
teaching. "Rational creatures, receiving light," says
Cyril, "enlighten by imparting principles, which are
poured from their own mind into another intellect;
and such an illumination may be justly called teaching
rather than revelation. But the Word of God en-
lighteneth every man that cometh into the world, not
in the way of a teacher, as for instance Angels do or

men, but rather as God, in the way of a Framer, doth He sow in each whom He calls into being the seed of Wisdom, that is of divine knowledge, and implant a root of understanding," &c. Cyril. in Joan. xix. p. 75. Athan. speaks of this seed sometimes as natural, sometimes as supernatural, and indeed the one order of grace is parallel to the other, and not incompatible with it. Again, he speaks of " a reason combined and connatural with everything that came into being, which some are wont to call seminal, inanimate indeed and unreasoning and unintelligent, but operating only by external art according to the science of Him who sowed it." contr. Gent. 40. Thus there are three supernatural aids given to men of which the Word is the ἀρχὴ, that of instinct, of reason, and the " gratia Christi."

3. Even this is not all which is given us over and above nature. The greatest and special gift is the actual presence, as well as the power within us of the Incarnate Son as a principle or ἀρχὴ (vid. art. ἀρχὴ) of sanctification, or rather of deification. (vid. art. *Deif.*) On this point Athan. especially dwells in too many passages to quote or name.

E.g. " The Word of God was made man in order to sanctify the flesh." Orat. ii. § 10. (*Disc.* n. 114 fin.) " Ye say, ' He destroyed [the works of the devil] by not sinning ;' but this is no destruction of sin For not in Him did the devil in the beginning work sin, that by His coming into the world and not sinning sin was destroyed ; but whereas the devil had wrought sin by an after-sowing in the rational and spiritual nature of man, therefore it became impossible for nature, which was rational and had voluntarily sinned, and fell under the penalty of death, to recover itself into freedom (ἐλευθερίαν). . . . Therefore came the Son of God by Himself to establish [the flesh] in His own nature from a new beginning (ἀρχὴ) and a marvellous generation." Apoll. ii. § 6.

¶ "True, without His incarnation at all, God was able to speak the Word only and undo the curse . . . but then the power indeed of Him who gave command had been shown, but man would have fared but as Adam before the fall, by receiving grace only from without, not having it united to the body. . . Then, had he been again seduced by the serpent, a second need had arisen of God's commanding and undoing the curse ; and thus the need had been interminable, and men had remained under guilt just as before, being in slavery to sin, &c. Orat. ii. § 68. (*Disc.* n. 200); vid arts. *Incarnation* and *Sanctification.* And so in Incarn. § 7, he says that repentance might have been pertinent, had man merely offended, without *corruption* following ; but that that *corruption* involved the necessity of the Word's vicarious sufferings and intercessory office.

¶ "If the works of the Word's Godhead had not taken place through the body, man had not been made god; and again, had not the belongings of the flesh been ascribed to the Word, man had not been thoroughly delivered from them ; but though they had ceased for a little while, as I said before, still sin had remained in man and corruption, as was the case with mankind before He came ; and for this reason :—

K 2

Many, for instance, have been made holy and clean from all sin; nay, Jeremias was hallowed, even from the womb, and John, while yet in the womb, leapt for joy at the voice of Mary Mother of God; nevertheless *death reigned from Adam to Moses, even over those that had not sinned after the similitude of Adam's transgression;* and thus men remained mortal and corruptible as before, liable to the affections proper to their nature. But now the Word having become man and having appropriated the affections of the flesh, no longer do these affections touch the body, because of the Word who has come in it, but they are destroyed by Him, and henceforth men no longer remain sinners and dead according to their proper affections, but having risen according to the Word's power, they abide ever immortal and incorruptible. Whence also, whereas the flesh is born of Mary Mother of God, He Himself is said to have been born, who furnishes to others a generation of being; in order that, by His transferring our generation into Himself, we may no longer, as mere earth, return to earth, but as being knit into the Word from heaven, may be carried to heaven by Him." Orat. iii. 33. (*Disc.* n. 270.)

¶ "We could not otherwise," says S. Irenæus, "receive incorruption and immortality, but by being united to incorruption and immortality. But how could this be, unless incorruption and immortality had first been made what we are? that corruption might be absorbed by incorruption and mortal by immortality, that we might receive the adoption of Sons." Hær. iii. 19, n. 1. "He took part of flesh and blood, that

is, He became man, whereas He was Life by nature,
. . . that uniting Himself to the corruptible flesh
according to the measure of its own nature, ineffably,
and inexpressibly, and as He alone knows, He might
bring it to His own life, and render it partaker through
Himself of God and the Father. . . . For He bore our
nature, refashioning it into His own life; . . . He is
in us through the Spirit, turning our natural corruption into incorruption and changing death to its
contrary." Cyril. in Joan. lib. ix. cir. fin. pp. 883, 4.
This is the doctrine of S. Athanasius and S. Cyril,
one may say, *passim*.

¶ Vid. Naz. Epp. ad Cled. 1 and 2 (101, 102, ed.
Ben.); Nyssen. ad Theoph. in Apoll. p. 696. "Generatio
Christi origo est populi Christiani," says S. Leo; "for
whoso is regenerated in Christ," he continues, "has
no longer the propagation from a carnal father, but the
germination of a Saviour, who therefore was made Son
of man, that we might be sons of God." Serm. 26,
2. "Multum fuit a Christo recepisse formam, sed plus
est in Christo habere substantiam. Suscepit nos in
suam proprietatem illa natura," &c. &c. Serm. 72, 2;
vid. Serm. 22, 2; "ut corpus regenerati fiat caro Cruci-
fixi." Serm. 63, 6. "Hæc est nativitas nova dum homo
nascitur in Deo; in quo homine Deus natus est, carne
antiqui seminis susceptâ, sine semine antiquo, ut illam
novo semine, id est, spiritualiter, reformaret, exclusis
antiquitatis sordibus, expiatam." Tertull. de Carn.
Christ. 17; vid. Orat. iii. § 34.

¶ Such is the channel and mode in which spiritual
life and freedom is given to us. Our Lord Himself,

according to the Holy Fathers, is the ἀρχή of the new creation to each individual Christian. If it be asked of them, What real connexion can there possibly be between the sanctification of Christ's manhood and ours? how does it prove that human nature is sanctified because a particular specimen of it was sanctified in Him? S. Chrysostom explains: " He is born of our substance; you will say, 'This does not pertain to all;' yea, to all. He mingles (ἀναμίγνυσιν) Himself with the faithful individually, through the mysteries, and whom He has begotten those He nurses from Himself, not puts them out to other hands," &c. Hom. 82, 5. in Matt. And just before, "It sufficed not for Him to be made man, to be scourged, to be sacrificed; but He assimilates Himself to us (ἀναφύρει ἑαυτὸν ἡμῖν), nor merely by faith, but really, has He made us His body." Again, " That we are commingled (ἀνακερασθῶμεν) into that flesh, not merely through love, but really, is brought about by means of that food which He has bestowed upon us." Hom. 46. 3. in Joann. And so S. Cyril writes against Nestorius: " Since we have proved that Christ is the Vine, and we branches as adhering to a communion with Him, not spiritual merely but bodily, why clamours he against us thus bootlessly, saying that, since we adhere to Him, not in a bodily way, but rather by faith and the affection of love according to the Law, therefore He has called, not His own flesh the vine, but rather the Godhead?" in Joann. 10, p. 863, 4. And Nyssen: " As they who have taken poison, destroy its deadly power by some other preparation . . . so when we have tasted what

destroys our nature, we have need of that instead
which restores what was destroyed. . . . But what is
this? nothing else than that Body which has been
proved to be mightier than death, and was the beginning, κατήρξατο, of our life.   For a little leaven,"
&c. Orat. Catech. 37. " Decoctâ quasi per ollam carnis
nostræ cruditate, sanctificavit in æternum nobis cibum
carnem suam." Paulin. Ep. 23. 7.   Of course in such
statements nothing *material* is implied.   But without
some explanation of this nature, language such as
S. Athanasius's in the text seems a mere matter of
words.

GRACE OF GOD.

IT is a doctrine much insisted on by S. Athanasius, that, together with the act of creation, there was, on the part of the Creator, a further act conservative of the universo which He was creating. This was the communication to it of a blessing or grace, analogous to the grace and sonship purchased for us by our Lord's incarnation, though distinct in kind from it and far inferior to it; and in consequence the universe is not only γενητὸν but γεννητὸν, not only made, but in a certain sense begotten or generated, and, being moulded on the Pattern supplied by the Divine Nature, is in a true sense an Image or at least a Semblance of the Creator. (Vid. art. γεννητόν.)

In controversy with the Arians, he explains with great care the nature of this gift, because it was their device to reduce our Lord's Sonship, in which lay the proof of His Divinity, to the level of the supernatural adoption which has been accorded by the Creator first to the whole world on its creation, and again through the redemption of the fallen race of man upon the cross.

This grace of adoption was imparted in both cases by the ministration of the Eternal Son, in capacity of Primogenitus or First-born,—as through His Incarnation in the Gospel Economy so through His συγκατάβασις, or the coming in the beginning of His

Personal Presence into the world,—and was His type and likeness stamped upon the world, and a fulness of excellence enriching it from the source of all excellence. (Vid. πρωτότοκος.)

"Since God is self-existing and not composed of parts," says Athan., "such too is His Word also, being One Only-begotten God, who from a Father, as a Fount of Good, has gone forth (προελθὼν) Himself Good, and put into order and into consistency all things. The reason for this is truly admirable, and evidently befitting. For the nature of creatures, as coming into subsistence out of nothing, is dissoluble, and feeble, and, taken by itself, is mortal, but the God of the universe is good and of surpassing beauty in His nature. (vid. ῥευστός) . . Beholding then that all created nature was in respect of its own laws dissoluble and dissolving, lest this should happen to it, and the whole world fall back again into nothing, having made all things by His own Eternal Word, and having given substance to the creation, He refused to let it be carried away and wrecked (χειμάζεσθαι) by stress of its own nature, and, as a Good God, He governs and sustains it all by His own Word, who is Himself God, . . . through whom and in whom all things consist, visible and invisible," &c. contr. Gent. § 41.

Again, "In order that what came into being might not only be, but be good, it pleased God that His own Wisdom should condescend (συγκαταβῆναι) to the creatures, so as to introduce an impress and semblance of Its Image on all in common and on each, that what was made might be manifestly wise works and worthy of God. For as of the Son of God, considered as the Word, our word is an image, so of the same Son considered as Wisdom is the wisdom which is implanted in us an image; in which wisdom we, having the power of knowledge and thought, become recipients of the All-framing Wisdom and through It we are able to know Its Father." Orat. ii. 78. (*Disc.* n. 215.)

¶ S. Cyril, using another figure, says that the universe is grafted on the Word: " He is Only-begotten according to nature, as being alone from the Father, God from God, Light kindled from Light; and He is First-born for our sakes, that, *as if to some immortal root* the whole creation might be ingrafted and might bud forth from the Everlasting. For all things were made by Him, and *consist* for ever and are *preserved in Him.*" Thesaur. 25, p. 238.

Moreover, Athan. goes so far as to suggest that the universe does not evidence the Creator, except as being inhabited by the Son, and that what we see divine in it is His Presence. " He has said, ' The invisible things of Him from the creation of the world are clearly seen, being understood by the things that are made, His eternal Power and Divinity.' . . . Study the context, and ye will see that it is the Son who is signified. For after making mention of the creation, he naturally speaks of the Framer's Power as seen in it, which Power, I say, is the Word of God, by whom all things were made. *If indeed* the creation be sufficient of itself alone, without the Son, to make God known, see that you fall not into the further opinion that without the Son it came to be. But if through the Son it came to be, and *in Him all things consist, it must follow* that he who contemplates the creation rightly, is contemplating also the Word who framed it, and *through Him* begins to apprehend the Father. And on Philip's asking, *Show us the Father*, He *said not,* 'Behold the *creation*,' but, *He that hath seen Me, hath seen the Father."* Orat. i. § 11, 12. (*Disc.* n. 17.)

2. It is then the original συγκατάβασις of the Son, making Himself the First-begotten of the creation in the beginning, which breathes, and which stamps a sort of divinity upon the natural universe, and prepares us for that far higher grace and glory which is given to human nature by means of the Incarnation; this evangelical grace being not merely a gift from above, but an inhabitation of the Giver in man, a communication of His Person, and a participation, as it may be called, of the Virtue of that Person, similar to that, which, when He came upon earth He bestowed on individuals by contact with His hands or His garments for their deliverance from bodily ailments or injuries.

¶ Our Lord, then, came on earth, not merely as the physician of our souls, but as the First-born and the Parent of a new Family, who should be the principle of propagation of a new birth in a fallen world. "The flesh being first sanctified in Him, we have the sequel of the Spirit's grace, receiving out of His fulness." Orat. i. § 50 fin. (*Disc.* n. 83 fin.) "Therefore did He assume the body created and human, that, having renewed it as its Framer, He might make it god in Himself, and thus might introduce us all into the kingdom of heaven after His likeness." Orat. ii. § 70.

"How could we be partakers of that adoption of sons, unless through the Son we had received from Him that communion with Him, unless His Word had been made flesh, and had communicated it to us?" Iren. Hær. iii. 18, 7.

¶ Hence it is that the adoption of sons which is the gift which we gain by the Incarnation, is far more than an adoption in the ordinary sense of that word, and far stronger terms are used of it. Athan. says that we are made sons 'truly,' υἱοποιούμεθα ἀληθῶς. Decr. § 31. (Nic. n. 45.) Again S. Basil says, that we are sons, κυρίως, "properly," and πρώτως, "primarily," in opposition to ἐκ μεταφορᾶς and τροπικῶς, "figuratively," contr. Eunom. ii. 23, 24. S. Cyril too says, that we are sons "naturally," φυσικῶς, as well as κατὰ χάριν, vid. Suicer. Thesaur. v. υἱός, i. 3. Of these words, ἀληθῶς, φυσικῶς, κυρίως, and πρώτως, the first two are commonly reserved for our Lord; e. g. τὸν ἀληθῶς υἱὸν, Orat. ii. § 37. (Disc. n. 150 fin.) ἡμεῖς υἱοὶ, οὐκ ὡς ἐκεῖνος φύσει καὶ ἀληθείᾳ, Orat. iii. § 19. (Disc. n. 251.) Hilary indeed seems to deny us the title of "proper" sons, de Trin. xii. 15; but his "proprium" is a translation of ἴδιον, not κυρίως.

¶ The true statement is, that, whereas there is a primary and secondary sense in which the word Son is used,—the primary, when it has its formal meaning of continuation of nature, and the secondary when it is used nominally, or for an external resemblance to the first meaning,—it is applied to the regenerate, not in the secondary sense, but in the primary. S. Basil and S. Gregory Nyssen consider Son to be " a term of *rela-*

tionship according to *nature*" (vid. art. *Son*), also Basil in Psalm 28, 1. The actual presence of the Holy Spirit in the regenerate in *substance* (vid. Cyril. Dial. 7, p. 638), constitutes this relationship of nature; and hence after the words quoted from S. Cyril in the beginning of this note, in which he says, that we are sons φυσικῶς, he proceeds, " naturally, because *we are in Him*, and in Him alone," vid. Athan.'s words which follow in the text at the end of Decr. § 31. And hence Nyssen lays down, as a received truth, that " to none does the term ' proper,' κυριώτατον, apply, but to one in whom the name responds with truth to the nature." contr. Eunom. iii. p. 123. And he also implies, p. 117, the intimate association of our sonship with Christ's, when he connects together regeneration with our Lord's eternal generation, neither being διὰ παθοῦς, or, of the will of the flesh. If it be asked, what the *distinctive* words are which are incommunicably the Son's, since so much is man's, it is obvious to answer, ἴδιος υἰὸς and μονογενὴς, which are in Scripture, and the symbols " of the substance," and " one in substance," of the Council; and this is the value of the Council's phrases, that, while they guard the Son's divinity, they allow full scope, without risk of intrenching on it, to the Catholic doctrine of the fulness of the Christian privileges.

HAND.

GOD, the Creative Origin and Cause of all beings, acts by the mediation, ministration, or agency of His co-equal Son. To symbolize His numerical oneness with that Son, the Son is called His Hand.

E.g. by Athan. Dec. § 7, 17. Orat. ii. § 31, 71. iv. 26. Also Incarn. c. Ar. 12.

Also by Clem. Recogn. viii. 43. Hom. xvi. 12. Method ap. Phot. cod. 235, p. 937. Iren. Hær. iv. præf. 20, v. 1 and 5 and 6. Clem. Protr. (brachium) p. 93. Potter. Tertull. Herm. 45. Cyprian. Test. ii. 4. Euseb. in Psalm. 108, 27. Hilar. Trin. viii. 22. Basil. Eunom. v. p. 297. Cyril. in Joann. 476, 7, et *alibi*. Thesaur. p. 154. Job. ap. Phot. p. 582. August. in Joan. 48, 7 (though he prefers another use of the word), p. 323.

This image is in contrast with that of *instrument,* ὄργανον, which the Arians would use to express the relation of the Son to the Father, as implying separateness and subservience, whereas the word *Hand* implies His consubstantiality; *vid.* art. *Mediation.*

HERESIES.

¶ HERESIES are *partial* views of the truth, starting from some truth which they exaggerate, and disowning and protesting against other truth, which they fancy inconsistent with it.

¶ All heresies are partial views of the truth, and are wrong, not so much in what they directly say as in what they deny.

¶ All heresies seem connected together and to run into each other. When the mind has embraced one, it is almost certain to run into others, apparently the most opposite, it is quite uncertain which. Thus Arians were a reaction from Sabellians, yet did not the less consider than they that God was but one Person, and that Christ was a creature. Apollinaris was betrayed into his heresy by opposing the Arians, yet his heresy started with the tenet in which the Arians ended, that Christ had no human soul. His disciples became, and even naturally, some of them Sabellians, some Arians. Again, beginning with denying our Lord a soul, he came to deny Him a body, like the Manichees and Docetæ. The same passages from Athanasius will be found to refute both Eutychians and Nestorians, though diametrically opposed to each other : and these agreed together, not only in considering nature and person identical, but, strange to say, in holding, (and the Apollinarians too,) that our Lord's manhood existed before its union with Him, which is the special heresy of Nestorius. Again, the Nestorians were closely connected with the Sabellians and Samosatenes, and the latter with the Photinians and modern Socinians. And the Nestorians were connected with the Pelagians; and Aerius, who denied Episcopacy and prayers for the dead, with the Arians; and his opponent the Semi-Arian Eustathius with the Encratites. One reason of course of this peculiarity of heresy is, that when the mind is once unsettled, it may fall into any error. Another is that it *is* heresy; all heresies being secretly connected, as in temper, so in certain primary principles. And, lastly, the Truth only is a *real* doctrine, and therefore stable; everything false is of a transitory nature and has no stay, like reflections in a stream, one opinion continually passing into another, and creations being but the first stages of dissolution. Hence so much is said in the Fathers of orthodoxy being a narrow way. Thus S. Gregory speaks of the middle and "royal" way. Orat. 32, 6, also Damasc. contr. Jacob. iii. t. 1, p. 398; vid. also Leon. Ep. 85, 1, p. 1051; Ep. 129, p. 1254, "brevissimâ adjectione corrumpitur;" also Serm. 25, 1, p. 83; also Vigil. in Eutych. i. init. " Quasi inter duos latrones crucifigitur Dominus," &c. Novat. Trin. 30. vid. the promise, " Thine ears shall hear a word behind thee, saying, This is the way, walk ye in it, *and go not aside either to the right hand, or to the left.*" Is. xxx. 21.

¶ Heresies run into each other, (one may even say)

logically. No doctrines were apparently more opposed, whether historically or ethically, than the Arian and the Apollinarian or the Monophysite; nay, in statement, so far as the former denied that our Lord was God, the latter that He was man. But their agreement lay in this compromise, that strictly speaking He was neither God nor man. Thus in Orat. ii. § 8, Athan. hints that if the Arians gave the titles (such as Priest) which really belong to our Lord's manhood, to His pre-existent nature, what were they doing but removing the evidences of His manhood, and so far denying it? Vid. the remarkable passage of the Council of Sardica against Valens and Ursacius quoted supr. vol. i. p. 116. In the Arian Creed No. vii. or second Sirmian, it is implied that the Divine Son is passible, the very doctrine against which Theodoret writes one of his Anti-monophysite Dialogues, called Eranistes. He writes another on the ἄτρεπτον of Christ, a doctrine which was also formally denied by Arius, and is defended by Athan. Orat. i. § 35. Vid. art. *Eusebius*, who speaks of our Lord's taking a *body*, almost to the prejudice of the doctrine of His taking a perfect *manhood;* εἰ μὲν ψυχῆς δίκην, &c. Hence it is that Gibbon throws out (ch. 47, note 34), after La Croze, Hist. Christ. des Indes, p. 11, that the Arians invented the term θεοτόκος, which the Monophysites, in their own sense strenuously held, vid. Garner in Mar. Merc. t. 2, p. 299. If the opposites of connected heresies are connected together, then the doctrinal connexion of Arianism and Apollinarianism is shown in their respective opposition to the heresies of Sabellius and

Nestorius. Salig, (Eutych. ant. Eut. 10,) denies the connexion, but with very little show of reason. La Croze calls Apollinarianism "Arianismi tradux," Thes. Ep. Lacroz. t. 3, p. 276.

¶ It was the tendency of all the heresies concerning the Person of Christ to explain away or deny the Atonement. The Arians, after the Platonists, insisted on the pre-existing Priesthood, as if the incarnation and crucifixion were not of its essence. The Apollinarians resolved the Incarnation into a manifestation, Theod. Eran. i. The Nestorians denied the Atonement, Procl. ad Armen. p. 615. And the Eutychians, Leon. Ep. 28, 5.

¶ It is remarkable that the Monophysites should have been forced into their circumscription of the Divine Nature by the limits of the human, considering that Eutyches their Patriarch began with asserting for reverence-sake that the Incarnate Word was not under the *laws* of human nature, vid. infra art. *Specialties,* &c. This is another instance of the running of opposite heresies into each other. Another remarkable instance will be found in art. *Ignorance,* viz. the Agnoetæ, a sect of those very Eutychians, who denied or tended to deny our Lord's manhood with a view of preserving His Divinity, yet who were characterized by holding that He was ignorant as man.

¶ "This passage of the Apostle," Rom. i. 1, "[Marcellus] I know not why perverts, instead of *declared,* ὁρισθέντος, making it *predestined,* προορισθέντος, that the Son may be such as they who are predestined according to foreknowledge." Euseb. contr. Marc. i. 2.

Paul of Samosata also considered our Lord Son by foreknowledge, προγνώσει. vid. Routh, Reliqu. t. 2, p. 466; and Eunomius, Apol. 24.

¶ In spite of their differing diametrically from each other in their respective heresies about the Holy Trinity, that our Lord was not really the Divine Word was the point in which Arians and Sabellians agreed. vid. infr. Orat. iv. init.; also ii. § 22, 40, also Sent. D. 25. Ep. Æg. 14 fin. Epiph. Hær. 72, p. 835.

¶ Heretics have frequently assigned reverence as the cause of their opposition to the Church; and if even Arius was obliged to affect it, the plea may be expected in any others. "O stultos et impios metus," says S. Hilary, "et irreligiosam de Deo sollicitudinem." de Trin. iv. 6. It was still more commonly professed in regard to the Catholic doctrine of the Incarnation. Thus Manes, "Absit ut Dominum nostrum Jesum Christum per naturalia mulieris descendisse confitear; ipse enim testimonium dat, quia de sinibus Patris descendit." Archel. Disp. t. iii. p. 601. "We, as saying that the Word of God is incapable of defilement, even by the assumption of mortal and vulnerable flesh, fear not to believe that He is born of a Virgin; ye" Manichees, "because with impious perverseness ye believe the Son of God to be capable of it, dread to commit him to the flesh." August. contr. Secund. 9. Faustus "is neither willing to receive Jesus of the seed of David, nor made of a woman . . . nor the death of Christ itself, and burial, and resurrection," &c. August. contr. Faust. xi. 3. As the Manichees denied our Lord a body, so the Apollinarians denied Him a rational soul, still under pretence of reverence, because, as they said, the soul was necessarily sinful. Leontius makes this their main argument, ὁ νοῦς ἁμαρτητικός ἐστι, de Sect. iv. p. 507; vid. also Greg. Naz. Ep. 101, ad Cledon. p. 89; Athan. in Apoll. i. 2, 14; Epiph. Ancor. 79, 80. Athan. and others call the Apollinarian doctrine Manichean in consequence. vid. in Apoll. ii. 8, 9, &c. Again, the Eranistes in Theodoret, who advocates a similar doctrine, will not call our Lord *man*. " I consider it important to acknowledge an assumed *nature*, but to call the Saviour of the world *man* is to impair our Lord's glory." Eranist. ii. p. 83. Eutyches, on the other hand, would call our Lord *man*, but refused to admit His human *nature*, and still with the same profession. " Ego," he says, " sciens sanctos et beatos patres nostros refutantes *duarum naturarum* vocabulum, et non *audens* de naturâ tractare Dei Verbi, qui in carnem venit, in veritate non in phantasmate *homo* factus," &c. Leon. Ep. 21, 1 fin. " Forbid it," he says at Constantinople, " that I should say that the Christ was of two natures, or should discuss the nature, φυσιολογεῖν, of my God." Concil. t. 2, p. 157. And so in this day popular Tracts have been published, ridiculing St. Luke's account of our Lord's nativity under pretence of reverence towards the God of all, and interpreting Scripture allegorically on Pantheistic principles. A modern argument for Universal Restitution takes the same form; " Do not *we* shrink from the notion of another's being sentenced to eternal punishment; *are we more merciful than God?* " vid. Matt. xvi. 22, 23.

¶ That heresies before the Arian appealed to Scripture we learn from Tertullian, de Præscr. 42, who warns Catholics against indulging themselves in their own view of isolated texts against the voice of the Catholic Church. vid. also Vincentius, who specifies *obiter* Sabellius and Novatian. Commonit. 2. Still Arianism was contrasted with other heresies on this point, as in these two respects; (1.) they appealed to a *secret tradition*, unknown, even to most of the Apostles, as the Gnostics, Iren. Hær. iii. 1 ; or they professed a gift of prophecy introducing fresh *revelations*, as Montanists, Syn. § 4, and Manichees, Aug. contr. Faust. xxxii. 6.   (2.) The Arians availed themselves of certain texts as objections, argued keenly and plausibly from them, and would not be driven from them.   Orat. ii. § 18, c.; Epiph. Hær. 69, 15.   Or rather they took some words of Scripture, and made their own deductions from them; viz. "Son," "made," " exalted," &c.

¶ "They who do not pertinaciously defend their opinion, false and perverse though it be, especially when it does ·not spring from the audacity of their own presumption, but has come to them from parents seduced and lapsed into error, while they seek the truth with cautious solicitude, and are prepared to correct themselves when they have found it, are by no means to be ranked among heretics." August. Ep. 43, init.; vid. also de Bapt. contr. Don. iv. 20.

HERETICS.

REVEALED truth, to be what it professes, must
have an uninterrupted descent from the Apostles; its
teachers must be unanimous, and persistent in their
unanimity; and it must bear no human master's name
as its designation.

On the other hand, first novelty, next discordance,
vacillation, change, thirdly sectarianism, are consequences and tokens of religious error.

These tests stand to reason; for what is over and
above nature must come from divine revelation; and,
if so, it must descend from the very date when it was
revealed, else it is but matter of opinion; and
opinions vary, and have no warrant of permanence,
but depend upon the relative ability and success of
individual teachers, one with another, from whom they
take their names.

The Fathers abound in passages which illustrate
these three tests.

¶ "Who are you?" says Tertullian, "whence and
when came ye? what do ye on my property, being
none of mine? by what right, O Marcion, cuttest thou
my wood? by what licence, O Valentinus, turnest thou
my springs? by what power, O Apelles, movest thou
my landmarks? Mine is possession. . . . I possess of
old, I have prior possession. . . . I am heir of the

Apostles." Tertull. de Præscr. 37. "Tardily for me hath this time of day put forth these, in my judgment, most impious doctors. Full late hath that faith of mine, which Thou hast taught me, encountered these Masters. Before these names were heard of, I thus believed in Thee, I thus was new born by Thee, and thenceforth I thus am Thine." Hil. de Trin. vi. 21. "What heresy hath ever burst forth, but under the name of some certain men, in some certain place, and at some certain time ? who ever set up any heresy, who first divided not himself from the consent of the universality and antiquity of the Catholic Church ? " Vincent. Lir. Commonit. 24. "I will tell thee my mind briefly and plainly, that thou shouldest remain in that Church which, being founded by the Apostles, endures even to this day. When thou hearest that those who are called Christ's, are named, not after Jesus Christ, but after some one, say Marcionites, Valentinians, &c., know then it is not Christ's Church, but the synagogue of Antichrist. For by the very fact that they are formed afterwards, they show that they are those who the Apostle foretold should come." Jerom. in Lucif. 27. "If the Church was not . . . whence hath Donatus appeared ? from what soil has he sprung ? out of what sea hath he emerged ? from what heaven hath he fallen ? " August. de Bapt. contr. Don. iii. 2. vid. art. *Catholic*, &c.

¶ "However the error was, certainly," says Tertullian ironically, "error reigned so long as heresies were not. Truth needed a rescue, and looked out for Marcionites and Valentinians." "Meanwhile, gospelling was nought,

faith was nought, nought was the baptism of so many
thousand thousand, so many works of faith performed,
so many virtues, so many gifts displayed, so many
priesthoods, so many ministries exercised, nay, so many
martyrdoms crowned." Tertull. Præscr. 29. "'Profane novelties,' which if we receive, of necessity the
faith of our blessed ancestors, either all or a great part
of it, must be overthrown; the faithful people of all
ages and times, all holy saints, all the chaste, all the
continent, all the virgins, all the Clergy, the Deacons,
the Priests, so many thousands of confessors, so great
armies of martyrs, so many famous populous cities and
commonwealths, so many islands, provinces, kings,
tribes, kingdoms, nations, to conclude, almost now the
whole world, incorporated by the Catholic Faith to
Christ their head, must needs be said, so many hundred
years, to have been ignorant, to have erred, to have
blasphemed, to have believed they knew not what."
Vinc. Comm. 24. "O the extravagance! the wisdom,
hidden until Christ's coming, they announce to us to-
day, which is a thing to draw tears. For if the faith
began thirty years since, while near four hundred are
past since Christ was manifested, nought hath been
our gospel that long while, and nought our faith, and
fruitlessly have martyrs been martyred, and fruitlessly
have such and so great rulers ruled the people. Greg.
Naz. ad Cledon. Ep. 102, p. 97.

¶ "They know not to be reverent even to their
leaders. And this is why commonly schisms exist not
among heretics; because while they are, they are not
visible. Schism is their very unity. I am a liar if

they do not dissent from their own rules, while every man among them equally alters at his private judgment (suo arbitrio) what he has received, just as he who gave to them composed it at his private judgment. The progress of the thing is true to its nature and its origin. What was a right to Valentinus, was a right to Valentinians, what to Marcion was to the Marcionites, to innovate on the faith at their private judgment. As soon as any heresy is thoroughly examined, it is found in many points dissenting from its parent. Those parents for the most part have no Churches; they roam about without mother, without see, bereaved of the faith, without a country, without a home." Tertull. Præscr. 42.

¶ "Faith is made a thing of dates rather than Gospels, while it is written down by years, and is not measured by the confession of baptism." Hil. ad Const. ii. 4. "We determine yearly and monthly creeds concerning God, we repent of our determinations; we defend those who repent, we anathematize those whom we have defended; we condemn our own doings in those of others, or others in us, and gnawing each other, we are well-nigh devoured one of another." ibid. 5. "It happens to thee," says S. Hilary to Constantius, "as to unskilful builders, always to be dissatisfied with what thou hast done; thou art ever destroying what thou art ever building." contr. Constant. 23. "O miserable state! with what seas of cares, with what storms are they tossed! for now at one time, as the wind driveth them, they are carried away headlong in error; at another time, coming again to themselves, they are beaten back like contrary waves; sometimes with rash presumption, they allow such things as seem uncertain, at another time of pusillanimity they are in fear even about those things which are certain; doubtful which way to take, which way to return, what to desire, what to avoid, what to hold, what to let go, &c." Vincent. Comm. 20. "He writes," says Athan. of Constantius, "and while he writes repents, and while he repents is exasperated; and then he grieves again, and not knowing how to act, he shows how bereft the soul is of understanding." Hist. Arian. 70; vid. also ad Ep. Æg. 6.

¶ "The Emperor [Theodosius] had a conversation with Nectarius, Bishop [of Constantinople], in what way to make Christendom concordant, and to unite the Church. . . This made Nectarius anxious; but Sisinnius, a man of ready speech and of practical experience, and thoroughly versed in the interpretation of the sacred writings and in the doctrines of philosophy, having a conviction that disputation would but aggravate the party-spirit of the heresies instead of reconciling schisms, advised him to avoid dialectic engagements, and to appeal to the statements of the ancients, and to put the question to the heresiarchs from the Emperor, whether they made any sort of account of the doctors who belonged to the Church before the division, or came to issue with them as aliens from Christianity; for if they made their authority null, therefore let them venture to anathematize them. But if they did venture, then they would be driven out by the people." Socr. v. 10.

HIERACAS.

HIERACAS was a Manichæan. He compared the Two Divine Persons to the two lights of one lamp, where the oil is common and the flame double, thus implying a third substance distinct from Father and Son, or to a flame divided into two by (for instance) the papyrus which was commonly used instead of a wick. vid. Hilar. de Trin. vi. 12.

¶ This doctrine is also imputed to Valentinus, though in a different sense, by Nazianzen, Orat. 33, 16. vid. also Clement. Recogn. i. 69.

HOMOUSION, HOMŒUSION.

Vid. ὁμοούσιον, Nicene Tests, Semi-Arians, &c.

HYPOCRISY, HYPOCRITES.

THIS is almost a title of the Arians, (with an apparent allusion to 1 Tim. iv. 2. vid. Socr. i. p. 13. Athan. Orat. i. § 10, ii. § 1 and § 19, iii. § 16. Syn. § 32. Ep. Enc. 6. Ep. Æg. 18. Epiph. Hær. 73, 1,) and that in various senses. The first meaning is that, being heretics, they nevertheless used orthodox phrases and statements to deceive and seduce Catholics. The term is thus used by Alexander in the beginning of the controversy. vid. Theod. Hist. i. 3, pp. 729, 746. Again, it implies that they agreed with Arius, but would not confess it; professed to be Catholics, but would not anathematize him. vid. Athan. ad Ep. Æg. 20, or alleged untruly the Nicene Council as their ground of complaint, ibid. § 18. Again, it is used of the hollowness and pretence of their ecclesiastical proceedings, with the Emperor at their head; which were a sort of make-belief of spiritual power, or piece of acting, δραματούργημα. Ep. Encycl. 2 and 6. It also means general insincerity, as if they were talking about what they did not under-stand, and did not realize what they said, and were blindly implicating themselves in evils of a fearful cha-racter. Thus Athan. calls them (as cited supr.) τοὺς τῆς Ἀρείου μανίας ὑποκριτάς, Orat. ii. § 1, init.; and he speaks of the evil spirit making them his sport, τοῖς ὑποκρινομένοις τὴν μανίαν αὐτοῦ, ad Serap. i. 1. And

hence further it is applied, at Syn. § 32, as though
with severity, yet to those who were near the truth,
and who, though in sin, would at length come to it or
not, according as the state of their hearts was. He is
here anticipating the return into the Church of those
whom he thus censures. In this sense, though with
far more severity in what he says, the writer of a
Tract imputed to Athan. against the Catholicizing
Semi-Arians of 363, entitles it " on the *hypocrisy* of
Meletius and Eusebius of Samosata." It is remarkable that what Athan. here predicts was fulfilled to
the letter, even of the worst of these " hypocrites."
For Acacius himself, who in 361 signed the Anomœan
Confession above recorded, was one of those very men
who accepted the Homoüsion with an explanation
in 363.

HYPOSTASIS.

ὑπόστασις, subsistence, person.   It is remarkable how
seldom this word occurs in Athanasius except as found
in Hebr. i. 3 ; and the more so, because it is a term little
known outside Christian theology, and within that
theology after Athan.'s time so important and authentic.
It is not found, I believe, in his first two Orations ; twice
in the third ; in the fourth, which seems a distinct work
from the three, by contrast five times, and often in S.
Alexander's Letter in Theodoret, to his namesake
at Constantinople.   Vid. art. εἶδος and οὐσία, which
Athan. seems to use instead of it.

It would seem as if there were a class of words
which, in the first age, before the theological ter-
minology was fixed by ecclesiastical determinations,
admitted of standing either for the Divine Being or a
Divine Person as the occasion settled ; and this, as
being one of them, was not definite or precise enough
for a mind so clear as Athan's. vid. Orat. iii. § 66. iv. § 1.
25, 33, 35.   vid. art. οὐσία.

IDOLATRY OF ARIANISM.

ARIANS considered our Lord a creature, with a beginning of existence, with a probation, and during it a liability to fall. Yet it was one of their fundamental tenets that He was creator of the universe, and created with this very end. Accordingly Athan. and the other Fathers rightly charge them with idol worship.

"We must take reverent heed," says Athanasius, "lest transferring what is proper to the Father to what is unlike Him, and expressing the Father's godhead by what is unlike in kind and alien, we introduce another being foreign to Him, as if capable of the properties of the first, and lest we be silenced by God Himself, saying, *My glory I will not give to another,* and be discovered worshipping this alien God." Syn. § 50. "Who told them after abandoning the worship of creatures, after all to draw near and to worship a creature and a work?" Orat. i. § 8. vid. also Orat. ii. § 14. Ep. Ægypt. 4 and 13. Adelph. 3. Serap. i. 29.

This point, as might be expected, is insisted on by other Fathers, vid. Cyril. Dial. iv. p. 511, &c. v. p. 566. Greg. Naz. Orat. 40, 42. Hil. Trin. viii. 28. Ambros. de Fid. i. n. 69 and 104. Theod. in Rom. i. 25.

¶ The Arians were in the dilemma of holding two Gods, or worshipping the creature, unless they denied to the Lord both divinity and worship. Hence Athan.

says, φάσκοντες, οὐ λέγομεν δύο ἀγένητα, λέγουσι δύο θεούς, Orat. iii. 16. But "every substance," says S. Austin, "which is not God, is a creature, and which is not a creature, is God," de Trin. i. 6. And so S. Cyril, "We see God and creation and besides nothing; for whatever falls external to God's nature, is certainly made; and whatever is clear of the definition of creation, is certainly within the definition of the Godhead." In Joan. p. 52. vid. also Naz. Orat. 31, 6. Basil. contr. Eunom. ii. 31.

¶ Petavius gives a large collection of passages, de Trin. ii. 12, § 5, from other Fathers, in proof of the worship of Our Lord evidencing His Godhead.

IGNORANCE ASSUMED ECONOMICALLY BY OUR LORD.

"It is plain that He knows the hour of the end of all things," says Athan., "as the Word, though as man He is ignorant of it, for ignorance belongs to man." Orat. iii. § 43, and Serap. ii. 9.

¶ S. Basil, on the general question being asked him, of our Lord's infirmities, by S. Amphilochius, says that he shall give him the answer he had "heard from a boy from the fathers," but which was more fitted for pious Christians than for cavillers, and that is, that "Our Lord says many things to men in His human aspect, as ' Give Me to drink,' . . . yet He who asked was not flesh without a soul, but Godhead using flesh which had one." Ep. 236, 1. He goes on to suggest another explanation about His ignorance which is mentioned below. And S. Cyril, " Let them [the heretics] strip the Word openly of the flesh and what it implies, and destroy outright the whole Economy [Incarnation] and then they will clearly see the Son as God; or, if they shudder at this as impious and absurd, why blush they at the conditions of the manhood, and determine to find fault with what especially befits the economy of the flesh?" Trin. pp. 623, 4. vid. also Thes. p. 220. "As He submitted as man to hunger and thirst, so . . . to be ignorant," p. 221. Vid. also Naz.

Orat. 30, 15. Theodoret expresses the same opinion very strongly, speaking of a gradual revelation to the manhood from the Godhead, but in an argument when it was to his point to do so, in Anath. 4, t. v. p. 23, ed. Schulze. Theodore of Mopsuestia also speaks of a revelation made by the Word. ap. Leont. iii. c. Nest. (Canis. i. p. 579).

¶ Though our Lord, as having two natures, had a human as well as a divine knowledge, and though that human knowledge was not only limited because human, but liable to ignorance in matters in which greater knowledge was possible; yet it is the received doctrine, that *in fact* He was not ignorant even in His human nature, according to its capacity, since it was from the first taken out of its original and natural condition, and "deified" by its union with the Word. As then (infra art. *Specialties*, part 5) His manhood was created, yet He may not be called a creature even in His manhood, and as (*ibid.* part 6) His flesh was in its abstract nature a servant, yet He is not a servant in fact, even as regards the flesh; so, though He took on Him a soul which left to itself had been partially ignorant, as other human souls, yet as ever enjoying the Beatific Vision from its oneness with the Word, it never was ignorant in fact, but knew all things which human soul can know. vid. Eulog. ap. Phot. 230, p. 884. As Pope Gregory expresses it, "Novit in naturâ, non ex naturâ humanitatis." Epp. x. 39. However, this view of the sacred subject was received by the Church after S. Athanasius's day, and it cannot be denied that he and others of the most eminent

Fathers use language which *primâ facie* is inconsistent with it. They certainly seem to impute ignorance to our Lord as man, as Athan. in the passage cited above. Of course it is not meant that our Lord's soul had the same perfect knowledge which He has as God. This was the assertion of a General of the Hermits of S. Austin at the time of the Council of Basil, when the proposition was formally condemned, "animam Christi Deum videre tam clarè et intensè quàm clarè et intensè Deus videt seipsum." vid. Berti Opp. t. 3, p. 42. Yet Fulgentius had said, "I think that in no respect was full knowledge of the Godhead want-ing to that Soul, whose Person is one with the Word,—whom Wisdom so assumed that it is itself that same Wisdom," ad Ferrand. Resp. iii. p. 223. ed. 1639; though, ad Trasimund. i. 7, he speaks of ignorance attaching to our Lord's human nature.

¶ S. Basil takes the words οὐδ' ὁ υἰὸς, εἰ μὴ ὁ πατήρ, to mean, "nor does the Son know, except the Father knows," or "nor would the Son but for, &c." or "nor does the Son know, except as the Father knows." "The cause of the Son's knowing is from the Father." Ep. 236, 2. S. Gregory alludes to the same interpreta-tion, οὐδ' ὁ υἰὸς ἢ ὡς ὅτι ὁ πατήρ, "Since the Father knows, therefore the Son." Naz. Orat. 30, 16. S. Irenæus seems to adopt the same when he says, "The Son was not ashamed to *refer* the knowledge of that day to the Father;" Hær. ii. 28, n. 6, as Naz. supr. uses the words ἐπὶ τὴν αἰτίαν ἀναφερέσθω. And so Photius distinctly, εἰς ἀρχὴν ἀναφέρεται. "'Not the Son, but the Father,' that is, whence knowledge

comes to the Son as from a fountain." Epp. p. 342.
ed. 1651.

¶ Origen considers such answer an economy. " He
who knows what is in the heart of men, Christ Jesus,
as John also has taught us in his Gospel, asks, yet is not
ignorant. But since He has now taken on Him man,
He adopts all that is man's, and among them the asking
questions. Nor is it strange that the Saviour should
do so, since the very God of all, accommodating Himself to the habits of man, as a father might to his son,
inquires, for instance, 'Adam, where art thou?' and
'Where is Abel thy brother?'" in Matt. t. 10, § 14;
vid. also Pope Gregory and Chrysost. infr.

¶ S. Chrysostom, S. Ambrose, and Pope S. Gregory,
in addition to the instances in Orat. iii. § 50, refer to " I
will go down now, and *see whether* they have done, &c.
and if not, I will *know*." Gen. xviii. 21. " The Lord
came down *to see* the city and the tower, &c." Gen.
xi. 5. " God looked down from heaven upon the
children of men *to see, &c.*" Ps. liii. 3. " *It may be*
they will reverence My Son." Matt. xxi. 37. Luke
xx. 13. " Seeing a fig tree afar off, having leaves,
He came, *if haply* He *might find*, &c." Mark xi. 13,
" Simon, lovest thou Me?" John xxi. 15. Vid. Ambros.
de Fid. v. c. 17. Chrys. in Matt. Hom. 77, 3. Greg.
Epp. x. 39. Vid. also the instances Athan. Orat. iii. § 37.
Other passages may be added, such as Gen. xxii. 12. vid.
Berti Opp. t. 3, p. 42. But the difficulty of Mar. xiii. 32,
lies in its signifying that there is a sense in which the
Father knows what the Son knows not. Petavius,
after S. Augustine, meets this by explaining it to mean

that our Lord, *as sent* from the Father on a mission, was not to reveal all things, but to observe a silence and profess an ignorance on those points which it was not good for His brethren to know. *As* Mediator and Prophet He was ignorant. He refers in illustration of this view to such texts as, " I have not *spoken of Myself;* but the Father which sent Me, He gave Me commandment *what* I should say and *what* I should speak. . . . . *Whatsoever* I speak therefore, even as the Father said unto Me, *so* I speak." John xii. 49, 50.

¶ It is a question to be decided, whether our Lord speaks of actual ignorance in His human Mind, or of the natural ignorance of that Mind considered as human; ignorance " in " or " ex naturâ ;" or, which comes to the same thing, whether He spoke of a real ignorance, or of an economical or professed ignorance, in a certain view of His incarnation or office, as when He asked, " How many loaves have ye ? " when " He Himself knew what He would do," or as He is called sin, though sinless. Thus Ath. seems, Orat. ii. § 55 fin. to make His infirmities altogether imputative, not real ; " He is said to be infirm, not being infirm himself," as if showing that the subject had not in his day been thoroughly worked out. In like manner S. Hilary, who, if the passage be genuine, states so clearly our Lord's ignorance, de Trin. ix. fin. yet, as Petavius observes, seems elsewhere to deny to Him those very affections of the flesh to which he has there paralleled it. And this view of Athan.'s meaning is favoured by the turn of his expressions. He says, such a defect belongs to *"that human nature* whose property it is to be ignorant;" Orat. iii. § 43; that "since He was made man, He is not *ashamed*, because of the flesh which is ignorant, *to say* 'I know not;'" ibid. And § 45, that "as *showing* His manhood, in that to be ignorant is *proper* to man, and that He had *put on* a flesh *that was ignorant*, being in which, He *said* according to the flesh, 'I know not;'" "that He might *show* that as man He knows not," § 46; viz. *as* man (i.e. on the *ground* of being man, not in the *capacity* of man,) "He knows not," ibid.; and that "He *asks* about Lazarus humanly," even when "He was *on His way* to raise him," which implied surely knowledge in His human nature. The reference to the parallel of S. Paul's professed ignorance when he really knew, § 47, leads us to the same suspicion. And so, "for *our profit*, as I think, did He this." § 48—50.

The natural want of precision on such questions in the early ages was shown or fostered by such words as οἰκονομικῶς, which, in respect of this very text, is used by S. Basil to denote both our Lord's Incarnation, Ep. 236, 1 fin. and His gracious accommodation of Himself and His truth, Ep. 8, 6; and with the like variety of meaning, with reference to the same text, by Cyril. Trin. p. 623; and Thesaur. p. 224. (And the word *dispensatio* in like manner, Ben. note on Hil. Trin. x. 8.) In the latter Ep. S. Basil suggests that our Lord "economizes by a feigned ignorance." And S. Cyril. in Thesaur. l.c. (in spite of his strong language ibid. p. 221), "The Son knows all things, though economically He says He is ignorant of something," Thesaur. p. 224. And even in de Trin. vi. he seems

to recognize the distinction laid down just now between
the natural and actual state of our Lord's humanity;
" God would not make it known even to the Son Himself, were He a *mere* man upon earth, as they say, and
not having it in His nature to be God." p. 629. And
S. Hilary arguing that He must as man know the day of
judgment, for His then coming is as man, says, " Since
He is Himself a sacrament, let us see whether He be
ignorant in the things which He knows not. For if
in the other respects a profession of ignorance is not
an intimation of not knowing, so here too He is not
ignorant of what He knows not. For since His ignorance, in respect that all treasures of knowledge lie hid
in Him, is rather an economy (dispensation) than an
ignorance, you have a cause why He might be ignorant
without an actual intimation of not knowing." Trin. ix.
62. And he gives reasons why He professed ignorance,
n. 67. viz. as S. Austin words it, " Christum se dixisse
nescientem, in quo alios facit occultando nescientes."
Ep. 180. 3. S. Austin follows Hilary, saying, " Hoc
nescit quod nescientes facit." Trin. i. n. 23. Pope Gregory says that the text " is most certainly to be referred
to the Son not as He is Head, but as to His body which
we are." Ep. x. 39. And S. Ambrose distinctly; " The
Son which took on Him the flesh, assumed our affections, so as to say that He knew not with our ignorance;
not that He was ignorant of anything Himself, for,
though He seemed to be man in truth of body, yet He
was the life and light, and virtue went out of Him, &c."
de Fid. v. 222. And so Cæsarius, Qu. 20. and Photius
Epp. p. 336, &c. Chrysost. in Matth. Hom. 77, 3. Theo-

doret, however, but in controversy, is very severe on the principle of Economy. "If He knew the day, and wishing to conceal it, said He was ignorant, see what a blasphemy is the result. Truth tells an untruth." l.c. pp. 23, 24.

¶ The expression, Orat. iii. § 48, &c. "for our sake," which repeatedly occurs, surely implies that there was something economical in our Lord's profession of ignorance. He said it with a purpose, not as a mere plain fact or doctrine. And so S. Cyril, "He says that He is ignorant, *for our sake* and among us, as man;" Thes. p. 221. "economically effecting, οἰκονομῶν, something profitable and good." ibid. And again, after stating that there was an objection, and paralleling His words with His question to S. Philip about the loaves, he says, "Knowing as God the Word, He *can*, as man, be ignorant." p. 223. "It is not a sign of ignorance, but of wisdom, for it was inexpedient that we should know it." Ambros. de Fid. v. 209. S. Chrysostom seems to say the same, denying that the Son was ignorant, Hom. 77, 1. And Theophylact, "Had He said, 'I know, but I will not tell you,' they had been cast down, as if despised by Him; but now in saying 'not the Son but the Father only,' He hinders them asking . . . . for how can the Son be ignorant of the day?" Theophyl. in loc. Matt. "Often little children see their fathers holding something in their hands, and ask for it, but they will not give it. Then the children cry as not receiving it. At length the fathers hide what they have got and show their empty hands to their children, and so stop their crying. . . . .

For our profit hath He hid it." ibid. in loc. Marc. "For thee He is ignorant of the hour and day of judgment, though nothing is hid from the Very Wisdom. . . . . But he economizes this because of thy infirmity, &c." supr. Basil, Ep. 8, 6.

¶ It is the doctrine of the Church that Christ, as man, was perfect in knowledge from the first, as if ignorance were hardly separable from sin, and were the direct consequence or accompaniment of original sin. "That ignorance," says S. Austin, "I in no wise can suppose existed in that Infant, in whom the Word was made flesh to dwell among us; nor can I suppose that that infirmity of the mind belonged to Christ as a babe, which we see in babes. For in consequence of it, when they are troubled with irrational emotions, no reason, no command, but pain sometimes and the alarm of pain restrains them, &c." de Pecc. Mer. ii. 48. As to the limits of Christ's perfect knowledge as man, we must consider "that the soul of Christ knew all things that are or ever will be or ever have been, but not what are only *in posse,* not in fact." Petav. Incarn. xi. 3, 6.

¶ Leporius, in his Retractation, which S. Augustine subscribed, writes, "That I may in this respect also leave nothing to be cause of suspicion to any one, I then said, nay I answered when it was put to me, that our Lord Jesus Christ was ignorant as He was man (secundùm hominem). But now not only do I not presume to say so, but I even anathematize my former opinion expressed on this point, because it may not be said, that the Lord of the Prophets was ignorant even as He was man." ap. Sirmond. t. i. p. 210. A subdivision also of the Eutychians were called by the name of Agnoetæ from their holding that our Lord was ignorant of the day of judgment. "They said," says Leontius, "that He was ignorant of it, as we say that He underwent toil." de Sect. 5. circ. fin. Felix of Urgela held the same doctrine according to Agobard's testimony, as contained adv. Fel. 6, Bibl. Patr. Max. t. xiv. p. 244. The Ed. Ben. observes, Ath. Orat. iii. § 44, that the assertion of our Lord's ignorance "seems to have been condemned in no one in ancient times, unless joined to other error." And Petavius, after drawing out the authorities for and against it, says, "Of these two opinions, the latter, which is now received both by custom and by the agreement of divines, is deservedly preferred to the former. For it is more agreeable to Christ's dignity, and more befitting His character and office of Mediator and Head, that is, Fountain of all grace and wisdom, and moreover of Judge, who is concerned in knowing the time fixed for exercising that function. In consequence, the former opinion, though formerly it received the countenance of some men of high eminence, was afterwards marked as a heresy." Incarn. xi. 1. § 15.

¶ The mode in which Athan. expresses himself, is as if he only ascribed apparent ignorance to our Lord's soul, and not certainly in the broad sense in which heretics have done so:—as Leontius, e. g. reports of Theodore of Mopsuestia, that he considered Christ "to be ignorant so far, as not to know, when He was tempted, who tempted Him;" contr. Nest. iii. (Canis. t. i. p. 579,) and Agobard of Felix the Adoptionist that he held "Our Lord Jesus Christ according to the flesh *truly* to have been ignorant of the sepulchre of Lazarus, when He said to His sisters, 'Where have ye laid him?' and was *truly* ignorant of the day of judgment; and was *truly* ignorant what the two disciples were saying as they walked by the way, of what had been done at Jerusalem; and was *truly* ignorant whether He was more loved by Peter than by the other disciples, when He said, 'Simon Peter, Lovest thou Me more than these?'" Bibl. Patr. Max. t. xiv. p. 244. The Agnoetæ have been noticed above.

¶ It is remarkable, considering the tone of his statements, Orat. iii. § 42—53, that there and in what follows upon it Athan. should resolve our Lord's advance in wisdom merely into its gradual manifestation through the flesh; and it increases the proof that his statements are not to be taken in the letter, and as if fully brought out and settled. Naz. says the same, Ep. ad Cled. 101. p. 86, which is the more remarkable since he is chiefly writing against the Apollinarians, who considered a $\phi a\nu\epsilon\rho\omega\sigma\iota\varsigma$ the great end of our Lord's coming; and Cyril. c. Nest. iii. p. 87. Theod. Hær. v. 13. On the other hand, S. Epiphanius speaks of Him as growing in wisdom as man. Hær. 77, p. 1019-24, and S. Ambrose, Incarn. 71-74. Vid. however Ambr. de Fid. as quoted supr. p. 167. The Ed. Ben. in Ambr. Incarn. considers the advancement of knowledge spoken of to be that of the "scientia experimentalis" alluded to in Hebr. v. 8, which is one of the three kinds of knowledge possessed by Christ as man. vid. Berti Opp. t. 3, p. 41. Petavius, however, omits the consideration of this knowledge, (which S. Thomas at first denied in our Lord, and in his Summa ascri s to Him,) as lying beyond his province. "De hac ute neutram in partem pronuntiare audeo," says Petavius, "hujusmodi enim quæstiones ad Scholas relegandæ sunt; de quibus nihil apud antiquos liquidi ac definiti reperitur." Incarn. xi. 4, § 9.

ILLUSTRATIONS.

¶ " Is there any cause of fear," says Athan., "lest, because the offspring from men are one in substance, the Son, by being called One in substance, be Himself considered as a human offspring too? perish the thought ! not so ; but the explanation is easy. For the Son is the Father's Word and Wisdom; whence we learn the impassibility (ἀπαθὲς) and indivisibility (ἀμέριστον) of such a generation from the Father. For not even is man's word part of Him, nor proceeds from Him according to passion; much less God's Word; whom the Father has declared to be His own Son: lest, on the other hand, if we merely heard of ' Word,' we should suppose Him, such as is the word of man, unsubsistent (ἀνυπόστατον); therefore we are told that He is Son, that we may acknowledge Him to be a living Word and a substantive (ἐνούσιον) Wisdom. Accordingly, as in saying ' Offspring,' we have no human thoughts, and, though we know God to be a Father, we entertain no material ideas concerning Him, but while we listen to these illustrations and terms, we think suitably of God, for He is not as man, so in like manner, when we hear of ' consubstantial,' we ought to transcend all sense, and, according to the Proverb, *understand by the understanding that is set before us;* so as to know, that not by the Father's will, but in eternal truth, is

He genuine Son of the Father, as Life from Fountain, and Radiance from Light. Else why should we understand ' Offspring ' and ' Son,' in no corporeal way, while we conceive of ' One in substance ' as after the manner of bodies ? especially since these terms are not here used about different subjects, but of whom " offspring " is predicated, of Him is " one in substance also." Syn. § 41, 42.

" For whereas men beget with passion, so again when at work they work upon an existing subject matter, and otherwise cannot make. Now if we do not understand creation in a human way, when we attribute it to God, much less seemly is it to understand generation in a human way, or to give a corporeal sense to Consubstantial; instead, as we ought, of receding from things generate, casting away human images, nay, all things sensible, and ascending to the Father, lest we rob the Father of the Son in ignorance, and rank Him among His own creatures." Syn. § 51.

¶ S. Athanasius's doctrine is, that, God containing in Himself all perfection, whatever is excellent in one created thing above another, is found in its perfection in Him. If then such generation as radiance from light is more perfect than that of children from parents, that belongs, and transcendently, to the All-perfect God.

¶ The question is not, whether in matter of fact, in the particular case, the rays would issue after, and not with the initial existence of the luminous body; for the illustration is not used to show *how* such a thing may be, or to give an *instance* of it, but to convey to the mind a correct *idea* of what it is proposed to teach in the Catholic doctrine.

¶ Athanasius guards against what is defective in his illustration, Orat. iii. § 5, of an Emperor and his image, but independent of such explanation a mistake as to his meaning would be impossible; and the passage affords a good instance of the imperfect and partial character of all illustrations of the Divine Mystery. What it is taken to symbolize is the unity of the Father and Son, for the Image is not a Second Emperor but the same. Vid. Sabell. Greg. 6; still no one, who bowed before the Emperor's Statue can be supposed to have really worshipped it; whereas our Lord is the Object of supreme worship, which terminates in Him, as being really one with Him whose Image He is.

¶ " Whoso uses the particle *as*, implies, not identity, nor equality, but a likeness of the matter in question, viewed in a certain respect. This we may learn from our Saviour Himself, when He says " As Jonas," &c. Orat. iii. 22, 23. "Even when the analogy is solid and well founded, we are liable to fall into error, if we suppose it to extend farther than it really does. . . . . Thus because a just analogy has been discerned between the metropolis of a country, and the heart in the animal body, it has been sometimes contended that its increased size is a disease, that it may impede some of its most important functions, or even be the means of its dissolution." Copleston on Predestination, p. 129. The principle here laid down, in accordance with S. Athan., of course *admits* of being made an excuse for denying the orthodox meaning of " Word, Wis-

dom, &c.," under pretence that the figurative terms
are not confined by the Church within their proper
limits; but here the question is about the *matter of
fact, which* interpretation is right, the Church's or the
objector's? Thus a late writer says, " The most
important words of the N. T. have not only received an
indelibly false stamp from the hands of the old Schoolmen, but those words having, since the Reformation,
become common property in the language of the
country, are, as it were, thickly incrusted with the
most vague, incorrect, and vulgar notions. . . . . Any
word · . . . . if habitually repeated in connexion with
certain notions, will appear to reject all other signi-
fications, as it were, by a natural power." Heresy and
Orthod. pp. 21, 47. Elsewhere he speaks of words
" which were used in a language now dead to represent
objects . . . . which are now supposed to express
figuratively something spiritual and quite beyond the
knowledge and comprehension of man." P. 96. Of
course Athan. assumes that, *since* the figures and
parallels given us in Scripture have but a partial application, *therefore* there is given us also an interpreter
in order to apply them. Vid. art. *Economical.*

¶ Again, just as S. Athan. says, " A figure is but a
parallel, . . . if we too become one, *as* the Son in the
Father, we shall not therefore be *as* the Son, nor
equal to Him, for He and we are but parallel," so
again Dr. Copleston thus proceeds, " Analogy does not
mean the similarity of two things, but the similarity
or sameness of two relations. . . . . Things most
unlike and discordant in their nature may be strictly

analogous to one another. Thus a certain *proposition* may be called the *basis* of a system . . . . it serves a similar *office* and *purpose* . . . . the system *rests* upon it; it is *useless to proceed* with the argument till this is well established : if this were *removed,* the system must fall." On Predest. pp. 122, 123.

IMAGE

Is used to signify our Lord's relation to the Eternal Father: and first in Scripture,—

1. We find Him called εἰκών, imago, in 2 Cor. iv. 4; and Col. i. 15. In a verse following the former of these passages it is said in like manner that the glory of God is in the face of Jesus Christ. This carries us to Heb. i. 3, where we read of Him as the ἀπαύγασμα of God's glory, and find in the word χαρακτὴρ, figura, impress, a synonym for the word *Image*. St. John confirms St. Paul; he speaks of our Lord's glory "quasi Unigeniti a Patre," and says that the "Son who is in the bosom of the Father, hath declared Him."

These modes of expressing the nature and office of the Son, as the revealed and revealing God, as the Light, the Glory, the Image, the Impress, the Face of the Almighty, are exemplified with still greater variety and fulness of language in the Book of Wisdom, ch. vii., in a passage too long to quote, in which, among other attributes and prerogatives, Wisdom, that is, our Lord, is called a πνεῦμα ἅγιον, μονογενές, φιλάγαθος, φιλάνθρωπος, the ἀπόρροια τῆς τοῦ παντοκράτορος δόξης, the ἀπαύγασμα φωτὸς ἀϊδίου, the ἔσοπτρον ἀκηλίδωτον τῆς τοῦ θεοῦ ἐνεργείας, and the εἰκὼν τῆς ἀγαθότητος αὐτοῦ.

It is impossible that the Holy Apostles, when they

spoke of our Lord as the Word, Image, and Splendour of God, should not have had in mind this passage, so overpowering in its force and significance, and were not investing with personality and substance what they thus viewed as all-perfect, immutable, co-eternal, consubstantial with Him.

2. S. Athanasius and the other Fathers take up and insist upon this definite theology, thus found in Scripture.

"We must conceive of necessity," says Athan., "that in the Father is the eternal, the everlasting, the immortal; and in Him, not as foreign to Him, but as in a Fount abiding (ἀναπαυόμενα) in Him, and also in the Son. When then you would form a conception of the Son, learn what are the things in the Father, and believe that they are in the Son too. If the Father is creature or work, these attributes are also in the Son, &c. . . . He who honours the Son, is honouring the Father who sent Him, and he who receives the Son, is receiving with Him the Father, &c." In illud Omn. 4. "As the Father is I Am (ὁ ὤν) so His Word is I Am and God over all." Serap. i. 28. "Altogether, there is nothing which the Father has, which is not the Son's; for therefore it is that the Son is in the Father, and the Father in the Son; because the things of the Father, these are in the Son, and still the same are understood as being in the Father. Thus is understood, 'I and the Father are One;' since not these things are in Him and those in the Son, but the things which are in the Father those are in the Son, and what thou seest in the Father, because thou seest in the Son, thereby is rightly understood ' He that hath seen Me, hath seen the Father.' " Serap. ii. 2.

Again : " Such as the parent, such of necessity is the offspring; and such as is the Word's Father, such must be also His Word . . . God is not as man, as Scripture has said, but is existing (ὤν ἐστι) and is ever, therefore His Word also is existing, and is ever-lastingly with the Father, as radiance with light. . . . As radiance from light, so is He perfect offspring from perfect. Hence He is also God, as being God's Image. Orat. ii. § 35. "It was fitting that, whereas God is One, that His Image should be One also, and His Word One, and One His Wisdom." Ibid. § 36.

¶ "He is likeness and image of the sole and true God, being Himself sole also," § 49. μόνος ἐν μόνῳ, Orat. iii. § 21. ὅλος ὅλου εἰκών, Serap. i. 16. "The Offspring of the Ingenerate," says S. Hilary, "is One from One, True from True, Living from Living, Perfect from Perfect, Power of Power, Wisdom of Wisdom, Glory of Glory," de Trin. ii. 8; τέλειος τέλειον γεγέννηκεν, πνεῦμα πνεῦμα. Epiph. Hær. lxxvi. p. 945. "As Light from Light, and Life from Life, and Good from Good; so from Eternal Eternal." Nyss. contr. Eunom. i. p. 164. App. "De Deo nascitur Deus, de Ingenito Unigenitus, de Solo Solus, de Toto Totus, de Vero Verus, de Perfecto Perfectus, Totum Patris habens, nihil derogans Patri." Zenon. Serm. ii. 3.

¶ "A man will see the extravagance of this heresy still more clearly, if he considers that the Son is the Image and Radiance of the Father, and Impress and Truth. For if, when Light exists, there be withal its Image, viz. Radiance,—and a Subsistence existing, there be of it the entire Impress,— and a Father existing, there be His true representation,—let them consider what depths of impiety they fall into, who make time the measure of the Image and Countenance of the Godhead. For if the Son was not before His generation, Truth was not always in God, which it were a sin to say; for, since the Father was, there was ever in Him the Truth, which is the Son, who says, *I am the Truth.* And the Subsistence existing, of course there was forthwith its Impress and Image; for God's Image is not delineated from without, but God Himself hath begotten It; in which seeing Himself, He has delight, as the Son Himself says, *I was His delight.* When then did the Father not see Himself in His own Image? or when had He not delight in Him, that a man should dare to say, 'The Image is out of nothing,' and 'The Father had not delight before the Image was generated?' and how should the Maker and Creator see Himself in a created and generated substance? for such as is the Father, such must be the Image. Proceed we then to consider the attributes of the Father, and we shall come to know whether this Image is really His. The Father is eternal, immortal, powerful, light, King, Sovereign, God, Lord, Creator, and Maker. These attributes must be in the Image, to make it true, that *he that hath seen* the Son, *hath seen the Father."* Orat. i. § 20, 21.

¶ " If God be ingenerate, His Image is not generate [made,] but an Offspring, which is His Word and His Wisdom," ibid. § 31.

Athan. argues from the very name Image for our Lord's eternity. An Image, to be really such, must be an impress from the Original, not an external and detached imitation. It was attempted to secure this point before Nicæa by the epithets *living* and ἀπαράλ-λακτος, unsuccessfully, vid. Decr. § 20. Thus S. Basil, "He is an Image not made with the hand, or a work of art, but a living Image," &c. vid. art. ἀπαράλλακτον, also contr. Eunom. ii. 16, 17. Epiph. Hær. 76, 3. Hilar. Trin. vii. 41 fin. Origen observes that man, on the contrary, is an example of an external or improper image of God. Periarch. i. 2, § 6. vid. Theod. Hist. i. 3, pp. 737, 742.

¶ S. Gregory Naz. argues from the name of Image to our Lord's consubstantiality. "He is Image as ὁμοούσιον . . . for this is the nature of an image to be a copy of the archetype." Orat. 30, 20.

¶ Vid. S. Athan.'s doctrine concerning Wisdom, Orat. ii. § 80, &c. He says, Gent. 34, "The soul as in a mirror contemplates the Word the Image of the Father, and in Him considers the Father, whose Image the Saviour is . . . or if not . . . yet from the things that are seen, the creation is such, as by letters signifying and heralding its Lord and Maker by means of its order and harmony." And "As by looking up to the heaven . . . we have an idea of the Word who set it in order, so considering the Word of God, we cannot but see God His Father." 45. And Incarn. 11, 41, 42, &c. Vid. also Basil. contr. Eunom. ii. 16.

¶ On the Arian objection, that, if our Lord be the Father's Image, He ought to resemble Him in being

a Father, vid. article, "Father Almighty." The
words "like" and much more "image," would be in-
appropriate, if the Second Divine Person in nothing
differed from the First. Sonship is just that one
difference which allows of likeness being predicated
of Him.

IMPERIAL TITLES AND HONOURS.

¶ EUSEBIUS was emphatically the court bishop, but he did but observe the ecclesiastical rule in calling Constantine " most pious," § 14, Lett. App. Decr. "most wise and most religious," § 4, "most religious," § 8, § 10. (*Nic.* n. 47, &c.) He goes in his Vit. Const. further than this, and assigns to him the office of determining the faith (Constantine being as yet unbaptized). E. g. "When there were differences between persons of different countries, the Emperor, as if some common bishop appointed by God, convened Councils of God's ministers; and, not disdaining to be present, and to sit amid their conferences," &c. i. 44. When he came into the Nicene Council, " it was," says Eusebius, " as some heavenly Angel of God," iii. 10, alluding to the brilliancy of the imperial purple. He confesses, however, he did not sit down until the Bishops bade him. Again at the same Council, " with pleasant eyes, looking serenity itself into them all, collecting himself, and in a quiet and gentle voice," he made an oration to the Fathers upon peace. Constantine had been an instrument in conferring such vast benefits, humanly speaking, on the Christian body, that it is not wonderful that other writers of the day besides Eusebius should praise him. Hilary speaks of him as " of sacred memory," Fragm. 5, init.

Athanasius calls him "most pious," Apol. contr. Arian. 9, "of blessed memory," Ep. Æg. 18, 19. Epiphanius "most religious and of ever-blessed memory," Hær. 70, 9. Posterity, as was natural, was still more grateful.

¶ Up to the year 356, when Constantius took up the Anomœans, this was Athan.'s tone in speaking of him also. In his Apol. contr. Arian. init. (A.D. 350,) ad Ep. Æg. 5, (356,) and his Apol. ad Constant. passim. (356,) he calls the Emperor most pious, religious, &c. At the end of the last-mentioned work, § 27, the news comes to him while in exile of the prosecution of the Western Bishops and the measures against himself. He still in the peroration calls Constantius, "blessed and divinely favoured Augustus," and urges on him that he is a " Christian, φιλόχριστος, Emperor." Vid. supr. art. *Athanasius.*

¶ The honour paid to the Imperial Statues is well known. "He who crowns the Statue of the Emperor of course honours him, whose image he has crowned." Ambros. in Psalm 118, x. 25. vid. also Chrysost. Hom. on Statues, Oxf. Tr. pp. 355, 6, &c. Fragm. in Act. Conc. vii. (t. 4, p. 89, Hard.). Chrysostom's second persecution arose from his interfering with a statue of the Empress which was so near the Church, that the acclamations of the people before it disturbed the services. Socr. vi. 18. The Seventh Council speaks of the images sent by the Emperors into provinces instead of their coming in person; Ducange in v. Lauratum. Vid. a description of the imperial statues and their honours in Gothofred, Cod. Theod. t. 5, pp. 346, 347, and in

Philostorg, ii. 18, xii. 10. vid. also Molanus de Imaginibus ed. Paquot, p. 197.

¶ From the custom of paying honour to the Imperial Statues, the Cultus Imaginum was introduced into the Eastern Church. The Western Church, not having had the civil custom, resisted. vid. Döllinger, Church History, vol. iii. p. 55. E. Tr. Certain Fathers, e. g. S. Jerome, set themselves against the civil custom, as idolatrous, comparing it to that paid to Nebuchadnezzar's statue, vid. Hieron. in Dan. iii. 18. Incense was burnt before those of the Emperors; as afterwards before the Images of the Saints.

THE INCARNATION,

1. *Considered in its purpose.*

" THE need of man preceded His becoming man," says Athan., "apart from which He had not put on flesh. And what the need was for which He became man, He Himself thus signifies, *I came down from heaven . . . to do the will of Him that sent Me. And this is the will of Him that sent Me, that of all which He hath given Me, I should lose nothing ; but, &c. &c.* (John vi. 38—40), and again, *I am come a Light into the World, &c.,* and again, *To this end was I born, &c., that I should bear witness unto the truth* (John xviii. 37), and John hath written, *For this was manifested the Son of God, that He might destroy the works of the devil* (1 John iii. 8). To give a witness, then, and for our sakes to undergo death, to raise men up and loose the works of the devil, the Saviour came, and this is the reason of His Incarnate Presence." Orat. ii. § 54.

¶ However, there are theologians of great name, who consider that the decree of the Incarnation was independent of Adam's fall ; and certainly by allowing that it was not absolutely necessary (vid. infra) for the divine forgiveness of sin, and that it was the actual and immediate means of the soul's renewal and sanctification, as we shall see presently, Athan. goes far towards countenancing that belief. "Dico ex vi præsentis decreti," says Viva (Curs. Theol. de Incarn. p. 74), "Adamo non peccante Verbum fuisse incarnatum; atque adeo motivum Incarnationis non fuit sola redemptio, sed etiam et principalius ipsa Christi excellentia ac *humanæ naturæ exaltatio.* Ita Scotistæ, Suar. Martinon. et alii contra Thomistas. Angelicus vero qu. 1 a. 3 sententiam nostram censet probabilem, quamvis probabiliorem putet oppositam."

¶ It is the general teaching of the Fathers in accordance with Athan., that our Lord would not have been incarnate had not man sinned. "Our cause was the occasion of His descent, and our transgression called forth the Word's love of man. Of His incarnation we became the ground." Athan. de Incarn. V. D. 4. vid. Thomassin, at great length de Incarn. ii. 5—11, also Petav. de Incarn. ii. 17, 7—12. Vasquez. in 3 Thom. Disp. x. 4 and 5.

¶ "Without His sojourning here at all, God was able to speak the word only and undo the curse . . . . but then the power indeed of Him who gave command had been shown, but man, though restored to what Adam was before the fall, had received grace only from without, not had it united to his body. . . . Then, had he been again seduced by the serpent, a second need had arisen of God's commanding and undoing the curse; and this had gone on without limit, and men had remained under guilt just as before, being in slavery to sin; and ever sinning, they had ever needed pardon, and never been made free, being in themselves carnal, and ever defeated by the Law by reason of the infirmity of the flesh." Orat. ii. 68. And so in Incarn. 7, he says that repentance might have been pertinent, had man merely offended, without *corruption* following (supra *Freedom*). vid. also 14. Athan. is supported by Naz. Orat. 19, 13; Theod. adv. Gent. vi. p. 876-7. Aug. de Trin. xiii. 13. The contrary view is taken by St. Anselm, but St. Thomas and the Schoolmen side with the Fathers. vid. Petav. Incarn. ii. 13.

¶ On the subject of God's power, as contrasted with His acts, vid. Petav. de Deo, v. 6.

¶ There were two reasons then for the Incarnation, viz. atonement for sin, and renewal in holiness, and these are ordinarily associated with each other by Athanasius.

These two ends of our Lord's Incarnation, that He might die for us, and that He might renew us, answer nearly to those specified in Rom. iv. 25, "who was delivered for our offences and raised again for our justification." The general object of His coming, including both of these, is treated of in Incarn. 4—20, or rather in the whole Tract, and in the two books against Apollinaris. It is difficult to make accurate references under the former head, (vid. supra, art. *Atonement,*) without including the latter. "Since all men had to pay the debt of death, on which account especially He came on earth, therefore after giving proofs of His Divinity from His works, next He offered a sacrifice for all, &c.," the passage then runs on into the other fruit of His death. Incarn. 20. Vid. also Orat. § ii. 7—9, where he speaks of our Lord as offering Himself, as offering His flesh to God; also Decr. § 14. And Orat. iv. § 6, he says, "When He is said to hunger, to weep and weary and to cry Eloi, which are human affections, He receives them from us and offers to His Father, interceding for us, that in Him they may be annulled." And so Theodoret, "Whereas He had an immortal nature, He willed according to equity to put a stop to death's power, taking on Himself first from those who were exposed to death a first fruit; and preserving this immaculate and guiltless of sin, He surrenders it for death to seize upon as well as others, and satiate its insatiableness; and then on the ground of its want of equity against that first-fruit, He put a stop to its iniquitous tyranny over others." Eran. iii. p. 196, 7. Vigil. Thaps. contr. Eutych. i. § 9, p. 496 (Bibl. Patr. ed. 1624).

And S. Leo speaks of the whole course of redemption, i.e. incarnation, atonement, regeneration, justification, &c. as one sacrament, not drawing the line distinctly between the several agents, elements, or stages in it, but considering it to lie in the intercommunion of Christ's person and ours. Thus he says that our Lord "took on Him all our infirmities which come of sin without sin;" and "the most cruel pains and death," because "none could be rescued from mortality, unless He, in whom our common nature was innocent, allowed Himself to die by the hands of the impious;" "unde," he continues, "in se credentibus et *sacramentum* condidit et exemplum, ut unum apprehenderent *renascendo*, alterum sequerentur imitando." Serm. 63, 4. He speaks of His fortifying us against our passions and infirmities, both "*sacramento susceptionis*" and "exemplo." Serm. 65, 2, and of a "duplex remedium cujus aliud in

sacramento, aliud in exemplo." Serm. 67, 5, also 69, 5.
Elsewhere he makes the strong statement, "The
Lord's passion is continued on [producitur] even to
the end of the world; and as in His Saints He is
honoured Himself, and Himself is loved, and in the
poor He Himself is fed, is clothed Himself, so in all who
endure trouble for righteousness' sake, does He Himself suffer together ["compatitur"], Serm. 70, 5. vid.
also more or less in Serm. pp. 76, 93, 98, 99, 141, 249,
257, 258, 271, fin. and Epist. pp. 1291, 1363, 1364. At
other times, however, the atonement is more distinctly
separated from its circumstances, pp. 136, 198, 310 ;
but it is very difficult to draw the line. The tone of
his teaching is throughout characteristic of the
Fathers, and very like that of S. Athanasius. vid. art.
Atonement and *Freedom.*

2. *Considered in itself.*

THE Two natures, the divine and human, both perfect,
though remaining distinct, are in the Christ intimately
and for ever one.

"Two natures," says S. Leo, "met together in our
Redeemer, and, while what belonged to each remained,
so great a unity was made of either substance, that from
the time that the Word was made flesh in the Blessed
Virgin's womb, we may neither think of Him as God
without that which is man, nor as man without that
which is God," &c. Vid. art. *Two Natures.*

¶ And the principle of unity, viz. that in which they
were united, was the Person of the Son. From this
unity of Person it comes to pass, first, that one and the

same act on the part of our Lord may be both divine and human; e. g. His curing with a touch, this is called the θεανδρικὴ ἐνέργεια; and secondly, that the acts and attributes of one nature may safely be ascribed as personal to the other; this is called the ἀντίδοσις ἰδιωμάτων. Thus it is true that "the Creator is the Lamb of God," though there can be no intrinsic union of attribute or act in Him who both in the beginning created and in the fulness of time suffered.

That Person which our Lord is after the Incarnation, He was before; His human nature is not a separate being; that is the heresy of the Nestorians. vid. *Unity*, &c. It has no personality belonging to it; but that human nature, though perfect as a nature, lives in and belongs to and is possessed by Him, the second Person of the Trinity, as an attribute or organ or inseparable accident of being, not as what is substantive, independent, or co-ordinate. Vid. Articles ὄργανον and παραπέτασμα.

¶ Personality is not necessary in order to a nature being perfect, as we see in the case of brute animals.

¶ Nothing then follows from the union of the two natures, which circumscribes or limits the Divine Son; so to teach was the heresy of the Monophysites, who held that the Divinity and Manhood of Christ made up together one nature, as soul and body in man are one compound nature; from which it follows that neither of them is perfect. Vid. Article Μία φύσις.

THE DIVINE INDWELLING.

OUR Lord, by becoming man, has found a way whereby to sanctify that nature, of which His own ' manhood is the pattern specimen. He inhabits us personally, and this inhabitation is effected by the channel of the Sacraments.

" Since the Word bore our body," says Athanasius, "and came to be in us (γέγονεν), therefore, by reason of the Word in us, is God called our Father." Decr. § 31. Vid. τὸν ἐν ἡμῖν υἱόν. Orat. ii. § 59, ὁ λόγος θεὸς ἐν σαρκὶ . . . ἕνεκα τοῦ ἁγιάζειν τὴν σάρκα γέγονεν ἄνθρωπος. ibid. § 10, also § 56, and τὸν ἐν αὐτοῖς οἰκοῦντα λόγον, § 61. Also Orat. i. § 50, iii. 23—25, iv. § 21. " We rise from the earth, the curse of sin being removed, because of Him who is in us," iii. § 33.

¶ In thus teaching Athan. follows the language of Scripture, in which ἐν means *in* our nature, not merely *among* us; vid. ὄντως ἐν ἡμῖν θεός, 1 Cor. xiv. 25. ἐν ἐμοί, Gal. i. 24. ἐντὸς ὑμῶν, Luke xvii. 21. ἐσκήνωσεν ἐν ἡμῖν, John i. 14; also xiv. 17, 23; 1 Cor. vi. 20; 1 John iii. 24, &c.

By this indwelling our Lord is the immediate ἀρχὴ of spiritual life to each of His elect individually. Οὐκ ὁ λόγος ἐστὶν ὁ βελτιούμενος, εἶχεν γὰρ πάντα, ἀλλ' οἱ ἄνθρωποι οἱ ἀρχὴν ἔχοντες τοῦ λαμβάνειν ἐν αὐτῷ

καὶ δι᾽ αὐτοῦ. Orat. i. 48.   Vid. also what he says on
the phrase ἀρχὴ ὁδῶν. Orat. ii. 48, &c.   Also the note
of the Benedictine editor on Justin's Tryphon. 61,
referring to Tatian. c. Gent. S. Athenag. Apol. 10.
Iren. Hær. iv. 20, n. 4. Origen in Joan. tom. i. S9.
Tertull. Prax. 6, and Ambros. de Fid. iii. 7.

¶ " Flesh being first sanctified in Him," says Athan.,
" and He being said on account of it to have received as
man [the anointing], we have the sequel of the Spirit's
grace receiving *out of His fulness*." Orat. i. 50. vid. art.
Grace.   Other Fathers use still stronger language.   S.
Chrysostom explains ; " He is born of our substance :
you will say, ' This does not pertain to all ; yea, to all.
He mingles (ἀναμίγνυσιν) Himself with the faithful
individually, through the mysteries, and whom He has
begotten those He nurses from Himself, not puts them
out to other hands," &c.   Hom. 82, 5, in Matt., &c., &c.
vid. art. *Freedom*.

In Orat. iii. § 33 S. Athanasius uses the strong phrase
λογωθείσης τῆς σαρκὸς, of regenerate human nature.
Damascene speaks of the λόγωσις of the flesh, but he
means principally our Lord's flesh, F. O. iv. 18, p. 286,
ed. Ven.   For the words θεοῦσθαι, &c. vid. supr. art.
Deification ; also vid. *Flesh*.

¶ Nor is this all; we must go on to the results
of this doctrine, as indicated in the following passages of Scripture which are referred to above.
" Know ye not that ye are the temple of God, and
that the Spirit of God dwelleth in you ? "   1 Cor.
iii. 16, 17 ; vi. 15—20.   2 Cor. vi. 16, &c.   It is plain
that there is a special presence of God in those who are

real members of our Lord. To this St. Paul seems to refer when he says, "They glorified God in me," Gal. i. 24. To this and to other passages noted *supr.* Athanasius refers, when he says, "Because of our relationship to His Body we too have become God's temple, and in consequence are made God's sons, so that even in us the Lord is now worshipped, and beholders report, as the Apostle says, that God is in them of a truth." Orat. i. § 43. And S. Basil, arguing for the worship of the Holy Spirit, says, "Man in common is crowned with glory and honour, and glory and honour and peace is reserved in the promises for every one who doeth good. And there is a certain glory of Israel peculiar, and the Psalmist speaks of a glory of his own, 'Awake up my glory;' and there is a glory of the sun, and according to the Apostle even a ministration of condemnation with glory. So many then being glorified, choose you that the Spirit alone of all should be without glory?" de Sp. S. c. 24.

¶ We are led on to a farther remark :—If even while we are in the flesh, soul and body become, by the indwelling of the Word, so elevated above their natural state, so sacred, that to profane them in a sacrilege, is it wonderful that the Saints above should so abound in prerogatives and privileges, and should claim a religious *cultus,* when once in the *pleroma,* and in the sight as in the fruition of the exuberant infinitude of God?

MARCELLUS.

¶ MARCELLUS was Bishop of Ancyra in Galatia. In the early years of S. Athanasius's episcopate, he wrote his Answer to the Arian Asterius and others, which was the occasion, and forms the subject of Eusebius's "contra Marcellum" and "Ecclesiastica Theologia," and which is the only existing document of his opinions. "Now he replies to Asterius," says Eusebius, "now to the great Eusebius [of Nicomedia] "and then he turns upon that man of God, that indeed thrice blessed person Paulinus [of Tyre]. Then he goes to war with Origen. . . Next he marches out against Narcissus, and pursues the other Eusebius," himself. "In a word, he counts for nothing all the Ecclesiastical Fathers, being satisfied with no one but himself." contr. Marc. i. 4. He was in consequence condemned in several Arian Councils, and retired to Rome, as did S. Athanasius, about the year 341, when both of them were formally acquitted of heterodoxy by the Pope in Council. Both were present, and both were again acquitted at the Council of Sardica in 347. From this very date, however, the charges against him, which had hitherto been confined to the Arians, begin to find a voice among the Catholics. S. Cyril in his Catechetical Lectures, A.D. 347, speaks of the heresy which had lately arisen in Galatia, which denied Christ's eternal reign, a description which both from country and tenet is evidently levelled at Marcellus. He is followed by S. Paulinus at the Council of Arles, and by S. Hilary, in the years which follow; but S. Athanasius seems to have acknowledged him down to about A.D. 360. At length the latter began to own that Marcellus "was not far from heresy," vid. below, and S. Hilary and S. Sulpicius say that he separated from his communion. S. Hilary adds (Fragm. ii. 21.) that Athanasius was decided in this course, not by Marcellus's work against Asterius, but by publications posterior to the Council of Sardica. Photinus, the disciple of Marcellus, who had published the very heresy imputed to the latter before A.D. 345, had now been deposed, with the unanimous consent of all parties, for some years. Thus for ten years Marcellus was disowned by the Saint with whom he had shared so many trials; but in the very end of S. Athanasius's life a transaction took place between himself, S. Basil, and the Galatian school, which issued in his being induced again to think more favourably of Marcellus, or at least to think it right in charity to consider him in communion with the Church. S. Basil had taken a strong part against him, and wrote to S. Athanasius on the subject, Ep. 69, 2, thinking that Athanasius's apparent countenance of him did harm to the Catholic cause. Upon this the accused party sent a deputation to Alexandria, with a view of setting themselves right with Athanasius. Eugenius, deacon of their Church, was their representative, and he in behalf of his brethren subscribed a statement in vindication of his and their orthodoxy, which was countersigned by the clergy of Alexandria and apparently by S. Athanasius, though his name does not appear among the extant signatures. This important document, which was brought to light and published by Montfaucon, speaks in the name of "the Clergy and the others assembled in Ancyra of Galatia, with our father Marcellus." He, as well as Athanasius himself, died immediately after this transaction, Marcellus in extreme age, being at least twenty years older than Athanasius, who himself lived till past the age of seventy. One might trust that the life of the former was thus prolonged, till he really recanted the opinions which go under his name; yet viewing him historically, and not in biography, it still seems right, and is in accordance with the usage of the Church in other cases, to consider him rather in his works and in his school and its developments, than in his own person and in his penitence. Whether S. Athanasius wrote the controversial passages which form Orat. iv. against him or against his school, in either case it was prior to the date of the explanatory document signed by Eugenius; nor is its interpretation affected by that explanation. As to S. Hilary's statement, that S. Athanasius did not condemn the particular work of Marcellus against Asterius, of which alone portions remain to us, his evidence in other parts of the history is not sufficiently exact for us to rely on his evidence in Marcellus's favour, against the plainly heretical import of the statements made in that work. Those statements were as follows:—

Marcellus held, according to Eusebius, that (1) there

was but one person, πρόσωπον, in the Divine Nature;
but he differed from Sabellius in maintaining, (2) not
that the Father was the Son and the Son the Father,
(which is called the doctrine of the υἱοπάτωρ,) but that
(3) Father and Son were mere names or titles, and
(4) not expressive of essential characteristics,—names
or titles given to Almighty God and (5) to His Eternal
Word, on occasion of the Word's appearing in the
flesh, in the person, or subsistence (ὑπόστασις) of Jesus
Christ, the Son of Mary.   The Word, he considered,
was from all eternity in the One God, being analogous
to man's reason within him, or the ἐνδιάθετος λόγος of
the philosophical schools.   (6) This One God or μόνας
has condescended to extend or expand Himself,
πλατύνεσθαι, to effect our salvation.   (7 and 8) The
expansion consists in the action, ἐνεργεία, of the λόγος,
which then becomes the λόγος προφορικὸς or voice of
God, instead of His inward Reason.   (9) The incarnation is a special divine expansion, viz. an expansion in
the flesh of Jesus, Son of Mary; (10) in order to
which the Word went forth, as at the end of the
dispensation He will return.   Consequently the λόγος
is not (11) the Son, nor (12) the Image of God, nor
the Christ, nor the First-begotten, nor King, but Jesus
is all these; and if these titles are applied to the Word
in Scripture, they are applied prophetically, in anticipation of His manifestation in the flesh.   (13) And
when He has accomplished the object of His coming, they will cease to apply to Him; for He will
leave the flesh, return to God, and be merely the
Word as before; and His Kingdom, as being the

Kingdom of the flesh or manhood, will come to an end.

This account of the tenets of Marcellus comes, it is true, from an enemy, who was writing against him, and moreover from an Arian or Arianizer, who was least qualified to judge of the character of tenets which were so opposite to his own. Yet there is no reason to doubt its correctness on this account. Eusebius supports his charges by various extracts from Marcellus's works, and he is corroborated by the testimony of others. Moreover, if Athanasius's account of the tenets against which he himself writes in his fourth Oration, answers to what Eusebius tells us of those of Marcellus, as in fact they do, the coincidence confirms Eusebius as well as explains Athanasius. And further, the heresy of Photinus, the disciple of Marcellus, which consisted in the very doctrines which Eusebius deduces from the work of Marcellus, gives an additional weight to such deductions.

¶ He wrote his work against Asterius not later than 335, the year of the Arian Council of Jerusalem, which at once took cognizance of it, and cited Marcellus to appear before them. The same year a Council held at Constantinople condemned and deposed him, about the time that Arius came thither for re-admission into the Church. From that time his name is frequently introduced into the Arian anathemas, vid. Macrostich, Syn. § 26. By adding those " who communicate with him," in that document the Eusebians intended to strike at the Roman see, which had acquitted Marcellus in a Council held in June of the same year.

¶ The Arians of Alexandria, writing to Alexander, (Syn. § 16) speak of the Son as "not as existing before, and afterwards generated or new created into a Son." One school of theologians may be aimed at, who held our Lord's συγκατάβασις to create the world was His γέννησις, and certainly such language as that of Hippol. contr. Noet. § 15, favours the supposition. But a class of the Sabellians may more probably be intended, who held that the Word became the Son on His incarnation, such as Marcellus, vid. Euseb. Eccles. Theol. i. 1. contr. Marc. ii. 3. vid. also Eccles. Theol. ii. 9, p. 114. b. μηδ' ἄλλοτε ἄλλην κ. τ. λ. Also the Macrostich says, " We anathematize those who call Him the mere Word of God, . . . not allowing Him to be Christ and Son of God before all ages, but from the time He took on Him our flesh . . . such are the followers of Marcellus and Photinus, &c." Syn. § 26. Again, Athanasius, Orat. iv. 15, says that, of those who divide the Word from the Son, some called our Lord's manhood the Son, some the two Natures together, and some said "that the Word Himself became the Son when He was made man." It makes it the more likely that Marcellus is meant, that Asterius seems to have written against him before the Nicene Council, and that Arius in other of his writings borrowed from Asterius, vid. de Decret. § 8; though it must not be forgotten that some of the early Fathers spoke unadvisedly on this subject, vid. the author's *Theological Tracts*.

¶ In the fourth (Arian) Confession of Antioch (supr. vol. i. p. 101) words are used, which answer to those added in the second General Council (381) to the Creed, and are directed against the doctrine of Marcellus, who taught that the Word was but a divine energy, manifested in Christ and retiring from Him at the consummation of all things, when the manhood or flesh of Christ would consequently no longer reign. "How can we admit," says Marcellus in Eusebius, "that that flesh, which is from the earth and profiteth nothing, should co-exist with the Word in the ages to come as serviceable to Him?" de Eccl. Theol. iii. 8. Again, "If He has received a beginning of His Kingdom not more than four hundred years since, it is no paradox that He who gained that Kingdom so short a while since, should be said by the Apostle to deliver it up to God. What are we to gather about the human flesh, which the Word bore for us, not four hundred years since? will the Word have it in the ages to come, or only to the judgment season?" iii. 17. And, "Should any ask whether that flesh which is in the Word has become immortal, we say to him, that we count it not safe to pronounce on points of which we learn not for certain from divine Scripture." Ibid. 10.

¶ Pope Julius acquitted Marcellus, Athan. Apol. Ar. 32, A.D. 341, but it would seem that he did not eventually preserve himself from heresy, even if he deserved a favourable judgment at that time. Athan. also sides with him, de Fug. 3. Hist. Arian. 6, but Epiphanius records, that, once on his asking Athan. what he (Athan.) thought of Marcellus, a smile came on his face, as if he had an opinion of him which he did not like to express, or which Epiphanius ought not to have asked for. Hær. 72, 4. And S. Hilary says that

Athan. separated Marcellus from his communion, because he agreed with his disciple, Photinus. He is considered heretical by Epiphanius, l.c.; by Basil, Epp. 69, 125, 263, 265; Chrysost. in Heb. i. 8; Theod. Hær. ii. 10; by Petavius, far more strongly by Bull. Montfaucon defends him, Tillemont, and Natal. Alex.

THE BLESSED MARY.

1. *Mary Ever-Virgin.*

THIS title is found in Athan. Orat. ii. § 70. "Let those who deny that the Son is from the Father by nature and proper to His substance, deny also that He took true human flesh of Mary Ever-Virgin." Vid. also Athan. Comm. in Luc. in Collect. Nov. t. 2, p. 43. Epiph. Hær. 78, 5. Didym. Trin. i. 27 p. 84. Rufin. Fid. i. 43. Lepor. ap. Cassian. Incarn. i. 5. Leon. Ep. 28, 2. Pseudo-Basil, t. 2, p. 598. Cæsarius has ἀειπαῖς. Qu. 20. On the doctrine itself, vid. the controversial Tract of S. Jerome against Helvidius; also a letter of S. Ambrose and his brethren to Siricius, and the Pope's letter in response. Coust. Ep. Pont. t i. p. 669—682.

Pearson, Bishop of Chester, writes well upon this subject. Creed, Art. 3. A passage from him is incidentally quoted infr. art. εὐσεβεία. He also says, "As we are taught by the predictions of the Prophets that a Virgin was to be Mother of the promised Messias, so are we assured by the infallible relation of the Evangelists, that this Mary 'was a Virgin when she bare him.' . . . . Neither was her act of parturition more contradictory to virginity, than that former [act] of conception. Thirdly, we believe the Mother of our

Lord to have been, not only before and after His nativity, but also for ever, the most immaculate and blessed Virgin. . . . . The peculiar eminency and unparalleled privilege of that Mother, the special honour and reverence due unto her Son and ever paid by her, the regard of that Holy Ghost who came upon her, the singular goodness and. piety of Joseph, to whom she was espoused, have persuaded the Church of God in all ages to believe that she still continued in the same virginity, and therefore is to be acknowledged as the Ever-Virgin Mary." Creed, Art. 3.

He adds that "many have taken the boldness to deny this truth, because not recorded in the sacred writ," but "with no success." He replies to the argument from "until" in Matt. i. 25 by referring to Gen. xxviii. 15, Deut. xxxiv. 6, 1 Sam. xv. 35, 2 Sam. vi. 23, Matt. xxviii. 20.

He might also have referred to Psalm cix. 1, and 1 Cor. xv. 25, which are the more remarkable, because they were urged by the school of Marcellus as a proof that our Lord's kingdom would have an end, and are explained by Euseb. himself, Eccl. Theol. iii. 13, 14. Vid. also Cyr. Cat. 15, 29, Naz. Orat. 30, 4, where the true force of "until" is well brought out,—"He who is King *before* He subdued.His enemies, how shall He not *the rather* be King, after He has got the mastery over them?"

¶ I have said in a note on the word in the *Aurea Catena*, that the word "till" need not imply a termination at a certain point of time, but may be given as information up to a certain point from which onwards there is already no doubt. Supposing an Evangelist thought the very notion shocking that Joseph should have considered the Blessed Virgin as his wife, *after* he was witness of her bearing the Son of God, he would only say that the vision had its effect upon him up to that date, when the idea was monstrous. If one said of a profligate, that, in consequence of some awful occurrence, he was in the habit of saying a prayer, every night up to the time of his conversion, no one would gather thence that he left off praying on being converted. " Michal the daughter of Saul had no child *to* the day of her death;" had she children after it? This indeed is one of Pearson's references. Vid. also Suicer de Symb. Niceno-Const. p. 231. Spanheim, Dub. Evang. part i. 28, 11.

¶ Athan. elsewhere compares the Virgin's flesh to the pure earth of Paradise out of which Adam was formed. She is ἀνέργαστος γῆ. Orat. ii. § 7, and so Iren. Hær. iii. 21 fin., and Tertullian, "That virgin earth, not yet watered by rains, nor impregnated by showers, from which man was formed in the beginning, from which Christ is now born according to the flesh from a Virgin." Adv. Jud. 13, vid. de Carn. Christ. 17. "Ex terra virgine Adam, Christus ex virgine." Ambros. in Luc. lib. iv. 7. Vid. also the parallel drawn out t. v. Serm. 147. App. S. August. and in Proclus, Orat. 2, pp. 103, 4, ed. 1630, vid. also Chrysost. t. 3, p. 113, ed. Ben. and Theodotus at Ephesus, "O earth unsown, yet bearing a salutary fruit, O Virgin, who didst surpass the very Paradise of Eden," &c. Conc. Eph. p. 4 (Hard. t. i. p. 1643). And so Proclus again, "She, the flowering and incorruptible Paradise, in whom the Tree of Life," &c. Orat. 6, p. 227. And Basil of Seleucia, "Hail, full of grace, the amarantine Paradise of purity, in whom the Tree of Life, &c." Orat. in Annunc. p. 215. And p. 212, "Which, think they, is the harder to believe, that a virgin womb should be with child, or the ground should be animated?" &c. And Hesychius, " Garden unsown, Paradise of immortality." Bibl. Patr. Par. 1624. t. 2; pp. 421, 423.

¶ Vid. the well-known passage in S. Ignatius, ad Eph. 19, where the devil is said to have been ignorant of the Virginity of Mary, and the Nativity and the Death of Christ; Orig. Hom. 6. in Luc. Basil. (if Basil,) Hom. in t. 2, App. p. 598, ed. Ben. and Jerome in Matt. i. 18, who quote it. vid. also Leon. Serm. 22, 3. Clement Eclog. Proph. p. 1002, ed. Potter.

¶ " Many," says Athanasius, "have been made holy and clean from all sin; nay, Jeremias was hallowed even from the womb, and John, while yet in the womb, leapt for joy at the voice of Mary Mother of God." Orat. iii. § 33. vid. Jer. i. 5. And so S. Jerome, S. Leo, &c. as mentioned in Corn. à Lap. in loc. who adds that S. Ephrem considers Moses also sanctified in the womb, and S. Ambrose Jacob. S. Jerome implies a similar gift in the case of Asella (ad Marcell. Ep. 24, 2). And so S. John Baptist, Maldon. in Luc. i. 15.

¶ It is at first strange that these instances of special exemptions should be named by early writers, without our Lady also being mentioned; or rather it would be strange, unless we bore in mind how little is said of her at all by Scripture or the Fathers up to the Council of Ephesus, A.D. 431. It would seem as if till our Lord's glory called for it, it required an effort for the reverent devotion of the Church to speak much about her or to make her the subject of popular preaching; but, when by her manifestation a right faith in her Divine Son was to be secured, then the Church was to be guided in a contrary course. It must be recollected that there was a *disciplina arcani* in the first centuries, and, if it was exercised, as far as might be, as regards the Holy Trinity and the Eucharist, so would it be as regards the Blessed Virgin.

I have insisted upon this deep sentiment of reverence in matters of sacred doctrine in my " History of the Arians," written long before I was a Catholic, and I may fairly quote here one of several passages contained in it, in solution of a difficulty with which at that time I was not concerned. For instance, I say, ch. 2, § 1:—" The meaning and practical results of deep-seated religious reverence were far better understood in the primitiue times than now, when the infidelity of the world has corrupted the Church. Now, we allow ourselves publicly to canvass the most solemn truths in a careless or fiercely argumentative way; truths, which it is as useless as it is unseemly to discuss before men, as being attainable only by the sober and watchful, by slow degrees, with dependence on the giver of wisdom, and with strict obedience to the light which has already been granted. Then, they would scarcely express in writing, what now is not only preached to the mixed crowds who frequent our churches, but circulated in prints among all ranks and classes of the unclean and the profane, and pressed upon all who choose to purchase. Nay, so perplexed is the present state of things, that *the Church is obliged to change her course of acting,* after the spirit of the alteration made at Nicæa, and unwillingly to take part in the theological discussions of the day, as a man crushes venomous creatures of necessity, powerful to do it, but loathing the employment." I am corroborated in my insistance on this principle by the words of Sozomen, who says, "I formerly deemed it necessary to transmit the confession drawn up by the unanimous consent of the Nicene Council, in order that posterity might possess a public record of the truth; but subsequently I was persuaded to the contrary by some godly and learned men, who represented that such matters ought to be kept secret, as only requisite to be known by disciples and their instructors." Hist. i. 20.

In an Anglican Sermon of a later date, I apply this instinctive feeling to the fact of the silence of Scripture about the Blessed Virgin in its narrative of the Resurrection. "Here perhaps," I say, "we learn a lesson from the deep silence which Scripture observes concerning the Blessed Virgin after the Resurrection; as if she, who was too pure and holy a flower to be more than seen here on earth, even during the season of her Son's humiliation, was altogether drawn by the Angels within the veil on His Resurrection, and had her joy in Paradise with Gabriel, who had been the first to honour her, and with those elder saints who arose after the Resurrection, appeared in the Holy City, and then vanished away." Par. Serm. vol. iv. 23. And I refer in a note to the following passage in the Christian Year.

> " God only, and good angels, look
>   Behind the blissful screen,—
> As when, triumphant o'er His woes,
> The Son of God by moonlight rose,
>   By all but Heaven unseen ;
> As when the Holy Maid beheld
>   Her risen Son and Lord,
> Thought has not colours half so fair,
> That we to paint that hour may dare,
>   In silence best adored."

Such doubtless were the spirit and the tone of the Church till Nestorius came forward to deny that the Son of God was the Son of Mary. Thenceforward her title of Theotocos, already in use among Christian writers, became dogmatic.

2. *Mary Theotocos.*

Mater Dei. Mother of God. Vid. Art. ἀντίδοσις ἰδιωμάτων. Athanasius gives the title to the Blessed Virgin, Orat. iii. § 14, § 29, § 33. Orat. iv. 32. Incarn. c. Ar. 8, 22.

¶ As to the history of this title, Theodoret, who from his party would rather be disinclined towards it, says that " *the most ancient* (τῶν πάλαι καὶ πρόπαλαι) heralds

of the orthodox faith taught to name and believe the
Mother of the Lord θεοτόκος, according to *the Apostolical tradition*." Hær. iv. 12. And John of Antioch,
whose championship of Nestorius and quarrel with
S. Cyril are well known, writes to the former, " This
title no ecclesiastical teacher has put aside ; those who
have used it are many and eminent, and those who have
not used it have not attacked those who used it."
Concil. Eph. part i. c. 25. (Labb.) And Alexander,
the most obstinate or rather furious of all Nestorius's
adherents, who died in banishment in Egypt, fully
allows the ancient reception of the word, though only
into popular use, from which came what he considers
the doctrinal corruption. " That in festive solemnities,
or in preaching and teaching, θεοτόκος should be unguardedly said by the orthodox without explanation,
is no blame, because such statements were not dogmatic, nor said with evil meaning. But now after the
corruption of the whole world," &c. Lup. Ephes. Epp.
94. He adds that it, as well as ἀνθρωποτόκος, " was used
by the great doctors of the Church." Socrates Hist.
vii. 32. says that Origen, in the first tome of his Commentary on the Romans (vid. de la Rue in Rom. lib. i. 5.
the original is lost), treated largely of the word ; which
implies that it was already in use. " Interpreting," he
says, " *how* θεοτόκος is used, he discussed the question
at length." Constantine implies the same with an
allusion to pagan mythology of an unpleasant kind ; he
says, " When He had to draw near to a body of this
world, and to tarry on earth, the need so requiring, He
contrived a sort of irregular birth of Himself, νόθην

τινὰ γένεσιν; for without marriage was there conception, and childbirth, εἰλείθυια, from a pure Virgin, and a maid, the Mother of God, θεοῦ μήτηρ κόρη." Ad. Sanct. Cœt. p. 480. The idea must have been familiar to Christians before Constantine's date to be recognized by him, a mere catechumen, and to be virtually commented on by such a parallelism.

¶ For instances of the word θεοτόκος, besides Origen. ap. Socr. vii. 32, vid. Euseb. V. Const. iii. 43, in Psalm cix. 4, p. 703, Montf. Nov. Coll.; Alexandr. Ep. ad Alex. ap. Theodor. Hist. i. 3, p. 745; Athan. (supra); Cyril. Cat. x. 19; Julian Imper. ap. Cyril. c. Jul. viii. p. 262; Amphiloch. Orat. 4, p. 41 (if Amphil.) ed. 1644; Nyssen. Ep. ad Eustath. p. 1093; Chrysost. apud Suicer Symb. t. ii. p. 240; Greg. Naz. Orat. 29, 4; Ep. 101, p. 85, ed. Ben. Antiochus and Ammon. ap. Cyril. de Recta Fid. pp. 49, 50; Pseudo-Dion. contr. Samos. 5, p. 240; Pseudo-Basil. Hom. t. 2, p. 600, ed. Ben.

¶ Pearson on the Creed (notes on Art. 3), arguing from Ephrem. ap. Phot. Cod. 228, p. 775, says the phrase *Mater Dei* originated with St. Leo. On the contrary, besides in Constantine's Oration as above, it is found, before S. Leo, in Ambros. de Virg. ii. 7; Cassian. Incarn. ii. 5, vii. 25; Vincent. Lir. Commonit. 21. It is obvious that θεοτόκος, though framed as a test against Nestorians, was equally effective against Apollinarians and Eutychians, who denied that our Lord had taken human flesh at all, as is observed by Facundus Def. Trium Cap. i. 4. And so S. Cyril, " Let it be carefully observed, that nearly this whole contest about the faith has been created against us for

our maintaining that the Holy Virgin is Mother of God ;
now, if we hold," as was the calumny, " that the Holy
Body of Christ our common Saviour was from heaven,
and not born of her, how can she be considered as
Mother of God ?" Epp. pp. 106, 7. Yet these sects, as
the Arians, maintained the term. Vid. supr. *Heresies.*

¶ As to the doctrine, which the term implies and
guards, the following are specimens of it. Vid. S. Cyril's
quotations in his de Recta Fide, p. 49, &c. "The
fleshless," says Atticus, " becomes flesh, the impalpable
is handled, the perfect grows, the unalterable advances,
the rich is brought forth in an inn, the coverer of
heaven with clouds is swathed, the king is laid in a
manger." Antiochus speaks of Him, our Saviour "with
whom yesterday in an immaculate bearing Mary
travailed, the Mother of life, of beauty, of majesty, the
Morning Star," &c. "The Maker of all," says S.
Amphilochius, " is born to us to-day of a Virgin."
" She did compass," says S. Chrysostom, " without
circumscribing the Sun of righteousness. To-day the
Everlasting is born, and becomes what He was not.
He who sitteth on a high and lofty throne is placed in
a manger, the impalpable, incomposite, and immaterial
is wrapped around by human hands, He who snaps the
bands of sin, is environed in swathing bands." And
in like manner S. Cyril himself, "As a woman, though
bearing the body only, is said to bring forth one who
is made up of body and soul, and that will be no injury
to the interests of the soul, as if it found in flesh the
origin of its existence, so also in the instance of the
Blessed Virgin, though she is Mother of the Holy

Flesh, yet she bore God of God the Word, as being in truth one with it." Adv. Nest i. p. 18. "God dwelt in the womb, yet was not circumscribed; whom the heaven containeth not, the Virgin's frame did not straiten." Procl. Orat. i. p. 60. "When thou hearest that God speaks from the bush, and Moses falling on his face worships, believest thou, not considering the fire that is seen, but God that speaks? and yet, when I mention the Virgin womb, dost thou abominate and turn away? ... In the bush seest thou not the Virgin, in the fire the loving-kindness of Him who came?" Theodotus of Ancyra ap. Conc. Eph. (p. 1529, Labb.). "Not only did Mary bear her Elder," says Cassian in answer to an objector, "but her Author, and giving birth to Him from whom she received it, she became parent of her Parent. Surely it is as easy for God to give nativity to Himself, as to man; to be born of man as to make men born. For God's power is not circumscribed in His own Person, that He should not do in Himself what He can do in all." Incarn. iv. 2. "The One God Only-begotten, of an ineffable origin from God, is introduced into the womb of the Holy Virgin, and grows into the form of a human body. He who contrives all, .. is brought forth according to the law of a human birth; He at whose voice Arch-angels tremble .. and the world's elements are dis-solved, is heard in the wailing of an infant, &c." Hil. Trin. ii. 25. "'My beloved is white and ruddy;' white truly, because the Brightness of the Father, ruddy, because the Birth of a Virgin. In Him shines and glows the colour of each nature; .. He did not begin from a Virgin, but the Everlasting came into a Virgin." Ambros. Virgin. i. n. 46. " Him, whom, coming in His simple Godhead, not heaven, not earth, not sea, not any creature had endured, Him the inviolate womb of a Virgin carried." Chrysost. ap. Cassian. Incarn. vii. 30. "Happily do some understand by the ' closed gate,' by which only ' the Lord God of Israel enters,' that Prince on whom the gate is closed, to be the Virgin Mary, who both before and after her bearing remained a Virgin." Jerom. in Ezek. 44 init. " Let them tell us," says Capreolus of Carthage, " how is that Man from heaven, if He be not God conceived in the womb ? " ap. Sirm. Opp. t. i. p. 216. " He is made in thee," says S. Austin, " who made thee . . . nay, through whom heaven and earth is made ; . . the Word of God in thee is made flesh, receiving flesh, not losing Godhead. And the Word is joined, is coupled to the flesh, and of this so high wedding thy womb is the nuptial chamber, &c." Serm. 291, 6. " Say, O blessed Mary," says S. Hippolytus, " what was It which by thee was conceived in the womb, what carried by thee in that virgin frame ? It was the Word of God, &c." ap. Theod. Eran. i. p. 55. " There is one physician," says S. Ignatius, " fleshly and spiritual, generate and ingenerate, God come in the flesh, in death true life, both from Mary and from God, first passible, then impassible, Jesus Christ our Lord." Ep. ad Eph. 7.

MEDIATION.

GOD, the Origin and Cause of all things, acts by the mediation, ministration, or operation of His Son, as signified by the Son's names of Word and Wisdom. Vid. art. *Eternal Son.*

"It belongs to the Son," says Athanasius, " to have the things of the Father; and to be such that the Father is seen in Him, and that through Him all things were made, and that the salvation of all comes to pass and consists in Him." Orat. ii. § 24. " Men were made through the Word, when the Father Himself willed." Orat. i. § 63. " Even if God compounded the world out of materials, . . . still allow the Word to work those materials, though at the bidding and in the service of God, προστατόμενος καὶ ὑπουργῶν; but if by His own Word He calls into existence things which existed not, then the Word is not in the number of things not existing," &c. Orat. ii. § 22. "With whom did God speak," (saying *Let us make*, &c.) " so as even to speak with a command," προστάττων ? " He bids, προστάττει, and says, *Let us make* men. . . . Who was it but His Word ? " c. *Gent.* § 46. " A Word then must exist, to whom God gives command, ἐντέλλεται ὁ θεός," de Decr. § 9.

¶ The language of Catholics and heretics is very much the same on this point of the Son's ministration, with this essential difference of sense, that Catholic writers mean a ministration internal to the divine substance and an instrument connatural with the Father, and Arius meant an external and created medium of operation. vid. arts. *Hand* and ὄργανον. Thus S. Clement calls our Lord "the All-harmonious Instrument (ὄργανον) of God." Protrept. p. 6. Eusebius, "an animated and living instrument (ὄργανον ἔμψυχον,) nay, rather divine and . . . . vivific of every substance and nature." Demonstr. iv. 4. S. Basil, on the other hand, insists that the Arians reduced our Lord to "an inanimate instrument," ὄργανον ἄψυχον, though they called Him ὑπουργὸν τελειότατον, "most perfect minister or underworker." adv. Eunom. ii. 21. Elsewhere he says, "the nature of a cause is one, and the nature of an instrument, ὀργανου, another; . . . foreign then in nature is the Son from the Father, since so is an instrument from an artist." de Sp. S. n. 6 fin. vid. also n. 4 fin. and n. 20. Afterwards he speaks of our Lord as "not intrusted with the ministry of each work by particular injunctions in detail, for this were ministration," λειτουργικὸν, but as being "full of the Father's excellences," and "fulfilling not an instrumental, ὀργανικὴν, and servile ministration, but accomplishing the Father's will like a Maker, δημιουργικῶς." ibid. n. 19. And so S. Gregory, "The Father signifies, the Word accomplishes, not servilely, nor ignorantly, but with knowledge and sovereignty, and, to speak more suitably, in the Father's way, πατρικῶς." Orat. 30, 11. And S. Cyril, "There is nothing abject in the Son, as in a minister, ὑπουργῷ, as they say; for

218 MEDIATION.

the God and Father injoins not, ἐπιτάττει, on His Word, 'Make man,' but as one with Him, by nature, and inseparably existing in Him as a co-operator," &c., in Joann. p. 48. Explanations such as these secure for the Catholic writers some freedom in their modes of speaking; e.g. we have seen supr. that Athan. speaks of the Son, as "enjoined and ministering," προσταττόμενος, καὶ ὑπουργῶν, Orat. ii. § 22. Thus S. Irenæus speaks of the Father being well-pleased and commanding κελεύοντος, and the Son doing and framing. Hær. iv. 38, 3. S. Basil too, in the same treatise in which are some of the foregoing protests, speaks of "the Lord ordering, προστάσσοντα, and the Word framing." de Sp. S. n. 38. S. Cyril of Jerusalem, of "Him who bids, ἐντέλλεται, bidding to one who is present with Him," Cat. xi. 16. vid. also ὑπηρετῶν τῇ βουλῇ, Justin. Tryph. 126, and ὑπουργὸν, Theoph. ad Autol. ii. 10 (Galland. t. 2, p. 95), ἐξυπηρετῶν θελήματι, Clem. Strom. vii. p. 832.

¶ As to these words προσταττόμενος καὶ ὑπουργῶν, it is not quite clear that Athan. accepts these words in his own person, as has been assumed supr. Vid. de Decr. § 7, and Orat. ii. § 24 and 31, which, as far as they go, are against their use. Also S. Basil objects to ὑπουργος, contr. Eunom. ii. 21, and S. Cyril in Joan. p. 48, though S. Basil speaks of τὸν προστάττοντα κύριον, as noticed above, and S. Cyril of the Son's ὑποταγὴ, Thesaur. p. 255. Vid. "ministering, ὑπηρετοῦντα, to the Father of all." Just. Tryph. n. 60. "The Word become minister, ὑπηρέτης, of the Creator," Origen in Joan. t. 2, p. 67, also Constit.

Ap. viii. 12, but Pseudo-Athan. objects to ὑπηρετῶν, de Comm. Essent. 30, and Athan. apparently, Orat. ii. § 28. Again, "Whom did he order, præcepit?" Iren. Hær. iii. 8, n. 3. "The Father bids ἐντέλλεται (allusion to Ps. 33. 9), the Word accomplishes . . . He who commands, κελεύων, is the Father, He who obeys, ὑπακούων, the Son . . . the Father willed, ἠθέλησεν, the Son did it." Hippol. c. Noet. 14, on which vid. Fabricius's note. S. Hilary speaks of the Son as "subditus per obedientiæ obsequelam," Syn. 51. Origen contr. Cels. ii. 9. Tertull. adv. Prax. 12. fin. Patres Antioch. ap. Routh t. 2. p. 468. Prosper in Psalm. 148. Hilar. Trin. iv. 16. "That the Father speaks and the Son hears, or contrariwise, that the Son speaks and the Father hears, are expressions for the sameness of nature and the agreement of Father and Son." Didym. de Sp. S. 36. "The Father's bidding is not other than His Word; so that 'I have not spoken of Myself,' He perhaps meant to be equivalent to 'I was not born from Myself.' For if the Word of the Father speaks, He pronounces Himself, for He is the Father's Word, &c." August. de Trin. i. 26. On this mystery vid. Petav. Trin. vi. 4.

¶ Athan. says that it is contrary to all our notions of religion that Almighty God cannot create, enlighten, address, and unite Himself to His creatures immediately. This seems to be implied when it was said by the Arians that the Son was created for creation, illumination, &c.; whereas in the Catholic view the Son is but that Divine Person, who in the Economy of grace is creator, enlightener, &c. God is represented as all-perfect, but acting according to a certain divine order. Here the remark is in point about the right and wrong sense of the words "commanding," "obeying," &c.

Hence our Lord is the βούλησις and the βουλὴ, and ζῶσα βουλὴ, of the Father. Orat. iii. 63 fin. and so Cyril Thes. p. 54, who uses βουλὴ expressly, (as it is always used by implication,) in contrast to the κατὰ βούλησιν of the Arians, though Athan. uses κατὰ τὸ βούλημα, e. g. Orat. iii. 31. And so αὐτὸς τοῦ πατρὸς θέλημα, Nyss. contr. Eunom. xii. p. 345.

¶ The bearing of the above teaching of the early Fathers on the relation of the Second to the First Person in the Holy Trinity, is instructively brought out by Thomassinus in his work, *de Incarnatione*, from which I have made a long extract in one of my Theological Tracts:—part of it I will make use of here.

"It belongs to the Father to be without birth, but to the Son to be born. Now innascibility is a principle of concealment, but birth of exhibition. The former withdraws from sight, the latter comes forth into open day; the one retires into itself, lives to itself, and has no outward start; the other flows forth and extends itself and is diffused far and wide. It corresponds then to the idea of the Father, as being ingenerate, to be self-collected, remote, unapproachable, invisible, and in consequence to be utterly alien to an incarnation. But to the Son, considered as once for all born, and ever coming to the birth, and starting into view, it especially belongs to display Himself, to be prodigal of Himself, to bestow Himself as an object for sight and enjoyment, because in the fact of being born He has burst forth into His corresponding act of self-diffusion. . . .

"Equally . . . incomprehensible is in His nature the Son as the Father. Accordingly we are here considering a personal property, not a natural. It is especially congenial to the Divine Nature to be good, beneficent, and indulgent; and for these qualities there is no opening at all without a certain manifestation of their hiding-place, and outpouring of His condescending Majesty. Wherefore, since the majesty and goodness of God, in the very bosom of His nature, look different ways, and by the one He retires into Himself, and by the other He pours Himself out, it is by the different properties of the Divine Persons that this contrariety is solved," &c., &c. vid. Thomassin. Incarn. ii. 1, p. 89, &c.

MELETIUS was Bishop of Lycopolis in the Thebais, in the first years of the fourth century. He was convicted of sacrificing to idols in the persecution, and deposed by a Council under Peter, Bishop of Alexandria and subsequently martyr. Meletius separated from the communion of the Church, and commenced a schism; at the time of the Nicene Council it included as many as twenty-eight or thirty Bishops; in the time of Theodoret, a century and a quarter later, it included a number of monks. Though not heterodox, they supported the Arians on their first appearance, in their contest with the Catholics. The Council of Nicæa, instead of deposing their Bishops, allowed them on their return a titular rank in their sees, but forbade them to exercise their functions.

¶ The Meletian schismatics of Egypt formed an alliance with the Arians from the first. Athan. imputes the alliance to ambition and avarice in the Meletians, and to zeal for their heresy in the Arians. Ep. Æg. 22, vid. also Hist. Arian. 78. In like manner after Sardica the Semi-Arians attempted a coalition with the Donatists of Africa. Aug. contr. Cresc. iii. 34 (n. 38).

¶ Epiphanius gives us another account of the circumstances under which Meletius's schism originated.

¶ There was another Meletius, Bishop of Antioch, in the latter part of the same century. He at one time belonged to the Semi-Arian party, but joined the orthodox, and was the first president of the second Ecumenical Council.

TWO NATURES OF EMMANUEL.

¶ "Two natures," says S. Leo, "met together in
our Redeemer, and, while what belonged to each respectively remained, so great a unity was made of either
substance, that from the time that the Word was made
flesh in the Blessed Virgin's womb, we may neither
think of Him as God without that which is man, nor as
man without That which is God. Each nature certifies
its own reality under distinct actions, but neither of
them disjoins itself from connexion with the other.
Nothing is wanting from either towards other; there
is entire littleness in majesty, entire majesty in littleness; unity does not introduce confusion, nor does what
is special to each divide unity. There is what is
passible, and what is inviolable, yet He, the Same, has
the contumely whose is the glory. He is in infirmity
who is in power; the Same is both the subject and
the conqueror of death. God then did take on Him
whole man, and so knit Himself into man and man into
Himself in His mercy and in His power, that either
nature was in other, and neither in the other lost its
own attributes." Serm. 54, 1. "Suscepit nos in
suam proprietatem illa natura, quæ nec nostris sua,
nec suis nostra consumeret," &c. Serm. 72. p. 286. vid.
also Ep. 165, 6. Serm. 30, 5. Cyril. Cat. iv. 9. Amphiloch. ap. Theod. Eran. i. p. 66, also pp. 60, 87, 88.

¶ "All this belongs to the Economy, not to the
Godhead. On this account He says, 'Now is My soul

troubled,' . . . . so troubled as to seek for a release, if escape were possible. . . . . As to hunger is no blame, nor to sleep, so is it none to desire the present life. Christ had a body pure from sins, but not exempt from physical necessities, else it had not been a body." Chrysost. in Joann. Hom. 67. 1 and 2. "He used His own flesh as an instrument for the works of the flesh and for physical infirmities and for other infirmities which are blameless," &c. Cyril. de Rect. Fid. p. 18. "As a man He doubts, as a man He is troubled ; it is not His power (virtus) that is troubled, not His Godhead, but His soul," &c. Ambros. de Fid. ii. n. 56. Vid. a beautiful passage in S. Basil's Hom. iv. 5 (de Divers.), in which he insists on our Lord's having wept to show us how to weep neither too much nor too little.

"Being God, and existing as Word, while He remained what He was, He became flesh, and a child, and a man, no change profaning the mystery. The Same both works wonders, and suffers ; by the miracles signifying that He is what He was, and by the sufferings giving proof that He had become what He had framed." Procl. ad Armen. p. 615. "Without loss then to what belongs to either nature and substance (salvâ proprietate, and so Tertullian, " Salva est utriusque proprietas substantiæ," &c., in Prax. 27), "yet with their union in one Person, Majesty takes on it littleness, Power infirmity, Eternity mortality, and, to pay the debt of our estate, an inviolable Nature is made one with a nature that is passible ; that, as was befitting for our cure, One and the Same Mediator between God and man, the man Jesus Christ, might both be capable of death from the one, and incapable from the other." Leo's Tome (Ep. 28, 3), also Hil. Trin. ix. 11 fin. "Vagit infans, sed in cœlo est," &c., ibid. x. 54. Ambros. de Fid. ii. 77. "Erat vermis in cruce sed dimittebat peccata. Non habebat speciem, sed plenitudinem divinitatis," &c. Id. Epist. i. 46, n. 5. Theoph. Ep. Pasch. 6, ap. Conc. Ephes. p. 1404. Hard.

¶ Athanasius, Orat. iv. § 33, speaks of the Word as "putting on the first fruits of our nature, and blended (ἀνακραθεὶς) with it;" vid. note on Tertull. Oxf. Tr. vol. i. p. 48; and so ἡ καινὴ μίξις, θεὸς καὶ ἄνθρωπος, Greg. Naz. as quoted by Eulogius ap. Phot. Bibl. p. 857; "immixtus," Cassian. Incarn. i. 5; "commixtio," Vigil. contr. Eutych. i. 4. p. 494 (Bibl. Patr. 1624); "permixtus," Au- gust. Ep. 137, 11; "ut naturæ alteri altera misceretur," Leon. Serm. 23, 1. There is this strong passage in Naz. Ep. 101, p. 87 (ed. 1840), κιρναμένων ὥσπερ τῶν φύσεων, οὕτω δὴ καὶ τῶν κλήσεων, καὶ περιχωρουσῶν εἰς ἀλλήλας τῷ λόγῳ τῆς συμφυΐας; Bull says that in using περιχωρουσῶν Greg. Naz. and others "minùs propriè loqui." Defens. F. N. iv. 4, § 14. Petavius had allowed this, but proves the doctrine intended amply from the Fathers. De Incarn. iv. 14. Such oneness is not "confusion," for οὐ σύγχυσιν ἀπεργασάμενος, ἀλλὰ τὰ δύο κεράσας εἰς ἕν, says Epiph. Ancor. 81 fin. and so Eulog. ap. Phot. Bibl. p. 831 fin. οὐ τῆς κράσεως σύγχυσιν αὐτῷ δηλούσης. Vid. also on the word μίξις, &c. Zacagn. Monum. p. xxi.—xxvi. Thomassin. de Incarn. iii. 5 iv. 15.

THE NICENE TESTS OF ORTHODOXY.

WHAT were the cardinal additions, made at Nicæa, to the explicit faith of the Church, will be understood by comparing the Creed, as there recorded and sanctioned, with that of Eusebius, as they both are found (vol. i. *supr.* pp. 55—57) in his Letter to his people. His Creed is distinct and unexceptionable, as far as it goes; but it does not guard against the introduction of the Arian heresy into the Church, nor could it, as being a creed of the primitive age, and drawn up before the heresy. On the other hand, we see by the anathematisms appended to the Nicene Creed what it was that had to be excluded, and by the wording of the additions to the Creed, and by Eusebius's forced explanation of them, how they acted in effecting its exclusion. The following are the main additions in question :—

1. The Creed of Eusebius says of our Lord, ἐκ τοῦ πατρὸς γεγεννημένον; but the Nicene says, γεννηθέντα οὐ ποιηθέντα, because the Arians considered generation a kind of creation, as Athan. says, Orat. ii. § 20, " Ye say that an offspring is the same as a work, writing ' generated *or* made.' " And more distinctly, Arius in his letter to Eusebius uses the words, πρὶν γεννηθῇ ἤτοι κτισθῇ ἢ ὁρισθῇ ἢ θεμελιωθῇ. Theodor. Hist. i. 4, p. 750. And to Alexander, ἀχρόνως γεννηθεὶς καὶ πρὸ αἰώνων κτισθεὶς καὶ θεμελιωθείς. De Syn. § 16.

And Eusebius to Paulinus, κτιστὸν καὶ θεμελιωτὸν καὶ γεννητόν. Theod. Hist. i. 5, p. 752. These different words profess to be scriptural, and to explain each other; "created" being in Prov. viii. 22; "made" in the speech of St. Peter, Acts ii. 22; "appointed" or "declared" in Rom. i. 4; and "founded" or "established" in Prov. viii. 23; vid. Orat. ii. § 72, &c., vid. also § 52.

2. We read in the Nicene Creed, "from the Father, *that is*, from the substance of the Father," whereas in Eusebius's Letter it is only "God from God." According to the received doctrine of the Church all rational beings, and in one sense all beings whatever, are "from God," over and above the fact of their creation, and in a certain sense sons of God, vid. *Arian tenets, Adam*, and *Eusebius*. And of this undeniable truth the Arians availed themselves to explain away our Lord's proper Sonship and Divinity.

3. But the chief test at Nicæa was the word ὁμοούσιον, its special force being that it excludes the maintenance of *more than one* divine οὐσία or substance, which seems to be implied or might be insinuated even ⸍in Eusebius's creed; "We believe," he says, "each of these [Three] to be and to exist, the Father *truly* Father, the Son *truly* Son, the Holy Ghost truly Holy Ghost;" for if there be Three substances or *res* existing, either there are Three Gods or two of them are not God. The ἐξ οὐσίας, important and serviceable as it was, did not exclude the doctrine of a divine emanation, and was consistent with Semi-Arianism, and with belief in two or in three substances; vid. the art

ὁμοούσιον. " It is the precision of this phrase," says Athan., " that detects their pretence, whenever they use the phrase 'from God,' and that excludes all the subtleties with which they seduce the simple. For, whereas they contrive to put a sophistical construction on all other words at their will, this phrase only, as detecting their heresy, do they dread, which the Fathers did set down as a bulwark against their impious speculations one and all," de Syn. § 45.   And Epiphanius calls it σύνδεσμος πίστεως, Ancor. 6.   And again he says, " Without the confession of the ' One in substance' no heresy can be refuted; for as a serpent hates the smell of bitumen, and the scent of sesame-cake, and the burning of agate, and the smoke of storax, so do Arius and Sabellius hate the notion of the sincere profession of the ' One in substance.' "   And Ambrose, " That term did the Fathers set down in their formula of faith, which they perceived to be a source of dread to their adversaries; that they themselves might unsheath the sword which cut off the head of their own monstrous heresy." de Fid. iii. 15.

This is very true, but a question arises whether another and a better test than the *homoüsion* might not have been chosen, one eliciting less opposition, one giving opportunities to fewer subtleties; and on this point a few words shall be said here.

Two ways then lay before the Fathers at Nicæa of condemning and eliminating the heresy of Arius, who denied the proper divinity of the Son of God.   By means of either of the two a test would be secured for guarding the sacred truth from those evasive professions and pretences of orthodoxy, which Arius himself, to do him justice, did not ordinarily care to adopt. Our Lord's divinity might be adequately defined either (1) by declaring Him to be in and of the essence of the Father, or (2) to be with the Father from everlasting, that is, to be either consubstantial or co-eternal with God. Arius had denied both doctrines; "He is not eternal," he says, "or co-eternal, or co-ingenerate with the Father, nor has He His being together with Him." And "The Son of God is not consubstantial with God." Syn. § 15, 16 (vid. also Epiph. Hær. 69, 7). Either course then would have answered the purpose required: but the Council chose that which at first sight seems the less advisable, the more debatable of the two; it chose the "Homoüsion" or "Consubstantial," not the Co-eternal.

Here it is scarcely necessary to dwell on a statement of Gibbon, which is strange for so acute and careful a writer. He speaks as if the enemies of Arius at Nicæa were at first in a difficulty how to find a test to set before the Council which might exclude him from the Church, and then accidentally became aware that the *Homoüsion* was such an available term. He says that in the Council a letter was publicly read and ignominiously torn, in which the Arian leader, Eusebius of Nicomedia, "*ingenuously* confessed that the admission of the Homoüsion, a word already familiar to the Platonists, was incompatible with the principles of his theological system. The *fortunate opportunity* was eagerly embraced by the bishops who governed the resolutions of the Synod," &c., ch. xxi.

He adds in a note, " We are indebted to Ambrose (vid.
de Fid. iii. 15,) for the knowledge of this *curious*
anecdote." This comes of handling theological subjects with but a superficial knowledge of them; it is
the way in which foreigners judge of a country which
they enter for the first time. Who told Gibbon that
Arius's enemies and the governing bishops did not
know from the first of the Arian rejection of this word
" consubstantial"? who told him that there were not
other formulæ which Arius rejected quite as strongly
as it, and which would have served as a test quite as
well? As I have quoted above, he had publicly said,
" The Son is not equal, no, nor consubstantial with
God," and " Foreign to the Son in substance is the
Father;" and, as to matter already provided by him for
other tests, he says in that same Thalia, " When
the Son was not yet, the Father was already God;"
" Equal, or like Himself, He [the Father] has
none " (vid. Syn. § 15), &c., &c. S. Ambrose too was
not baptized till A.D. 374, a generation after the
Nicene Council, and his report cannot weigh against
contemporary documents; nor can his words at this
time receive Gibbon's interpretation. It was not
from any dearth of tests, that the Fathers chose the
Homoüsion; and the question is, why did they prefer
it to συναίδιον, ἄναρχον, ἀγένητον, &c., &c.?

The first difficulty attached to " consubstantial "
was that it was not in Scripture, which would have
been avoided, had the test been " from everlasting,"
" without beginning," &c.; a complaint, however, which
came with a bad grace from the Arians, who had begun.

the controversy with phrases of their own devising, and not in Scripture. But, if the word was not Scriptural, it had the sanction of various Fathers in the foregoing centuries, and was derived from a root, ὁ ὤν, which was in Scripture. Nor could novelty be objected to the word. Athanasius, ad. Afros 6, speaks of the use of the word " by ancient Bishops, about 130 years since;" and Eusebius, supr. Decr. App. § 7, confirms him as to its ancient use in the Church: and, though it was expedient to use the words of Scripture in enunciations of revealed teaching, it would be a superstition to confine ourselves to them, as if the letter could be allowed to supersede the sense.

A more important difficulty lay in the fact that some fifty or sixty years before, in the Councils occasioned by the heretical doctrine of Paulus, Bishop of Antioch, the word had actually been proposed in some quarter as a *tessera* against his heresy and then withdrawn by the Fathers as capable of an objectionable sense. Paulus, who was a sharp disputant, seems to have contended that the term either gave a material character to the Divine nature, or else, as he wished himself to hold, that it implied that there was no real distinction of Persons between Father and Son. Any how, the term was under this disadvantage, that in some sense it had been disowned in the greatest Council which up to the Nicene the Church had seen. But its inexpedience at one time and for one purpose was no reason why it should not be expedient at another time and for another purpose, and its imposition at Nicæa showed by the event that it was the fitting word, and justified those who selected it. Even still the question occurs why it was that the Nicene Fathers selected a term which was not in Scripture, and had on a former occasion been considered open to objection, while against "co-eternal" or "from everlasting" no opposition could have been raised short of the heretical denial of its truth ; and again, whether it was not rather a test against Tritheism, of which Arius was not suspected. "Consubstantial" was a word needing a definition ; "co-eternal" spoke for itself.

Arius, it is true, had boldly denied the "consubstantial," but he had still more often and more pointedly denied the "co-eternal.' The definition of the Son's eternity *a parte ante* would have been the destruction of the heresy. Arius had said on starting, according to Alexander, that " God was not always a Father ; " "the Word was not always." " He said," says Socrates, "if the Father begot the Son, he that was begotten had a beginning of existence." Arius himself says to his friend Eusebius, " Alexander has driven us out of our city for dissenting from his public declaration, 'As God is eternal, so is His Son.' " Again, to Alexander himself, as quoted supr., " The Son is not eternal, or co-eternal, or co-ingenerate with the Father." Vid. also Decr. § 6. Would it not, then, have avoided all the troubles which, for a long fifty or sixty years, followed upon the reception of the Homoüsion by the Nicene Council, would it not have been a far more prudent handling of the Creed of the Church, to have said " begotten *from everlasting,* not made," instead of introducing into it a word of doubtful meaning, already discredited, and at best unfamiliar to Catholics? This is what may be asked, and, with a deep feeling of our defective knowledge of the ecclesiastical history of the times, I answer, under correction, as follows :—

There are passages, then, in the history of the Ante-Nicene times which suggest to us that the leading bishops in the Council were not free to act as they might wish, or as they might think best, and that the only way to avoid dangerous disputes in an assemblage of men, good and orthodox, but jealous in behalf of their own local modes of thought and expression and traditional beliefs, was to meet indirectly the heresy which they all agreed to condemn, which all wished to destroy. So it was, that various writers, some of them men of authority and influence, and at least witnesses to the sentiments of their day, had, in the course of the three centuries past, held the doctrine of the temporal *gennesis*, a doctrine which gave an excuse and a sort of shelter to the Arian misbelief. (Vid. supr. art. *Arians*, 3.) I am not denying that these men held with the whole Catholic Church that our Lord was in personal existence from eternity as the Word, connatural with the Father, and in His bosom; but they also held, with more or less distinctness, that He was not fully a Son from eternity, but that, when the creation according to the Divine counsels was in immediate prospect, and with reference to it, the Word was born into Sonship, and became the Creator, the Pattern, and the Conservative Power of all that was created. These writers were such as Justin, Tatian,

Theophilus, Tertullian, and Hippolytus; and if the
Fathers of the Nicene Council had spoken uncon-
ditionally and abruptly of the Son's eternity, they
would have given an opening to the Arians, who dis-
believed in the eternity of the Personal Word, to gain
over to their side, and to place in opposition to the
Alexandrians, many who substantially were orthodox
in their belief. They did not venture then, as it
would seem, to pronounce categorically that the
gennesis was from everlasting, lest they should
raise unnecessary questions :—at the same time,
by making the "consubstantial" the test of orthodoxy, they provided for the logical and eventual
acceptance of the Son's à *parte ante* eternity, on the
principle which Athan. is continually insisting on,
"What God is, that He ever was;" and by including
among the parties anathematized at the end of the
Creed " those who said that our Lord ' was not in being
before He was born,' " they both inflicted an additional
blow upon the Arians, and indirectly recognized the
orthodoxy, and gained the adhesion, of those who, by
speaking of the temporal *gennesis,* seemed at first
sight to ascribe to our Lord a beginning of being.

OMNIPRESENCE OF GOD.

¶ ATHAN. says, Decr. § 11, "Men, being incapable of self-existence, are enclosed in place, and consist in the Word of God; but God is self-existent, inclosing all things, and inclosed by none,—within all according to His own goodness and power, yet outside all in His own nature." Vid. also Incarn. § 17. This contrast is not commonly found in ecclesiastical writers, who are used to say that God is present everywhere, in substance as well as by energy or power. Clement, however, expresses himself still more strongly in the same way, " In substance far off (for how can the generate come close to the Ingenerate?), but most close in power, in which the universe is embosomed." Strom. ii. 2, but the parenthesis explains his meaning. Vid. Cyril. Thesaur. 6, p. 44. The common doctrine of the Fathers is, that God is present everywhere in *substance*. Vid. Petav. de Deo, iii. 8 and 9. It may be remarked that S. Clement continues, "*neither inclosing* nor inclosed."

¶ Athan., however, explains himself in Orat. iii. 22, saying that when our Lord, in comparing the Son and creatures, "uses the word 'as,' He signifies those who become from afar *as* He is *in* the Father; . . for in place nothing is far from God, but only in nature all things are far from Him." When, then, he says

"outside all in His nature," he must mean as here
"far from all things considered in His nature." He
says here distinctly, "in place nothing is far from
God." S. Clement, loc. cit., gives the same explanation, as above noticed. It is observable that the
Tract Sab. Greg. (which the Benedictines consider
not Athan.'s) speaks as Athan. does supr., "not by
being co-extensive with all things, does God fill all;
for this belongs to bodies, as air; but He comprehends
all as a power, for He is an incorporeal, invisible power,
not encircling, not encircled." 10. Eusebius says the
same thing, "Deum circumdat nihil, circumdat Deus
omnia non corporaliter; virtute enim incorporali adest
omnibus," &c. De Incorpor. i. init. ap. Sirm. Op.
t. i. p. 68. vid. S. Ambros. "Quomodo creatura in Deo
esse potest," &c. de Fid. i. 16.

PAUL OF SAMOSATA.

MENTION of this Paul and of his sect is frequently made by Athan. There is some difficulty in determining what his opinions were. As far as the fragments of the Antiochene Acts state or imply, he taught, more or less, as follows :—that the Son's pre-existence was only in the divine foreknowledge, Routh, Rell. t. 2. p. 466; that to hold His substantial pre-existence was to hold two Gods, ibid. p. 467; that He was, if not an instrument, an impersonal attribute, p. 469; that His manhood was not "unalterably made one with the Godhead," p. 473; "that the Word and Christ were not one and the same," p. 474; that Wisdom was in Christ as in the prophets, only more abundantly, as in a temple; that He who appeared was not Wisdom, p. 475; in a word, as it is summed up, p. 484, that "Wisdom was born with the manhood, not substantially, but according to quality." vid. also p. 476, 485. All this plainly shows that he held that our Lord's personality was in His Manhood, but does not show that he held a second personality in His godhead; rather he considered the Word impersonal, though the Fathers in Council urge upon him that he ought to hold two Sons, one from eternity, and one in time, p. 485.

Accordingly the Synodal Letter after his deposition

speaks of him as holding that Christ came not from Heaven, but from beneath. Euseb. Hist. vii. 30. S. Athanasius's account of his doctrine is altogether in accordance, (vid. vol. i. supr. p. 25, note 1.) viz., that Paul taught that our Lord was a mere man, and that He was advanced to His divine power, ἐκ προκοπῆς.

However, since there was a great correspondence between Paul and Nestorius, (except in the doctrine of the personality and eternity of the Word, which the Arian controversy determined and the latter held,) it was not unnatural that reference should be made to the previous heresy of Paul and its condemnation when that of Nestorius was on trial. Yet the Contestatio against Nestorius which commences the Acts of the Council of Ephesus, Harduin. Conc. t. i. p. 1272, and which draws out distinctly the parallel between them, says nothing to show that Paul held a double personality. And though Anastasius tells us, Hodeg. c. 7, p. 108, that the "holy Ephesian Council showed that the tenets of Nestorius agreed with the doctrine of Paul of Samosata," yet in c. 20, p. 323, 4, he shows us what he means, by saying that Artemon also before Paul "divided Christ in two." Ephrem of Antioch too says that Paul held that "the Son before ages was one, and the Son in the last time another," ap. Phot. p. 814; but he seems only referring to the words of the Antiochene Acts, quoted above. Again, it is plain from what Vigilius says in Eutych. t. v. p. 731. Ed. Col. 1618, (the passage is omitted in Ed. Par. 1624.) that the Eutychians considered that Paul and Nestorius differed; the former holding that our Lord was a mere man, the latter a mere man only till He was united to the Word. And Marius Mercator says, " Nestorius circa Verbum Dei, *non* ut Paulus sentit, qui non substantivum, sed prolatitium potentiæ Dei efficax Verbum esse definit." part 2, p. 17. Ibas, and Theodore of Mopsuestia, though more suspicious witnesses, say the same, vid. Facund. vi. 3, iii. 2, and Leontius de Sectis, iii. p. 504. To these authorities may be added Nestorius's express words, Serm. 12, ap. Mar. Merc. t. 2, p. 87, and Assemani takes the same view, Bibl. Orient. t. 4, p. 68, 9.

The principal evidence in favour of Paul's Nestorianism consists in the Letter of Dionysius to Paul and his answer to Paul's Ten Questions, which are certainly spurious, as on other grounds, so on some of those urged against the professed Creed of Antioch (in my " Theol. Tracts ") but which Dr. Burton in his excellent remarks on Paul's opinions, Bampton Lectures, Note 102, admits as genuine. And so does the accurate and cautious Tillemont, who in consequence is obliged to believe that Paul held Nestorian doctrines ; also Bull, Fabricius, Natalis Alexander, &c. In holding these compositions to be certainly spurious, I am following Valesius, Harduin, Montfaucon, Pagi, Mosheim, Cave, Routh, and others.

PERSONAL ACTS AND OFFICES OF OUR LORD.

THERE are various (and those not the least prominent and important) acts and offices of our Lord, which, as involving the necessity of both His natures in concurrence and belonging to His Person, may be said to be either θεανδρικὰ (vid. art. under that heading), or instances of ἀντίδοσις ἰδιωμάτων (vid. art.). Such are His office and His acts as Priest, as Judge, &c., in which He can be viewed neither as simply God, nor as simply man, but in a third aspect, as Mediator, the two natures indeed being altogether distinct, but the character, in which He presents Himself to us by the union of these natures, belonging rather to His Person, which is composite.

¶ Athanasius says, Orat. ii. § 16, " Since we men would not acknowledge God through His Word, nor serve the Word of God our natural Master, it pleased God to show in man His own Lordship, and so to draw all men to Himself. But to do this by a mere man beseemed not; lest, having man for our Lord, we should become worshippers of man. Therefore the Word Himself became flesh, and the Father called His Name Jesus, and so 'made' Him Lord and Christ, as much as to say, 'He made Him to rule and to reign;' that while in the name of Jesus, whom ye crucified, every knee bows, we may acknowledge as Lord and King both the Son and through Him the Father." Here the renewal of mankind is made to be the act, primarily indeed of the Word, our natural Master, but not from Him, as such, simply, but as given to Him to carry out by the Father, when He became incarnate, by virtue of His *Persona composita*.

¶ He says again that, though none could be "a beginning" of creation, who was a creature, yet still that such a title belongs not to His essence. It is the name of an *office* which the Eternal Word alone can fill. His Divine Sonship is both superior and necessary to that office of a "Beginning." Hence it is both true (as he says) that "if the Word is a creature, He is not a beginning;" and yet that that "beginning" is "in the number of the creatures." Though He becomes the "beginning," He is not "a beginning as to His *substance*;" vid. Orat. ii. § 60, where he says, "He who is *before all*, cannot be a *beginning of all*, but is other than all." He is the beginning in the sense of *Archetype*.

¶ And so again of His Priesthood (vid. art. upon it) the Catholic doctrine is that He is Priest, neither as God nor as man simply, but as being the Divine Word in and according to His manhood.

¶ Again S. Augustine says of judgment; "He judges by His divine power, not by His human, and yet man himself will judge, as the Lord of glory was crucified." And just before, "He who believes in Me, believes not in that which He sees, lest our hope should be in a creature, but in Him who has taken on Him the creature, in which He might appear to human eyes." Trin. i. 27, 28.

¶ And so again none but the Eternal Son could be πρωτότοκος, yet He is so called only when sent as Creator and as incarnate, Orat. ii. § 64.

¶ The phrase λόγος, ᾗ λόγος ἐστί, is frequent in Athan. as denoting the distinction between the Word's original nature and His offices. vid. Orat. i. § 43, 44. 47, 48. ii. § 8. 74. iii. § 38, 39. 41. 44. 52. iv. § 23.

PHILOSOPHY.

ATHAN. says, speaking of ἀγέννητον, "I am *told* the word has different senses." Decr. § 28.

And so de Syn. § 46, "we have on *careful inquiry* ascertained, &c." Again, "I have acquainted myself on their account [the Arians'] with the meaning of ἀγέννητον." Orat. i. § 30. This is remarkable, for Athan. was a man of liberal education. In the same way S. Basil, whose cultivation of mind none can doubt, speaks slightingly of his own philosophical knowledge. He writes of his "neglecting his own weakness, and being utterly unexercised in such disquisitions;" contr. Eunom. init. And so in de Sp. S. n. 5, he says, that "they who have given time" to vain philosophy, "divide causes into principal, co-operative," &c. Elsewhere he speaks of having "expended much time on vanity, and wasted nearly all his youth in the vain labour of pursuing the studies of that wisdom which God has made foolishness." Ep. 223. 2. In truth Christianity has a philosophy of its own. Thus at the commencement of his Viæ Dux, Anastasius says, "It is a first point to be understood that the tradition of the Catholic Church does not proceed upon, or follow the philosophical definitions in all respects of the Greeks, and especially as regards the mystery of Christ and the doctrine of the Trinity,

but a certain rule of its own, evangelical and apostolical;" p. 20. In like manner, Damascene, speaking
of the Jacobite use of φύσις and ὑπόστασις, says, " Who
of holy men ever thus spoke ? unless ye introduce to
us your St. Aristotle, as a thirteenth Apostle, and prefer the idolater to the divinely inspired." contr. Jacob.
10, p. 399. and so again Leontius, speaking of Philo-
ponus, who from the Monophysite confusion of nature
and hypostasis was led into Tritheism. " He thus
argued, taking his start from Aristotelic principles ;
for Aristotle says that there are of individuals particular substances as well as one common." de Sect. v. fin.

¶ " What our Fathers have delivered," says Athan,
" this is truly doctrine ; and this is truly the token of
doctors, to confess the same thing with each other, and
to vary neither from themselves nor from their fathers ;
whereas they who have not this character, are not to
be called true doctors but evil. Thus the Greeks, as
not witnessing to the same doctrines, but quarrelling
one with another, have no truth of teaching ; but the
holy and veritable heralds of the truth agree together,
not differ. For though they lived in different times,
yet they one and all tend the same way, being prophets of the one God, and preaching the same Word
harmoniously." Decr. § 4.

S. Basil says the same of the Grecian Sects,
" We have not the task of refuting their tenets, for
they suffice for the overthrow of each other." Hexaem,
i. 2. vid. also Theod. Græc. Affect. i. p. 707. &c.
August. Civ. Dei, xviii. 41. and Vincentius's celebrated
Commonitorium *passim*.

PRIESTHOOD OF CHRIST.

"The expressions *He became* and *He was made*," says Athanasius, on Hebr. iii. 2 (vid. Orat. ii. § 8) must not be understood as if the Word, considered as the Word, were *made*, (vid. art. *Personal Acts*, &c.,) but because the Word, being Framer of all, afterwards was made High Priest, by putting on a body which was made." ·

¶ In a certain true sense our Lord may be called a Mediator before He became incarnate, but the Arians, even Eusebius, seem to have made His mediatorship consist essentially in His divine nature, instead of holding that it was His office, and that He was made Mediator when He came in the flesh. Eusebius, like Philo and the Platonists, considers Him as made in the beginning the "Eternal Priest of the Father," Demonst. v. 3. de Laud. C. p. 503 fin. "an intermediate divine power," p. 525, "mediating and joining generated substance to the Ingenerate," p. 528.

¶ The Arians considered that our Lord's Priesthood preceded His Incarnation, and belonged to His Divine Nature, and was in consequence the token of an inferior divinity. The notice of it therefore in Heb. iii. 1, 2, did but confirm them in their interpretation of the words *made*, &c. For the Arians, vid. Epiph. Hær. 69, 37. Eusebius too had distinctly declared, " Qui

videbatur, erat agnus Dei; qui occultabatur sacerdos
Dei." advers. Sabell. i. p. 2, b. vid. also Demonst. i. 10,
p. 38, iv. 16, p. 193, v. 3, p. 223, vid. contr. Marc.
pp. 8 and 9, 66, 74, 95.   Even S. Cyril of Jerusalem
makes a similar admission, Catech. x. 14.   Nay S.
Ambrose calls the Word, "plenum justitiæ sacerdota-
lis," de fug. Sæc. 3. 14.   S. Clement Alex. before them
speaks once or twice of the λόγος ἀρχιερεὺς, e. g.
Strom. ii. 9 fin. and Philo still earlier uses similar language, de Profug. p. 466 (whom S. Ambrose follows),
de Somniis, p. 597. vid. Thomassin. de Incarn. x. 9.
Nestorius on the other hand maintained that the Man
Christ Jesus was the Priest; Cyril adv. Nest. p. 64.
And Augustine and Fulgentius may be taken to countenance him, de Consens. Evang. i. 6, and ad Thrasim.
iii. 30.   The Catholic doctrine is, that the Divine
Word is Priest *in* and *according to* His manhood. vid.
the parallel use of πρωτότοκος infr. art. in voc. "As He
is called Prophet and even Apostle for His humanity,"
says S. Cyril Alex. " so also Priest."   Glaph. ii. p. 58.
And so Epiph. loc. cit. Thomassin loc. cit. makes a
distinction between a divine Priesthood or Mediatorship, such as the Word may be said to sustain between
the Father and all creatures, and an earthly and sacri-
ficial for the sake of sinners. vid. also Huet. Origenian.
ii. 3. § 4, 5.

PRIVATE JUDGMENT ON SCRIPTURE.

(Vid. art. *Rule of Faith.*)

THE two phrases by which Athan. denotes private judgment on religious matters, and his estimate of it, are τὰ ἴδια and ἃ ἤθελον, e. g.

¶ "Laying down their private (τὴν ἰδίαν) impiety as some sort of rule (ὡς κανόνα τινὰ, i.e. as a Rule of Faith) they wrest all the divine oracles into accordance with it." Orat. i. § 52. And so ἰδίων κακονοιῶν, Orat. ii. § 18. ταῖς ἰδίαις μυθοπλαστίαις. Orat. iii. § 10, and, "they make the language of Scripture their pretence; but, instead of the true sense, sowing upon it (Matt. xiii. 25. vid. art. ἐπίσπειρας) the private (τὸν ἴδιον) poison of their heresy." Orat. i. § 53. And so, κατὰ τὸν ἴδιον νοῦν. Orat. i. § 37. τὴν ἰδίαν ἀσέβειαν. iii. § 55. And, " He who speaketh of his own, ἐκ τῶν ἰδίων, speaketh a lie." contr. Apoll. i. fin.

¶ And so other writers: "They used to call the Church a virgin," says Hegesippus, "for it was not yet defiled by profane doctrines . . . the Simonists, Dosithians, &c. . . . each privately (ἰδίως) and separately has brought in a private opinion." ap. Euseb. Hist. iv. 22. Ruffinus says of S. Basil and S. Gregory, "Putting aside all Greek literature, they are said to have passed thirteen years together in studying the Scriptures alone, and followed out their sense not *from their private opinion*, but by the writings and authority of the Fathers, &c." Hist. ii. 9. Sophronius at Seleucia cried out, "If to publish day after day our own private (ἰδίαν) will, be a profession of faith, accuracy of truth will fail us." Socr. ii. 40.

"We must not make an appeal to the Scriptures, nor take up a position for the fight, in which victory cannot be, or is doubtful, or next to doubtful. For though this conflict of Scripture with Scripture did not end in a drawn battle, yet the true order of the subject required that that should be laid down first, which now becomes but a point of debate, viz. *who have a claim to the faith itself, whose are the Scriptures.*" Tertull. de Præscr. 19. "Seeing the Canon of Scripture is perfect, &c. what need we join unto it the authority of the Church's understanding and interpretation? because the Scripture being of itself so deep and profound, all men do not understand it in one and the same sense, but *so many men, so many opinions* almost may be gathered out of it; for Novatian expounds it one way, Photinus another, Sabellius, &c." Vincent. Comm. 2. Hippolytus has a passage very much to the same purpose, contr. Noet. 9 fin.

As to the phrase ὡς οὗτοι θέλουσι, vid. λέγοντες μὴ οὕτως .. ὡς ἡ ἐκκλησία κηρύσσει, ἀλλ' ὡς αὐτοὶ θέλουσι. Orat. iii. § 10, words which follow ἰδίαις μυθοπλαστίαις, quoted just above. Vid. also iii. § 8 and 17. This is a common phrase with Athan. ὡς ἐθέλησεν, ἅπερ ἐθέλησαν, ὅταν θέλωσι, οὓς ἐθέλησαν, &c., &c., the proceedings of the heretics being self-willed from first to

last. Vid. Sent. Dion. 4 and 16. Mort. Ar. fin. Apoll.
ii. 5. init. in contrast with the εὐαγγελικὸς ὅρος. Also
Decr. § 3. Syn. § 13. Ep. Æg. § 5. 19. 22. Apol.
Arian. § 2. 14. 35. 36. 73. 74. 77. Apol. Const. § 1.
de Fug. § 2. 3. 7. Hist. Arian. § 2. 7. 47. 52. 54. 59–
60.

In like manner ἃ βουλονται, &c. Ep. Enc. 7. Ap.
Arian. § 82. 83. Ep. Æg. § 6. Apol. Const. § 32.
de Fug. § 1. Hist. Ar. 15. 18.

THE RULE OF FAITH.

(VID. art. *Private Judgment.*) The recognition of this rule is the basis of St. Athanasius's method of arguing against Arianism. It is not his aim ordinarily to *prove* doctrine by Scripture, nor does he appeal to the private judgment of the individual Christian in order to determine what Scripture means; but he assumes that there is a tradition, substantive, independent and authoritative, such as to supply for us the true sense of Scripture in doctrinal matters—a tradition carried on from generation to generation by the practice of catechising, and by the other ministrations of Holy Church. He does not care to contend that no other meaning of certain passages of Scripture besides this traditional Catholic sense is possible or is plausible, whether true or not, but simply that any sense inconsistent with the Catholic is untrue, untrue because the traditional sense is apostolic and decisive. What he was instructed in at school and in church, the voice of the Christian people, the analogy of faith, the ecclesiastical φρόνημα, the writings of saints; these are enough for him. He is in no sense an inquirer, nor a mere disputant; he has received, and he transmits. Such is his position, though the expressions and turn of sentences which indicate it are so delicate and indirect, and so scattered about his pages, that it is difficult to collect them and to analyse what they imply. Perhaps the most obvious proof that what I have stated is substantially true, is that on any other supposition he seems to argue illogically. Thus he says : " The Arians, looking at what is human in the Saviour, have judged him to be a creature. . . . But let them learn, however tardily, that *the Word became flesh ;*" and then he goes on to show that he does not rely simply on the inherent, unequivocal force of St. John's words, satisfactory as that is, for he adds, " Let us, as possessing τὸν σκόπον τῆς πίστεως, acknowledge that this is the right (ὀρθὴν, orthodox) understanding of what they understand wrongly." Orat. iii. § 35.

Again, " What they now allege from the Gospels they explain in an unsound sense, as we may easily see *if we will but avail ourselves* of τὸν σκόπον τῆς καθ' ἡμᾶς πίστεως, and using this ὥσπερ κανόνι, apply ourselves, as the Apostle says, to the reading of inspired Scripture." Orat. iii. 28.

And again : " Since they pervert divine Scripture in accordance with their own private (ἴδιον) opinion, we must *so far* (τοσοῦτον) answer them as (ὅσον) to justify its word, and to show that its sense is orthodox, ὀρθήν." Orat. i. 37.

For other instances, vid. art. ὀρθός; also vid. supr., vol. i. pp. 36, 235, 390, fin. 407 ; also Serap. iv. § 15, Gent. § 6, 7, and 33.

¶ In Orat. ii., § 5, after showing that "made" is used in Scripture for "begotten," in other instances besides that of our Lord, he says," "Nature and truth

draw the meaning to themselves " of the sacred text—
that is, while the style of Scripture *justifies* us in thus
interpreting the word "made," doctrinal truth *obliges*
us to do so. He considers the Regula Fidei the
principle of interpretation, and accordingly he goes on
at once to apply it.

¶ It is his way to start with some general exposition
of the Catholic doctrine which the Arian sense of the
text in dispute opposes, and thus to create a *præju-
dicium* or proof against the latter; vid. Orat. i. 10, 38,
40, init. 53, § ii. § 12 init. 32—34. 35. 44. init., which
refers to the whole discussion (18—43.) 73. 77. iii. 18.
init. 36 init. 42. 51. init. &c. On the other hand
he makes the ecclesiastical sense the rule of interpretation, τούτῳ (τῷ σκοπῷ, the general drift of Scripture
doctrine) ὥσπερ κανόνι χρησάμενοι, as quoted just
above. This illustrates what he means when he says
that certain texts have a " good," " pious," " orthodox " sense, i. e. they can be interpreted (in spite, if so
be, of appearances) in harmony with the Regula
Fidei.

¶ It is with a reference to this great principle, that he
begins and ends his series of Scripture passages, which
he defends from the misinterpretation of the Arians.
When he begins he refers to the necessity of interpreting them according to that sense which is not the
result of private judgment, but is orthodox. "This,"
he says, " I conceive is the meaning of this passage,
and that a meaning *especially ecclesiastical.*" Orat. i.
§ 44. And he ends with : " Had they dwelt on these
thoughts, and recognized the ecclesiastical scope as an

anchor for the faith, they would not of the faith have made shipwreck. Orat. iii. § 58.

¶ It is hardly a paradox to say that in patristical works of controversy the conclusion in a certain sense proves the premisses. As then he here speaks of the ecclesiastical scope "as an anchor for the faith;" so when the discussion of texts began, Orat. i. § 37, he introduces it as already quoted by saying, "Since they allege the divine oracles and force on them a misinterpretation *according to their private sense*, it becomes necessary to meet them *so far* as to do justice to these passages, and to show that they bear an orthodox sense, and that our opponents are in error." Again Orat. iii. 7, he says, "What is the *difficulty*, that one *must need* take such a view of such passages?" He speaks of the σκόπος as a κανών or rule of interpretation, supr. iii. § 28. vid. also § 29 init. 35 Serap. ii. 7. Hence too he speaks of the "ecclesiastical sense," e g. Orat. i. 44, Serap. iv. 15, and of the φρόνημα, Orat. ii. 31 init. Decr. 17 fin. In ii. § 32, 3, he makes the general or Church view of Scripture supersede inquiry into the force of particular illustrations.

SABELLIUS.

Eusebius, Eccles. Theol. i. 20, p. 91, as well as the Macrostich Confession, supr. Syn. § 26, says that Sabellius held the Patripassian doctrine. Epiph. however, Hær. p. 398. denies it, and imputes the doctrine to Noetus. Whatever Sabellius taught, it should be noticed, that, in the reason which the Arian Macrostich alleges against his doctrine, it is almost implied that the divine nature of the Son suffered on the Cross. The Arians would naturally fall into this notion directly they gave up their belief in our Lord's absolute divinity. It would as naturally follow to hold that our Lord had no human soul, but that His pre-existent nature stood in the place of it:—also that His Priesthood was no peculiarity of His Incarnation.

¶ It is difficult to decide what Sabellius's doctrine really was; nor is this wonderful, considering the perplexity and vacillation which is the ordinary consequence of abandoning Catholic truth. Also we must distinguish between him and his disciples. He is considered by Eusebius, Eccl. Theol. i. p. 91, Patripassian, i.e. as holding that the Father was the Son; also by Athan. Orat. iii. 36 init. de Sent. Dion. 5 and 9. By the Eusebians of the Macrostich Creed ap. Athan. de Syn. 26 vol. 1 supr. By Basil. Ep. 210, 5. Ruffin. in

Symb. 5. By Augustine de Hær. 41. By Theodor.
Hær. ii. 9. And apparently by Origen. ad Tit. t. 4.
p. 695. And by Cyprian. Ep. 73. On the other
hand, Epiphanius seems to deny it, ap. August. l. c.
and Alexander, by comparing Sabellianism to the emanation doctrine of Valentinus, ap. Theod. Hist. i. 3,
p. 743.

¶ Sabellians, as Arians, denied that the Word was a
substance, and as the Samosatenes, who, according
to Epiphanius, considered our Lord the internal, ἐν
διάθετος, word and thought, Hær. 65.

All Sabellians, except Patripassians, mainly differed
from Arians only at this point, viz. *when* it was that
our Lord came into being. Both parties considered
Him a creature, and the true Word and Wisdom but
attributes or energies of the Almighty. This Lucifer
well observes to Constantius, with the substitution
of Paulus and Photinus for Sabellius, " Quid interesse
arbitraris inter te et Paulum Samosatenum, vel eum tum
ejus discipulum tuum conscotinum, nisi quia tu 'ante
omnia' dicas, ille vero 'post omnia'"? p. 203, 4. A
subordinate difference was that the Samosatenes, Photinians, &c. considered our Lord to be really gifted
with the true Word, whereas Arians did scarcely more
than admit Him to be formed after its pattern.

The Sabellians agreed with the Arians, as far as
words went, in considering the Logos as a creative
attribute, vid. Sent. D. 25. Ep. Ægypt. 14 fin.
Epiph. Hær. 72, p. 835; but such of them as held
that the Logos actually took flesh, escaped the mystery of God subsisting in Two Persons, only by

falling into the heterodox notion that His nature was compounded of substance and attribute or quality, σύνθετον τὸν θέον ἐκ ποιότητος καὶ οὐσίας. They virtually‧ denied, with many Trinitarians outside the Church in this day, that the Son and again the Spirit is ὅλος θεός; but, if Each is not ὅλος θεὸς, God is σύνθετος.

SANCTIFICATION.

ATHANASIUS insists earnestly on the merciful dispensation of God, who has not barely given us through Christ justification, but has made our sanctification to be included in the gift, and sanctification through the personal presence in us of the Son. After saying, Incarn. § 7, that to accept mere repentance from sinners would not have been fitting, εὔλογον, he continues, " Nor does repentance recover us from our state of nature, it does but arrest the course of sin. Had there been but a fault committed, and not a subsequent *corruption*, repentance had been well, but if," &c. vid. *Incarnation* and *Freedom.*

" While it is mere man who receives the gift, he is liable to lose it again (as was shown in the case of Adam, for he received and he lost), but that the grace may be irrevocable, and may be kept sure by men, therefore it is the Son who Himself appropriates the gift." Orat. iii. § 38.

He received gifts in order " that strong by Him (δι᾽ αὐτὸν) men might henceforward upon earth have power against devils, as ' having become partakers of a divine nature,' and in heaven might, as ' being delivered from corruption,' reign everlastingly ; . . . and, whereas the flesh received the gift in Him, henceforth by It for us also that gift might abide secure." Orat. iii. § 40.

" The Word of God, who loves man, put on Himself created flesh, at the Father's will, that, whereas the first man had made the flesh dead through the transgression, He Himself might quicken it in the Blood of His own body." Orat. ii. § 65. Vid. also Orat. i. § 48. 51, ii. § 56.

¶ " How could we be partakers of the adoption of sons, unless through the Son we had received from Him that communion with Him, unless His Word had been made flesh, and had communicated that Flesh to us ? " Iren. Hær. iii. 19. " He took part of flesh and blood, that is, He became man, whereas He was Life by nature, . . . that, uniting Himself to the corruptible flesh according to the measure of its own nature, ineffably and inexpressibly, and as He alone knows, He might bring it to His own life, and render it partaker through Himself of God and the Father. . . . For He bore our nature, refashioning it into His own life. . . . He is in us through the Spirit, turning our natural corruption into incorruption, and changing death to its contrary." Cyril. in Joan. ix. cir. fin.

¶ " The Word having appropriated the affections of the flesh, no longer do those affections touch the body, because of the Word who has come in it, but they are destroyed by Him, and henceforth men . . . abide ever immortal and incorruptible." Orat iii. 33. vid. also Incarn. c. Ar. § 12. contr. Apoll. i. 17. ii. 6. " Since God the Word willed to annul the passions, whose end is death, and His deathless nature was not capable of them, ... He is made flesh of the Virgin in the way He knoweth, &c." Procl. ad. Armen. p. 616.

Also Leon. Serm. 22. pp. 69. 71. Serm. 26. p. 88.
Nyssen. contr. Apoll. t. 2. p. 696. Cyril. Epp. p. 138, 9.
in Joan. p. 95. Chrysol. Serm. 148.

¶ " His body is none other than His, and is a natural
recipient of grace; for He received grace as far as
man's nature was exalted, which exaltation was its being
deified." Orat. i. § 45. vid. *Indwelling* and *Deification*.

SCRIPTURE CANON.

ATHAN. will not allow that the *Pastor* is canonical, Decr. § 18. "In the *Shepherd* it is written, since they [the Arians] allege this book also, though it is not in the Canon;" yet he uses the formula, "It is written."

¶ And so in Ep. Fest. fin. he enumerates it with Wisdom, Ecclesiasticus, Esther, Judith, Tobit, and others, "not canonized but appointed by the Fathers to be read by late converts and persons under teaching." He calls it elsewhere a most profitablê book. Incarn. 3.

¶ As to the phrase, "it is written," or "he says" —τάδε λέγει, the Douay renders such phrases by "he," διὸ λέγει, "wherefore *he* saith," Eph. v. 14; εἴρηκε περὶ τῆς ἑβδόμης οὕτω, "*he* spoke," Heb. iv. 4; and 7, "*he* limiteth." And we may take in explanation, "As the Holy Ghost saith, To-day," &c. Heb. iii. 7. Or understand with Athan. διελέγξει λέγων ὁ Παῦλος. Orat. i. § 57. ὡς εἶπεν ὁ Ἰωάννης. Orat. iii. § 30. vid. also iv. § 31. On the other hand, "doth not the *Scripture* say," John vii. 42; "what saith the *Scripture?*" Rom. iv. 3; "do you think that the *Scripture* saith in vain," James iv. 5. And so Athan. οἶδεν ἡ θεια γραφὴ λέγουσα. Orat. i. § 56. ἔθος τῇ θειῇ γραφῇ .. φησί. Orat. iv. § 27. λέγει ἡ γραφή, Decr. § 22. φησὶν ἡ γραφή, Syn. § 52.

AUTHORITY OF SCRIPTURE.

ATHANASIUS considers Scripture sufficient for the proof of such fundamental doctrines as came into contro- versy during the Arian troubles; but, while in con- sequence he ever appeals to Scripture, (and indeed has scarcely any other authoritative document to quote,) he ever speaks against interpreting it by a private rule instead of adhering to ecclesiastical tradition. Tradition is with him of supreme authority, including therein catechetical instruction, the teaching of the *schola,* ecumenical belief, the φρόνημα of Catholics, the ecclesiastical scope, the analogy of faith, &c.

"The holy and inspired Scriptures are sufficient of themselves for the preaching of the truth; yet there are also many treatises of our blessed teachers com- posed for this purpose." contr. Gent. init. "For studying and mastering the Scriptures, there is need of a good life and a pure soul, and virtue according to Christ," Incarn. 57. "Since divine Scripture is suffi- cient more than anything else, I recommend persons who wish to know fully concerning these things," (the doctrine of the blessed Trinity,) "to read the divine oracles," ad Ep. Æg. 4. "The Scriptures are suffi- cient for teaching; but it is good for us to exhort each other in the faith, and to refresh each other with discourses." Vit. S. Ant. 16. "We must seek before

all things whether He is Son, and on this point
specially search the Scriptures, for this it was, when
the Apostles were questioned, that Peter answered,"
&c. Orat. ii. § 73. And passim in Athan. Vid.
Serap. i. 32 init. iv. fin. contr. Apoll. i. 6, 8, 9, 11,
22. ii. 8, 9, 13, 14, 17—19.

¶ "The doctrine of the Church should be proved,
not announced, (ἀποδεικτικῶς οὐκ ἀποφαντικῶς;) therefore show that Scripture thus teaches." Theod. Eran.
p. 199. "We have learned the rule of doctrine
(κανόνα) out of divine Scripture." ibid. p. 213.
" Do not believe me, let Scripture be recited. I
do not say of myself ' In the beginning was the
Word,' but I hear it; I do not invent, but I read;
what we all read, but not all understand." Ambros.
de Incarn. 14. " Non recipio quod extra Scripturam de
tuo infers." Tertull. Carn. Christ. 7. vid. also 6.
" You departed from inspired Scripture and therefore
didst fall from grace." Max. de Trin. Dial. v. 29. "The
Children of the Church have received from their holy
Fathers, that is, the holy Apostles, to guard the faith ;
and withal to deliver and preach it to their own
children. . . . Cease not, faithful and orthodox men,
thus to speak, and to teach the like from the divine
Scriptures, and to walk, and to catechise, to the confirmation of yourselves and those who hear you;
namely, that holy faith of the Catholic Church, as the
holy and only Virgin of God received its custody from
the holy Apostles of the Lord; and thus, in the case
of each of those who are under catechising, who are to
approach the Holy Laver, ye ought not only to preach

faith to your children in the Lord, but also to teach them expressly, as your common mother teaches, to say : ' We believe in One God,' " &c. Epiph. Ancor. 119, fin. who thereupon proceeds to give at length the Niceno-Constantinopolitan Creed. And so Athan. speaks of the orthodox faith, as " issuing from Aposto lical teaching and the Fathers' tradition, and confirmed by New and Old Testament." ad Adelph. 6, init. Cyril Hier. too as " declared by the Church and esta-blished from all Scripture." Cat. v. 12. " Let us guard with vigilance what we have *received*. . . . . What then have we received from the *Scriptures* but altogether this ? that God made the world by the Word," &c. &c. Procl. ad Armen. Ep. 2. p. 612. " That God the Word, after the union, remained such as He was, &c. so clearly hath divine Scripture, and more-over the doctors of the Churches, and the lights of the world taught us." Theodor. Eran. p. 175, init. " That it is the tradition of the Fathers is not the whole of our case ; for they too followed the meaning of Scripture, starting from the testimonies, which just now we laid before you from Scripture." Basil de Sp. S. n. 16. vid. also a remarkable passage in Athan. Synod. § 6, fin.

¶ S. Gregory says in a well-known passage ; " Why art thou such a slave to the letter, and takest up with Jewish wisdom, and pursuest sylla-bles to the loss of things ? For if thou wert to say, ' twice five,' or ' twice seven,' and I concluded ' ten ' or ' fourteen ' from your words, or from ' a rea-sonable mortal animal ' I concluded ' man,' should I seem to you absurd ? how so, if I did but give your meaning? for words belong as much to him who demands them as to him who utters." Orat. 31. 24. vid. also Hil. contr. Constant. 16. August. Ep. 238. n. 4—6. Cyril Dial. i. p. 391. Petavius refers to other passages, de Trin. iv. 5. § 6.

¶ In interpreting Scripture, Athan. always assumes that the Catholic teaching is true and the Scripture must be explained by it, vid. art. *Rule of Faith.* Thus he says, Orat. ii. 3. "If He be Son, as indeed He is, let them not question about the terms which the sacred writers use of Him. . . . For terms do not disparage His Nature but rather that Nature draws to itself those terms and changes them." And presently "Nature and truth draw the meaning to themselves; This being so, why ask, is He a work; it is proper to ask of them first, is he a Son?" ii. 5.

¶ The great and essential difference between Catholics and non-Catholics was, that Catholics interpreted Scripture by Tradition, and non-Catholics by their own private judgment.

¶ That not only Arians, but heretics generally, professed to be guided by Scripture, we know from many witnesses.

¶ Heretics in particular professed to be guided by Scripture. Tertull. Præscr. 8. For Gnostics vid. Tertullian's grave sarcasm, "Utantur hæretici omnes scripturis ejus, cujus utuntur etiam mundo." Carn. Christ. 6. For Arians, vid. supr. *Arian tenets.* And so Marcellus, "We consider it unsafe to lay down doctrine concerning things which we have not learned with exactness from the divine Scriptures." (leg.

περὶ ὧν . . . παρὰ τῶν.) Euseb. Eccl. Theol. p. 177.
And Macedonians, vid. Leont. de Sect. iv. init.   And
Monophysites, "I have not learned this from Scripture; and I have a great fear of saying what it is
silent about." Theod. Eran. p. 215.   S. Hilary brings
a number of these instances together with their respective texts, Marcellus, Photinus, Sabellius, Montanus, Manes; then he continues, "Omnes Scripturas
sine Scripturæ sensu loquuntur, et fidem sine fide
prætendunt.   Scripturæ enim non in legendo sunt,
sed in intelligendo, neque in prævaricatione sunt sed
in caritate." ad Const. ii. 9.   vid. also Hieron. c.
Lucif. 27.   August. Ep. 120, 13.

SCRIPTURE PASSAGES.

¶ 1. GEN. i. 26.—" Let us make man," &c.

The Catholic Fathers, as is well known, interpret such texts as this in the general sense which we find taken above (vol. i. de Syn. § 27, p. 112) by the first Sirmian Council convened against Photinus, Marcellus, &c. It is scarcely necessary to refer to instances; Petavius, however, cites the following. First, those in which the Eternal Father is considered in Gen. i. 26 to speak to the Son. Theophilus, ad Autol. ii. 18. Novatian, de Trin. 26. Tertullian, Prax. 12. Synod. Antioch. contr. Paul. Samos. ap. Routh, Reliqu. t. 2, p. 468. Basil. Hexaem. fin. Cyr. Hieros. Cat. x. 6. Cyril. Alex. Dial. iv. p. 516. Athan. contr. Gentes, 46. Orat. iii. § 29 fin. Chrysost. in Genes. Hom. viii. 3. Hilar. Trin. iv. 17, v. 8. Ambros. Hexaëm. vi. 7. Augustin. c. Maxim. ii. 26 n. 2. Next those in which Son and Spirit are considered as addressed. Theoph. ad Autol. ii. 18. Basil. contr. Eunom. v. 4, p. 315. Pseudo-Chrysost. de Trin. t. i. p. 832. Cyril. Thesaur. p. 12. Theodor. in Genes. 19. Hær. v. 3, and 9. But even here, where the Arians agree with Catholics, they differ in this remarkable respect, that in the Canons they pass in their Councils, they place certain interpretations of Scripture under the sanction of an anathema, showing how far less *free* the system of heretics is than that of the Church.

¶ 2. Gen. xviii. 1.—"The Lord appeared to Abraham," &c.

The same Sirmian Council anathematizes those who say that Abraham saw "not the Son, but the Ingenerate God."

This again, in spite of the wording, which is directed against the Catholic doctrine, and is of an heretical implication, is a Catholic interpretation. vid. (besides Philo de Somniis, i. 12, p. 1139.) Justin. Tryph. 56, and 126. Iren. Hær. iv. 10 n. 1. Tertull. de Carn. Christ. 6. adv. Marc. iii. 9. adv. Prax. 16. Novat. de Trin. 18. Origen. in Gen. Hom. iv. 5. Cyprian. adv. Jud. ii. 5. Antioch. Syn. contr. Paul. apud Routh, Rell. t. 2, p. 469. Athan. Orat. ii. 13. Epiph. Ancor. 29 and 39. Hær. 71. 5. Chrysost. in Gen. Hom. 41, 6 and 7. These references are principally from Petavius ; also from Dorscheus, who has written an elaborate commentary on this Council. The implication alluded to above is, that the Son is of a visible substance, and thus is naturally the manifestation of the Invisible God. Bull (Def. F. N. iv. 3) denies what Petavius maintains, that this doctrine is found in Justin, Origen, &c. The Catholic doctrine is that the Son manifests Himself (and thereby His Father) by means of material representations. Augustine seems to have been the first who changed the mode of viewing the texts in question, and considered the divine appearance, not God the Son, but a created Angel. vid. de Trin.

ii. passim.   Jansenius considers that he did so from a suggestion of S. Ambrose, that the hitherto received view had been the " origo hæresis Arianæ," vid. his Augustinus, lib. prooem. c. 12. t. 2, p. 12.

¶ 3. Exodus xxxiii. 23.—" Thou shalt see My back, but My face," &c. τὰ ὀπίσω μου, and not τὸ πρόσωπον. Gregory Naz. interprets τὸ ὀπίσω (ὀπίσθια) to mean God's works in contrast with His εἶδος.

¶ 4. Deut. xxviii. 66.—" Thy Life shall be hanging before thee."

Athanasius says, " His crucifixion is denoted by "Ye shall see your Life hanging," Orat. ii. 16, sup. p. 268.

Vid. Iren. Hær. iv. 10. 2. Tertull. in Jud. 11. Cyprian. Testim. ii. 20. Lactant. Instit. iv. 18. Cyril. Catech. xiii. 19. August. contr. Faust. xvi. 22, which are referred to in loc. Cypr. (Oxf. Tr.)   To which add Leon. Serm. 59, 6. Isidor. Hisp. contr. Jud. i. 35, ii. 6.   Origen. in Cels. ii. 75.   Epiph. Hær. 24. p. 75.   Damasc. F. O. iv. 11. fin.   This interpretation I am told by a great authority is recommended even by the letter, which has תלאים לך מנגד, ἀπέναντι τῶν ὀφθαλμῶν σου, in Sept. " Pendebit tibi a regione," vid. Gesenius, who also says, " Since things which are à regione of a place, are necessarily a little removed from it, it follows that מנגד signifies at the same time to be at a small distance," referring to the case of Hagar, who was but a bow-shot from her child.   Also, though the word here is תלא, yet תלה which is the same root,

is used for hanging on a stake, or crucifixion, e. g.
Gen. 20, 19. Deut. 21, 22. Esth. 5, 14; 7, 10.

¶ 5. Psalm xliv. 9.—" Therefore God, Thy God, hath
anointed Thee," &c.

" *Wherefore*," says Athan. " does not imply reward
of virtue or conduct in the Word, but the reason why
He came down to us, and of the Spirit's anointing
which took place in Him for our sakes. For he says
not, 'Wherefore He anointed Thee in order to Thy
being God or King or Son or Word;' for so He was
before and is for ever, as has been shown; but rather,
' Since Thou art God and King, therefore Thou wast
anointed, since none but Thou couldest unite man to
the Holy Ghost, Thou the Image of the Father, in
which we were made in the beginning; for Thine also
is the Spirit.' . .'. That as through Him we have come
to be, so also in Him all men might be redeemed from
their sins, and by Him all things might be ruled."
Orat. i. § 49. supr. vol. i. p. 228.

The word " wherefore " denotes the fitness why the
Son of God should become the Son of man. His
Throne, as God, is for ever; He has loved righteousness; *therefore* He is *equal* to the anointing of the
Spirit, as man. And so S. Cyril in Joan. lib. v.
2. " In this ineffable unity," says St. Leo, " of the
Trinity, whose words and judgments are common in
all, the Person of the Son has fitly undertaken to
repair the race of man, that, since He it is by whom
all things were made, and without whom nothing is
made, and who breathed the truth of rational life into

men fashioned of the dust of the earth, so He too should restore to its lost dignity our nature thus fallen from the citadel of eternity, and should be the reformer of that of which He had been the maker." Leon. Serm. 64. 2. vid. Athan. de Incarn. 7 fin. 10. In illud Omn. 2. Cyril. in Gen. i. p. 13.

¶ 6. Prov. viii. 22.—"The Lord created Me in the beginning of His ways, for His works."

The long and beautiful discourse left us by Athanasius on the First-born and His condescension, may be said to have grown out of what must be considered a wrong reading of this verse, *created* for *possessed*, ἔκτισε for ἔκτησατο being the Septuagint translation of the Hebrew קנה, as also in Gen. xiv. 19, 22. Such too is the sense of the word given in the Chaldee, Syriac, and Arabic versions, and the greater number of primitive writers. In consequence we find that it was one of the passages relied upon by the forerunners of the Arians in the 3rd century, vid. supr. vol. i. pp. 45—47. On the rise of Arianism, Eusebius of Nicomedia appealed to it against Alexander; and the other Eusebius in Demonstr. Evan. v. p. 212, &c. It was still insisted on in A.D. 350.

On the other hand Aquila translates ἔκτήσατο, and so read Basil c. Eunom. ii. 20, Nyssen c. Eunom. i. p. 34, Jerome in Is. xxvi. 13; and the Vulgate translates *possedit*, vid. also Gen. iv. 1, and Deut. xxxii. 8. The Hebrew sense is also recognized by Eusebius, Eccl. Theol. iii. 2, p. 153, and Epiph. Hær. 69, 24.

Athanasius, assuming the word *created* to be correct, interprets it of our Lord's human nature, as do Epiph. Hær. 69, 20—25. Basil. Ep. viii. 8. Naz. Orat. 30, 2. Nyss. contr. Eunom. vid. supra. et al. Cyril. Thesaur. p. 155. Hilar. de Trin. xii. 36 —49. Ambros. de Fid. i. 15. August. de Fid. et Symb. 6.

¶ Our Lord is ἀρχὴ ὁδῶν, says Athan. Orat. ii. 47, fin. in contrast with His proper Sonship; and so Justin understands the phrase, according to the Benedictine Ed. vid. supr. art. *Indwelling*.

¶ 7. Isa. liii. 7.—"He shall be led as a sheep to the slaughter."

Athan. says, Orat. i. § 54, supr. vol. i. p. 234, as elsewhere, that the error of heretics in their interpretation of Scripture arises from their missing the person, time, circumstances, &c., which Scripture has in view, and which, as I understand him to imply, Tradition, that is, the continuous teaching of the Church, supplies; just as the Jews, as regards Isa. liii. instead of learning from Philip, as he says, the meaning of the chapter, conjecture its words to be spoken of Jeremias or some other of the Prophets.

¶ The more common evasion on the part of the Jews was to interpret the prophecy of their own sufferings in captivity. It was an idea of Grotius that the prophecy received a first fulfilment in Jeremiah. vid. Justin. Tryph. 72 et al. Iren. Hær. iv. 33. Tertull. in Jud. 9. Cyprian Testim. in Jud. ii. 13. Euseb. Dem. iii. 2, &c.

¶ 8. Jerem. xxxi. 22.—"The Lord hath created a new salvation," &c.

This is the Septuagint version, as Athan. notices Expos. F. § 3, Aquila's being "The Lord hath created a new thing in the woman." The Vulgate, ("a new thing upon the earth, a woman shall compass a man,") is with the Hebrew. Athan. has preserved Aquila's version in three other places, Ps. xxx. 12, lix. 5, and lxv. 18.

¶ 9. Matt. i. 25.—"And he knew her not, *until,*" &c., that is, until then, when it became impossible, and need not be denied.

Supposing it was said, "He knew her not till her death," would not that mean, "He never knew her"? and in like manner, if she was "the Mother of God," it was an impossible idea, and the Evangelist would feel it to be so. They only can entertain the idea, who in truth do not believe our Lord's divinity, who do not believe literally that the Son of Mary is God. Vid. art. *Mary.*

¶ 10. Matt. iii. 17.—"This is My well-beloved Son," ἀγαπητός, &c. "Only-begotten and Well-beloved are the same," says Athan. . . . "hence the Word, with a view of conveying to Abraham the idea only-begotten, says, 'Offer thy Son, thy Well-beloved.'" Orat. iv. § 24. He adds, ibid. iv. § 29, "The word 'Well-beloved' even the Greeks who are skilful in grammar know to be equivalent with 'Only-begotten.' For Homer speaks thus of Telemachus, who was the only-begotten of Ulysses, in the second book of the Odyssey :—

O'er the wide earth, dear youth, why seek to run,
An only child, a well-beloved son ? (μοῦνος ἐὼν ἀγαπητός.)
He whom you mourn, divine Ulysses, fell,
Far from his country, where the strangers dwell.

Therefore he who is the only son of his father is called well-beloved."

'Αγαπητὸς is explained by μονογενὴς by Hesychius, Suidas, and Pollux; it is the version in the Sept. equally with μονογενὴς of the Hebrew יָחִיד. Homer calls Astyanax 'Εκτορίδην ἀγαπητόν; Plutarch notices the instance of Telemachus, "Ομηρος ἀγαπητὸν ὀνομάζει μοῦνον τηλύγετον, τουτέστι μὴ ἔχουσι ἕτερον γονεῦσι μήτε ἕξουσι γεγεννημένον, as quoted by Wetstein in Matt. iii. 17. Vid. also Suicer in voc.

¶ 11. Matt. xii. 32.—" Whosoever shall speak a word," &c.

This passage, which is commented on at Orat. i. § 50, Athan. explains at some length in Serap. iv. 8, &c., supr. vol. i. p. 229. Origen, he says, and Theognostus understand the sin against the Holy Ghost to be apostasy from the grace of Baptism, referring to Heb. vi. 4. So far the two agree; but Origen went on to say, that the proper power or virtue of the Son extends over rational natures alone, e. g. heathens, but that of the Spirit only over Christians; those then who sin against the Son or their reason, have a remedy in Christianity and its baptism, but nothing remains for those who sin against the Spirit. But Theognostus, referring to the text, "I have many things to say but ye cannot bear them now; howbeit when He, the Spirit of Truth," &c., argued that to sin against the Son was to sin against inferior light, but against the Spirit was to reject the full truth of the Gospel.

¶ 12. Matt. xiii. 25.—"His enemy came and over-sowed cockle," &c. ἐπίσπειρας, Decr. § 2. Orat. i. § 1, &c., &c. supr. vol. i. pp. 14, 153.

An allusion to this parable is very frequent in Athan. chiefly with a reference to Arianism. He draws it out at length, Orat. ii. § 34. " What is sown in every soul from the beginning is that God has a Son, the Word, the Wisdom, the Power, that is, His Image and Radiance; from which it at once follows that He is always; that He is from the Father; that He is like; that He is the eternal offspring of His substance; and there is no idea involved in these of creature or work. But when the man who is an enemy, while men slept, made a second sowing, of 'He is a creature,' and 'There was once when He was not,' and 'How can it be?' thenceforth the wicked heresy of Christ's enemies rose." Elsewhere, he uses the image for the evil influences introduced into the soul upon Adam's fall, contr. Apoll. i. § 15, as does S. Irenæus, Hær. iv. 40. n. 3, using it of such as lead to backsliding in Christians, ibid. v. 10. n. 1. Gregory Nyssen, of the natural passions and of false reason misleading them, de An. et Resurr. t. ii. p. 640. vid. also Leon. Ep. 156. c. 2.

¶ Tertullian uses the image in a similar but higher sense when he applies it to Eve's temptation, and goes on to contrast it with Christ's birth from a Virgin. "In virginem adhuc Evam irrepserat verbum ædificatorium mortis; in Virginem æque introducendum erat Dei Verbum exstructorium vitæ. . . . Ut in doloribus pareret, verbum diaboli semen illi fuit; contra Maria," &c. de Carn. Christ. 17. S. Leo, as Athan, makes "seed" in the parable apply peculiarly to *faith* in contrast with *obedience,* Serm. 69, 5, init.

¶ 13. John i. 1.—"In the beginning," &c. vid. Orat. i. § 11, supr. vol. i. p. 165.

If "beginning" in this verse be taken, not to imply time, but origination, then the first verse of St. John's Gospel may be interpreted "In the Beginning," or Origin, i. e. in the Father, "was the Word." Thus Athan. himself understands the text, Orat. ii. 57. Orat. iv. § 1. vid. also Orat. iii. § 9. Origen. in Joan. tom. 1, 17. Method. ap. Phot. cod. 235, p. 940. Nyssen. contr. Eunom. iii. p. 106. Cyril. Thesaur. 32, p. 312. Euseb. Eccl. Theol. ii. 11 and 14. pp. 118, 123, and Jerome in Calmet on Ps. 109.

¶ 14. John i. 3.—"Without Him was nothing made that was made." Vid. Orat. i. § 19. supr. p. 177.

The words "that was made" which end this verse were omitted by the ancient citers of it, as Irenæus, Clement, Origen, Eusebius, Tertullian, nay Augustine; but because it was abused by the Eunomians, Mace-

donians, &c. as if derogatory to the divinity of the
Holy Spirit, it was quoted in full, as by Epiphanius,
Ancor. 75, who goes so far as to speak severely of the
ancient mode of citation, vid. Fabric. and Routh, ad
Hippol. contr. Noet. 12.

Also vid. Simon. Hist. Crit. Comment. pp. 7, 32, 52.
Lampe in loc. Joann. Fabric. in Apocryph. N. T. t. 1. p.
384. Petav. de Trin. ii. 6, § 6. Ed. Ben. in Ambros. de Fid.
iii. 6. Wetstein in loc. Wolf. Cur. Phil. in loc. The
verse was not ended as we at present read it, especially
in the East, till the time of S. Chrysostom, according to
Simon, (vid. Ben. Præf. in Joann. § iv.) though, as
has been said above, S. Epiphanius had spoken strongly
against the ancient reading.   S. Ambrose loc. cit.
refers it to the Arians, Lampe refers it to the Valentinians on the strength of Iren. Hær. i. 8. n. 5.
Theophilus in loc. (if the Commentary on the Gospels
is his) understands by οὐδὲν "an idol," referring to
1 Cor. viii. 4.   Augustine, even at so late a date,
adopts the old reading, vid. de Gen. ad lit. v. 29—31.
It was the reading of the Vulgate, even at the time it
was ruled by the Council of Trent to be authentic, and
of the Roman Missal.   The verse is made to end after
"in Him," (thus, οὐδ᾽ ἓν ὃ γέγονεν ἐν αὐτῷ) by Epiph.
Ancor. 75.   Hil. in Psalm 148, 4.   Ambros. de Fid.
iii. 6. Nyssen in Eunom. i. p. 84. app., which favours
the Arians. The counterpart of the ancient reading,
which is very awkward, ("What was made in Him
was life,") is found in August. loc. cit. and Ambrose
in Psalm xxxvi. 35, but he also notices "What was made,
was in Him," de Fid. loc. cit. It is remarkable that

St. Ambrose attributes the present punctuation to the Alexandrians (in loc. Psalm.) in spite of Athan.'s and Alexander's (Theod. Hist. i. 3. p. 733.), nay Cyril's (in loc. Joann.) adoption of the ancient.

¶ 15. John ii. 4.—" Woman," &c. "He chid His Mother," says Athan.

'Επέπληττε; and so ἐπετίμησε, Chrysost. in loc. Joann. Hom. 21. 3, and Theophyl. ὡς δεσπότης ἐπιτιμᾷ, Theodor. Eran. ii. p. 106. ἐντρέπει, Anon. ap. Corder. Cat. in loc. μέμφεται, Alter Anon. ibid. ἐπιτιμᾷ οὐκ ἀτιμάζων ἀλλὰ διορθούμενος, Euthym. in loc. οὐκ ἐπέπληξεν, Pseudo-Justin. Quæst. ad Orthod. 136. It is remarkable that Athan. dwells on these words as implying our Lord's humanity, (i. e. because Christ appeared to *decline* a miracle,) when one reason assigned for them by the Fathers is that He wished, in the words τί μοι καί σοι, to remind our Lady that He was the Son of God and must be " about His Father's business." " Repellens ejus intempestivam festinationem," Iren. Hær. iii. 16, n. 7, who thinks she desired to drink of His cup; others that their entertainer was poor, and that she wished to befriend him. Nothing can be argued from S. Athan.'s particular word here commented on how he would have taken the passage. That the tone of our Lord's words is indeed (judging humanly and speaking humanly) cold and distant, is a simple fact, but it may be explained variously. It is observable that ἐπιπλήττει and ἐπιτιμᾷ are the words used by Theophylact (in Joan. xi. 34, vid. infra, art. *Specialties*,) for our Lord's treatment of His own sacred body.

But they are very vague words, and have a strong meaning or not, as the case may be.

¶ 16. John x. 30.—"I and My Father are One."

"They contend," says Athan. Orat. iii. § 10, supr. vol. i. p. 367, "that the Son and the Father are not in such wise one as the Church preaches . . but that, since what the Father wills, the Son wills also, and . . is in all respects concordant, (σύμφωνος) with Him . . . therefore it is that He and the Father are one. And some of them have dared to write as well as to say this ;" viz. Asterius ; vid. Orat. iii. § 2, supr. vol. i. p. 356.

We find the same doctrine in the Creed, said to be Lucian's, as translated above Syn. § 23, supr. vol. i. p. 97, where vid. note 2 ; vid. also infra, art. ὅμοιον. Besides Origen, Novatian, the Creed of Lucian, and (if so) Hilary, (as mentioned in the note at vol. i. p. 97,) "one" is explained as oneness of will by S. Hippolytus, contr. Noet. 7, where he explains John x. 30. by xvii. 22. like the Arians ; and, as might be expected, by Eusebius, Eccl. Theol. iii. 19, p. 193, and by Asterius ap. Euseb. contr. Marc. pp. 28. 37. The passages of the Fathers in which this text is adduced are collected by Maldonat. in loc.

¶ 17. John x. 30. 38. xiv. 9.—"I and the Father are One." "The Father is in Me, and" &c. "He that seeth Me," &c.

These three texts are found together frequently in Athan., particularly in Orat. iii., where he considers the doctrines of the "Image" and the περιχώρησις ; vid.

de Decr. § 21, § 31. de Syn. § 45. Orat. iii. 3. 5, 6. 10. 16 fin. 17. Ep. Æg. 13. Sent. D. 26. ad Afr. 7, 8, 9. vid. also Epiph. Hær. 64. 9. Basil. Hexaem. ix. fin. Cyr. Thes. xii. p. 111. Potám. Ep. ap. Dacher. t. 3. p. 299. Hil. Trin. vii. 41. Vid. also Animadv. in Eustath. Ep. ad Apoll. Rom. 1796. p. 58.

In Orat. iii. § 5, these three texts, which so often occur together, are recognized as "three;" so are they by Eusebius, Eccl. Theol. iii. 19, and he says that Marcellus and "those who Sabellianize with him," among whom he included Catholics, were in the practice of adducing them, θρυλλοῦντες; which bears incidental testimony to the fact that the doctrine of the περιχώρησις was the great criterion between orthodox and Arian. To the many instances of the joint use of the three which are given supr. may be added Orat. ii. 54 init. 67 fin. iv. 17, Serap. ii. 9, Serm. Maj. de fid. 29. Cyril. de Trin. p. 554, in Joann. p. 168. Origen, Periarch. p. 56. Hil. Trin. ix. 1. Ambros. Hexaem. vi. 7. August. de Cons. Ev. i. 7.

¶ 18. John xiv. 28.—"The Father is greater than I."

Athan. explains these words by comparing them with, "*Made so much better than the Angels,*" Hebr. i. 1. "He says not '*the Father is better than I,*' lest we should conceive Him to be foreign to His Nature," as Angels are foreign in nature to the Son; "but greater, not indeed in greatness nor in time, but because of His generation from the Father Himself," Orat. i. § 58, that is, on account of the *principatus* of the Father, as the ἀρχὴ and πηγὴ θεότητος, and of His own *filietas.*

¶ 19. Acts x. 36.—"God sent the word to the children of Israel. . . . You know the word," &c.

So the Vulgate, but the received Greek runs with Athan. Orat. iv. § 30. τὸν λόγον, ὃν ἀπέστειλε . . . οὗτός ἐστι . . . ὑμεῖς οἴδατε τὸ γενόμενον ῥῆμα. The followers of Paul of Samosata, with a view to their heresy, interpreted these words, as Hippolytus before them, as if τὸν λόγον were either governed by κατὰ or attracted by ὃν, οὗτος agreeing with ὁ λόγος understood. Dr. Routh in loc. Hipp. (vid. Noët 13) who at one time so construed it, refers to 1 Pet. ii. 7, John iii. 34, as parallel, also Matt. xxi. 42. And so 'Urbem quam statuo,' &c. vid. Raphel. in Luc. xxi. 6. vid. also τὴν ἀρχὴν ὅτι καὶ λαλῶ ὑμῖν, John viii. 25, with J. C. Wolf's remarks, who would understand by ἀρχὴν omnino, which Lennep however in Phalar. Ep. says it can only mean with a negative. The Vulgate is harsh in understanding λόγος and ῥῆμα as synonymous, and the latter as used merely to connect the clauses. Moreover, if λόγος be taken for ῥῆμα, τὸν λόγον ἀπέστειλε is a harsh phrase; however, it occurs Acts xiii. 26. If λόγος on the other hand has a theological sense, a *primâ facie* countenance is given to the distinction between "the Word" and "Jesus Christ," which the Samosatenes wished to deduce from the passage.

¶ 20. Rom. i. 20. — "His Eternal Power and Divinity."

Athanasius understands this of our Lord. Orat. i. § 11. Syn. § 49. vid. Justinian's Comment. in Paul.

Epp. for its various interpretations. It was either a received interpretation, or had been adduced at Nicæa, for Asterius had some years before these Discourses replied to it, vid. Syn. § 18, supr. vol. i. p. 88, and Orat. ii. § 37, p. 295.

SEMI-ARIANS.

THE Semi-Arian symbols admitted of an orthodox interpretation, but they also admitted of an heretical. They served as a shelter for virtual Arians, and as a refuge for those who feared the orthodox *homoüsion,* as either materialistic or Sabellian. In the first years of the controversy they were tokens of a falling short of the true faith, in the later years tokens of an approaching it. Hence Athanasius is severe with Eusebius and Asterius, and kind in his treatment of Basil and his party.

Accordingly, these symbols in no way served the necessity of the time as a test to secure the Church against a dangerous and insidious heresy. Eusebius of Cæsarea could have no difficulty in professing our Lord was God, and like in His nature to the Father, yet his heterodoxy has been shown in art. *Eusebius.* Still more openly heterodox was Eusebius of Nicomedia; yet such statements as occur in the Semi-Arian Councils and Creeds would give him no annoyance. These men did but scruple at the one word *homoüsion.*

The Catholic Theologians taught, with our Lord, that " He and the Father are one;" and, when asked in what sense one, they answered "numerically one, else were there two Gods;" that is, they were ὁμοούσιοι. The Arians considered them numerically two, and only in agreement one. Either then they held that there were two Gods, or that our Lord was God only in name and not true God. They would answer that that dilemma was none of their making; that is, the idea of incomprehensibility in the Infinite, and of mystery in what was predicated of Him, does not seem to have had a place in their reasonings.

So far Semi-Arians agreed with Arians, in holding a greater God and a less, a true God and a so-called God; a God of all, and a Divine Mediator and representative God; but when Catholics questioned them more closely on their belief, as, for instance, whether the Son was a creature, and what was meant by His being "like" the Father, the Arians proper said boldly that He was a creature, though the first of creatures and unlike other creatures, and not the Son of God except figuratively, as men were His sons, and that, moreover, as a creature He had been liable to fall, as the Angels fell and Adam; but from such blasphemy others shrank, and were in consequence called Semi-Arians, holding that, though our Lord was not in being from everlasting, and though He had been brought into being at the will of the Father, still a *gennesis* was a divine act in kind different from a creation; not indeed an emanation, else, He was not only like, but the same as the Father in essence, and if so why had Euseb. Nic. from the first protested against ἐξ ἀπορροίας and μέρος ὁμοούσιον, and why did Euseb. Cæs. so evidently evade the ἐξ οὐσίας (as shown supr. art. *Eusebius*) ? In short they were driven by their remaining religiousness, unlike the Arians proper, (who in the later shape of Eunomianism expressly denied that God was incomprehensible) into the admission that there was mystery in the revealed doctrine. And this Eusebius confesses in a passage which will be quoted infr. art. *Son of God.*

Recurring to the dilemma insisted on against the Arian disputant, it will be observed that the clear-headed Arians grasped fearlessly the conclusion that our Lord was not God, while the more pious and timid Semi-Arians could not extricate themselves from the charge of holding two Gods.

Eusebius (vid. art. *Euseb.*) calls our Lord a second substance, another God, a second God. And it was in this sense his co-religionists used such epithets as τέλειος of our Lord, and called Him, as in Lucian's creed, " perfect from perfect, king from king," &c. viz. under the impression or with the insinuation, that the ὁμοούσιον diluted belief in His divinity into a sort of Sabellianism. Whether in giving these high titles to our Lord they used them in a Catholic sense, would also be seen in their use and interpretation of the word περιχώρησις, co-inherence, (vid. art. *Coinherence*), which was a practical equivalent to ὁμοούσιον, though it too they could explain away, and they did. Accordingly viewing Father and Son as distinct substances, and rejecting both ὁμοούσιον and περιχώρησις, they certainly considered them, as far as words go, to be distinct Gods. Such strong expressions as ὁμοιούσιος, and ἀπαράλλακτος εἴκων, which they used, would but increase the evil, as Athanasius argues against them. " If all that is the Father's is the Son's, as in an Image and Impress," he says, "let it be considered dispassionately, whether a substance foreign to the Father's substance admits of such attributes ; and whether such a one can possibly be other in nature and alien in substance, and not rather one in substance with the Father." Syn. § 50. vid. also Orat. iii. 16. vid. art. *Idolatry.*

However, Athan., and Hilary too, saw enough of what was good and promising in the second generation of Semi-Arians to adopt a kind tone towards them, which they could not use in speaking of the followers of Arius. Athan. calls certain of them "brethren" and "beloved," and Hilary "sanctissimi," and the events in many cases justified their anticipation.

They guard, however, their words, lest more should be understood by others than the language of charity and hope. Athan. speaks severely of Eustathius and Basil. Ep. Æg. 7, and Hilary explains himself in his notes upon his de Syn., from which it appears that he had been expostulated with on his conciliatory tone. Indeed all throughout he had betrayed a consciousness that he should offend some parties, e. g. § 6. In § 77, he had spoken of "having expounded the faithful and religious sense of 'like in substance,' which is called Homœüsion." On this he observes, note 3, "I think no one need be asked to consider why I have said in this place '*religious* sense of like in substance,' except that I meant that there was also an *irreligious ;* and that therefore I said that 'like' was not only *equal* but the 'same.' vid. supr. vol. i. pp. 133, 4, notes. In the next note he speaks of them as not more than hopeful. Still it should be observed how careful the Fathers of the day were not to mix up the question of doctrine, which rested on Catholic tradition, with that of the adoption of a certain term which rested on a Catholic injunction. Not that the term was not in duty to be received, but it was to be received mainly on account of its Catholic sense, and where the Catholic sense was held, the word might for a while by a sort of dispensation be waived. It is remarkable that Athanasius scarcely mentions the word "One in substance" in his three Orations, as has been already observed; nor does it occur in S. Cyril's Catecheses, of whom, as being suspected of Semi-Arianism, it might have been required, before his writings were received as of authority. The word was not imposed upon Ursacius and Valens, A.D. 349, by Pope Julius; nor, in the Council of Aquileia in 381, was it offered by St. Ambrose to Palladius and Secundianus. S. Jerome's account of the apology made by the Fathers of Ariminum is of the same kind. "We thought," they said, "the sense corresponded to the words, nor in the Church of God, where there is simplicity, and a pure confession, did we fear that one thing would be concealed in the heart, another uttered by the lips. We were deceived by our good opinion of the bad." ad Lucif. 19.

SON OF GOD.

I UNDERSTAND Athanasius, (always after accepting and assuming the doctrine as true and indisputable because revealed,) to go on to argue about it thus :—

The Son of God must be God, granting that the human word "Son" is to guide us to the knowledge of what is heavenly; for on earth we understand by a son one who is the successor and heir to a given nature. A continuation or communication of nature enters into the very idea of γέννησις; if there is no participation of nature there is no sonship, "Μία ἡ φύσις, οὐ γὰρ ἀνόμοιον τὸ γέννημα τοῦ γεννήσαντος, εἴκων γὰρ ἐστιν αὐτοῦ." Orat. iii. § 4. Hence he speaks of "οἰκειότης τῆς φύσεως," ibid. § 4, 16, &c.

This is the teaching also of the great theologians who followed Athanasius. Basil says that *Father* is "a term of relationship," οἰκειώσεως, in Eunom. ii. 24, *init.* and that a father may be defined, "one who gives to another the origin of being, *according to a nature like his own,* ibid. 22. And Gregory Nyssen, that "the title 'Son' does not simply express the being from another, but *relationship according to nature*," c. Eunom. ii. p. 91. And Cyril says that the term "Son" denotes the "*substantial* origin from the Father."

Dial. v. p. 573. This was why the Fathers at Nicæa were not content with " from the Father," but wrote " from the substance of the Father."

The Son then participates in the Divine Nature, and since the Divine Nature is none other than the One individual Living Personal true God, He too is that God, and, since He is thus identical with that One True God, and since that One True God is eternal and never had a beginning of existence, therefore He is eternal and without beginning.

¶ Again, such a real Son is made necessary by considering what the very Nature of God, the existence of an Infinite, all-abounding, all-perfect Being, implies. We cannot be surprised to be told that the infinite Essence of God necessarily flows out, in consequence of His very immensity, into a reflexion or perfect image or likeness of Himself, which in all respects is His reiteration, except in not being He. There are then at least two Selves (so to speak) in God, that is, a First and Second Person.

Now this infinite Image of God is not external to the First Person, because the First is infinite. The image is commensurate, but no more than commensurate, with the Original. The Second cannot extend beyond the First or be external to Him. The First and Second cannot become Two except as viewed in their relation of Father and Son. As eternity *a parte ante* is not doubled by being added to eternity *a parte post*, but *before* and *after* are two only when contrasted with each other, so, though God and His Image are relatively two, an Image of God does not make two Gods. Indeed we cannot apply ideas arising out of number to the Illimitable.

¶ This Image, as being the Effluence and Expression and Likeness of the Almighty, may equally well be called Word or Son, and, whether we use one of these names or the other, we mean to express, though under a distinct aspect in each of them, a Second Person in the Godhead. The name of Image teaches us that the Second is commensurate and coequal with the First; that of Son that He is co-eternal, for the nature of God cannot alter or vary; and the Word, that in Him is represented and exercised the intelligence, living force, and operative energy of the Supreme Being. Hence it is that in the history, (if I may use the word,) of the Creator and His creatures, the Second Person of the Blessed Trinity is the chief Agent manifested to us, and that the offices which are assigned to Him occupy a far larger portion of revealed teaching than even what belongs to His original Divine Nature.

¶ The Arians joined issue with Catholics on the question as to what was involved in the title "Son." They put aside Word, Image, &c., as figures of speech, said that Son was his real name, and then explained "Son" away, maintaining that whatever else Sonship might teach us, even at first sight it was plain that a Son could not but be posterior in time to his Father; but if so, if Our Lord was not eternal *a parte ante*, He was only a creature. The Catholics replied that that could not be the essential true meaning of a word which it did not always hold; now the Arian argument from the word

"Son" involved the existence of *time*, which was a
condition which was not always present in the instance
of the Almighty; either then God had no son, or else
that Son was co-eval, co-eternal with Him. Moreover
there could be no change in the Divine Essence; what
He was once, that He ever was. Once a Father, always
a Father. The Arians replied that the Almighty was
not always Creator, He became a Creator in time, and so
it was with the *gennesis* of the Son, that it was not from
eternity but in time; that *gennesis* was some unknown
kind of creation, and that to connect it with the Divine
οὐσία was to introduce material notions into the idea
of God. The Catholics of course answered that the
notion of materiality was quite as foreign to any right
conception of God as that of time was, and that as the
Divine Sonship was eternal, so was it simply spiritual,
being taught under material images, only because
from the conditions of our knowledge we could not
speak of it in any other way. vid. art. *Arian tenets.*

Here Eusebius makes an apposite remark which
ought to have led him farther:—As we do not know
how God can create out of nothing, so, he says, we are
utterly ignorant of the Divine Generation. We do
not understand innumerable things which lie close to
us; how the soul is joined to the body, how it enters
and leaves it, what its nature, what the nature of
Angels. It is written, He who believes, not he who
knows, has eternal life. Divine generation is as
distinct from human, as God from man. The sun's
radiance itself is but an earthly image, and gives us no
true idea of that which is above all images. Eccl.

Theol. i. 12. So too S. Greg. Naz. Orat. 29. 8. vid. also Hippol. in Noet. 16. Cyril, Cat. xi. 11. and 19, and Origen, according to Mosheim, Ante-Const. p. 619. And instances in Petav. de Trin. v. 6. § 2, and 3. vid. art. *Illustrations, Image,* &c.

¶ "There are not many Words, but one only Word of the One Father, and one Image of the one God." Orat. ii. § 27.

¶ "The Son does not live by the *gift* of life, for He *is* life, and does but give it, not receive." Orat. iii. § 1. S. Hilary uses different language with the same meaning, "Vita viventis [Filii] in vivo [Patre] est," de Trin. ii. 11. Other modes of expression for the same mystery are found in art. *Coinherence,* "the whole being of the Son is proper to the Father's substance;" Orat. iii. 3. "the Son's being, because from the Father, is therefore in the Father;" ibid. also 6 init. "the fulness of the Father's Godhead is the being of the Son." 5. and Didymus ἡ πατρικὴ θεότης. Trin. i. 27, p. 82, and S. Basil, ἐξ οὗ ἔχει τὸ εἶνα, contr. Eunom. ii. 12, fin. Thus the Father is the Son's life because the Son is from Him, and the Son the Father's because the Son is in Him. All these are but different ways of signifying the περιχώρησις.

¶ The Second Person in the Holy Trinity is not a quality or attribute or relation, but the One Eternal Essence; not a part of the First Person, but whole or entire God, all that God is; nor does the *gennesis* impair the Father's Essence, which is already whole and entire God. Thus there are two infinite Persons, in Each Other because they are infinite. Each of Them being wholly one and the same Divine Being, yet not being merely separate aspects of the Same. Each is God as absolutely as if the Others were not. Such a statement indeed is not so much a contradiction in the terms used, as in our conceptions, from the inability of our minds to deal with infinites; yet not therefore a contradiction in fact, unless we would maintain that human words can express in one formula, or human thought grasp and contemplate, the Incomprehensible, Self-existent First cause.

¶ "Man," says S. Cyril, inasmuch as He had a beginning of being, also has of necessity a beginning of begetting, as what is from Him is a thing generate, but . . . if God's substance transcend time, or origin, or interval, His generation too will transcend these; nor does it deprive the Divine Nature of the power of generating that He doth not this in time. For other than human is the manner of divine generation; and together with God's existing is His generating implied, and the Son was in Him by generation, nor did His generation precede His existence, but He was always, and that by generation. Thesaur. v. p. 35.

SPECIAL CHARACTERISTICS OF OUR LORD'S MANHOOD.

1. His manhood had no personality, but was taken up into His divinity as Second Person of the Holy Trinity.

That is, according to the words of the *Symbolum S. Athan.*, "Unus, non conversione divinitatis in carnem, sed assumptione humanitatis in Deum." That personality, which our Lord had had from eternity in the Holy Trinity, He had still after His incarnation. His human nature subsisted in His divine, not existing as we exist, but, so to say, grafted on Him, or as a garment in which He was clad. We cannot conceive of an incarnation, except in this way; for, if His manhood had not been thus after the manner of an attribute, if it had been a person, an individual, such as one of us, if it had been in existence before He united it to Himself, He would have been simply two beings under one name, or else, His divinity would have been nothing more than a special grace or presence or participation of divine glory, such as is the prerogative of saints.

He then is one, as He was from eternity,—the same " He " to whom also belong body and soul, and all their powers and affections, as well as the possession of divinity. He it is, God the Son, who was born, who had a mother, who shed His blood, who died and rose again.

His manhood loses the privilege of a personality of its own, in order to gain the special prerogative of belonging to the Second Person of the Divine Trinity, and all for our sake, that He may be the medium of a spiritual union between us and His Father.

¶ This was the question which came into discussion in the Nestorian controversy, when it was formally determined that all that took place in respect to the Eternal Word as man, belonged to His *Person*, and therefore might be predicated of Him; so that it was heretical not to confess the Word's body, (or the body of God in the Person of the Word,) the Word's death, the Word's blood, the Word's exaltation, and the Word's or God's Mother, who was in consequence called θεοτόκος, the tessera on which the controversy mainly turned. "The Godhead," says Athan. elsewhere, "dwelt in the flesh bodily; which is all one with saying, that, being God, He had a proper body, (ἴδιον,) and using this as an instrument, ὀργάνῳ, He became man, for our sakes; and because of this things proper to the flesh are said to be His, since He was in it, as hunger, thirst, suffering, fatigue, and the like, of which the flesh is capable, δεκτική; while the works proper to the Word Himself, as raising the dead, and restoring sight to the blind, and curing the issue of blood, He did Himself through His body, &c.' " Orat. iii. 31. vid. the whole passage, which is as precise as if it had been written after the Nestorian and Eutychian controversies, though without the technical words then adopted.

2. He took on Him our fallen nature, vid. art. *Flesh*, to which add here from Petavius, "Verbum corpus et

naturam hominis ex eâdem, quæ in corruptelam defluxerat, massâ sibi formare et assumere voluit; tametsi in eâ, unde genitus est Deus, carne Virginis repurgatum illud fuerit." Incarn. v. 14, 6. He says this, quoting Irenæus; and elsewhere, quoting Leontius, "Recte Leontius ejusmodi assumpsisse carnem asserit Verbum, qualem habuit Adam post peccatum damnatus, et qualem nos habemus ex eâdem massâ procreati." Incarn. x. 3, 8. Vid. on this subject Perrone de Incarn, part ii. c. 2. Coroll. iv.

3. His manhood was subject to death, and to the other laws of human nature.

¶ Athanasius, Orat. ii. 66, says that our Lord's body was subject to death; and so elsewhere, "His body, as having a common substance with all men, for it was a human body (though by a new marvel, it subsisted of the Virgin alone), yet being mortal, died after the common course of the like natures." Incarn. 20, also 8, 18, init. Orat. iii. 56. And so τὸν ἄνθρωπον σαθρωθέντα. Orat. iv. 33. And so S. Leo. in his Tome lays down that in the Incarnation, "suscepta est ab æternitate mortalitas." Ep. xxviii. 3. And S. Austin, "Utique vulnerabile atque mortale corpus habuit" [Christus], contr. Faust. xiv. 2. A Eutychian sect denied this doctrine (the Aphthartodocetæ), and held that our Lord's manhood was naturally indeed corrupt, but became from its union with the Word incorrupt from the moment of conception; and in consequence they held that our Lord did not suffer and die, except by miracle. vid. Leont. c. Nest. ii. (Canis. t. i. pp. 563, 4, 8.) vid. supr. art. *Adam*.

¶ It was a point in controversy with the extreme Monophysites, that is, the Eutychians, whether our Lord's body was naturally subject to death, the Catholics maintaining the affirmative, as Athanasius, Orat. i. § 44. Eutyches asserted that our Lord had not a human nature, by which he meant among other things that His manhood was not subject to the *laws* of a body, but so far as He submitted to them, did so by an act of will in each particular case; and this, lest it should seem that He was moved by the πάθη against His will ἀκουσίως; and consequently that His manhood was not subject to death. But the Catholics maintained that He had voluntarily placed Himself *under* those laws, and died *naturally,* vid. Athan. contr. Apoll. i. 17, and that after the resurrection His body became incorruptible, not according to nature, but by grace. vid. Leont. de Sect. x. p. 530. Anast. Hodeg. c. 23. To express their doctrine of the ὑπερφυὲς of our Lord's manhood the Eutychians made use of the Catholic expression "ut voluit," vid. Athan. l. c. Eutyches ap. Leon. Ep. 21. "quomodo voluit et scit" twice; vid. also Theod. Eranist. i. p. 10. ii. p. 105. Leont. contr. Nest. i. p. 544. Pseudo-Athan. Serm. adv. Div. Hær. § viii. (t. 2. p. 560.)

4. Yet He suspended those laws, when He pleased.

¶ This our Lord's either suspense or permission, at His will, of the operations of His manhood, is a great principle in the doctrine of the Incarnation. "That He might give proof of His human nature," says Theophylact, on John xi. 34, "He allowed It to do its own work, and chides It and rebukes It by the power of the Holy Spirit. The Flesh then, not bearing the rebuke, is troubled and trembles and thus gets the better of Its grief." And S. Cyril: "When grief began to be stirred in Him, and His sacred flesh was on the verge of tears, He suffers it not to be affected freely, as is our custom, but 'He was vehement (ἐνεβριμήσατο) in the Spirit,' that is, He in some way chides His own Flesh in the power of the Holy Ghost; and It, not bearing the movement of the Godhead united to It, trembles, &c. . . . For this I think is the meaning of 'troubled Himself.'" fragm. in Joan. p. 685. "Sensus corporei vigebant sine lege peccati, et veritas affectionum sub moderamine Deitatis et mentis." Leon. Ep. 35, 3. "Thou art troubled against thy will; Christ is troubled, because He willed it. Jesus hungered, yes, but because He willed it; Jesus slept, yes, but because He willed it; Jesus sorrowed, yes, but because He willed it; Jesus died, yes, but because He willed it. It was in His power to be affected so or so, or not to be affected." Aug. in Joan. xlix. 18. The Eutychians perverted this doctrine, as if it implied that our Lord was not subject to the laws of human nature; and that He suffered *merely* "by permission of the Word." Leont. ap. Canis. t. 1. p. 563. In like manner Marcion or Manes said that His "flesh appeared from heaven in resemblance, ὡς ἠθέλησεν." Athan. contr. Apoll. ii. 3.

¶ "To be troubled was proper to the flesh," says Athan., "but to have power to lay down His life, and to take it again, when He will, was no property of men, but of the Word's power. For man dies, not by his own power, but by necessity of nature and against his will; but the Lord, being Himself immortal, but having a mortal flesh, had power, as God, to become separate from the body and to take it again, when He would. Concerning this too speaks David in the Psalm, *Thou shalt not leave My soul in hell, neither shalt Thou suffer Thy Holy One to see corruption.* For it beseemed, that the flesh, corruptible as it was, should no longer after its own nature remain mortal, but because of the Word who had put it on, should abide incorruptible." Orat. iii. § 57.

¶ This might be taken as an illustration of the "ut voluit," vid. supr. p. 296. And so the expressions in the Evangelists, "Into Thy hands I *commend* My Spirit," "He *bowed the head*," "He *gave up* the ghost," are taken to imply that His death was His free act. vid. Ambros. in loc. Luc. Hieron. in loc. Matt. also Athan. Serm. Maj. de Fid. 4. It is Catholic doctrine that our Lord, as man, submitted to death of His free will, and not as obeying an express command of the Father. "Who," says S. Chrysostom on John x. 18. Hom. 60. 2, "has not power to lay down His own life? for any one who will may kill himself. But He says not this, but how? 'I have power to lay it down in such sense that no one can do it against My will. . I alone have the disposal of My life,' which is not true of us." And still more appositely Theophylact, "It was open to Him not to suffer, not to die; for being without sin, He was not subject to death . . . If then He had not been willing, He had not been crucified." in Hebr. xii. 2. " Since this punishment is contained in the death of the body, that the soul, because it has deserted God with its will, deserts the body against its will . . . the soul of the Mediator proved how utterly clear of the punishment of sin was its coming to the death of the flesh, in that it did not desert the flesh unwillingly, but because it willed, and when it willed, and as it willed. . . And this did they specially admire, who were present, says the Gospel, that after that work, in which He set forth a figure of our sin, He forthwith gave up the ghost. For crucified men were commonly tortured by a lingering death. . . . But He was a wonder, (miraculo fuit,) because He was found dead." August. de Trin. iv. n. 16.

5. Though His manhood was of created substance, He cannot be called a creature.

¶ Athan. seems to say, Orat. ii. § 45, that it is both true that " The Lord created Me," and yet that the Son was not created. Creatures alone are created, and He was not a creature. Rather something belonging or relating to Him, something short of His substance or nature, was created. However, it is a question in controversy whether even His Manhood can be called a creature, though many of the Fathers, (including Athan. in several places,) seem so to call it. The difficulty may be viewed thus; that our Lord, even as to His human nature, is the natural, not the adopted, Son of God, (to deny which is the error of the Adoptionists,) whereas no creature can be His natural and true Son; and again, that His human nature is worshipped, which would be idolatry, if it were a creature. The question is discussed in Petav. de

Incarn. vii. 6, who determines that the human nature, though in itself a created substance, yet viewed as deified in the Word, does not in fact exist as a creature. Vasquez, however, considers that our Lord may be called creature, viewed as man, in 3 Thom. Disp. 66, and also Raynaud Opp. t. 2. p. 84, expressing his opinion strongly. And Berti de Theol. Disc. xxvii. 5, who adds, however, with Suarez after S. Thomas (in 3 Thom. Disput. 35. Opp. t. 16, p. 489,) that it is better to abstain from the use of the term. Of the Fathers, S. Jerome notices the doubt, and decides it in favour of the term; "Since," he says, "Wisdom in the Proverbs of Solomon speaks of Herself as created a beginning of the ways of God, and many through fear lest they should be obliged to call Christ a creature, deny the whole mystery of Christ, and say that not Christ, but the world's wisdom is meant by this Wisdom, we freely declare, that there is no hazard in calling Him creature, whom we confess with all the confidence of our hope to be "worm," and "man," and "crucified," and "curse." In Eph. ii. 10. He is supported by Athan. Orat. ii. § 46. Ep. Æg. 17. Expos. F. 4 (perhaps), Serap. ii. 8, fin. Naz. Orat. 30, 2, fin. 38, 13. Nyss. in Cant. Hom. 13, t. i. p. 663, init. Cyr. Hom. Pasch. 17, p. 233. Max. Mart. t. 2, p. 265. Damasc. F. O. iii. 3. Hil. de Trin. xii. 48. Ambros. Psalm. 118. Serm. 5. 25. August. Ep. 187, n. 8. Leon. Serm. 77, 2. Greg. Mor. v. 63. The principal authority on the other side is S. Epiphanius, who ends his argument with the words, "The Holy Church of God worships not a creature, but the Son, who is begotten, Father in Son, &c." Hær. 69, 36. And S. Proclus too speaks of the child of the Virgin as being " Him who is worshipped, not the creature," Orat. v. fin.

¶ On the whole it would appear, (1.) that if " creature," like " Son," be a *personal* term, then He is not a creature; but if it be a word of *nature*, He is a creature ; (2.) that our Lord is a creature in respect to the flesh (vid. Orat. ii. § 47.) ; (3.) that since the flesh is infinitely beneath His divinity, it is neither natural nor safe to call Him a creature, (according to St. Thomas's example, " non dicimus, quod Æthiops est albus, sed quod est albus secundum dentes ") ; and (4.) that, if the flesh is worshipped, still it is worshipped as in the Person of the Son, not by a separate act of worship. " A creature worship not we," says Athan., " perish the thought . . . but the Lord of creation made flesh, the Word of God; for though the flesh in itself be a part of creation, yet it has become God's body . . . who so senseless as to say to the Lord, Remove Thyself out of the body, that I may worship Thee ?" ad Adelph. 3. Epiphanius has imitated this passage, Ancor. 51, introducing the illustration of a king and his robe, &c.

¶ And hence Athanasius says, Orat. ii. § 47, that though our Lord's flesh is created, or He is created as to the flesh, it is not right to call Him a creature. This is very much what S. Thomas says above, that " Æthiops, albus secundum dentes, not est albus." But why may not our Lord be so called upon the principle of the *communicatio Idiomatum*, (vid. art. ἀντίδοσις ἰδιωμάτων) as He is said to be born of a Virgin, to have suffered, &c? The reason is this:—birth, passion, &c. confessedly belong to His human nature, without adding "according to the flesh;" but "creature" not implying humanity, might appear a simple attribute of His Person, if used without limitation. Thus, as S. Thomas adds, though we may not absolutely say "Æthiops iste albus," we may say "crispus est," or in like manner, "he is bald;" since "crispus," or "bald," can but refer to the hair. Still more does this remark apply in the case of "Sonship," which is a personal attribute altogether; as is proved, says Petav. de Incarn. vii. 6, fin. by the instance of Adam, who was in all respects a man like Seth, yet not a son. Accordingly, we may not call our Lord, even according to the manhood, an adopted Son.

6. In like manner we cannot call our Lord a servant.

¶ "The assumption of the flesh did not make of the Word a servant," says Athan. Orat. ii. § 14. οὐκ ἐδούλου τὸν λόγον, though, as he said, Orat, ii. § 11, the Word became a servant, as far as He was man. He says the same thing, Ep. Æg. 17. So say Naz. Orat. 32, 18. Nyssen. ad Simpl. (t. 2, p. 471.) Cyril. Alex. adv. Theodor. p. 223. Hilar. de Trin. xi. 13, 14. Ambros. 1. Epp. 46, 3. Athan. however seems to modify the statement when he says, Orat. ii. § 50, " Not that He was servant, but because He took a servant's form." Theodoret also denies it, Eran. ii. fin. And Damasc. F. O. iii. 21, who says, that our Lord " took on Him an ignorant and servile nature," but " that we may not call Him servant," though " the flesh is servile, had it not been united to God the Word." The parallel question of *ignorance*, here touched upon, has come under our notice already, vid. art. *Ignorance*. The latter view prevailed after the heresy of the Adoptionists, who seem to have made "servant" synonymous with "adopted son." Petavius, Incarn. vii. 9, distinguishes between the essence or (what is called) *actus primus* and the *actus secundus;* thus water may be considered in its *nature* cold, though certain springs are *in fact* always warm.

SPIRIT OF GOD.

THOUGH the Catholic doctrine of the Holy Trinity and the characteristics of the Three Persons have been taught from the first, there have been in the Church certain difficulties in determining what passages of Scripture belong to each, what are the limits of their respective offices, and what are the terms under which their offices and the acts of those offices are to be expressed. Thus the word " Spirit," if the Fathers are to be our expositors, sometimes means Almighty God, without distinction of Persons, sometimes the Son, and sometimes and more commonly the Holy Ghost. And, while the Son and Spirit divide, so to speak, the economy and mission of mercy between Them, it is not always clear how the line of division runs, and in what cases there is no assignable line.

It is with a view to remove some portion of this difficulty that Athan. observes, Serap. i. 4—7; that the Holy Ghost is never in Scripture called simply " Spirit" without the addition " of God," or " of the Father," or " from Me," or of the article, or of " Holy," or " Paraclete," or " of truth," or unless He has been spoken of just before. This rule, however, goes but a little way to remove the difficulty, as it exists in fact. One important class of questions is suggested at once by the Holy Ghost being *another* Paraclete, which implies that that office is common to Him and the Son. It is hence, I suppose, that in St. Paul's words, "ὁ κύριος τὸ πνεῦμά ἐστίν," 2 Cor. iii. 17, Spirit is understood of the third Divine Person by Origen. c. Cels. vi. 70. Basil. de Spir. S. n. 52. Pseudo-Athan. Comm. Ess. 6. But there are more important instances than this. "Spirit" is used more or less distinctly of our Lord's divine nature, whether in itself or as incarnate, in John vi. 64, Rom. i. 4, 1 Cor. xv. 45, 1 Tim. iii. 16, Hebr. ix. 14, 1 Pet. iii. 18, &c. Indeed, the early Fathers speak as if the "Holy Ghost" which came down on Mary might be considered the Word, e. g. Tertullian against the Valentinians, "If the Spirit of God did not descend into the womb *to partake in flesh from the womb*, why did He descend at all?" de Carn. Chr. 19. vid. also ibid. 5 and 14. contr. Prax. 26. Just. Apol. i. 33. Iren. Hær. v. 1. Cypr. Idol. Van. 6. (p. 19. Oxf. Tr.) Lactant. Instit. iv. 12. vid. also Hilar. Trin. ii. 26. Athan. λόγος ἐν τῷ πνεύματι ἔπλαττε τὸ σῶμα. Serap. i. 31, fin. ἐν τῷ λόγῳ ἦν τὸ πνεῦμα. ibid. iii. 6. And more distinctly even as late as S. Maximus, αὐτὸν, ἄντι σπορᾶς συλλαβοῦσα τὸν λόγον, κεκύηκε. t. 2. p. 309. The earliest ecclesiastical authorities are S. Ignatius ad Smyrn. init. and S. Hermas (even though his date were A.D. 150), who also says plainly, "Filius autem Spiritus Sanctus est." Past. iii. 5. n. 5. The same use of "Spirit" for the Word or Godhead of the Word is also found in Tatian. adv. Græc. 7. Athenag. Leg. 10. Theoph. ad Autol. ii. 10. Tertull. Apol. 23. Lact. Inst. iv. 6. 8. Hilar. Trin. ix. 3. and 14. Eustath. apud Theod. Eran. iii. p. 235.

Athan. de Incarn. etc. Ar. 22. (if it be Athan.'s), contr.
Apol. i. 8. Apollinar. ap. Theod. Eran. i. p. 71. and the
Apollinarists passim. Greg. Naz. Ep. 101. ad Cledon.
p. 85. Ambros. Incarn. 63. Severian. ap. Theod.
Eran. ii. p. 167. Vid. Grot. ad Marc. ii. 8. Bull. Def.
F. N. i. 2. § 5. Coustant. Præf. in Hilar. 57, &c.
Montfaucon in Athan. Serap. iv. 19.

Phœbadius too, in his remarks on 2nd Confession of
Sirmium (the " blasphemia ") supr. vol. i. p. 116 note,
in condemning the clause, " Hominem suscepisse per
quem *compassus* est," as implying that our Lord's higher
nature was not divine, but of the nature of a soul, uses
the word "spiritus" in the sense of Hilary and the
Ante-Nicene Fathers. "Impassibilis Deus," he says,
"quia Deus *Spiritus* . . . non ergo passibilis Dei
Spiritus, licet in homine suo passus."

¶ Again Athan. says that our Lord's Godhead was
the immediate anointing or chrism of the manhood He
assumed. "God needed not the anointing, nor was
the anointing made without God; but God both applied
it, and also received it in that body which was capable
of it." in Apollin. ii. 3. and τὸ χρῖσμα ἐγὼ ὁ λόγος, τὸ
δὲ χρισθὲν ὑπ᾽ ἐμοῦ ὁ ἄνθρωπος. Orat. iv. §. 36. vid.
Origen. Periarch. ii. 6. n. 4. And S. Greg. Naz. still
more expressly, and from the same text as Athan.,
"The Father anointed Him 'with the oil of gladness
above his fellows,' *anointing the manhood with the
Godhead.*" Orat. x. fin. Again, "This [the Godhead]
is the anointing of the manhood, not sanctifying by an
energy as the other Christs [anointed ones], but by a
presence of that Whole who anointed, ὅλου τοῦ χρίοντος;

whence it came to pass that what anointed was called man and what was anointed was made God." Orat. 30. 20. "He Himself anointed Himself; anointing as God the body with His Godhead, and anointed as man." Damasc. F. O. iii. 3. " Dei Filius, sicut pluvia in vellus, toto divinitatis unguento nostram se fudit in carnem." Chrysolog. Serm. 60. It is more common, however, to consider that the anointing was the descent of the Spirit, as Athan. says Orat. i. § 47, according to Luke iv. 18. Acts x. 38.

¶ Again, in explaining Matt. xii. 32, " Quicunque dixerit verbum contra Filium, &c., he considers our Lord to contrast the Holy Ghost with His own humanity, vid. Orat. i. § 50, but he gives other expositions in Serap. iv. 6, vid. supr. art. *Scripture passages*, No. 10.

¶ "The Spirit is God's gift," says Athan., θεοῦ δῶρον, Orat. ii. § 18. And so S. Basil, δῶρον τοῦ θεοῦ τὸ πνεῦμα. de Sp. S. 57, and more frequently the later Latins, as in the Hymn, "Altissimi Donum Dei;" also the earlier, e. g. Hil. de Trin. ii. 29. and August. Trin. xv. n. 29, who makes it the personal characteristic of the Third Person in the Holy Trinity; "non dicitur Verbum Dei, nisi Filius, nec Donum Dei, nisi Spiritus Sanctus." And elsewhere, "Exiit, non quomodo natus, sed quomodo datus, et ideo non dicitur Filius." ibid. v. 15, making it, as Petavius observes, His eternal property, "ut sic procedat, tanquam *donabile*," as being Love. Trin. vii. 13. § 20.

¶ It was an expedient of the Macedonians to deny that the Holy Spirit was God because it was not usual

x 2

to call Him Ingenerate; and perhaps to their form of
heresy, which was always implied in Arianism, and
which began to show itself formally among the Semi-
Arians ten years later, the Sirmian anathematism may
be traced; "Whoso speaking of the Holy Ghost as
Paraclete, shall speak of the Ingenerate God," &c., supr.
vol. i. p. 113. They asked the Catholics whether the
Holy Spirit was *Ingenerate, generate,* or *created,* for into
these three they divided all things. vid. Basil. in Sabell.
et Ar. Hom. xxiv. 6. But, as the Arians had first made
the alternative only between *Ingenerate* and *created,* and
Athan. de Decr. § 28, supr. vol. i. p. 50, shows that
generate is a third idea really distinct from one and the
other, so S. Greg. Naz. adds *proceeding,* ἐκπορευτὸν, as
an intermediate idea, contrasted with *Ingenerate,* yet
distinct from *generate.* Orat. xxxi. 8. In other words,
Ingenerate means, not only *not generate,* but *not from
any origin.* vid. August. de Trin. xv. n. 47, 8.

¶ "If the Word be not from God," says Athan.
"reasonably might they deny Him to be Son; but if
He is from God, how see they not that what exists from
any, is the son of that from whom it is?" Orat. iv. § 15.
In consequence it is a very difficult question in theology,
why the Holy Spirit is not called a "Son," and His
procession " generation." This was an objection of the
Arians, vid. ad Serap. i. 15—17, and Athan. only
answers it by denying that we may speculate. Other
writers apply, as in other cases, the theological language
of the Church to a solution of this question. It is
carefully discussed in Petav. Trin. vii. 13. 14.

¶ As the Arians objected, Orat. i. § 14, that the

First and Second Persons of the Holy Trinity ought to be considered brothers, ἀδελφοὶ, so, in the course of the controversy, did they say the same as to the Second and Third. vid. Serap. i. §. 15. iv. 2.

¶ "Is the Holy Spirit one," says Athan., "and the Paraclete another, and the Paraclete the later, as not mentioned in the Old Testament?" Orat. iv. § 29. A heresy of this kind is actually noticed by Origen, viz. of those "qui Spiritum Sanctum alium quidem dicant esse qui fuit in Prophetis, alium autem qui fuit in Apostolis Domini nostri Jesu Christi." In Tit. t. 4. p. 695. Hence in the Creed, "who spake by the prophets;" and hence the frequent epithet given by S. Justin to the Holy Spirit of προφητικόν; e. g. when speaking of baptism, Apol. i. 61 fin. Also Ap. i. 6. 13. Tryph. 49. On the other hand, he calls the Spirit of the Prophets "the Holy Spirit," e. g. Tryph. 54, 61.

THEOGNOSTUS.

THEOGNOSTUS was Master of the Catechetical school of Alexandria towards the end of the 3rd century, being a scholar, or at least a follower, of Origen. He is quoted by Athanasius, as being one of those theologians who, before the Council of Nicæa, taught that the οὐσία of the Son was not created, but from the οὐσία of the Father. Athan. calls him " a learned man," Decr. § 25, and " the admirable and excellent," Serap. iv. 9. His seven books of Hypotyposes treated of the Holy Trinity, of angels, and evil spirits, of the Incarnation and the Creation. Photius, who gives this account, Cod. 106, accuses him of heterodoxy on these points; which Athanasius in a measure admits, as far as the wording of his treatise went, speaking of his " investigating by way of exercise." Eusebius does not mention him at all.

TRADITION.

" See," says Athanasius, "we are proving that this view has been transmitted from Fathers to Fathers; but ye, O modern Jews and disciples of Caiaphas, whom can ye assign as Fathers to your phrases? Not one of the understanding and wise; for all abhor you, but the devil alone; none but he is your father in this apostasy, who both in the beginning scattered on you the seed of this irreligion, and now persuades you to slander the Ecumenical Council for committing to writing, not your doctrines, but that which ' from the beginning those who were eye-witnesses and ministers of the Word' have handed down to us. For the faith which the Council has confessed in writing, that is the faith of the Catholic Church; to assert this, the blessed Fathers so expressed themselves while condemning the Arian heresy; and this is a chief reason why these men apply themselves to calumniate the Council. For it is not the terms which trouble them, but that those terms prove them to be heretics, and presumptuous beyond other heresies." Decr. § 27.

¶ Elsewhere he speaks of the Arians " forcing on the divine oracles a misinterpretation according to their own private sense," Orat. i. § 37, and cries out, " Who heard in his first catechizings that God had a Son, without understanding it in our sense? who, on the

rise of this odious heresy, was not at once startled at
what he heard as strange to him ?"   Orat. ii. § 34.

For parallel passages from Athan. and many others,
vid. arts. on *Definitions, Heretics, Private Judgment, Rule
of Faith,* and *Scripture.* From these it would appear that
the two main sources of Revelation are Scripture and
Tradition; that these constitute one Rule of Faith, and
that, sometimes as a composite rule, sometimes as a
double and co-ordinate, sometimes as an alternative,
under the *magisterium,* of course, of the Church, and
without an appeal to the private judgment of individuals.

These articles, too, effectually refute the hypothesis
of some Protestants, who, to destroy the force of the evidence in favour of our doctrine of Tradition, wish to
maintain that by Tradition then was commonly meant
Scripture; and that when the Fathers speak of " Evangelical Tradition " they mean the Gospels, and when
they speak of "Apostolical" they mean the Epistles.
This will not hold, and it may be right, perhaps, here
to refer to several passages in illustration.

For instance, Irenæus says, " Polycarp, . . whom
we have seen in our first youth, . . was taught those
lessons which he learned from the Apostles, *which the
Church also transmits,* which alone are true. All the
Churches of Asia *bear witness* to them; and the
successors of Polycarp, down to this day, who is a
much more trustworthy and sure *witness* of truth
than Valentinus," &c.   Hær. iii. 3, § 4.   Here is not
a word about Scripture, not a hint that by " transmission " and " succession " Scripture is meant.   And

so Irenæus continues, contrasting "Traditio quæ est ab Apostolis" with Scripture; "Neque Scripturis neque Traditioni consentire;" "Traditio Apostolorum;" τὸ κήρυγμα τῶν ἀποστόλων καὶ τὴν παράδοσιν· ἣν ἀπὸ τῶν ἀποστόλων παράδοσιν εἰλήφει· "Apostolicam Ecclesiæ Traditionem;" "veterem Apostolorum Traditionem." Again, Theodoret says that the word θεοτόκος was used, κατὰ τὴν ἀποστολικὴν παράδοσιν; and no one would say that θεοτόκος was in Scripture. Hær. iv. 12. And S. Basil contrasts τὰ ἐκ τῆς ἐγγράφου διδασκαλίας with τὰ ἐκ τῆς τῶν ἀποστόλων παραδόσεως, de Sp. S. n. 66. Presently he speaks of οὔτε τῆς θεοπνεύστου γραφῆς, οὔτε τῶν ἀποστολικῶν παραδόσεων. n. 77. Origen speaks of a dogma, οὔτε παραδιδόμενον ὑπὸ τῶν ἀποστόλων, οὔτε ἐμφαινόμενόν που τῶν γραφῶν. Tom. in Matth. xiii. 1. Vid. also in Tit. t. 4, p. 696, and Periarchon. præf. 2, and Euseb. Hist. v. 23. So in S. Athanasius (de Synod. 21, fin.) we read of "the Apostolical Tradition and teaching which is acknowledged by all;" and soon after, of a believing conformably τῇ εὐαγγελικῇ καὶ ἀποστολικῇ παραδόσει." § 23, init. where παράδοσις means *doctrine*, not *books*, for the Greek would run τῇ εὐαγγ. καὶ τῇ ἀποστ. were the Gospels and Epistles intended. (Thus S. Leo, "secundum evangelicam apostolicamque *doctrinam*," Ep. 124, 1.) And he makes ἡ εὐαγγελικὴ παράδοσις and ἡ ἐκκλησιαστικὴ παρ. synonymous. Cf. contr. Apoll. i. 22, with ad Adelph. 2, init. In like manner, Neander speaks of two kinds of so-called Apostolical Traditions, doctrinal and ecclesiastical, Eccl. Hist. vol. ii. p. 333, transl. And Le Moyne considers the Apostolical Tradition of S.

Hippolytus to be what S. Irenæus means by it, doctrine, as distinct from Scripture. Var. Sacr. t. 2. p. 1062. Vid. also Pearson, Vindic. Ignat. i. 4, circ. fin.　In like manner, S. Augustine contrasts Apostolical Tradition with writings, De Bapt. contr. Don. ii. 7, v. 23, and he calls Infant Baptism an Apostolical Tradition. De Peccat. Mer. i. 26.　And S. Cyprian speaks of, not only wine, but the mixed Cup in the Holy Eucharist, as an "Evangelical truth" and "tradition of the Lord." Epist. 63. 14, 15.

Some instances indeed may be found in the Fathers of Scripture considered as a kind of Tradition, which it is: but these do not serve to make an unnatural or rather an impossible interpretation imperative in the case of such passages as the above. *E. g.* Athan. says, "The Apostolical Tradition teaches, blessed Peter saying, &c. and Paul writing, &c." Adelph. 6.　Suicer refers to Greg. Nys. de Virg. xi. fin. Cyril in Is. lxvi. 5, p. 909. Balsamon, ad Can. vi. Nic. 2, Cyprian, Ep. 74, &c.

THE HOLY TRINITY IN UNITY.

WHEN the Church speaks of Three Persons in One Divine Essence, it seems at first sight that she must imply and mean, if she would avoid contradiction of ideas, either that the " Three " or that the " One " expresses an abstraction of our minds.

If God is numerically one, if the Divine Essence is undivided and simple in that strict sense in which we speak of each man as an individual, then the term Person must surely denote nothing more than some aspect, character, office, or assemblage of attributes, which belongs to the Almighty, as when our Lord is spoken of as Prophet, Priest, and King, which are mere titles or appellatives, not existing *re* but *ratione*. But this is Sabellianism.

On the other hand, we may consider the Three Persons actually to exist, not being mere ideas or modes of our viewing God, but as realities, intrinsically distinct from each other, separate and complete one by one, *re* as well as *ratione*, Persons as we men are persons, or at least in some analogous way. In that case we should go on to consider, as a necessary inference, that " One " expressed only a logical unity, *Ens unum in multis*, a nature or class, as when we say " *Man* is mortal; " but this conclusion brings us either to Arianism or to Tritheism.

There is no incompatibility of ideas involved in the doctrine of Sabellian, Arian, or Tritheist, that is, no mystery; but the Catholic believes and holds as an article of faith that the Divine Three, and again the Divine One, both as One and as Three exist *re* not *ratione*; and therefore he has to answer the objection, " Either the word ' Trinity' denotes a mere abstraction, or the word 'Unity' does; for it cannot be at once a fact that Each of Three, who are eternally distinct one from another, is really God, and also a fact that there really is but one God." This however is the doctrine of the creed of S. Athanasius, and certainly is to be received and held by every faithful member of the Church, viz. that the Father is God and all that God is, and so too is the Son, and so too is the Holy Ghost, yet there is but one God; that the word God may be predicated of an objective Triad, yet also belong to only One Being, to a being individual and sole, all-perfect, self-existent and everlasting.

To state this in the language of Petavius, who is the most learned expositor of the doctrine of the Fathers as distinct from the medieval Church, " Non omittendum Personas Tres, etsi invicem *reapse* distant, *re* tamen *idem* esse cum essentia, et ab eâ *non nisi ratione* discrepare." de Trin. iii. 11, 7. It is a Three or Triad, Each of whom is intrinsically and everlastingly distinct from Each, (as Prophet, Priest, and King are not, but as Priest and his people, King and his subjects, Teacher and taught are), yet each one and the same individual Divine Essence.

Let it be observed the mystery lies, not in any one

of the statements which constitute the doctrine, but in their combination. The meaning of each proposition is on a level with our understanding. There is no intellectual difficulty in apprehending any one of them. "God is a Father; God is a Son; God is a Holy Spirit; The Father is not the Son; the Son is not the Holy Ghost; the Holy Ghost is not the Father: God is numerically One; there are not Three Gods." In which of these propositions do we not understand what is meant to be told us? For devotion, then (and for devotion we may conceive these high truths to be revealed to us), the mystery is no difficulty; such understanding of its separate constituent propositions as we have is sufficient for devotion, which lives and thrives upon single objects rather than on a collection.

The difficulty then is not in understanding each sentence of which the doctrine consists, but in its incompatibility, (taken as a whole, and in the only words possible for conveying it to our minds) with certain of our axioms of thought indisputable in themselves, but foreign and inapplicable to a sphere of existences of which we have no experience whatever.

What in fact do we know of pure spirit? What do we know of the infinite? Of the latter just a little, by means of mathematical science, that is, under the conditions of number, quantity, space, distance, direction, and shape; just enough to tell us how little we know, and how little we are able to draw arguments and inferences when infinites are in question. Mathematical science tells us that one and one infinite do not, put together, make two; that there may be innumerable infinites, and that all put together are not greater than one of them; that there are orders of infinites. It is plain we are utterly unable to determine what is possible and what is impossible in this high region of realities. And then again, in the case of infinitesimals, do not three lines become one line when one is placed upon another? yet how can we say, supposing them respectively coloured white, red, and blue, that they would not remain three, after they had coalesced into one, as they were really three before?

Nor in its doctrine of infinites only, does mathematical science illustrate the mysteries of Theology. Geometry, for instance, may be used to a certain point as an exponent of algebraical truth; but it would be irrational to deny the wider revelations of algebra, because they do not admit of a geometrical expression. The fourth power of a quantity may be received as a fact, though a fourth dimension in space is inconceivable. Again, a polygon or an ellipse is a figure different in kind from a circle; yet we may tend towards a conception of the latter by using what we know of either of the former. Thus it is by economical expedients that we teach and transmit the mysteries of religion, separating them into parts, viewing them in aspects, adumbrating them by analogies, and so approximating to them by means of words which say too much or too little. And if we consent to such ways of thought in our scientific treatment of " earthly things," is it wonderful that we should be forced to them in our investigation of " heavenly " ?

¶ " You have the Son, you have the Father ; fear not

duality. . . . . There is one God, because Father is One, and Son is God, having identity as Son towards Father. . . . . The Father is the whole fulness of Godhead as Father, and the Son is the whole fulness of Godhead as Son. . . . . The Father has Being perfect and without defect, being root and fount of the Son and the Spirit; and the Son is in the fulness of Godhead, a Living Word and Offspring of the Father without defect. And the Spirit is full of the Son, not being part of another, but whole in Himself; . . Let us understand that the Face (nature εἶδος) is One of Three truly subsisting, beginning in Father, beaming in Son, and manifested through Spirit." Pseudo-Ath. c. Sab. Greg. 5—12. "I hardly arrive at contemplaing the One, when I am encircled with the radiance of the Three; I hardly arrive at distinguishing the Three, when I am carried back to the One. When I have imaged to myself One of the Three, I think It the whole, and my sight is filled, and what is more escapes me. . . . And when I embrace the Three in my contemplation, I see but One Luminary, being unable to distinguish or to measure the Light which becomes One." Greg. Naz. Orat. 40, 41. "The fulness of Godhead is in the Father, and the fulness of Godhead is in the Son, yet not differing, but one Godhead. . . . . If of all believers there was one soul and one heart . . . . if every one who cleaves to the Lord is one spirit, ... if man and wife are one flesh, if all of us men in respect of nature are of one substance, if Scripture thus speaks of human things, that many are one, of which there can be no comparison with

things divine, how much more are Father and Son
one in Godhead, where there is no difference of substance or of will, &c." Ambros. de Fid. i. n. 18.
" This Trinity is of one and the same nature and substance, not less in Each than in All, nor greater in
All than in Each; but so great in Father alone or in
Son alone, as in Father and Son together . . . . For
the Father did not lessen Himself to have a Son for
Himself, but as begat of Himself another self, as to
remain whole in Himself, and to be in the Son as great
as He is by Himself. And so the Holy Ghost, whole
from whole, doth not precede That whence He proceeds, but is as great with Him as He is from Him,
and neither lessens Him by proceeding nor increases
by adhering. . . . . Moreover, He who hath given to
so many hearts of His faithful to be one heart, how
much more doth He maintain in Himself that these
Three and Each of Them should be God, and yet all
together, not three gods, but One God?" August.
Ep. 170, 5.

¶ It is no inconsistency to say that the Father is first,
and the Son first also, for comparison or number is not
equal to the expression of this mystery. Since Each is
ὅλος θεός, Each, as contemplated by our finite reason, at
the moment of contemplation excludes the Other.
Though we profess Three Persons, Person cannot be
made one abstract *idea*, certainly not as containing
under it three individual subjects, but it is a *term* applied
to the One God in three ways. It is the doctrine of the
Fathers, that, though we use words expressive of a
Trinity, yet that God is beyond our numbering, and that

Father, Son, and Holy Ghost, though eternally distinct from each other, can scarcely be viewed together in common, except as *One* substance, as if they could not be generalized into Three Any whatever; and as if it were, strictly speaking, incorrect to speak of *a* Person, or otherwise than of *the* Person, whether of Father, or of Son, or of Spirit. The question has almost been admitted by S. Austin, whether it is not possible to say that God is *One* Person (Trin. vii. 8), for He is wholly and entirely Father, and at the same time wholly and entirely Son, and wholly and entirely Holy Ghost. Vid. also Orat. iv. § 1 and 2, where Athan. argues against the Sabellian hypothesis as making the Divine Nature compound (the Word being a something in It), whereas the Catholic doctrine preserves unity because the Father is the One God simply and entirely, and the Son the One God singly and entirely (vid. next paragraph); the Word not a sound, he says, which is nothing, nor a quality which is unworthy of God, but a substantial Word and a substantial Wisdom. "As," he continues, "the Origin is One substance, so Its Word and Wisdom is One, substantial and subsistent; for as from God is God, and from Wise Wisdom, and from Rational (λογικοῦ) a Word, and from Father a Son, so from a subsistence is He subsistent, and from substance substantial and substantive, and from existing existent," &c. Vid. art. *Coinherence.*

¶ Nothing is more remarkable than the confident tone in which Athan. accuses Arians, as in Orat. ii. § 38, and Sabellians, Orat. iv. § 2, of considering the Divine Nature as compound, as if the Catholics were in no respect open to such a charge. Nor are they; though in avoiding it, they are led to enunciate the most profound and ineffable mystery. vid. supr. art. *Son of God.* The Father is the One Simple Entire Divine Being, and so is the Son. They do in no sense share divinity between Them; Each is ὅλος Θεός. This is not ditheism or tritheism, for They are the same God; nor is it Sabellianism, for They are eternally distinct and substantive Persons; but it is a depth and height beyond our intellect, how what is Two in so full a sense can also in so full a sense be One, or how the Divine Nature does not come under number in the sense in which we have earthly experience of it. Thus, " being uncompounded in nature," says Athan., " He is Father of One Only Son," Decr. § 11. In truth the distinction into Persons, as Petavius remarks, " avails especially towards the unity and simplicity of God," vid. de Deo ii. 4, 8.

¶ " The Father," says Athan., " having given all things to the Son, in the Son still hath all things ; and the Son having, still the Father hath them; for the Son's Godhead is the Father's Godhead, and thus the Father in the Son takes the oversight of all things." Orat. iii. 36. Thus iteration is not duplication in respect to God; though *how* this is, is the inscrutable Mystery of the Trinity in Unity. Nothing can be named which the Son is in Himself, as distinct from the Father ; but we are told His relation towards the Father; and distinct from and beyond that relation, He is but the One God, who is also the Father. Such statements are not here intended to explain, but to bring home to the mind *what* it is which faith receives. We say, "Father, Son, and Spirit," a transcendant Three, but when we would abstract a general idea of Them in order to number Them as we number things on earth, our abstraction really does but carry us back to the One Substance. There will be different ways of expressing this, but such seems the meaning of such passages as the following. "Those who taunt us with tritheism must be told that we confess One God not in number, but in nature. For what is one in number is not really one, nor single in nature; for instance, we call the world one in number, but not one in nature, for we divide it into its elements; and man again is one in number, but compounded of body and soul. . . . If then we say that God is in nature one, how do they impute number to us, who altogether banish it from that blessed and spiritual nature? For number belongs to quantity, and number is connected with matter, &c." Basil. Ep. 8, 2. "That which saveth us, is faith, but number has been devised to indicate quantity . . . . We pronounce Each of the Persons once, but when we would number them up, we do not proceed by an unlearned numeration to the notion of a polytheism." (vid. the whole passage,) ibid. de Sp. S. c. 18. "Why, passing by the First Cause, does he [S. John] at once discourse to us of the Second? We will decline to speak of 'first' and 'second;' for the Godhead is higher than number and succession of times." Chrysost. in Joan. Hom. ii. 3 fin. "In respect of the Adorable and most Royal Trinity, 'first' and 'second' have no place; for the Godhead is

higher than number and times." Isid. Pel. Ep. 3, 18.
" He calls," says S. Maximus, commenting on Pseudo-
Dionysius, " fecundity, the Father's incomprehensible
progression to the production of the Son and the Holy
Ghost; and suitably does he say, ' *as* a Trinity,' since
not number, but glory is expressed in ' The Lord God
is one Lord.' " in Dionys. Opp. t. 2. p. 101. " We do
not understand ' one ' in the Divine Substance, as in
the creatures; in whom what is properly one is not to
be seen; for what is one in number, as in our case, is
not properly one. . . . It is not one in number, or as the
beginning of number, any more than It is as magnitude
or as the beginning of magnitude. . . . That One is
ineffable and indescribable; since It is itself the cause
of all that is one, πάσης ἑνάδος ἑνοποιόν." Eulog. ap.
Phot. 230. p. 864. " Three what? I answer, Father
and Son and Holy Ghost. See, he urges, you have
said Three; but explain Three what? Nay, do you
number, for I have said all about the Three, when I
say, Father and Son and Holy Ghost. Not, as there
are two men, so are They two Gods; for there is here
something ineffable, which cannot be put into words,
viz. that there should both be number, and not
number. For see if there does not seem to be number,
Father and Son and Holy Spirit, a Trinity. If Three,
Three what? number fails. Then God neither is
without number, nor is under number. . . . They
imply number, only relatively to Each Other, not in
Themselves." August. in Joan. 39, 3 and 4. " We
say Three ' Persons,' as many Latins of authority have
said in treating the subject, because they found no
more suitable way of declaring an idea in words which

they had without words. Since the Father is not the Son, and the Son not the Father, and the Holy Ghost neither Father nor Son, there are certainly Three; but when we ask, Three what? we feel the great poverty of human language. However, we say Three 'Persons,' not for the sake of saying that, but of not saying nothing." Aug. de Trin. v. 10. " Unity is not number, but is itself the principle of all things." Ambros. de Fid. i. n. 19. "That is truly one, in which there is no number, nothing in It beyond That which is. . . . There is no diversity in It, no plurality from diversity, no multitude from accidents, and therefore no number . . . . but unity only. For when God is thrice repeated, and Father, Son, and Holy Ghost is named, three Unities do not make plurality of number in Him which They are. . . . This repetition of Unities is iteration rather than numeration. . . . A trine numeration does not make number, which they rather run into who make some difference between the Three." Boeth. Trin. unus Deus, p. 959.

¶ The last remark is also found in Naz. Orat. 31, 18. Many of these passages are taken from Thomassin de Trin. 17. Petavius, de Trin. iv. 16. fin., quotes St. Anselm as saying, " Though there be not many eternities, yet, if we say eternity in eternity, there is but one eternity. And so whatever is said of God's essence, if returned into itself, does not increase quantity, nor admit number. Since there is nothing out of God, when God is born of God." Infinity does not add to infinity; the treatment of infinities is above us. With this remark I end as I began.

UNITY OF EMMANUEL.

IT is well known that the illustration in the Athan.
Creed, " As the reasonable soul and flesh is one man,
so God and man is one Christ," was taken by the
Monophysites to imply that the Divine Nature was
made dependent on the flesh, and was influenced and
circumscribed by it.   Man is partly soul and partly
Body; he is *of* body and soul, not body and soul; but
Christ is wholly God, and wholly man, ὅλος Θεὸς, ὅλος
ἄνθρωπος, Orat. iv. 35.   He is as simply God as if
He were not man, as simply man as if He were not
God; "unus atque idem est," says S. Leo, " et totus
hominis filius propter carnem, et totus Dei filius propter unam cum Patre deitatem," Ep. 165, 8.   Athan. has
anticipated the heresy which denied this doctrine in a
very distinct passage written apparently even before
the rise of Arianism.   " It is the function of the soul,"
he says, " to contemplate in its thoughts what is within
its own body; but not to operate in things beyond its
own body, or to act by its presence on what is far from
the body.   Certainly man at a distance never moves
or transposes such things; nor could a man sit at home
and think of things in heaven, and thereby move the
sun, or turn the heaven round. . . . Not thus is the
Word of God in man's nature; for He was not bound
up with the body (συνεδέδετο), but rather He hath

Himself dominion over it, so that He was not in it only, but in all things ; nay, He was external to the whole universe and in the sole Father," Incarn. V. D. 17. The same passage occurs in Serm. Maj. de Fid. 11.

It could not be otherwise. The Divine Word was not a mere presence or manifestation of God in man, but He was God Himself incarnate. He was still what He had ever been, and will be from first to last, One,—one and the same, impassible, immutable, in His αὐτότης, so to speak, as one of the Eternal Trinity. His Divine Nature carried with It on His incarnation that αὐτότης or Personality. So necessary, so cardinal is this truth for the right holding of the great doctrine under consideration, that the Alexandrians, St. Cyril at least, and perhaps St. Athanasius, spoke of there being only One Nature in the Incarnate Lord, by " one Nature " meaning one Person (for Person and Nature could not be divided; and, if our Lord's Nature was divine, His person was divine also), and by saying " only one," meaning that, in comparison of the Divine Person who had taken flesh, what He had taken was not so much a nature, though it was strictly a nature, as the substance of a manhood which was not substantive.

Whereas the Apostle says, " One Lord Jesus Christ," that unity does not lie in the unity of two natures, but in His Person, which brings the two natures together, which is and ever has been indivisible from His Divine Nature, and has absorbed into Itself, and is sovereign over, not destroying thereby, but perpetuating, Its human nature.

¶ Hence, while it be true to say "Man is God," as well as to say "God is man," it is not true that "man became God," or "took on him divinity," as it is true to say "God became man," because from first to last the Son and Word is supreme, independent, and one and the same; and it is a first point in all orthodox teaching of the Incarnation to make this clear and definite. He is "Jesus Christ," indeed, but at the same time, "heri, et hodie, ipse et in sæcula;" He is now, and He was from everlasting.

¶ "While He received no hurt (οὐδὲν ἐβλάπτετο) Himself by bearing our sins in His body on the tree, we men were redeemed from our affections (παθῶν), Orat. iii. § 31. And so ἐβλάπτετο μὲν αὐτὸς οὐδὲν, Incarn. § 54, μὴ βλαπτόμενος, ibid. § 34. In these passages αὐτὸς means "in that which is Himself," i.e., in His own Person or Divine Self, αὐτὸς being used when the next century would have used "Person." "For the sun, too, which He made and we see, makes its circuit in the sky and is not defiled by touching, &c.," Incarn. § 17. "As the rays of sun-light would not suffer at all, though filling all things and touching bodies dead and unclean, thus and much more the spiritual virtue of God the Word would suffer nothing in substance nor receive hurt, &c," Euseb. de Laud. Const. p. 536, and 538; also Dem. Evang. vii. p. 348. "The insults of the passion even the Godhead bore, but the passion His flesh alone felt; as we rightly say that a sunbeam or a body of flame can be cut indeed by a sword but not divided. . . . I will speak yet more plainly; the Godhead [divinitas] was fixed with nails, but could not

Itself be pierced, since the flesh was exposed and offered room for the wound, but God remained invisible, &c.," Vigil. contr. Eutych. ii. 9, p. 503 (Bibl. Patrum, ed. 1624). "There were five together on the Cross, when Christ was nailed to it ; the sun-light, which first received the nails and the spear, and remained undivided from the Cross and unhurt by the nails, next, &c.," Anast. Hodeg. c. 12, p. 220 (ed. 1606); also p. 222; vid. also the beautiful passage in Pseudo-Basil : "God in flesh, not working with aught intervening as in the prophets, but having taken to Him a manhood con-natural with Himself ($\sigma\nu\mu\phi\nu\hat{\eta}$, i. e. joined to His nature), and made one, and, through His flesh akin to us, drawing up to Him all humanity. . . . . What was the manner of the Godhead in flesh ? as fire in iron, not transitively, but by communication. For the fire does not dart into the iron, but remains there and communicates to it of its own virtue, not impaired by the communication, yet filling wholly its recipient." Basil, t. 2, p. 596, ed. Ben. Also Ruffin. on Symb. 12 ; Cyril, *Quod unus*, t. v. p. 776 ; Dam. F. O., iii. 6 fin.; Aug. Serm. 7, p. 26, ed. 1842, Suppl. It is to show at once the intimacy of the union of natures and the absolute sovereignty of the divine, that such strong expressions are in use as God's body, God's death, God's mother, &c.

¶ $\theta\epsilon o\hat{v}$ $\hat{\eta}\nu$ $\sigma\hat{\omega}\mu a$, Orat. iii. § 31 ; also ad Adelph. 3. ad. Max. 2, and so $\tau\grave{\eta}\nu$ $\pi\tau\omega\chi\epsilon\acute{v}\sigma a\sigma a\nu$ $\phi\acute{v}\sigma\iota\nu$ $\theta\epsilon o\hat{v}$ $\acute{o}\lambda\eta\nu$ $\gamma\epsilon\nu o\mu\acute{e}\nu\eta\nu$, c. Apoll. ii. 11. $\tau\grave{o}$ $\pi\acute{a}\theta os$ $\tau o\hat{v}$ $\lambda\acute{o}\gamma ov$, ibid. 16, $\sigma\grave{a}\rho\xi$ $\tau o\hat{v}$ $\lambda\acute{o}\gamma ov$, Orat. iii. 34. $\sigma\hat{\omega}\mu a$ $\sigma o\phi\acute{\iota}as$, 53, also $\theta\epsilon\grave{o}s$ $\grave{\epsilon}\nu$ $\sigma a\rho\kappa\grave{\iota}$, Orat. ii. § 10 ; $\theta\epsilon\grave{o}s$ $\grave{\epsilon}\nu$ $\sigma\acute{\omega}\mu a\tau\iota$, ii. § 12, and 15 ; $\lambda\acute{o}\gamma os$ $\grave{\epsilon}\nu$ $\sigma a\rho\kappa\grave{\iota}$, iii. 54 ; $\lambda\acute{o}\gamma os$ $\grave{\epsilon}\nu$ $\sigma\acute{\omega}\mu a\tau\iota$, Sent. D. 8 fin.

πάθος Χριστοῦ τοῦ θεοῦ μου, Ignat. Rom. 6. ὁ θεὸς
πέπονθεν, Melit. ap. Anast. Hodeg. 12.   Dei passiones,
Tertull. de Carn. Christ. 5.   Dei interemptores, ibid.
caro Deitatis, Leon. Serm. 65 fin.   Deus mortuus et
sepultus, Vigil. c. Eut. ii. p. 502.   Vid. supr. p. 294.
Yet Athan. objects to the phrase, "God suffered in the
flesh," i. e. as used by the Apollinarians. Vid. contr.
Apoll. ii. 13 fin.   Vid. article μία φύσις.

VAPOUR.

Vid. art. ἀπόῤῥοή.

TWO WILLS IN CHRIST.

THE Monothelite question does not come into the range of doctrine included in the foregoing Treatises; but Athanasius has one passage bearing upon it, to which I have added passages from Anastasius and others.

"And as to His saying, *If it be possible, let the cup pass,* observe how, though he thus spake, He rebuked Peter, saying, *Thou savourest not the things that be of God, but those that be of men.* For He willed what He deprecated, for therefore had He come; but His was the willing, (since for it He came,) but the terror belonged to the flesh. Wherefore as man He utters this speech also, and yet both were said by the Same, to show that He was God, willing in Himself, but when He had become man, having a flesh that was in terror. For the sake of this flesh He combined His own will with human weakness, that destroying this affection He might in turn make man undaunted in the thought of death." Orat. iii. § 57.

"I say not, perish the thought, that there are two wills in Christ at variance with each other, as you consider, and in opposition; nor at all a will of flesh, or of passion, or evil. . . But, since it was perfect man that He took on Him, that He might save him whole, and He is perfect in manhood, therefore we call that sovereign disposal of His orders and commands by the name of the Divine will in Christ, and we understand by human will the intellectual soul's power of willing, given it after the image and likeness of God, and breathed into it by God, when it was made, by means of this power to prefer and to obey, and to do the divine will and the divine orders. If then the soul of Christ was destitute of the power of reason, will, and preference, it is not indeed after the image of God, nor consubstantial with our souls .... and Christ cannot be called perfect in manhood. Christ then, being in the form of God, has, according to the Godhead, that lordly will which is common to Father and Holy Ghost ; and, as having taken the form of a servant, He does also the will of His intellectual and immaculate soul, &c. . . . . Else if this will be taken away, He will according to the Godhead be subject, and fulfil the Father's will as a servant . . . . as if there were two wills in the Godhead of Father and of Son, the Father's that of a Lord, the Son's that of a servant." Anast. Hodeg. i. p. 12.

¶ It is observable that, as we see elsewhere Athan. speaks of the *nature* of the Word, and not also of the *nature* of man as united to Him, but of *flesh, humanity,* &c. (vid. infra art. μία φύσις), so here, instead of using the word "will," he speaks of the Word's *willing* and His human *weakness, terror,* &c. In another place he says still more pointedly, "The *will* was of the Godhead alone ; since the whole *nature* of the Word was manifested in the second Adam's *human form* and visible *flesh.*" contr. Apoll. ii. 10. Yet elsewhere, he distinctly expresses the Catholic view ; thus,

" When He says, ' Father, if it be possible,' &c. and ' the spirit is willing,' &c., He makes mention of *two* wills, the one human, which belongs to the flesh, the other Divine, which belongs to God; for the human, because of the weakness of the flesh, prays against the passion, but His divine will is ready." de Incarn. c. Ar. 21. S. Leo on the same passage begins, like Athan. in the first passage, vaguely, but ends, as in Athan.'s second passage, distinctly; " The first request is one of infirmity, the second of power; the first He asked in our [character], the second in His own .... The inferior will gave way to the superior," &c. Serm. 56, 2. vid. a similar passage in Nyssen, Antirrh. adv. Apol. 32. vid. also 31. An obvious objection may be drawn from such passages, as if the will "of the flesh" were represented as contrary (vid. above, p. 331) to the will of the Word. It is remarkable, as Petavius observes, Dogm. tom. v. ix. 9, that Athan. compares, Orat. iii. § 57, the influence of our Lord's divine will on His human, (vid. the passage from the Incarn. l. c.) to His rebuke of St. Peter, "Get thee behind Me, &c." vid. supr. *Specialties*, n. 4. But this is but an analogous instance, not a direct resemblance. The whole of our Lord's prayer is offered by Him as man, because it is a prayer; but the former part expresses the sinless infirmity of our nature, the latter is from His human will expressing its acquiescence in His Father's, that is, in His own Divine Will. "His Will," says S. Greg. Naz. "was not contrary to God, being all deified, θεωθὲν ὅλον."

WISDOM.

¶ ATHAN. considers that the Eternal Wisdom, one of the proper appellatives of the Son, is that Wisdom which in Prov. ix. 1, viii. 22, &c. is said to be created, and that this creation is to be understood of His taking on Him a created nature. He says, " *Wisdom has made herself a house ;* it is plain that our body, which it took upon itself to become man, is Wisdom's House." Orat. ii. § 44. And he is followed by St. Leo, " ut intra intemerata viscera ædificante sibi sapentiâ domum, Verbum caro fieret." Leon. Epist. 31,2. Also Didymus de Trin. iii. 3, p. 337 (ed. 1769) August. Civ. D. xvii. 20. Cyril. in Joann. iv. 4, p. 384, 5. Max. Dial. iii. p. 1029 (ap. Theod. ed. Schulz) Hence Clem. Alex. ὁ λόγος ἑαυτὸν γεννᾷ. Strom. v. 3. vid. art. *Holy Spirit.*

But without denying that our Lord is signified in the above passage, as the Prototype, Author, and Pattern of all wisdom, it is more natural to apply it, as Athan. also does, to the attribute or grace called wisdom as displayed in the creation, whether in the original creation or the new. Hence he says, " The Only-begotten and very Wisdom of God is Creator and Framer of all things ; for *in Wisdom hast Thou made them all,* he says, and *the earth is full of Thy creation.* But that what came into being might not only be, but be good, it pleased God that His own Wisdom should con-

descend to the creatures, so as to introduce an impress
and semblance of Its Image in all in common and in
each, that what was made might be manifestly wise
works and worthy of God.   For, as of the Son of God,
considered as the Word, our word is an image, so of
the same Son, considered as Wisdom, is the wisdom
which is implanted in us an image; in which wisdom
we, having the power of knowledge and thought,
become recipients of the All-framing Wisdom, and
through It we are able to know Its Father." Orat. ii.
§ 78.

¶ As Athan. in the above passage considers wisdom as
the image of the Creator in the Universe, so elsewhere he
explains it of the Church, de Incarn. contr. Ar. 6, if it be
his (and so Didym. Trin. iii. 3 fin.), where his teaching
about the Word is very much the same as in Orat. ii.
§ 56.   S. Jerome applies it to the creation of the new
man in holiness, "'Put ye on Christ Jesus;' for He
is the new man, in whom all we believers ought to be
clad and attired.   For what was not new in the man
which was taken on Him by our Saviour ? . . . He therefore who can imitate His conversation and bring out in
himself all virtues, he has put on the new man, and
can say with the Apostle, 'Not I, but Christ liveth
in me.' . . . Only in great deeds and works the word
'creation' is used. . . The new man is the great work
of God, and excels all other creatures, since he is said to
be framed, as the world is said to be, and is created the
beginning of God's ways, and in the commencement
of all the elements." in Eph. iv. 23, 24.   Naz. alludes to
the interpretation by which Wisdom is the plan, system,

or the laws of the Universe, Orat. 30, 2, though he does not so explain it himself. Epiphanius says, "Scripture has nowhere confirmed this application of Prov. 8. 22, nor has any Apostle referred it to Christ." (vid. also Basil. contr. Eunom. ii. 20.) He adds, "How many wisdoms of God are there, improperly so called! but One Wisdom is the Only-begotten, not improperly so called, but in truth . . . . The very word ' wisdom ' does not oblige me to speak of the Son of God." Hær. 69, pp. 743—745. He proceeds to show how it may apply to Him.

¶ Didymus argues at length in favour of interpreting the passage of created wisdom, Trin. iii. l. c. He says that the context makes this interpretation necessary, as speaking of " the fear of God " being the " beginning " of it, of " doing it," and of " kings and rulers " reigning by means of it. Again it is said that wisdom was with the Creator who was Himself the Son and Word. " The Son and Word, the Framer of all seeing and being able from the first, long suffering and waiting for repentance in the unrighteous and wrong-thinking multitude, when He had finished all, delighted in wisdom which was in His creatures and was glad in it, rejoicing in His own work." p. 336. He contrasts with this the more solemn style used by the sacred writer when he speaks of the Uncreated Wisdom ; ὑπερφυῶς καὶ ὥσπερ ὑπ᾽ ἐκπλήξεως θαυμάζων ἀναφθέγγεται, e. g. Prov. xxx. 3, p. 338.

THE WORD

Logos, *verbum*, being a term already used in the schools of heathen philosophy, was open to various misunderstandings on its appearance in the theology of Revealed teaching. In the Church it was both synonymous with and corrective of the term "Son;" but heretics had almost as many senses of the term as they had sects.

¶ It is a view familiar to the Fathers, viz., that in this consists our Lord's Sonship, that He is the Word, or as S. Augustine says, "Christum ideo Filium quia Verbum." Aug. Ep. 102, n. 11. "If God is the Father of a Word, why is not He who is begotten a Son?" de Decr. § 17 : Orat. iv. § 12. "If I speak of Wisdom, I speak of His Offspring." Theoph. ad Autolyc. i. 3. "The Word, the genuine Son of Mind." Clem. Protrept. p. 78; and Dionysius, "ἔστιν ὁ μὲν οἷον πατὴρ ὁ νοῦς τοῦ λόγου, Sent. Dion. § 23, fin. Petavius discusses this subject accurately with reference to the distinction between Divine generation and Divine Procession, de Trin. vii. 14.

¶ But the heretics, says Athan., "dare to separate Word and Son, and to say that the Word is one and the Son another, and that first was the Word and then the Son. Now their presumption takes various forms; for some say that the man whom the Saviour assumed is the Son; and others both that the man and the Word then became Son when they were united. And others say that the Word Himself then became Son when He became man; for from being Word, they say, He became Son, not being Son before, but only Word." Orat. iv. § 15. The Valentinians, in their system of Eons, had already divided the Son from the Word; but they considered the μονογενὴς first, the λόγος next.

The title "Word" implies the ineffable mode of the Son's generation, as distinct from *material* parallels, vid. Gregory Nyssen, contr. Eunom. iii. p. 107; Chrysostom in Joan. Hom. 2, § 4; Cyril Alex. Thesaur. 5, p. 37. Also it implies that there is but *One* Son.

¶ "As there is one Origin," says Athan., "and therefore one God, so one is that Substance and Subsistence (οὐσία καὶ ὑπόστασις) which indeed and truly and really is, and which said *I am that I am*, and not two, that there be not two Origins; and from the One, a Son in nature and truth is Its proper Word, Its Wisdom, Its Power, and inseparable from It. And as there is not another substance, lest there be two Origins, so the Word which is from that One Substance has no dissolution, nor is a sound significative, but is a substantial Word and substantial Wisdom, which is the true Son. For were He not substantial, God would be speaking into the air, and having a body in nothing different from that of men; but since He is not man, neither is His Word according to the infirmity of man. For as the Origin is one Substance, so Its Word is one, substantial, and subsisting, and Its Wisdom. For as He is God from God, and Wisdom from the Wise, and Word from the

Rational, and Son from Father, so is He from Subsistence Subsistent, and from Substance Substantial and Substantive, and Being from Being." Orat. iv. § 1.

For the contrast between the Divine Word and the human which is Its shadow, vid. also Orat. iv. 1, above, Iren. Hær. ii. 13, n. 8. Origen. in Joan. t. i., p. 23, 25, Euseb. Demonstr. v. 5, p. 230; Cyril. Cat. xi. 10; Basil, Hom. div. xvi. 3; Nyssen contr. Eunom. xii. p. 350. Orat. Cat. i. p. 478; Damasc. F. O. i. 6; August. in Psalm. 44, 5.

¶ "Men have many words, and after those many, not any one of them all; for the speaker has ceased, and thereupon his word fails. But God's Word is one and the same, and as it is written, *remaineth for ever*, not changed, not first one and then another, but existing the same always. For it behoved that God being one, one should be His Image, one His Word, one His Wisdom." Orat. ii. § 36. vid. contr. Gent. 41. ad Ep. Æg. 16. Epiph. Hær. 65. 3. Nyss. in Eun. xii. p. 349. Origen (in a passage, however, of questionable doctrine) says, "as there are gods many, but to us one God the Father, and many lords, but to us one Lord Jesus Christ, so there are many words, but we pray that in us may exist the Word that was in the beginning, with God, and God," in Joan. tom. ii. 3. "Many things, it is acknowledged, does the Father speak to the Son," say the Semi-Arians at Ancyra, "but the words which God speaks to the Son are not sons. They are not substances of God, but vocal energies; but the Son, though a Word, is not such, but, being a Son, is a substance." Epiph. Hær. 73. 12. The Semi-Arians are here speaking against Sabellianism, which took the same ground here as Arianism.

¶ Vid. the article on the *Nicene Tests* for those ante-Nicene theologians, who, though they undoubtedly were upholders of the Homoüsion and good Catholics when they wrote, nevertheless seem to have held that the Word, after existing from eternity, was born to be a Son at the beginning and on the beginning of time, and then became the Creator, the Pattern, the conservative power of the whole universe. These writers were such as Justin, Tatian, Tertullian, Novatian, &c. There was a parallel theory to theirs, and by which they were apparently influenced, in the heathen and Jewish schools. The view of the Logos as ἐνδιάθετος and as προφορικὸς, as the Word conceived and the Word uttered, the Word mental and the Word active and effectual—to distinguish the two senses of Logos, thought and speech — came from the Stoics, and is found in Philo, and was under certain limitations allowed in Catholic theology. Damasc. F. O. ii. 21. To use, indeed, either of the two absolutely and to the exclusion of the other, would have involved some form of Sabellianism, or Arianism, as the case might be; but each might correct the defective sense of either. That the use was not oversafe would appear from its history in the Church, into which the above theologians, by their mode of teaching the γέννησις of the Word, introduce us. Theophilus does not scruple, in teaching it, to use the very terms, endiathetic and prophoric. God made all things out of nothing," he says. . . . " Having His own Word *endiathetic* in His

own womb, He begat Him together with His own Wisdom, bringing Him forth before the universe was."
Again he speaks of "the Word of God, who also
is His Son, who was ever (διαπαντὸς) *endiathetic* in
the heart of God, . . . God begat Him to be *prophoric*,
the first-born of all creation." ad Autol. ii. 10, 22.

While S. Theophilus speaks of our Lord as both endiathetic and prophoric, S. Cyril seems to consider Him
endiathetic, in Joan. i. 4, p. 39, though he also says, "This
word of ours, προφορικὸς, is generated from mind and
unto mind, and seems to be other than that which stirs in
the heart, &c., &c. . . . so too the Son of God proceeding from the Father without division, is the *expression*
and likeness of what is proper to Him, being a subsistent
Word, and living from a Living Father." Thesaur.
p. 47. When the Fathers deny that our Lord is the
προφορικὸς λόγος, they only mean that that title is not,
even as far as its philosophical idea went, an adequate
representative of Him, a word spoken being insubstan-
tive, vid. Athan. Orat. ii. 35. Hil. de Syn. 46. Cyr.
Catech. xi. 10. Damas. Ep. ii. p. 203, "nec prolativum,
ut generationem ei demas," for this was the Arian doctrine. The first Sirmian Council of the Arians anathematizes those who use of the Son either name. So does
the Arian Macrostich. "The Son," said Eunomius, "is
other than the endiathetic Word, or Word in intellectual action, of which partaking and being filled He is
called the Prophoric Word, and expressive of the
Father's substance, that is, the Son." Cyril in Joan.
p. 31. The Gnostics seem to have held the λόγος προφορικός. Iren. Hær. ii. 12, n. 5. Marcellus is said by

Eusebius to have considered our Lord as first the one and then the other. Eccl. Theol. ii. 15. Sabellius thought our Lord the προφορικὸς, according to Epiph. Hær. p. 398. cf. Damasc. Hær. 62. Paul of Samosata the ἐνδιάθετος. Epiph. Hær. 65, passim. Eusebius, Eccles. Theol. ii. 17, describes our Lord as the προφορικὸς while disowning it.

¶ Athan. speaks, contr. Gent. of man as "having" besides grace, of the Giver, also his own natural virtue proper from the Father's Word;" of the mind "seeing the Word, and in Him the Word's Father also," 2; of "the way to God being, not as God Himself, above us and far off, or external to us, but in us," 30, &c., &c. vid. also Basil. de Sp. S. n. 19. Athan. also speaks of the seed of Wisdom as being " a reason combined and connatural with every-thing that came into being, which some are wont to call seminal, inanimate indeed and unreasoning and unintelligent, but operating only by external art ac-cording to the science of Him who sowed it." contr. Gent. 40.

This is drawn out somewhat differently, and very strikingly in contr. Gent. 43, &c. The Word indeed is regarded more as the Governor than as the Life of the world, but He is said to be, ὁ παραδοξοποιὸς καὶ θαυμα-τοποιὸς τοῦ θεοῦ λόγος φωτίζων καὶ ζωοποιῶν . . . . ἑκαστῷ τὴν ἰδίαν ἐνέργειαν ἀποδιδούς, &c. 44. Shortly before the Word is spoken of as the Principle of per-manence, 41 fin.

¶ " For it was fitting," says Athan. above, "whereas God is One, that His Image should be One also, and

His Word One, and One His Wisdom. Wherefore I am in wonder how, whereas God is One, these men, after their private notions, introduce many images and wisdoms and words, and say that the Father's proper and natural Word is other than the Son, by whom He even made the Son, and that He who is really Son is but notionally called Word, as vine, and way, and door, and tree of life; and that He is called Wisdom also only in name, the proper and true Wisdom of the Father, which co-exists ingencrately with Him, being other than the Son, by which He even made the Son, and named Him Wisdom as partaking of Wisdom." . Orat. ii. § 37. That is, they allowed Him to be really the Son, though they went on to explain away the name, and argued that He was but by a figure the Word, πολλοὶ λόγοι, since these were, and He was not οὐδ' ἐκ πολλῶν εἷς, Sent. D. 25. Also Ep. Æg. 14; Origen in Joan. tom. ii. 3; Euseb. Demonstr. v. 5, p. 229, fin.; contr. Marc. p. 4, fin.; contr. Sabell. i. p. 4.; August. in Joan. Tract. i. 8. Also vid. Philo's use of λόγοι for Angels as commented on by Burton, Bampt. Lect. p. 556. The heathens called Mercury by the name of λόγος. Vid. Benedictine note f. in Justin, Ap. i. 21.

¶ "If the Wisdom which is in the Father is other than the Lord, Wisdom came into being in Wisdom; and if God's Word is Wisdom, the Word too has come into being in a Word; and if God's Word is the Son, the Son too has been made in the Son." Ep. Æg. 14. vid. also, Decr. § 8, and Orat. iii. 2, 64. And so S. Austin, "If the Word of God was

Himself made, by what other Word was He made? If you say, that it is the Word of the Word, by whom that Word is made, this I say is the only Son of God. But if you say the Word of the Word, grant that He is not made by whom all things are made ; for He could not be made by means of Himself, by whom are made all things," in Joan. Tract. i. 11. Vid. a parallel argument with reference to the Holy Spirit. Athan. Serap. i. 25.

ANNOTATIONS

ON GREEK TERMS IN THE FOREGOING TREATISES

ALPHABETICALLY ARRANGED.

The 'Aγέννητον, or Ingenerate.

It had been usual in the schools of Philosophy, as we contrast Creator and creatures, the Infinite and the finite, the Eternal and the temporal, so in like manner to divide all beings into the Unoriginate or Ingenerate, the ἄναρχα or ἀγένητα, on the one hand, and those on the other which have an origin or beginning. Under the ingenerate, which was a term equivalent to "uncreate," fell, according as particular philosophies or heresies determined, the universe, matter, the soul of man, as well as the Supreme Being, and the Platonic *ideas*. Again, the Neoplatonists spoke of Three Principles as beyond time, that is, eternal, the Good, Intellect, and the Soul of the world.   (Theod. Affect. Cur. ii. p. 750.) Plotinus, however, in his Enneads, seems to make Good the sole ἀρχή; ἡ ἀρχὴ ἀγέννητος, (5. Enn. iv. 1,) while Plato says, εἴτε ἀρχὴν εἴτε ἀρχάς (Theod. *ibid.* p. 749, Tim. p. 48), and in his Phædrus, p. 246, he calls the soul of man ingenerate or ἀγένητον. The Valentinians (Tertull. contr. Valent. 7, and Epiph. Hær. 31, 10), and Basilides (Epiph. Hær. 24) applied the term to the Supreme God. The word thus selected to denote the First Principle or Cause, seems to have been spelt sometimes with one ν, sometimes with two. Vid. art. γένητος.

¶ And so too with Christian writers, and with like variety in the spelling, this was the word expressing the contrast between the First Cause or causes, and all things besides. Ignatius distinctly applies it to our Lord in His Divine Nature, doubling the ν in the *Cod. Med.* "There is One Physician, generate and ingenerate, ... from Mary and from God." (Ephes. 7.) vid. Athan. Syn. § 47. Theophilus says, ὁ γενητὸς καὶ προσδεής ἐστι· ὁ δὲ ἀγένητος οὐδενὸς προσδεῖται, (ad Autol. ii. 10.) Clement of Alexandria, ἓν τὸ ἀγένητον, in contrast to our Lord (Strom. vi. 7, p. 769). Dionysius Alex. even entertains the hypothesis that ἀγεννησία is the very οὐσία of God (Euseb. Præp. vii. 19), which the Arians took advantage of for the purposes of their heresy, (vid. Epiph. Hær. 76,) laying it down as a fundamental axiom that nothing γεννητὸν could be God. Hence Eusebius of Nicomedia, in the beginning of the controversy, rested his heresy on the *dictum,* ἓν τὸ ἀγέννητον, adding ἓν δὲ τὸ ὑπ' αὐτοῦ ἀληθῶς, καὶ οὐκ ἐξ' οὐσίας αὐτοῦ. Theod. Hist. i. 5. Eusebius of Cæsarea too speaks of the Supreme Being as ἀγεννητὸς καὶ τῶν ὅλων ποιητῆς θεός. (Ev. Dem. iv. 7, p. 167.)

The word ἀρχή expressed the same attribute of the Divine Being, and furnished the same handle to the Arian disputant for his denial of our Lord's Divinity. The ἀρχὴ of all was ἄναρχος; how then could our Lord be the ἀρχή, that is, God, if He was a Son? But the solution of both forms of the question was obvious, as easy as that of the stock fallacies inserted, half as exercises, half as diversions for the student, to relieve a dry treatise on Logic. It was enough for Catholics to answer that ἀρχή had notoriously two meanings, origin and beginning; that in the philosophical schools these senses were understood to go together, but that Christianity had introduced a separation of them; that our Lord's Sonship involved His having no beginning because He was God, but His having an origin, because He was Son. And in like manner, the Son of God was, as God, ingenerate, that is without a beginning, and as Son generate, that is, with an origin.

Thus Clement calls Him ἄναρχος ἀρχὴ, and Arius scoffingly ἀγεννητογενής.

As to the assumption that nothing generate could be God, Athan. maintains on the contrary that our Lord cannot but be God because He is generate. vid. Art. *Son*.

The 'Αειγεννές.

ATHAN., as the other Fathers, insists strongly on the perfection and the immutability of the Divine Being; from which it follows that the birth of the Son must have been from eternity, for, if He exists now, He must have existed ever. " I am the Lord, I change not." It was from dimness and inaccuracy even in orthodox minds, in apprehending this truth, that Arianism arose and had its successes.

Athan. says, "Never was the substance of the Father incomplete, so that what belonged to it should be added afterwards; on the contrary, whereas it belongs to men to beget in time, from the imperfection of their nature, God's offspring is eternal, for God's nature is ever perfect." Orat. i. § 14. (*Disc.* n. 24.) " Though a parent be distinct in time from his son, as being man, who himself has come into being in time, yet he too would have had his child ever co-existent with him except that his nature was a restraint, and made it impossible. Let these say what is to restrain God from being always Father of the Son?" Orat. i. § 26, 27; iv. § 15.

"Man," says S. Cyril, inasmuch as He had a beginning of being, also has of necessity a beginning of begetting, as what is from Him is a thing generate, but . . . . if God's substance transcend time, or

origin, or interval, His generation also will transcend
these; nor does it deprive the Divine Nature of the
power of generating, that He doth not generate in time.
For other than human is the manner of divine generation; and together with God's existing is His
generating implied, and the Son was in Him by generation, nor did His generation precede His existence,
but He was always, and that by generation." Thesaur.
v. p. 35. vid. also p. 42, and Dialog. ii. fin. This was
retorting the objection; the Arians said, "How can
God be ever perfect, who added to Himself a Son?"
Athan. answers, "How can the Son not be eternal,
since God is ever perfect?" vid. Greg. Nyssen. contr.
Eunom. Append. p. 142. Cyril. Thesaur. x. p. 78. As
to the Son's perfection, Aetius objects ap. Epiph. Hær.
76, p. 925, 6, that growth and consequent accession
from without were essentially involved in the idea of
Sonship; whereas S. Greg. Naz. speaks of the Son as
not ἀτελῆ πρότερον, εἶτα τέλειον, ὥσπερ νόμος τῆς
ἡμετέρας γεννέσεως. Orat. 20, 9, fin. In like manner,
S. Basil argues against Eunomius, that the Son is
τέλειος, because He is the Image, not as if copied,
which is a gradual work, but as a χαρακτήρ, or impression of a seal, or as the knowledge communicated
from master to scholar, which comes to the latter and
exists in him perfect, without being lost to the former.
contr. Eunom. ii. 16 fin.

It follows from this perfection and unchangeableness
of the Divine Nature, that, if there is in the beginning a *gennesis* of the Son, it is continual:—that is the
doctrine of the ἀειγεννές. Athan. says that there is no

παῦλα τῆς γεννήσεως. Orat. iv. § 12. Again, "Now man, begotten in time, in time also himself begets the child; and whereas from nothing he came to be, therefore his word also is over and continues not. But God is not as man, as Scripture has said; but is existing and is ever; therefore also His Word is existing and is everlastingly with the Father, as radiance from light." vid. Orat. ii. § 35.

¶ In other words, by the Divine γέννησις is not meant so much an act, as an eternal and unchangeable fact, in the Divine Essence. Arius, not admitting this, objected at the outset of the controversy to the phrase "always Father, always Son," Theod. Hist. i. 4, p. 749, and Eunomius argues that, "if the Son is co-eternal with the Father, the Father was never such in act, ἐνεργὸς, but was ἀργός." Cyril. Thesaur. v. p. 41. S. Cyril answers that *works*, ἔργα, are made ἔξωθεν, *from without*; but that our Lord is neither a "work" nor "from without." And hence he says elsewhere that, while men are fathers first in *posse* then in act, God is δυνάμει τε καὶ ἐνεργείᾳ πατήρ. Dial. 2, p. 458. Victorinus in like manner says, that God is "potentiâ et actione Deus sed in æternâ," Adv. Ar. i. 33; and he quotes S. Alexander, speaking apparently in answer to Arius, of a "semper generans generatio." And Arius scoffs at ἀειγεννὴς and ἀγεννητογενής. Theod. Hist. i. 4, p. 749. And Origen had said, ὁ σωτὴρ ἀεὶ γεννᾶται. ap. Routh. Reliq. t. 4, p. 304, and S. Dionysius calls Him the Radiance, ἄναρχον καὶ ἀειγενές. Athan. S. D. 15. And Athan. "As the Father is good always and by nature, so is He always generative by nature." Orat.

iii. § 66. S. Augustine too says, "Semper gignit Pater, et semper nascitur Filius." Ep. 238, n. 24. Petav. de Trin. ii. 5, n. 7, quotes the following passage from Theodorus Abucara, " Since the Son's generation does but signify His having His existence from the Father, which He has ever, therefore He is ever begotten. For it became Him, who is properly (κυρίως) the Son, ever to be deriving His existence from the Father, and not as we who derive its commencement only. In us generation is a way to existence ; in the Son of God it denotes the existence itself ; in Him it has not existence for its end, but it is itself an end, τέλος, and is perfect, τέλειον." Opusc. 26. Vid. art. *Father Almighty.*

Didymus however says, οὐκ ἔτι γεννᾶται, de Trin. iii. 3, p. 338, but with the intention of maintaining our Lord's perfection and eternity, as Hil. Trin. ii. 20. Naz. Orat. 20, 9 fin. Basil. de Sp. S. n. 20 fin. It is remarkable that Pope Gregory too objects to " Semper nascitur " as implying imperfection, and prefers Semper natus est. Moral. 29, 1 ; but this is a question of words.

Ἄθεος, ἀθεότης.

This epithet, in its passive sense, as used by St. Paul, Eph. ii. 12, (not in the sense of disowning or denying God, but of being disowned by Him,) is familiar with the Fathers in their denunciation of heretics and heathen, and with the heathen against Christians and others, who refused to worship their country's gods. Of course the active sense of the word is here and there more or less implied in the passive.

Thus Athan. says of Arius that "he is on all sides recognized as godless (atheist,) Arius Orat. i. § 4. And of Anomœan Aetius, "Aetius who was surnamed godless," Syn. § 6. Asterius too he seems to call atheist, including Valentinus and the heathen, Orat. iii. § 64. Eustathius calls the Arians ἀνθρώπους ἀθέους, who were attempting κρατῆσαι τοῦ θείου. Theod. Hist. i. 7, p. 760. And Arius complains that Alexander had expelled him and his from Alexandria, ὡς ἀνθρώπους ἀθέους ibid. i. 4.

¶ Since Christ was God, to deny Him was to deny God; but again, whereas the Son had revealed the "unknown God," and destroyed the reign of idols, the denial of the Son was bringing back idolatry and its attendant spiritual ignorance. Thus in the Orat. contr. Gent. § 29 fin, written before the Arian controversy, he speaks of "the Greek idolatry as full of all Atheism" or ungodliness, and contrasts with it the knowledge of "the Guide and Framer of the Universe, the Father's Word," "that through Him we may discern His Father, and the Greeks may know how far they have separated themselves from the truth." And, Orat. ii. § 43, he classes Arians with the Greeks, who, "though they have the name of God in their mouths, incur the charge of *Atheism,* because they know not the real and true God, *the Father of our Lord Jesus Christ.*" (vid. also Basil. in Eunom. ii. 22.) Shortly afterwards Athan. gives a further reason for the title, observing that Arianism was worse than previous heresies, such as Manicheism, inasmuch as the latter denied the Incarnation, but Arianism tore from God's substance His connatural Word, and, as far as its words went, infringed the perfections and being of the First Cause. And so ad Ep. Æg. § 17 fin. he says, that it alone, beyond other heresies, "has been bold against the Godhead Itself in a mad way, (μανικώτε-ρον,) denying that there is a Word, and that the Father was always Father."

¶ In like manner he says, ad Serap. iii. 2, that if a man says "that the Son is a creature, who is Word and Wisdom, and the Impress, and the Radiance, whom whoso seeth seeth the Father," he falls under the text, "Whoso denieth the Son, the same hath not the Father." "Such a one," he continues, "will in no long time say, *as the fool, There is no God.*" In like manner he speaks of those who think the Son to be the Spirit, as "without (ἔξω) the Holy Trinity, and atheists," Serap. iv. 6, "because they do not really believe in the God that is, and there is none other but He." And so again, " As the faith deliverèd [in the Holy Trinity] is one, and this unites us to God, and he who takes aught from the Trinity, and is baptized in the sole Name of the Father or of the Son, or in Father and Son without the Spirit, gains nothing, but remains empty and incomplete, both he and the professed administrator, (for in the Trinity is the perfection, [initiation,]) so whoso divides the Son from the Father, or degrades the Spirit to the creatures, hath neither the Son nor the Father, but is an atheist and worse than an infidel and anything but a Christian." Serap. i. 30.

¶ Elsewhere, he speaks more generally, as if Arianism introduced "an Atheism or rather Judaism *against the Scriptures*, being next door to Heathenism, so that its disciple cannot be even named Christian, for all such tenets are *contrary to the Scriptures ;*" and he makes this the reason why the Nicene Fathers stopped their ears and condemned it, Ep. Æg. § 13. Moreover, he calls the Arian persecution worse than the pagan *cruelties*, and therefore "a Babylonian Atheism," Ep. Encycl. § 5, as not allowing the Catholics the use of prayer and baptism, with a reference to Dan. vi. 11, &c. Thus too he calls Constantius atheist, for his treatment of Hosius, οὔτε τὸν θεὸν φοβηθεὶς ὁ ἄθεος, Hist. Arian. 45 ; and Nazianzen calls Lucius, on account of his cruelties in Alexandria, "this second Arius, the most copious river of the atheistic fountain." Orat. 25, 11. And Palladius, the Imperial officer, is ἀνὴρ ἄθεος. ibid. 12.

¶ Another reason for the title seems to have lain in the idolatrous character of Arian worship *on its own showing*, viz. as paying divine honours to One whom they yet maintained to be a creature.

¶ As to other heretics, Eusebius uses the word of Sabellius, Eccl. Theol. p. 63; of Marcellus, p. 80; of Phantasiasts, p. 64; of Valentinus, p. 114. Basil applies it to Eunomius.

¶ As to the heathen, Athan. speaks of the εἰδώλων ἀθεότητα, contr. Gent. § 14 and 46 init. Orat. iii. § 67, though elsewhere he contrasts apparently atheism with polytheism, Orat. iii. § 15 and 16. Nazianz. speaks of the πολύθεος ἀθεΐα, Orat. 25, 15. vid. also Euseb. Eccl. Theol. p. 73.

¶ On the other hand, Julian says that Christians preferred "atheism to godliness." vid. Suicer. Thes, in voc. It was a popular imputation upon Christians, as it had been before on philosophers and poets, some of whom better deserved it. On the word as a term of reproach, vid. Voet. Disput. 9. t. 1, pp. 115, &c. 195.

Αἰών.

By *αἰών*, age, seems to be meant duration, or the measure of duration, before or independent of the existence of motion, which is the measure of time. As motion, and therefore time, are creatures, so are the ages. Considered as the measure of duration, an age has a sort of positive existence, though not an *οὐσία* or substance, and means the same as "world," or an existing system of things viewed apart from time and motion. vid. Theodor. in Hebr. i. 2. Our Lord then is the Maker of the ages thus considered, as the Apostle also tells us, Hebr. xi. 3, and God is the King of the ages, 1 Tim. i. 17, or is before all ages, as being eternal, or *προαιώνιος*. However, sometimes the word is synonymous with eternity; "as time is to things which are under time, so ages to things which are everlasting," Damasc. Fid. Orth. ii. 1, and "ages of ages" stands for eternity; and then the "ages" or measures of duration, may be supposed to stand for the *ἰδέαι* or ideas in the Divine Mind, which seems to have been a Platonic or Gnostic notion. Hence Synesius, Hymn iii., addresses the Almighty as *αἰωνό-τοκε*, parent of the ages. Hence sometimes God Himself is called the Age, Clem. Alex. Hymn. Pæd. iii. fin., or the Age of ages, Pseudo-Dion. de Div. Nom. 5, p. 581, or again, *αἰώνιος*. Theodoret sums up what has been said thus: "Age is not any subsisting substance, but is an interval indicative of time, now infinite, when God is spoken of, now commensurate with creation, now with human life." Hær. v. 6. If then, as St. Paul says in Hebr. xi. 3, the Word is Maker of the ages, He is independent of duration altogether; He does not come to be in time, but is above and beyond it, or eternal. vid. Decr. 18. Elsewhere he says, " The words addressed to the Son in the 144th Psalm, ' Thy kingdom is a kingdom of all ages,' forbid any one to imagine any interval at all in which the Word did not exist. For if every interval is measured by ages, and of all the ages the Word is King and Maker, therefore, whereas no interval at all exists prior to Him, it were madness to say, ' There was once when the Everlasting (αἰώνιος) was not.' " Orat. i. 12. And so Alexander; " Is it not unreasonable that He who made times, and ages, and seasons, to all of which belongs 'was not,' should be said not to be? for, if so, that interval in which they say the Son was not yet begotten by the Father, precedes that Wisdom of God which framed all things." Theod. Hist. i. 3, p. 736. vid. also Basil. de Sp. S. n. 14. Hilar. de Trin. xii. 34.

The subject is treated of at length in Greg. Nyssen. contr. Eunom. i. t. 2. Append. p. 93—101. Vid. also Ambros. de Fid. i. 8—11. As time measures the material creation, so "ages" were considered to measure the immaterial, as the duration of Angels. This had been a philosophical distinction. Timæus says, εἰκών ἐστι χρόνος τῷ ἀγεννάτῳ χρόνῳ, ὂν αἰῶνα ποταγορεύομες. Vid. also Philo, p. 298, Quod Deus Immort. 6. Euseb. Laud. C. p. 501. Naz. Orat. 38, 8.

"Ακρατος,

SIMPLE, absolute, untempered, direct; an epithet applied
both by Catholics and Arians to the creative Hand of
God, as if the very contact of the Infinite with the finite,
which creation involves, would extinguish the nascent
creature which it was bringing into being. The
Arians attempted to find in this doctrine an argument
in favour of their own account of our Lord's nature.
They said that our Lord was created to be the instrument whereby the world could be created without that
perilous intervention of the Almighty Hand, which made
creation almost impossible. Decr. § 8, Orat. ii. § 25, 30.
Epiph. Hær. 76, p. 951. Cyril. Thes. pp. 150, 241. de
Trin. iv. p. 523. Basil. contr. Eunom. ii. 21, Orat. ii. 29.
But how was it, asked Catholics, that creation was possible at all, that is, in the case of our Lord Himself, on
supposing Him a creature? vid. Decr. § 8. Catholics on
their side had no difficulty to overcome: they considered that the Creator, by a special and extraordinary grace, supplied whatever was necessary for
bearing the mighty Hand of God, as also a parallel
grace is supplied for receiving safely the great privileges of the Gospel, especially the Holy Eucharist.

"Not as if He were a creature, nor as having any
relation in substance with the universe, is He called
First-born of it; but because, when at the beginning

He framed the creatures, He condescended to them that it might be possible for them to come into being. For they could not have endured His untempered nature and His splendour from the Father, unless, condescending by the Father's love for man, He had supported them and taken hold of them and brought them into substance." Orat. ii. § 64.

¶ He does not here say with Asterius that God could not create man immediately, for the Word is God, but that He did not create him without at the same time infusing a grace or presence from Himself into his created nature to enable it to endure His external plastic hand; in other words, that man was created *in Him*, not as something external to Him (in spite of the διὰ and ἐν in reference to the first and second creation, In Illud omn. 2). Vid. art. *Arian Tenets*, &c. and Gent. 47, where the συγκατάβασις is spoken of.

Ἀλήθεια,

Truth, whether true doctrine or reasoning, means the objective truth in contrast to subjective opinion or private judgment. Sometimes ἀλήθεια is used by itself, sometimes ἀληθείας λόγος, sometimes λόγος (vid. arts. *Rule of Faith* and ὀρθός). E. g. ὁ τῆς ἀληθείας λόγος ἐλέγχει, Orat. ii. 35. ὡς ὁ τῆς ἀληθείας ἀπῄτει λόγος, Ap. c. Ar. 36, where it is contrasted with ὡς ἤθελον (vid. above, art. *Private Judgment*); also Serap. ii. 2. Epiphanius; ὁ τῆς ἀλ. λ. ἀντιπίπτει αὐτῷ, Hær. 71, p. 830. Eusebius; ὁ τῆς ἀλ. λ. βοᾷ, Eccl. Theol. i. p. 62, and ἀντιφθέγξεται αὐτῷ μέγα βοήσας ὁ τῆς ἀλ. λ. ibid. iii. p. 164. And Council of Sardica; κατὰ τὸν τῆς ἀλ. λ. ap. Athan. Apol. contr. Ar. 46, where it seems equivalent to "fairness" or "impartiality." Asterius; οἱ τῆς ἀλ. ἀποφαίνονται λογισμοί, Orat. ii. 37. i. 32. de Syn. § 18 cir. fin, and so also τοῖς ἀλ. λογισμοῖς, Sent. D. 19. And so also, ἡ ἀλ. διήλεγξε, Orat. ii. § 18. ἡ φύσις καὶ ἡ ἀλ. "draw the meaning to themselves," § 5 init. τοῦ λόγου δεικνύντος, ibid. 3 init. ἐδείκνυεν ὁ λόγος, 13 fin. τῆς ἀλ. δειξάσης, 65 init. 60, ἐλέγχονται παρὰ τῆς ἀληθείας, 63, ἡ ἀλήθεια δείκνυσι, 70 init. τῆς ἀλ. μαρτυρησάσης, 1 init. τὸ τῆς ἀλ. φρόνημα μεγαληγορεῖν πρεπεῖ, § 31 init. and Decr. 17 fin. In some of these instances the words ἀλήθεια, λόγος, &c. are almost synonymous with the Regula Fidei; vid. παρὰ τὴν ἀλήθειαν, Orat. ii. § 36, and Origen de Princ. Præf. 1 and 2.

¶ " Had these expositions proceeded from orthodox men (ὀρθοδόξων), Hosius," &c. &c. Ep. Æg. 8. And, "Terms do not disparage His Nature ; rather that Nature draws to Itself those terms, and changes them." Orat. ii. § 3. Also de Mort. Ar. fin. And vid. Leont. contr. Nest. iii. 41. (p. 581, Canis.) He here seems alluding to the Semi-Arians, Origen, and perhaps the earlier Fathers.

¶ One of the characteristic points in Athanasius is his constant attention to the *sense* of doctrine, or the *meaning* of writers, in preference to the very words used. Thus he scarcely uses the symbol ὁμοούσιον, (one in substance,) throughout his Orations, and in the de Synod. acknowledges the Semi-Arians as brethren. Hence Decr. § 18, he says, that orthodox doctrine " is revered by all, though expressed in strange language, provided the speaker means religiously, and wishes to convey by it a religious sense." vid. also § 21. He says, that Catholics are able to " speak freely," or to expatiate, παῤῥησιαζόμεθα, " out of Divine Scripture." Orat. i. § 9. vid. de Sent. Dionys. § 20 init. Again : " The devil spoke from Scripture, but was silenced by the Saviour ; Paul spoke from profane writers, yet, being a saint, he has a religious meaning." de Syn. § 39. Again, speaking of the apparent contrariety between two Councils, " It were unseemly to make the one conflict with the other, for all their members are fathers ; and it were profane to decide that these spoke well and those ill, for all of them have slept in Christ." § 43 ; also § 47. Again : " Not the phrase, but the meaning and the religious life, is the recommendation of the faithful." ad Ep. Æg. § 9.

Ἀλογία, Ἄλογος.

THIS epithet is used by Athan. against the Arians, as if, by denying the eternity of the Logos (Reason or Word), first, they were denying the Intellectual nature of the Divine Essence; and, secondly, were forfeiting the source and channel of their own rational nature.

1. As to the first of these, he says, "Imputing to God's nature an absence of His Word, ἀλογίαν . . . they are most impious." Orat. i. § 14. Again, "Is the God, *who is*, ever without His rational Word?" Orat. i. § 24. iv. § 4 and 14. Also Sent. D. 16, 23, &c. Serap. ii. 2. Athenag. Leg. 11. Tat. contr. Græc. 5. Hipp. contr. Noet. 10. Nyssen. contr. Eunom. vii. p. 216. Orat. Catech. 1. Naz. Orat. 29, 17 fin. Cyril. Thesaur. xiv. p. 145. (vid. Petav. de Trin. vi. 9.)

¶ It must not be supposed from these instances that the Fathers meant that our Lord was literally what is called the *attribute* of reason or wisdom in the Divine Essence, or in other words that He was God merely viewed as God is wise; which would be a kind of Sabellianism. But, whereas their opponents said that He was but *called* Word and Wisdom *after* the attribute, they said that such titles marked, not only a typical resemblance to the attribute, but so full a correspondence and (as it were) coincidence in *nature* with it, that

whatever relation that attribute had to God, such in kind
had the Son ;—that the attribute was the Son's symbol, and not His mere archetype ;—that our Lord was
eternal and proper to God, because that attribute was
so, which was His title, vid. Athan. Ep. Æg. 14 ;—that
our Lord was that Essential Reason and Wisdom, not
by which the Father *is* wise, but *without* which the
Father was *not* wise ;—not, that is, in the way of a
formal cause, but in *fact*. Or, whereas the Father
Himself is Reason and Wisdom, the Son is the necessary issue of that Reason and Wisdom, so that, to say
that there was no Word, would imply there was no
Divine Reason ; just as a radiance supposes a light ; or,
as Petavius remarks, Trin. vi. 9, as the eternity of the
Original involves that of the Image ; τῆς ὑποστάσεως
ὑπαρχούσης, πάντως εὐθὺς εἶναι δεῖ τὸν χαρακτῆρα καὶ
εἰκόνα ταύτης. Orat. i. § 20. vid. also § 31. Decr. § 13.
Theod. Hist. i. 3, p. 737.

¶ Secondly, he says of the Arians themselves,
"Denying the Word of God, Reason have they forfeited." Decr. § 2. And again, " If they impute change
to the Word, their own reason is in peril." Orat. i.
§ 35. Hence Arianism, as denying the Word, is essentially madness. " Has not a man lost his mind who entertains the thought that God is wordless and wisdom-
less ?" Orat. ii. § 32. This will help us to understand
how it is he calls them ἀρειομανῖται. vid. art. *in voc.*

Ἄνθρωπος

In Greek and *homo* in Latin, are used by the Fathers to signify our Lord's manhood and again human nature, with an abruptness which, were it not so frequent, would be taken to give some sanction to Nestorianism.

Thus Athan., speaking of His receipt of grace, says "He, as far as *the man*, was exalted," Orat. i. § 5. "The Word being united to *the man*," Orat. iv. § 7. "Separating the hypostasis of God's Word from the Man from Mary," *ibid.* § 35. "I, the Word, am the Chrism, and that which has the Chrism from Me is the man," ibid. It illustrates this use of the word, that it is also used for human nature; e. g., "Of that was ὁ ἄνθρωπος in want, because of . . . the flesh and of death," Orat. i. § 41, vid. also iv. § 6.

¶ I will set down one or two specimens of the parallel use of *homo* among the Latins. ' Deus cum homine miscetur; hominem induit,' Cypr. Idol. ed. Ven. p. 538. 'Assumptus homo in Filium Dei,' Leon. Serm. 28, p.101. ' Suus [the Word's] homo,' ibid. 22, p. 70. ' Hic homo,' Ep. 31, p. 855. ' Hic homo, quem Deus suscepit.' Aug. Ep. 24, 3. vid. Tract. Theolog. μία φύσις, fin.

Ἀντίδοσις τῶν ἰδιωμάτων.

Since God and man are one Person, we are saved from the confusion which would otherwise follow from the union of two contrary natures. We may say intelligibly that God is man and man is God, because the attributes of those two contrary natures of Christ do not rest and abide in, and thereby destroy, each other, but belong to the one Person, and become one because they are His; and when we say that God becomes man, we mean that the Divine Person becomes man; and when we say that a man is the object of our worship, we mean that He is worshipped who is Himself also truly a man.

The word "Person," as the received term for expressing this union of natures, is later than Athan., who uses instead "He" and "His," the personal pronouns; but no writer can bring out the theological idea more forcibly than he.

¶ οὐκ ἄλλου, ἀλλὰ τοῦ κυρίου· and so οὐκ ἑτέρου τινὸς, Incarn. 18; also Orat. i. § 45, and iv. 35. Cyril. Thes. p. 197, and Anathem. 11, who defends this phrase against the Orientals.

¶ ἴδιον is another word by which Athan. signifies the later word "Person." "For when the flesh suffered, the Word was not external to it; and therefore is the passion said to be His: and when He did divinely His

Father's works, the flesh was not external to Him, but in the body itself did the Lord do them." Orat. iii. § 32, 3.

For ἴδιον, which occurs so frequently in Athan., vid. also Cyril. Anathem. 11. ἰδιοποιούμενον, Orat. iii. § 33 and 38. ad Epict. 6. fragm. ex Euthym. (t. i. p. 1275, ed. Ben.) Cyril. in Joann. p. 151. And οἰκείωται, contr. Apoll. ii. 16, Cyril. Schol. de Incarn. t. v. p. 782, Concil. Eph. t. 1. pp. 1644, 1697, (Hard.) Damasc. F. O. iii. 3, p. 208, ed. Ven. Vid. Petav. de Incarn. iv. 15.

For κοινὸν, opposed to ἴδιον. vid. Orat. iii. § 32, 51. Cyril. Epp. p. 23; "communem," Ambros. de Fid. i. 94.

Vid. Orat. iv. 6. This interchange is called theologically the ἀντίδοσις or communicatio ἰδιωμάτων. "Because of the perfect union of the flesh which was assumed, and of the Godhead which assumed it, the names are interchanged, so that the human is called from the divine and the divine from the human. Wherefore He who was crucified is called by Paul Lord of glory, and He who is worshipped by all creation of things in heaven, in earth, and under the earth, is named Jesus, &c." Nyssen. in Apoll. t. 2, pp. 697, 8.

"And on account of this, the properties of the flesh are said to be His, since He was in it, such as to hunger, to thirst, to suffer, to weary, and the like, of which the flesh is capable; while on the other hand the works proper to the Word Himself, such as to raise the dead, to restore sight to the blind, and to cure the woman with an issue of blood, He did through His own body. The Word bore the infirmities of the flesh,

as His own, for His was the flesh; and the flesh ministered to the works of the Godhead, because the Godhead
was in it, for the body was God's." Orat. iii. § 31.

"The birth of the flesh is a manifestation of human
nature, the bearing of the Virgin a token of divine
power. The infancy of a little one is shown in the
lowliness of the cradle, the greatness of the Highest is
proclaimed by the voices of Angels. He has the rudi-
ments of men whom Herod impiously plots to kill, He
is the Lord of all whom the Magi delight suppliantly
to adore, &c. &c. To hunger, thirst, weary, and sleep
are evidently human; but to satisfy five thousand on five
loaves, and to give the Samaritan living water, &c. &c. . ."
Leon. Ep. 28. 4. Serm. 51. Ambros. de Fid. ii. n. 58.
Nyssen. de Beat. t. 1, p. 767. Cassian. Incarn. vi. 22.
Aug. contr. Serm. Ar. c. 8. Plain and easy as such
statements seem in this and some parallel notes, they
are of the utmost importance in the Nestorian and
Eutychian controversies.

¶ "If any happen to be scandalized by the swathing
bands, and His lying in a manger, and the gradual
increase according to the flesh, and the sleeping in a
vessel, and the wearying in journeying, and the hungering in due time, and whatever else happen to one who
has become really man, let them know that, making a
mock of the sufferings, they are denying the nature;
and denying the nature, they do not believe in the
economy; and not believing in the economy, they
forfeit the salvation." Procl. ad Armen. p. 2. p. 615, ed.
1630.

The Ἀπαράλλακτον,

Unvarying or *exact*, i. e. Image. This was a word used by the Fathers in the Nicene Council to express the relation of the Son to the Father, and if they eventually went farther, and adopted the formula of the Homoüsion, this was only when they found that the Arians explained its force away. " When the Bishops said that the Word . . . was the Image of the Father, like to Him in all things and ἀπαράλλακτον, &c. . . . the party of Eusebius were caught whispering to each other that ' like ' &c. were common to us and to the Son, and that it was no difficulty to agree to these . . . So the Bishops were compelled to concentrate the sense of the Scriptures, and to say that the Son is ' consubstantial,' or ' one in substance,' that is, the same in likeness with the Father." Decr. § 20.

¶ The Eusebian party allowed that our Lord was like, and the image of, the Father, but in the sense in which a picture is like the original, differing from it in substance and in fact. In this sense they even allowed the strong word ἀπαράλλακτος, *exact* image, which, as I have said, had been used by the Catholics, (vid. Alexander, ap. Theod. Hist. i. 3, p. 740,) as by the Semi-Arians afterwards, who even added the words κατ' οὐσίαν, or "according to substance." Even this strong phrase, however, κατ' οὐσίαν ἀπαράλλακτος εἰκὼν, or ἀπαραλλάκτως ὅμοιος, or ἀπαράλλακτος ταυτότης, did not appear to the Council an adequate safeguard of the doctrine. Athan. notices, Syn. § 53, that "like" applies to qualities rather than to substance. Also Basil. Ep. 8, n. 3. "In itself it is frequently used of faint similitudes, and falling very far short of the original." Ep. 9, n. 3. Accordingly, the Council determined on the word ὁμοούσιον as implying, as Athan. Decr. § 20 expresses it, "the same in likeness," ταὐτὸν τῇ ὁμοιώσει, that the likeness might not be analogical. vid. Cyril. in Joan. l. iii. p. 302.

¶ Athan. says that in consistency those who professed the ἀπαράλλακτον should go further one way or the other. Syn. § 38. When they spoke of "like," Athan. says, they could not consistently mean anything short of "likeness of substance," for this is the only true likeness; and while they used the words ἀπαράλλακτος εἰκών, unvarying image, to exclude all essential likeness, they were imagining instead an image varying utterly from its original. While then he allows it, he is far from satisfied with the phrase ὅμοιος κατ᾽ οὐσίαν or ὁμοιούσιος; he rejects it on the very ground that when we speak of "like," we imply qualities, not substance. Every image varies from the original because it is an image. Yet he himself frequently uses it, as do other Fathers; vid. Orat. i. § 26, ὅμοιος τῆς οὐσίας. And all human terms are imperfect; and "image" itself is used in Scripture.

¶ Ἀπαράλλακτος εἰκὼν κατ᾽ οὐσίαν was practically the symbol of Semi-Arianism, not because it did not admit of a religious explanation, but because it marked the limit of Semi-Arian approximation to the absolute truth. It was in order to secure the true sense of ἀπαράλλακτον that the Council adopted the word ὁμοούσιον. Ἀπαράλλακτον is accordingly used as a familiar word by Athan. de Decr. supr. § 20, 24. Orat. iii. § 36. contr. Gent. 41, 46 fin. Provided with a safe evasion of its force, the Arians had no difficulty in saying it after him. Philostorgius ascribes it to Asterius, and Acacius quotes a passage from his writings containing it. (vid. Epiph. Hær. 72, 6.) Acacius at the same time forcibly expresses what is meant by the word, τὸ ἔκτυπον καὶ τρανὲς ἐκμαγεῖον τοῦ θεοῦ τῆς οὐσίας. In this he speaks as S. Alexander, τὴν κατὰ πάντα ὁμοιότητα αὐτοῦ ἐκ φύσεως ἀπομαξάμενος Theod. Hist. i. 3, p. 740 (as, in the legend, the impression of our Lord's face on the cloth at His passion). Χαρακτήρ, Hebr. i. 3, contains the same idea. "An image not inanimate, not framed by the hand, nor work of art and imagination, (ἐπινοίας,) but a living image, yea, the very life (αὐτοοῦσα); ever preserving the unvarying (τὸ ἀπαράλλακτον), not in likeness of fashion, but in its very substance." Basil. contr. Eunom. i. 18. The Auctor de Trinitate says, speaking of the word in this very creed, "Will in nothing varying from will (ἀπαράλλακτος) is the *same* will; and power nothing varying from power is the *same* power; and glory nothing varying from glory is the *same* glory." The Macedonian replies, "Unvarying I say, the same I say not." Dial. iii. p. 993 (Theod. t. v.), Athan. de Decr. l. c. seems to say the same. That is, in the Catholic sense, the image was not ἀπαράλλακτος, if there was *any* difference, if He was not one with Him of whom He was the image. vid. Hil. de Syn. 91. ad Const. ii. 5. And the heretical party saw that it was impossible to deny the ὁμοούσιον and περιχώρησις, and yet maintain the ἀπαράλλακτον, without holding two Gods. Hence the ultimate resolution of the Semi-Arians, partly into orthodox, partly into Anomœans.

¶ "What sort of faith have they who stand neither to word nor writing, but alter and change everything according to the season? For if, O Acacius and Eudoxius, you do not decline the faith published at the Dedication, and in it is written that the Son is "Exact Image of God's substance," why is it ye write in Isauria, "we reject 'the Like in substance'"? for if the Son is not like the Father in respect of substance, how is He "exact image of the substance?" But if you are dissatisfied at having written "Exact Image of the substance," how is it that ye anathematize those who say that the Son is Unlike? for if He be not according to substance like, He is altogether unlike: and the Unlike cannot be an Image. And if so, then it does not hold that *he that hath seen* the Son, *hath seen the Father*, there being then the greatest difference possible between Them, or rather the One being wholly Unlike the Other. And Unlike cannot possibly be called Like. By what artifice then do ye call Unlike like, and consider Like to be unlike, and so pretend to say that the Son is the Father's Image? for if the Son be not like the Father in substance, something is wanting to the Image." Syn. § 38.

᾽Απαύγασμα,

RADIANCE or shine. This is St. Paul's word, Hebr. i. 3, taken from Wisdom vii. 26, and suggesting the "Light from Light" of the Nicene Creed. It is the familiar illustration used by Athan. to convey the idea of the Divine Sonship, as consubstantial and from eternity. He sometimes uses the image of fire, Orat. iv. § 2 and 10, but it is still fire and its *radiance*. However, we find the illustration of fire from fire, Justin. Tryph. 61 Tatian. contr. Græc. 5. At this early day the illustration of radiance might have a Sabellian bearing, as that of fire in Athan.'s had an Arian. Hence Justin protests against those who considered the Son as "like the sun's light in the heaven," which " when it sets, goes away with it," whereas it is as "fire kindled from fire." Tryph. 128. Athenagoras, however, like Athanasius, says "as Light from Fire," using also the word ἀπόῤῥοια, *effluence*. Vid. also Orig. Periarchon, i. 2, n. 4. Tertull. Apol. 21. Theogn. ap. Athan. Decr. § 25.

Ἀποῤῥοή.

THIS word, though in itself unobjectionable as an expression of the divine γέννησις, is generally avoided by the Fathers as being interpreted by the Arians in a material sense. "The offspring of men are portions of their fathers," says Athanasius, "and men ἀποῤῥέουσι in begetting, and gain substance in taking food; but God, being without parts, is Father of a Son without partition or passion, for there is neither ἀποῤῥοὴ in the Immaterial nor ἐπιῤῥοὴ, and, being uncompounded by nature, He is Father of One only Son. And He too is the Father's Word, from which may be understood the impassible nature of the Father, in that not even a human word is begotten with passion, much less the Word of God." Decr. § 11.

¶ S. Cyril, Dial. iv. init. p. 505, speaks of the θρυλλουμένη ἀποῤῥοή; and disclaims it, Thesaur. 6, p. 43. Athanasius disclaims it, Expos. § 1. Orat. i § 21. So does Alexander, ap. Theod. Hist. i. 3, p. 743. On the other hand, Athanasius quotes it in a passage which he adduces from Theognostus, Decr. § 25, and from Dionysius, de Sent. D. § 22, and Origen uses it, Periarchon, i. 2. It is derived from Wisd. vii. 25.

The passage of Theognostus is as follows:—

¶ "The substance of the Son is not anything gained from without, nor provided out of nothing, but it sprang from the Father's substance, as the radiance of light, as the vapour of water; for neither the radiance, nor the vapour, is the water itself or the sun itself, nor is it alien; but it is an effluence of the Father's substance, which, however, suffers no partition. For as the sun remains the same, and is not impaired by the rays poured forth by it, so neither does the Father's substance suffer change, though it has the Son as an Image of Itself." Decr. § 25. "Vapour" is also used in Wisdom vii., Origen, &c. as referred to *supr.*

¶ Hieracas the Manichæan compared the Two Divine Persons to the two lights of one lamp, where the oil is common and the flame double, thus implying a substance distinct from Father and Son of which each partook, or to a flame divided into two by (for instance) the papyrus which was commonly used instead of a wick. vid. Hilar. de Trin. vi. 12.

Ἀρειομανῖται,

A TITLE of the Arians. "The dumb ass forbade the *madness* of the prophet," παραφρονίαν. On the word Ἀρειομανῖται, Gibbon observes, "The ordinary appellation with which Athanasius and his followers chose to compliment the Arians, was that of Ariomanites," ch. xxi. note 61. Rather, the name originally was a state title, enjoined by Constantine, vid. Petav. de Trin. i. 8 fin. Naz. Orat. 43, 30, p. 794, note e., and thenceforth used by the general Church, e. g. Eustathius of Antioch, ap. Theod. Hist. i. 7. Constant. ap. Concil. t. i. p. 456, Hilar. de Trin. vii. n. 7. note, Julius ap. Athan. Apol. c. Ar. 23. Council of Egypt, ibid. 77. vid. also 6. Phœbadius contr. Arian. 22. Epiph. Hær. 69. 19. (ὁ μανιώδης Ἄρειος.) Greg. Naz. Orat. ii. 37. τὴν Ἀρείου καλῶς ὀνομασθεῖσαν μανίαν, and so ὁ τῆς μανίας ἐπώνυμος, Orat. 43. 30. vid. also Orat. 20. 5. and so Proclus, τὴν Ἀρείου μανίαν, ad Armen. p. 618 fin. And Athan. e. g. μανίαν διαβόλου, ad Serap. i. 1. also ad Serap. i. 17 fin. 19 init. 20, 24, 29. ii. 1 fin. iv. 5 init. 6 fin. 15 fin. 16 fin. In some of these the denial of the divinity of the Holy Ghost is the madness. In like manner Hilary speaks continually of their "furor," de Trin. i. 17.

¶ Several meanings are implied in this title; the real reason for it was the fanatical fury with which it spread and maintained itself; (cf. on' the other hand, ὁ μανικὸς ἐραστὴς τοῦ χριστοῦ, enthusiastic. Chrysost. in Esai. vi. 1. Hom. iv. 3, t. 6, p. 124.) Thus Athan. contrasts the Arian hatred of the truth, with the mere worldliness of the Meletians, Ep. Æg. 22. Hence they are ἀσεβεῖς, χριστομάχοι, and governed by κακόνοια and κακοφροσύνη.

Again, Socrates speaks of it as a flame which ravaged, ἐπενέμετο, provinces and cities. i. 6. And Alexander cries out, ὦ ἀνοσίου τύφου καὶ ἀμέτρου μανίας. Theod. Hist. i. 3, p. 741. vid. also pp. 735, 6. 747. And we read much of their eager spirit of proselytism. Theod. ibid. The word *mania* may be taken to express one aspect of it in English. Their cruelty came into this idea of their "mania;" hence Athan. in one place calls the Arian women, in the tumult under George of Cappadocia, *Mœnades.* "They, running up and down like Bacchanals and furies, μαινάδες καὶ ἐρινννύες, thought it a misfortune not to find opportunity for injury, and passed that day in grief in which they could do no harm." Hist. Arian. 59. Also, "profana Arianorum novitas velut quædam Bellona aut Furia." Vincent. Common. 4. Eustathius speaks of οἱ παράδοξοι τῆς ἀρείου θυμέλης μεσόχοροι. ap. Phot. 225, p. 759. And hence the strange paronomasia of Constantine, Ἄρες, ἄρειε, with an allusion to Hom. Il. v. 31.

¶ A second reason, or rather sense, of the appellation was what is noted, supr. art. ἀλογία, that, denying the Word, they have forfeited the gift of reason, e. g. τῶν 'Αρειομανιτῶν τὴν ἀλογίαν. de Sent.

Dion. init. vid. ibid. 24 fin. Orat. ii. § 32. iii. § 63 throughout. Hence in like manner Athan. speaks of the heathen as mad who did not acknowledge God and His Word. contr. Gent. fin. also 23 fin. Hence he speaks of εἰδωλομανία. contr. Gent. 10. and 21 fin. Again, Incarn. 47, he speaks of the *mania* of oracles, which belongs rather to the former sense of the word.

¶ Other heresies had the word *mania* applied to them, e. g. that of Valentinus, Athan. Orat. ii. § 70. κἂν μαινῆται. Epiphanius speaks of the ἐμμανὴς διδασκαλία of the Noetians. Hær. 57. 2. Nazianzen contrasts the sickness, νόσος, of Sabellius with the madness of Arius, Orat. 20. 5; but Athan. says, μαίνεται μὲν Ἄρειος, μαίνεται δὲ Σαβέλλιος, Orat. iv. 25. Manes also was called mad; "Thou must hate all heretics, but especially him who even in name is a maniac." Cyril. Catech. vi. 20. vid. also ibid. 24 fin.—a play upon the name. But this note might be prolonged indefinitely.

Ἀρχὴ,

First principle or *beginning*. This is a term employed both in expounding the doctrine of the Holy Trinity and in that of the Incarnation. For its employment in the former of these, *vid.* art. *Father Almighty.* As to the second, it expresses the great providential office of the Second Person towards the universe, spiritual and material, which He has created. The creature, as such, is insufficient for itself; and He who gave it being gives it also a grace above its nature to enable it to use and enjoy that being well and happily. Nor is it a mere gift of power or health, as a quality, but it is the very Presence of the Word, the Second Person of the Blessed Trinity, in the creature, of which Presence a certain perfection of being and a continuous life is the result. A still more wonderful dispensation or Economy is revealed to us pre-eminently in the Gospel, vid. *Deification, Grace, Sanctification, Indwelling,* &c.; but such a grace has been and is exercised in the first instance towards the material and Angelic world, and the title given to the Word in exercising this high Providential office is that of ἀρχή. Vid. also arts. ἄκρατος, συγκατάβασις, πρωτότοκος.

This office of the Word, it is plain, commences from the first moment of creation, and in its very nature implies divinity. It is spoken of in Scripture, viz. in the Proverbs,—" Dominus possedit Me in *initio* viarum suarum ;" a passage to which the Arians appealed in the controversy more than to any other place in Scripture. It is in refutation of their arguments that Athan. introduces his own grand dissertation upon the sense of *ἀρχή*. The Arians interpreted it as meaning that the Personal Word and Son of God was the work with which creation commenced, that is, He was the first creature. Athan. lays it down that He was not the beginning in the sense of being the first of the whole number of creatures, but as heading the creation of God. He could not have been the first of all, if He had been one of all. As being an *efficax initium,* or an *initium* that initiates, He is more than a beginning ; He is a cause : He could not initiate, unless He were divine. He entered creation by an act of condescension, in order to associate it with His own greatness. Vid. Orat. ii. § 49. And ibid. § 60, " He who is before all is not a beginning of all, but is other than all." Yet again, He is a beginning, because He begins the beginning.

In this there is an analogy to the circumstances of His Incarnation. His inhabiting and vivifying creation implies attributes of the Supreme Being : He could not be by office πρωτότοκος without first being μονογενής; and in like manner in the Gospel He is able to stoop to be our Mediator, and to be a Priest making atonement for us, and to be our brother gaining blessings for us, because, though man, He is more than mere man. vid. *Priesthood.* Such is the force, as Athan. says, of the " wherefore " in Ps. xliv.; *because* He is by nature God, *therefore* He was able to be exalted as Mediator.

In consequence of this close analogy between the circumstances of Creation and Redemption, our Lord is called ἀρχὴ by Athan. in both dispensations. There is an initial grace necessary for the redeemed, if they are to partake of the redemption, as well as for their having a place in creation. Vid. the passages quoted under *Spiritual Freedom.*

The Ἄτρεπτον,

THAT is, of a nature capable of change in ethical character. Arius maintained this of our Lord in the strongest language in the earlier statements of his heresy. "On being asked (says Alexander) whether the Word of God is capable of altering, as the devil altered, they scrupled not to say, 'Yes, he is capable.'" Socr. i. 6. vid. the anathema at Sirmium on those who said τὸν λόγον τροπὴν ὑπομεμενηκότα. supr. vol. i. p. 111, note 4.

It was indeed difficult, with their opinions, to exclude the notion that change of some kind belonged to Him; nay, that He was not only in nature τρεπτὸς, but in fact ἀλλοιούμενος. (vid. Decr. § 23. Orat. ii. § 6.) It would be strange if they stopped short of this, as soon as they came to hold that our Lord's superhuman nature took the place of a soul, and was dependent on the body; and they scarcely would encumber themselves with the mystery of a double ἡγεμονικὸν, when they had thrown aside the "mysterium pietatis." This they seem to have done even in S. Athanasius's lifetime; for he speaks of them in contr. Apoll. i. 15, as supposing that the Saviour took flesh only, and thus imputing suffering to the impassible Godhead. Vid. also Ambros. de Fid. iii. n. 38. Also an assumption of this tenet seems involved (vid. Macrostich 6,) in the ground assigned for condemning the Sabellians. vid. supr. vol. i. p. 106.

This tenet was the connecting point between Arians and Apollinarians. Both held that our Lord was a sort of man made up of a divine being and a brute animal, and what Athan. and other Fathers say against the Apollinarians serves against the Arians also. Ἄτρεπτος μένων &c. he says, Orat. ii. § 6, against the Arians, and so against Apollinaris he says, ὁ λόγος ἄνθρωπος γέγονε, μένων θεός. ii. 7. vid. also ibid. 3 circ. init. So ὃ μὲν ἦν, διέμεινεν· ὃ δὲ οὐκ ἦν, προσέλαβεν. Naz. Orat. 29, 19. οὐσία μένουσα ὅπερ ἐστί. Chrysost. ap. Theodor. Eran. p. 47. ὃ ἦν ἔμεινε δι' ἑαυτὸν, καὶ ὃ ἠθέλησε γέγονε δι' ἡμᾶς. Procl. ad Arm. Ep. ii. p. 615, ed. 1630. vid. also Maxim. Opp. t. 2, ed. 1675. ὅπερ ἦν διαμένων, καὶ γενόμενος ὅπερ οὐκ ἦν. p. 286. vid. also p. 264. "manens id quod erat, factus quod non erat." August. cons. Ev. i. n. 53 fin. "Non omiserat quod erat, sed cœperat esse quod non erat." Hilar. Trin. iii. 16. "non amittendo quod suum erat, sed suscipiendo quod nostrum erat." Vigil. contr. Eut. i. 13, p. 498, —(Bibl. P. ed. 1624,) and so Leo.

Βουλὴ, κατὰ βούλησιν.

ONE of the arguments, on which the Arians laid most stress in controversy, was the received doctrine, as it may be considered, that our Lord's *gennesis* was κατὰ τὸ βούλημα of the Father. Athanasius says that the doctrine is not only heretical in its application, but in its source, though still not necessarily heretical, viewed in itself. " The phrase," he says, " is from the heretics, and the words of heretics are suspicious." Orat. iii. § 59; and in corroboration he might allege various heterodox writers. E.g. of these, Tatian had said θελήματι προπηδᾷ ὁ λόγος. Gent. 5. Tertullian had said, "Ut primum voluit Deus ea edere, ipsum primum protulit Sermonem." adv. Prax. 6. Novatian, " Ex quo, quando ipse voluit, Sermo filius natus est." de Trin. 31. And Constit. Apost. τὸν πρὸ αἰώνων εὐδοκίᾳ τοῦ πατρὸς γεννηθέντα. vii. 41. Also Pseudo-Clem. " Genuit Deus voluntate præcedente." Recognit. iii. 10. And Eusebius, κατὰ γνώμην καὶ προαίρεσιν βουληθεὶς ὁ θεὸς and ἐκ τῆς τοῦ πατρὸς βουλῆς καὶ δυνάμεως. Dem. iv. 3. Arius, of course, θελήματι καὶ βουλῇ ὑπέστη, ap. Theod. Hist. i. 4, p. 750, and supr. vol. i. p. 84, Arius's Creed.

This is true, but far higher authorities can be cited in favour of the phrase, so that Athan. feels it necessary to guard and soften his adverse judgment upon it. Hence he says, " If any orthodox believer were to use these words in simplicity, there would be no cause to be suspicious of them, the orthodox intention prevailing over that somewhat simple use of words." Orat. iii. § 59 (*Disc.* n. 49). And, "Had these expositions of theirs proceeded from the great confessor Hosius, Maximinus, Philogonius, Eustathius, Julius, &c. &c." Ep. Æg. 8. But, after all, his admissions in favour of the phrase do not go far enough, as the following specimens of the use of it will show :—

S. Ignatius speaks of our Lord as " Son of God according to the will (θέλημα) and power of God." ad Smyrn. 1. S. Justin as "God and Son according to His will, βουλήν." Tryph. 127. and "begotten from the Father at His will, θελήσει." ibid. 61. and he says, δυνάμει καὶ βουλῇ αὐτοῦ. ibid. 128. S. Clement, " issuing from the Father's will itself quicker than light." Gent. 10 fin. S. Hippolytus, " Whom God the Father, having willed, βουληθείς, begat as He willed, ὡς ἠθέλησεν." contr. Noet. 16. Origen, ἐκ θελήματος. ap. Justin ad. Menn. (in Concil. Const. ii. p. 274, Hard.). vid. also "cum filius charitatis etiam voluntatis." Periarch. iv. 28.

But what is more to the purpose still, Athan. uses the phrase himself, and thereby necessarily sanctions the doctrine which it represents, in one passage in his Discourses, viz. in Orat. iii. § 31. " Our Lord was ever God," he says, " and hallowed those to whom He came, arranging all things κατὰ τὸ βούλημα τοῦ πατρός." And similarly he says, " Men came into being through the Word, ὅτε αὐτὸς ὁ πατὴρ ἠθέλησε." Orat. i. § 63.

¶ Now let us consider what the argument was which

the Arians founded on this phrase, and how it was to be refuted.

They threw it into the form of a dilemma thus: "Was our Lord's *gennesis* with or without the Father's will? If with, then He who willed the Son's existence, could have not willed it, or could unwill it now; if without, then it is the blind action of some unknown cause or fate, not the act of the Living Almighty God." If the first of these alternatives was accepted, then followed two conclusions, both contradictory of our Lord's divinity. "God is self-existent; but a son depends on his father's will:— God is eternal; but a son is posterior to his father's will. For both reasons the Son is not God." If the second alternative is taken, then Necessity is sovereign, and God ceases to be.

This reasoning, which in the first instance they applied to our Lord's *gennesis*, they proceeded to apply to all His divine acts also. As He was a being depending for his being, life, and powers on the will of the Supreme God, his Maker, so His great works in creation, conservation, and moral governance, in redemption and sanctification, were all done in obedience to definite commands and fiats of His Almighty Father.

Such was the Arian argument, yet it was not very difficult to expose its fallacy, while admitting the κατὰ τὸ βούλημα to be orthodox; and one can only suppose that Athan. in fact found Catholics perplexed and disturbed by the use the Arians made of it, and felt tender towards those who were not clear-headed. It was scarcely more than another form of the original objection that a son must be posterior to his father, as if the conditions of time existed in eternity. "Sooner" and "later" imply succession, and vanish when time is no longer. It is customary to lay down that with Omnipotence to say is to do: "He spake and it was done;" and if in creation, which is a work in time, to determine and to effect is one act, how much more really is succession unknown to the Ancient of days, who is at once the Alpha and Omega, the Beginning and the End! Then as to the alternative of the Divine acts being subject to necessity or fate, it is obvious to ask whether the Supreme Being is not good and just, omnipotent, and all-blessed, κατὰ τὸ βούλημα, yet could He change His nature? could He make virtue vice, and vice virtue? If He cannot destroy Himself, and would not be God if He could or would, why should He cease to be God, if He cannot be, nor can will to be, without a Son? Such thoughts are as profane as they are unmeaning; and in the presence of them, Athanasius begs God to pardon him, if his Arian opponents force him to entertain them.

The *gennesis*, he says, belongs to the Divine Nature, as the Divine Attributes do, and, as we cannot explain why and how the moral law is what it is, so neither can we understand how Father and Son are what They are. "They say," he observes, "'Unless the Son has by the Father's will come into being, it follows that the Father had a Son of necessity and against His good pleasure.' Who is it who imposes necessity on Him? ... What is contrary to will they see; but what is greater and transcends it, has escaped their perception.

For, as what is besides purpose is contrary to will, so what is according to nature transcends and precedes counselling. . . . The Son is not external to the Father, wherefore neither does [the Father] counsel concerning Him, lest He appear to counsel about Himself. As far then as the Son transcends the creature, by so much does what is by nature transcend the will. . . . For let them tell us, that God is good and merciful, does this attach to Him by will or not? if by will, we must consider that He began to be good, and that His not being good is possible. . . . Moreover, the Father Himself, does He exist, first having counselled, then being pleased, to exist, or before counselling?" Orat. iii. § 62, 63.

Thus he makes the question a nugatory one, as if it did not go to the point, and could not be answered, or might be answered either way, as the case might be. Really Nature and Will go together in the Divine Being, but in order, as we regard Him, Nature is first, Will second, and the generation belongs to Nature, not to Will. He says, "Whereas they deny what is by nature, do they not blush to place before it what is by will? If they attribute to God the willing about things which are not, why recognize they not that in God which lies above the will? now it is a something that surpasses will that He should be by nature, and should be Father of His proper Word." Orat. ii. § 2. In like manner S. Epiphanius: "He begat Him neither willing, θέλων, nor not willing, but in nature, which is above will, βουλήν. For He has the nature of the Godhead, neither needing will, nor acting without will." Hær. 69, 26. vid. also Ancor. 51, and Ambros. de Fid. iv. 4. Vid. others, as collected in Petav. Trin. vi. 8. § 14—16.

¶ It would seem then that the phrase "by the Father's will," is only objectionable, as giving rise to interpretations erroneous and dangerous. vid. Decr. § 18. Hence Athan. says, "It is all one to say 'at will,' and 'once He was not.'" Orat. iii. § 61. But as this needed not be the interpretation of the phrase, and it is well to keep to what has been received, therefore, as the earlier Fathers had used it, so did those who came after Arius. Thus Nyssen in the passage in contr. Eun. vii. referred to lower down. And S. Hilary, "Nativitatis perfecta natura est, ut qui ex substantiâ Dei natus est, etiam ex consilio ejus et voluntate nascatur." Hilar. Syn. 37. The same father says, "charitate Patris et virtute," in Psalm xci. 8, and "ut voluit qui potuit, ut scit qui genuit." Trin. iii. 4. And he addresses Him as "non invidum bonorum tuorum in Unigeniti tui nativitate." ibid. vi. 21. S. Basil too speaks of our Lord as αὐτοζωὴν καὶ αὐτοάγαθον, "from the quickening Fountain, the Father's goodness, ἀγαθότητος." contr. Eun. ii. 25. And Cæsarius calls Him ἀγάπην πατρός. Quæst. 39. Vid. Ephrem. Syr. adv. Scrut. R. vi. 1. Oxf. Trans. and note there. Maximus Taurin. says, that God is "per omnipotentiam Pater." Hom. de trad. Symb. p. 270, ed. 1784. vid. also Chrysol. Serm. 61. Ambros. de Fid. iv. 8. Petavius in addition refers to such passages as one just quoted from S. Hilary, speaking of God as not "invidus," so as not to communicate Himself, since He was able. "Si non potuit, infirmus; si noluit, invidus." August. contr. Maxim. ii. 7.

Hence, in order to secure the phrase from an heretical tendency, the Fathers adopted two safeguards, both of which are recognized by Athanasius. As regards the relation between the βούλημα and the γέννησις, they made a distinction between the βουλὴ προηγουμένη and the σύνδρομος, the precedent and the concomitant will; and as to the relation between the βούλημα and creation &c., they took care that the Son Himself should be called the βουλὴ or βούλημα of the Father. vid. supr. *Mediation*, p. 220.

¶ As to the *precedent* will, which Athan. notices, Orat. iii. § 60, it has been mentioned in Recogn. Clem. supr. p. 385. For Ptolemy vid. Epiph. Hær. p. 215. Those Catholics who allowed that our Lord was θελήσει, explained it as a σύνδρομος θέλησις, and not a προηγουμένη; as Cyril. Trin. ii. p. 450. And with the same meaning S. Ambrose, "nec voluntas ante Filium nec potestas." de Fid. v. n. 224. And S. Gregory Nyssen, "His immediate union, ἄμεσος συνάφεια, does not exclude the Father's will, βούλησιν, nor does that will separate the Son from the Father." contr. Eunom. vii. p. 206, 7. vid. the whole passage. The alternative which these words, σύνδρομος and προηγουμένη, expressed was this; whether an act of Divine Purpose or Will took place *before* the *gennesis* of the Son, or whether both the Will and the *gennesis* were eternal, as the Divine Nature was eternal. Hence Bull says, with the view of exculpating Novatian, " Cum Filius dicitur ex Patre, quando ipse voluit, nasci, *velle* illud

Patris æternum fuisse intelligendum," Defens. F. N. iii. 8. § 8, though Novatian's word *quando* is against this interpretation.

¶ Two distinct meanings may be attached to "by will," (as Dr. Clarke observes, Script. Doct. vol. iv. p. 142, ed. 1738,) either a concurrence or acquiescence, or a positive act. S. Cyril uses it in the former sense, when he calls it σύνδρομος, as referred to above ; in the latter, when he says that "the Father wills His own subsistence, θελητής ἐστι, but is not what He is from any will, ἐκ βουλήσεως τινὸς," Thes. p. 56 ; Dr. Clarke would apply to the *gennesis* the ἐκ βουλήσεως, with a view of inferring that the Son was subsequent to a Divine act, i. e. not eternal ; but what Athan. says leads to the conclusion, that it does not matter which sense is taken. He does not meet the Arian objection, "if not by will therefore by necessity," by speaking of a concomitant will, or by merely saying that the Almighty exists or is good, by will, with S. Cyril, but he says that "nature *transcends* will and necessity also." Accordingly, Petavius is even willing to allow that the ἐκ βουλῆς is to be ascribed to the γέννησις in the sense which Dr. Clarke wishes, i.e. he grants that it may precede the γέννησις, i.e. in *order*, not in time, viz. the succession of our ideas, Trin. vi. 8. § 20, 21 ; and follows S. Austin, Trin. xv. 20, in preferring to speak of our Lord rather as " voluntas de voluntate," than, as Athan. is led to do, as the " voluntas Dei."

¶ As to our Lord being the Father's βουλὴ, and thereby the concomitant βούλημα, Athan. declares it, Orat. ii. § 31. iii. § 63. Thus in the first of these places, " Since the Word is the Son of God by nature, and is from Him and in Him, so the Father without Him works nothing. *God said, Let there be light. . . . He spoke and it was done. . . .* He spoke, not that some under-worker might hear and learn His will who spoke, and go away and do it,. for the Word is the Father's Will."

¶ ζῶσα βουλή, supr. Orat. ii. 2. Cyril. in Joan. p. 213. ζῶσα δύναμις, Sabell. Greg. 5. ζῶσα εἰκὼν, Naz. Orat. 30, 20. ζῶσα ἐνέργεια, Syn. Antioch. ap. Routh, Reliqu. t. 2, p. 469. ζῶσα ἰσχὺς, Cyril. in Joan. p. 951. ζῶσα σοφία, Origen. contr. Cels. iii. fin. ζῶν λόγος, Origen. ibid.

¶ ἀγαθοῦ πατρὸς ἀγαθὸν βούλημα. Clem. Pæd. iii. p. 309. σοφία, χρηστότης, δύναμις, θέλημα παντοκρατορικόν. Strom. v. p. 546. " Voluntas et potestas patris." Tertull. Orat. 4. " Natus ex Patre velut quædam voluntas ejus ex mente procedens." Origen. Periarch. i. 2. § 6. S. Jerome notices the same interpretation of "by the will of God," in the beginning of Comment. in Ephes. S. Austin on the other hand, as just now referred to, says, " Some divines, to avoid saying that the Only-begotten Word is the Son of the counsel or will of God, have named Him the very Counsel or Will of the Father. But I think it better to speak of Him as Counsel from Counsel, Will from Will, as Substance from Substance, Wisdom from Wisdom." Trin. xv. 20. And so Cæsarius, ἀγάπη ἐξ ἀγάπης. Qu. 39. supr. vid. for other instances Tertullian's Works, Oxf. Tr. Note I.

¶ And so Cyril. Thes. p. 54, who uses it expressly, (as has been said above, p. 220,) in contrast to the κατὰ βούλησιν of the Arians, though Athan. uses κατὰ τὸ βούλημα, also (as in Orat. iii. 31.) :— αὐτὸς τοῦ πατρὸς θέλημα says Nyss. contr. Eunom. xii. p. 345. The principle to be observed in the use of such words is this; that we must ever speak of the Father's will, command, &c. and the Son's fulfilment, assent, &c. as if one act.

¶ Vid. de Decr. 9. contr. Gent. 46. Iren. Hær. iii. 8, n. 3. Origen contr. Cels. ii. 9. Tertull. adv. Prax. 12 fin. Patres Antioch. ap. Routh. t. 2, p. 468. Prosper in Psalm. 148. (149.) Basil. de Sp. S. n. 20. Hilar. Trin. iv. 16. vid. art. *Mediation.* "That the Father speaks and the Son hears, or contrariwise, that the Son speaks and the Father hears, are expressions for the sameness of nature and the agreement of Father and Son." Didym. de Sp. S. 36. "The Father's bidding is not other than His Word; so that 'I have not spoken of Myself' He perhaps meant to be equivalent to 'I was not born from Myself.' For if the Word of the Father speaks, He pronounces Himself, for He is the Father's Word, &c." August. de Trin. i. 26. On this mystery vid. Petav. Trin. vi. 4.

¶ "When God commands others, ... then the hearer answers, ... for each of these receives the Mediator Word which makes known the will of the Father; but when the Word Himself works and creates, there is no questioning and answer, for the Father is in Him, and the Word in the Father; but it suffices to will, and the work is done." Orat. ii. § 31. Such is the Catholic doctrine. For the contrary Arian view, even when it is highest, vid. Euseb. Eccl. Theol. iii. 3; (also vid. supra, art. *Eusebius.*) In the above passage, p. 164, the Father's νεύματα are spoken of, a word common with the Arians. Euseb. ibid. p. 75. de Laud. Const. p. 528. Eunom. Apol. 20 fin. The word is used of the Son's command given to the creation, in Athan. contr. Gent. e. g. 42, 44, &c. S. Cyril. Hier. frequently, as the Arians, uses it of the Father. Catech. x. 5. xi. passim. xv. 25, &c. The difference between the orthodox and Arian views on this point, is clearly drawn out by S. Basil. contr. Eunom. ii. 21.

Γέννημα,

Offspring. This word is of very frequent occurrence
in Athan. He speaks of it, Orat. iv. 3, as virtually
Scriptural. " If any one declines to say 'offspring,'
and only says that the Word exists with God, let such
a one fear lest, *declining an expression of Scripture,*
(τὸ λεγόμενον,) he fall into extravagance, &c." Yet
Basil, contr. Eunom. ii. 6—8, explicitly disavows the
word, as an unscriptural invention of Eunomius.
" That the Father begat we are taught in many places :
that the Son is an offspring we never heard up to this
day, for Scripture says, ' Unto us a *child* is born, unto
us a *son* is given.' " c. 7. He goes on to say that " it
is fearful to give Him names of our own, to whom God
has given a name which is above every name ;" and
observes that offspring is not the word which even a
human father would apply to his son, as for instance
we read, " Child, (τέκνον,) go into the vineyard," and
" Who art thou, my son ? " moreover that fruits of the
earth are called offspring, ("I will not drink of the
offspring of this vine,") rarely animated things, except
indeed in such instances as, " O generation (offspring)
of vipers." Nyssen defends his brother, contr. Eunom.
Orat. iii. p. 105. In the Arian formula " an offspring,
but not as *one of the offsprings*," it is synonymous with
" work " or " creature." On the other hand Epipha-

nius uses it, e. g. Hær. 76, 8, and Naz. Orat. 29, 2.
Eusebius, Demonstr. Ev. iv. 2. Pseudo-Basil. adv.
Eunom. iv. p. 280 fin. It may be added, too, that S.
Basil seems to have changed his mind, for he uses the
Word in Hom. contr. Sabell. t. 2, p. 192. It is
remarkable that this Homily in substance (i. e. the
contr. Sabell. Greg. which is so like it that it cannot
really be another, unless S. Basil copies it) is also given
to S. Athan.

The Γενητὸν, Γεννητόν.

In these Treatises γενητὸν and γεννητὸν seem to be
one word, whatever distinction was made at a later
date. So they were considered by S. Ignatius, by the
Neo-Platonists, and by the Arians, who availed themselves of the *equivoque* of meaning, in order to pronounce our Lord a creature, γέννημα, though not as
other creatures. So also by Athan. and Basil. Hence
perhaps it is that Basil is severe on the application of
γέννημα to our Lord, his brother Gregory supporting
him. Athanasius on the other hand uses it of our Lord
with an explanation. After a time the distinction was
made, and this will account for other Fathers, Nazianz.
&c., following Athanasius. vid. supr. art. γέννημα. Also
Damasc. F. O. i. 8, p. 135, and Le Quien's note; also
note in Cotelerius, in Ign. Eph. t. 2, p. 13.

¶ Athanasius considers that Scripture sanctions the
one and the two; and he considers the one and the
same word in its two forms, to have the meaning of
Son, but that " Son " admits of a primary sense and of a
secondary. He virtually says, " It is true that the
Word of God and the creatures whom He has made
may both be called γεννήματα, but both in a very
different sense. Both may be called ' Sons of God,'
but the Word of God is true γέννημα by nature,
whereas creatures are sons, γεννήματα, only by adoption,

and that adoption through a mere μετουσία or participation of the divine nature, which is a gift of grace; but our Lord possesses the very οὐσία of the Father, and is thereby His fulness, and has all His attributes."

Hence Athan. says, "Things generate, γεννητὰ, cannot receive this name, (God's handiwork though they be,) except so far as, *after* their making, they partake of the Son who is the True Generate, and are therefore said to have been generated also, not at all in their own nature, but because of their participation of the Son in the Spirit." Orat. i. § 56.

¶ It is by a like neglect of the one ν and the two, that our Lord is called μονογενής. And Athan. speaks of the γένεσις of human sons, and of the Divine, de Decr. § 11; and in de Syn. § 47, he observes that S. Ignatius calls the Son γενητὸς καὶ ἀγένητος, without a hint about the distinction of roots. Again, one of the original Arian positions was that our Lord was a γέννημα ἀλλ᾽ οὐκ ὡς ἓν τῶν γεννημάτων, which Athan. frequently notices and combats, vid. Orat. ii. 19. But instead of answering it by showing that our Lord's epithet should have a double ν and creatures a single, he allows γεννημάτων to be applied to creatures improperly, and only argues that there is a proper sense of it in which it applies to the Word, not *as one of a number*, as the Arians said, but solely, incommunicably, as being the μονογενής. It may be admitted, as evident even from this passage, that though Athan. does not distinguish between γενητὸν and γεννητὸν, yet he considers γεγεννῆσθαι or γέννημα as especially appropriate to the Son, γεγονέναι and γειόμενος to the creation.

Δημιουργός.

THE γεννησις of the Eternal Son is intimately connected with the idea of creation ; so much so that Origen
thought that the creation was eternal, because the Son
was; and Tertullian thought that the Son was not
eternal because the creation was not.

These were erroneous conclusions, but Catholic
theologians allow thus much of truth in them, not that
the Creator and the creation were co-eval, but that the
mission of the Son to create is included in the *gennesis ;*
so that, as by the Father's teaching the Son " doctum
et scientem genuisse " is meant and, as His committing
judgment to Him is " judicem ipsum gignere," so the
mission to create signifies the *gennesis* of a Son in
eternity who is in time to be Creator. vid. Petav. de
Trin. viii. 1. § 10. Hence S. Augustine says, "In
Verbo Unico Dei omnia præcepta sunt Dei, quæ ille
gignens dedit nascenti." contr. Max. ii. 14, 9, and still
more definitely S. Thomas says, "Importatur in Verbo
ratio factiva eorum quæ Deus facit." Summ. 1, qu.
34, art. 3.

Immediately upon the creation follows the second
act, viz. of conservation ; for the Divine Hand is of such
incomprehensible force and intensity in operation, that
the thing created needs, by the intervention of its
Creator, to be enabled to bear creation. " Things

created," says Athanasius, "could not have endured His absolute nature and His splendour from the Father, unless, condescending by the Father's love for man, He had supported them and taken hold of them, and brought them into substance, &c." Orat. ii. § 64. vid. ἄκρατος.

Διαβολικὸς,

Diabolical. This is Athan.'s judgment about the Arians. vid. Decr. § 5 fin. Orat. ii. § 38, 74. iii. § 17. Ep. Æg. § 4—6. de Sent. Dion. 27 fin., where he says, " Who then will continue to call these men Christians, whose leader is the devil, and not rather diabolical ? " and he adds, "not only Christ's foes, χριστομάχοι, but diabolical also." Again, " though the diabolical men rave," Orat. iii. § 8. "friends of the devil, and his spirits." ad Ep. Æg. 5.

¶ In Orat. iii. § 8, there seems an allusion to false accusation or lying, which is the proper meaning of the word; διαβάλλων occurs shortly before. And so in Apol. ad Const. when he calls Magnentius διάβολος, it is as being a traitor, 17; and soon after he says that his accuser was τὸν διαβόλου τρόπον ἀναλαβὼν, where the word has no article, and διαβέβλημαι and διεβλήθην have preceded ; vid. also Hist. Ar. 52 fin. And so in Sent. D. his speaking of the Arians' "father the devil," 3. is explained 4. by τοὺς πατέρας διαβαλλόντων and τῆς εἰς τὸν ἐπίσκοπον διαβολῆς.

¶ Another reason of his so accounting them, was their atrocious cruelty towards Catholics; this leads him elsewhere to break out, " O new heresy, that has put on the whole devil in irreligious doctrine *and conduct !* " Hist. Arian. § 66. also Alexander, " diabolical," ap. Theod. Hist. i. 3, p. 731. " satanical," ibid. p. 741. vid. also Socr. i. 9, p. 30 fin. Hilar. contr. Const. 17.

Εἶδος.

Ἑνὸς ὄντος εἴδους θεότητος, says Athan. Syn. § 52. The word εἶδος, face or countenance, is generally applied to the Son, as in what follows, and is synonymous with *hypostasis*; but it is remarkable that here as elsewhere it is almost synonymous with οὐσία or φύσις. Indeed in one sense nature, substance, and *hypostasis*, are all synonymous, i. e. as one and all denoting the Una Res, which is Almighty God. They differed, in that the word *hypostasis* regards the One God *as* He is the Son. The apparent confusion is useful then as reminding us of this great truth; vid. art. Μία φύσις.

In Orat. iii. § 6, first the Son's εἶδος is the εἶδος of the Father, then the Son is the εἶδος of the Father's Godhead, and then in the Son is the εἶδος of the Father. These expressions are equivalent, if Father and Son are, Each separately, ὅλος θεός. S. Greg. Naz. uses the word ὀπίσθια, (Exod. xxxiii. 23, which forms a contrast to εἶδος,) for the Divine Works. Orat. 28, 3.

¶ Vid. also in Gen. xxxii. 30, 31, Sept., where it is translated "facies," Vulg., though in John v. 37 "species." vid. Justin Tryph. 126. In Orat. iii. § 15, εἶδος is also used in composition for "kind." Athan. says as above, "there is but one face of Godhead;" yet the word is used of the Son as synonymous with "image." It would seem as if there were a certain class of words, all expressive of the One Divine Substance, which admit of more appropriate application, either ordinarily or under circumstances, to This or That Divine Person who is also that One Substance. Thus "Being" is more descriptive of the Father as the πηγὴ θεότητος, and He is said to be "the Being of the Son;" yet the Son is really the One Supreme Being also. On the other hand the word "form," μορφὴ, and "face," εἶδος, are rather descriptive of the Divine Substance in the Person of the Son, and He is called "the form" and "the face of the Father," yet there is but one Form and Face of Divinity, who is at once Each of Three Persons; while "Spirit" is appropriated to the Third Person, though God is a Spirit. Thus again S. Hippolytus says ἐκ [τοῦ πατρὸς] δύναμις λόγος, yet shortly before, after mentioning the Two Persons, he adds, δύναμιν δὲ μίαν. contr. Noet. 7 and 11. And thus the word "Subsistence," ὑπόστασις, which expresses the One Divine Substance, has been found more appropriate to express that Substance viewed personally. Other words may be used correlatively of either Father or Son; thus the Father is the Life of the Son, the Son the Life of the Father; or, again, the Father is in the Son and the Son in the Father. Others in common, as "the Father's Godhead is the Son's," ἡ πατρικὴ υἱοῦ θεότης, as indeed the word οὐσία itself. Other words on the contrary express the Substance in This or That Person only, as "Word," "Image," &c. The word εἶδος also occurs Orat. i. 20. Ep. Æg. 17. contr. Sabell. Greg. 8 and 12.

*Ενσαρκος παρουσία.

THIS phrase or its equivalent is very frequent with Athan. vid. Orat. i. § 8, 53, 59, 62 fin. ii. 6, 10, 55, 66 twice, 72 fin. iii. 28, 35. Incarn. 20. Sent. D. 9. Ep. Æg. 4. Serap. i. 3, 9. vid. also Cyril. Catech. iii. 11. xii. 15. xiv. 27, 30. Epiph. Hær. 77, 17. The Eutychians avail themselves of it at the Council of Constantinople, vid. Hard. Conc. t. 2, pp. 164, 236. Instead of it 'πιδημία is used Orat. i. § 59, three times; ἐπεδήμησεν, iii. 30.

'Εξαίρετον,

Or *prerogative*, Orat. ii. § 19, iii. 3, iv. 28, literally special, singular. Vid. also Euseb. Eccl. Th. pp. 47, 73, 89, 124, 129. Theod. Hist. p. 732. Nyssen. c. Eunom. iii. p. 133. Epiph. Hær. 76, p. 370. Cyr. Thes. p. 160.

The 'Εξουκόντιον,

FROM ἐξ οὐκ ὄντων, "out of nothing," one of the original Arian positions concerning the Son. Theodoret says that they were also called Exacionitæ, from the name of their place of meeting, Hær. iv. 3, and Du Cange confirms it so far as to show that there was a place or quarter of Constantinople called Exocionium or Exacionium. Some have thought that Exucontians and Exocionites are perhaps the same word corrupted. At the same time, since the Arians of Constantinople were of the violent sort who were called by various names, Anomœans, Aetians, Eunomians, Acacians, as well as pure Arians, it is not improbable that, in order to distinguish them from the more moderate heretics, they were also called in Constantinople from Exocionium, the district of the great metropolis to which they belonged.

Ἐπίνοια,

Κατ᾽ ἐπίνοιαν, ἐπινοεῖν, *conception*. This is a word very common with Athanasius. It expresses the view taken by the mind of theological realities, whether that view be the true view or not; thus it is used both in refereuce to heretical errpr and to Catholic faith. Thus Athan., Orat. i. init., speaks of heresies as ἐπινοή-σασαι μανίαν, implying that there is no objective truth corresponding to those conceptions which they so vehemently insist upon. And Socrates, speaking of the decree of the Council of Alexandria, 362, against Apollinaris; "for, not originating, ἐπινοήσαντες, any *novel* devotion, did they introduce it into the Church, but what from the beginning the *Ecclesiastical Tradi-tion* declared." Hist. iii. 7. And the Arians allowed what was imputed to them as far as this, that they were strenuous from the first in maintaining that the titles given to our Lord, viz. Word, Wisdom, &c., were not to be taken as expressing literal facts, but were mere names given to Him in honour and as a reward. Thus in the Thalia, "He is conceived in num-berless conceptions, ἐπινοίαις." de Syn. § 15. Hence Athan. says they held that "He who is really Son is but κατ᾽ ἐπίνοιαν Word, as He is Vine, and Way, and Door and Tree of life, and that He is called Wisdom also only in name (vid. art. Ὀνόματα), the proper and true Wisdom of the Father, which co-exists ingenerately with Him, being other than the Son, by which He even made the Son, and named Him Wisdom as partaking of it." Orat. ii. § 37. Not that they even allowed Him really to be Son, except in the sense that we are sons of God, that is, because adoption involves a gift of the Spirit, which is a real principle of a new birth. Thus Athan. quotes or charges Arius elsewhere as saying, " He is not the very and only Word of the Father, but is in name only called Word and Wisdom, and is *called by grace* Son and Power." Orat. i. § 9; and just after he contrasts " true " Son with the Arian tenet, Son " by adoption, which is from participation " of the Spirit "and κατ' ἐπίνοιαν." vid. also de Sent. D. 2. Ep. Æg. 12, 13, 14. Orat. iv. § 2.

The word, however, has also a good meaning and use, as expressive of the nearest approximation in human thought to the supernatural truths of Revelation, and thus equivalent to *economical* (vid. art. in voc.). Thus in our thoughts of the Almighty, though He is in reality most simple and uncompounded, without parts, passions, attributes, or properties, we consider Him as good or holy, or as angry or pleased, denoting some particular aspect in which our infirmity views, in which alone it can view, what is infinite and incomprehensible. That is, He is κατ' ἐπίνοιαν holy or merciful, being in reality a Unity which is all mercifulness and also all holiness, not in the way of qualities, but as one indivisible Perfection; which is too great for us to conceive as It is. And for the very reason that we cannot conceive It simply, we are bound to use thankfully these conceptions, which are true as far as they go, and our best possible; since some conceptions, however imperfect, are better than none. They stand for realities which they do not reach, and must be accepted for what they do not adequately represent. But when the mind comes to recognize this existing inadequacy, and to distrust itself, it is tempted to rush into the opposite extreme, and to conclude that because it cannot understand fully, it does not realize anything, · or that its ἐπίνοιαι are but ὀνόματα.

———

’Επισπείρας.

Vid. *Scripture Passages.*

Εὐσέβεια.

Εὐσέβεια, ἀσέβεια, &c., here translated *piety*, &c., stand for *orthodoxy* throughout, being taken from St. Paul's text, μέγα τὸ τῆς εὐσεβείας μυστήριον, 1 Tim. iii. 16, iv. 8. " Magnum *pietatis* mysterium," Vulg.

E. g. τὴν τῆς αἱρέσεως ἀσέβειαν, Decr. *init.* ὅσον εὐσεβοῦς φρονήσεως ἡ 'Αρειανὴ αἵρεσις ἐστέρηται. *ibid.* § 2. τί ἔλειπε διδασκαλίας εἰς εὐσέβειαν τῇ καθολικῇ ἐκκλησίᾳ; Syn. § 3. ἡ οἰκουμενικὴ σύνοδος τὸν "Αρειον ἐξεβάλε οὐ φέρουσα τὴν ἀσέβειαν. Orat. i. § 7, *et passim.* Hence Arius ends his letter to Eusebius Nic. with ἀληθῶς Εὐσέβιε. Theod. Hist. i. 4.

¶ A curious instance of the force of the word as a turning-point in controversy occurs in a Homily given to S. Basil by Petavius, Fronto Ducæus, Combefis, Du Pin, Fabricius, and Oudin, doubted of by Tillemont, and rejected by Cave and Garnier, where it is said that the denial of our Lady's perpetual virginity, though "lovers of Christ do not bear to hear that God's Mother ever ceased to be Virgin," yet " does no injury to the doctrine of *religion*," μηδὲν τῷ τῆς εὐσεβείας παραλυμαίνεται λόγῳ, i.e. (according to the above explanation of the word) to the orthodox view of the *Incarnation.* vid. Basil. Opp. t. 2, p. 599. vid. on the passage Petav. de Incarn. xiv. 3. § 7, and Fronto-Duc. in loc.   Pearson refers to this passage, and almost translates the λόγος εὐσεβείας by "mystery," Apost. Creed, Art. 3. " Although it may be thought *sufficient as to the mystery of the Incarnation*, that, when our Saviour was conceived and born, His Mother was a Virgin, though whatsoever should have followed after could have no reflective operation upon the first-fruit of her womb . . . yet the peculiar eminency, &c."

¶ John of Antioch again furnishes us with a definition of *pietas*, as meaning obedience to the word of God. He speaks, writing to Proclus, of a letter which evidenced caution and piety, i.e. orthodoxy; "piety, because you went along the royal way of. *Divine Scripture* in your remarks, rightly confessing the word of truth, not venturing to declare anything of *your own authority without Scripture testimonies;* caution, because *together with* divine Scripture you propounded also *statements of the Fathers* in order to prove what you advanced." ap. Facund. i. 1.

Θεανδρικὴ ἐνέργεια,

Operatio Deivirilis, "the Man-God's action." By the word ἐνέργεια is meant in theology the action or operation, the family of acts, which naturally belongs to and discriminates the substance or nature of a thing from that of other things ; and not only the mere operation, but also inclusively the faculty of such operation; as certain nutritive or medicinal qualities adhere, and serve as definitions, to certain plants and minerals, or as the ἐνέργεια and the ἔργον of a seraph may be viewed as being the adoration of the Holy Trinity.

This being laid down, it would seem to follow that our Lord, having two natures, has two attendant ἔργα and two ἐνέργειαι, and this in fact is the Catholic doctrine, whereas the Monothelites maintained He had but one, as if, with the Monophysites, they held but one nature of Christ, the divine and human energies making up one single third energy, neither the one nor the other,—for, in the Monophysite creed, God and man made one third and compound being, who would necessarily have one compound energy, and, as will is one kind of energy, one only will.

This one and only energy of our Lord, as proceeding from what they consider His one, compound nature, they denoted by the orthodox phrase, " ἐνέργεια θεανδρικὴ," diverting it from its true sense. Catholic

theologians, holding two energies, one for each nature, speak of them in three ways, viz. as a divine
energy, a human, and a union or concurrence of the
two; this last they call θεανδρικὴ, but in a sense quite
distinct from the use of the word by the Monothelites. Sometimes our Lord exerts His divine *energia*,
as when He protects His people; sometimes His
human, as when He underwent hunger and thirst;
sometimes both at once, as in making clay and restoring
sight, or in His suffering for His people; but in this
last instance, there is no intermingling of the divine
and the human, and, though it may be spoken of as a
double energy, still there are in fact two, not one.

It is this θεανδρικὴ ἐνέργεια that is spoken of in the
following passages :—

" And thus when there was need to raise Peter's
wife's mother who was sick of a fever, He stretched
forth His hand humanly, but He stopped the illness
divinely. And in the case of the man blind from the
birth, human was the spittle which He gave forth from
the flesh, but divinely did He open the eyes through
the clay. And in the case of Lazarus, He gave forth
a human voice, as man; but divinely, as God, did He
raise Lazarus from the dead." Orat. iii. 32.

" When He is said to hunger and thirst, and to toil,
and not to know, and to sleep, and to weep, and to
ask, and to flee, and to be born, and to deprecate the
chalice, and in a word to undergo all that belongs to
the flesh, let it be said, as is congruous, in each case,
' Christ's then hungering or thirsting *for us in the flesh*,
and saying He did not know, and being buffeted and

toiling *for us in the flesh,* and being exalted too, and born, and growing *in the flesh,* and fearing and hiding *in the flesh,* and saying, *If it be possible let this* chalice pass from Me, and being beaten and receiving gifts *for us in the flesh ;* and in a word, all such things *for us in the flesh,' "* &c.   Orat. iii. § 34.

"When He touched the leper, it was the man that was seen ; but something beyond man, when He cleansed him, &c." Ambros. Epist. i. 46, n. 7. Hil. Trin. x. 23 fin. vid. *Incarnation* and *Two Natures,* and S. Leo's extracts in his Ep. 165. Chrysol. Serm. 34 and 35. Paul. ap. Conc. Eph. t. iii. (p. 1620, Labbc.)

Θεομάχος, Χριστομάχος.

VID. Acts v. 39. xxiii. 9. text. rec. This epithet is of very frequent use in Athan., as is χριστομάχος, in speaking of the Arians, vid. *infra passim;* also ἀντιμαχόμενοι τῷ σωτῆρι. Ep. Encycl. § 5. And in the beginning of the controversy, Alexander ap. Socr. i. 6 p. 10, p. 11, p. 13. Theod. Hist. i. 3, p. 729. And so θεομάχος γλῶσσα. Basil. contr. Eunom. ii. 27 fin. χριστομάχων, in his Ep. 236 init. vid. also Cyril. Thesaur. p. 19, p. 24. θεομάχοι is used of other heretics, e. g. the Manichees, by Greg. Naz. Orat. 45. § 8.

¶ The title contains in Athan.'s use of it an allusion to the antediluvian giants; e.g. γίγαντας θεομαχοῦντας, Orat. iii. § 42. vid. also Naz., of the disorderly bishops during the Arian ascendency. Orat. 43, 26, and Socr. v. 10. Sometimes the mythological giants are spoken of. Orat. ii. § 32. In Hist. Arian. 74, he calls Constantius a γίγας.

¶ λογομαχία too is used with reference to the divine λόγος and the fight against Him, as χριστομαχεῖν and θεομαχεῖν. Thus λογομαχεῖν μελετήσαντες, καὶ λοιπὸν πνευματομαχοῦντες, ἔσονται μετ' ὀλίγον νεκροὶ τῇ ἀλογίᾳ. Serap. iv. 1.

Θεότης (vid. *Trinity*).

IF the doctrine of the Holy Trinity admits of being called contrary to reason, this must be on the ground of its being incompatible with some eternal truth, necessary axiom, &c., or with some distinct experience, and not merely because it is in its nature inconceivable and unimaginable ; for if to be inconceivable makes it untrue, then we shall be obliged to deny facts of daily experience, e.g. the action of the muscles which follows upon an act of the will.

However, clear as this is, the language by which we logically express the doctrine will be difficult to interpret and to use intelligently, unless we keep in mind the fundamental truths which constitute the mystery, and use them as a key to such language.

E.g. the Father's Godhead is the Son's, or is in the Son. Orat. i. § 52. Ἡ πατρικὴ αὐτοῦ θεότης. Orat. i. § 45, 49. ii. § 18, 73. iii. § 26. ἡ πατρικὴ φύσις αὐτοῦ. i. § 40. τὸ πατρικὸν φῶς ὁ υἱός. iii. § 53. ἡ θεότης καὶ ἡ ἰδιότης τοῦ πατρὸς τὸ εἶναι τοῦ υἱοῦ ἐστι. iii. § 5. The Son is worshipped κατὰ τὴν πατρικὴν ἰδιότητα. i. § 42. He has τὴν τῆς ὁμοιωσεως ἑνότητα. Syn. § 45. He is ὁ αὐτὸς τῇ ὁμοιώσει to the Father. Decr. § 20. He has τὴν ἑνότητα τῆς φύσεως καὶ τὴν ταυτότητα τοῦ φωτός. Decr. § 24. ταυτότητα τῆς φύσεως, Basil, Ep. 8, 3. τῆς οὐσίας, Cyril. in Joan. iii. p. 302. He is ἐξ οὐσίας οὐσιώδης. Orat. iv. § 1. ἡ οὐσία αὕτη τῆς οὐσίας τῆς πατρικῆς ἐστι γέννημα. Syn. § 48. And we are told of the prophet ἐκβοήσαντος τὴν πατρικὴν ὑπόστασιν περὶ αὐτοῦ. Orat. iv. § 33. vid. Tract μία φύσις, § 6 fin.

¶ φύσις seems sometimes in Athanasius to be used, not for οὐσία, as would be the ordinary application of the word, but for ὑπόστασις or person. Thus he says, "whereas the *nature* of the Son is less divisible relatively to the Father" than radiance is relatively to the sun, . . . "wherefore should not He be called consubstantial?" de Syn. § 52. And at least this is an Alexandrian use of the word. It is found in Alexander ap. Theod. Hist. i. 3. p. 740, and it gives rise to a celebrated question in the Monophysite controversy, as used in S. Cyril's phrase μία φύσις σεσαρκωμένη. S. Cyril uses the word both for person and for substance successively in the following passage. " Perhaps some one will say, ' How is the Holy and Adorable Trinity distinguished into three Hypostases, yet issues in *one nature* of Godhead?' Because, the Same in substance, necessarily following the *difference of natures*, recalls the minds of believers to *one nature* of Godhead." contr. Nest. iii. p. 91. In this passage " One nature" stands for one substance; but " three Natures" is the One Eternal Divine Nature viewed in that respect in which He is Three. And so S. Hilary, "naturæ ex naturâ gignente nativitas,". de Syn. 17; and " essentia de·essentiâ," August de Trin. vii. n. 3, and "de seipso genuit Deus id quod est," de Fid. et Symb. 4. i. e. He is the Adorable θεότης viewed as begotten. These phrases mean that the Son *who is* the Divine Substance, is from the Father *who is* the [same] divine substance. As, (to speak of what is *analogous*, not parallel,) we might say that "man is father of man," not meaning by man the same individual in both cases, but the same nature, so here we speak, not of the same Person in the two cases, but the same Individuum. All these expressions resolve themselves into the original mystery of the Holy Trinity, that Person and Individuum are not equivalent terms, and we understand them neither more nor less than we understand it. In like manner as regards the Incarnation, when St. Paul says "God was in Christ," he does not mean absolutely the Divine Nature, which is the proper sense of the word, but the Divine Nature as existing in the Person of the Son. Hence too, (vid. Petav. de Trin. vi. 10. § 6.) such phrases as "the Father begat the Son from *His* substance." And in like manner Athan. just afterwards, speaks of "the Father's Godhead *being in* the Son." Orat. i. § 52.

The μονὰς θεότητος is ἀδιαίρετος. Orat. iv. § 1, 2. Though in Three Persons, they are not μεμερισμέναι, Dion. ap. Basil. Sp. S. n. 72. Athan. Expos. F. § 2; not ἀπερρηγμέναι, Naz. Orat. 20, 6; not ἀπεξενωμέναι καὶ διεσπασμέναι, Orat. 23, 6, &c.; but ἀμέριστος ἐν μεμερισμένοις ἡ θεότης. Orat. 31, 14.

¶ Though the Divine Substance is both the Father Ingenerate and also the Only-begotten Son, it is not itself ἀγέννητος or γεννητή; which was the objection urged against the Catholics by Aetius, Epiph. Hær. 76. 10. Thus Athan. says, de Decr. § 30, "He has given the authority of all things to the Son, and, having given it, is *once more,* πάλιν, the Lord of all things through the Word." vol. i. p. 52. Again, "the Father having given all things to the Son, has all things once *again,* πάλιν . . . for the Son's Godhead is the Godhead of the Father." Orat. iii. § 36 fin. Hence ἡ ἐκ τοῦ πατρὸς εἰς τὸν υἱὸν θεοτὴς ἀῤῥεύστως καὶ ἀδιαιρέτως τυγχάνει. Expos. F. 2. "Vera et æterna substantia, in se tota permanens, totam se coæternæ veritati nativitatis indulsit." Fulgent. Resp. 7. And S. Hilary, "Filius in Patre est et in Filio Pater, non per transfusionem, refusionemque mutuam, sed per viventis naturæ perfectam nativitatem." Trin. vii. 31.

Θεοτόκος.

Vid. *Mary.*

Καταπέτασμα.

"As Aaron did not change," says Athanasius,
Orat. ii. 8, "by putting on his High-priest's dress, so
that, had any one said, 'Lo, Aaron has this day become High-priest,' he had not implied that he then had
been born man, . . . so in the Lord's instance the
words 'He became' and 'He was made' must not be
understood of the Word, considered as the Word,"
&c. &c.

This is one of those distinct protests by anticipation
against Nestorianism, which in consequence may be
abused to the purposes of the opposite heresy. Such
expressions as περιτιθέμενος τὴν ἐσθῆτα, ἐκαλύπτετο,
ἐνδυσάμενος σῶμα, were familiar with the Apollinarians,
against whom S. Athanasius is, if possible, even more
decided. Theodoret objects, Hær. v. 11, p. 422, to the
word προκάλυμμα, when applied to our Lord's manhood,
as implying that He had no soul; vid. also Naz. Ep.
102 fin. (ed. 1840.) In Naz. Ep. 101, p. 90, παραπέτασμα is used to denote an Apollinarian idea. Such
expressions were taken to imply that Christ was not
in nature man, only in some sense human; not a substance, but an appearance; yet S. Athan. (if Athan.)
contr. Sabell. Greg. 4. has παραπεπετασμένην, and
κάλυμμα, ibid. init.; S. Cyril Hieros. καταπέτασμα,
Catech. xii. 26. xiii. 32, after Hebr. x. 20, and Athan.

ad Adelph. 5 ; Theodor. παραπετασμα, Eran. 1, p. 22, and προκάλυμμα, ibid. p. 23, and adv. Gent. vi. p. 877 ; and στολὴ, Eran. l. c. S. Leo has "caro Christi velamen," Ep. 59, p. 979. vid. also Serm. 22, p. 70. Serm. 25, p. 84.

Κύριος, κυρίως.

THE meaning of κυρίως, when applied to language, on
the whole presents no difficulty. It answers to the
Latin *propriè*, and is the contrary to *impropriè*. Thus
Athan. says, "When the thing is a work or creature,
the words 'He made' &c. are used of it properly,
κυρίως; when an offspring, then they are no longer
used κυρίως." Orat. ii. § 3.

But the word has an inconvenient latitude (vid. art.
Father Almighty, fin.). Sometimes it is used in the sense
of archetypal or transcendent, as when Athan. says,
"The Father is κυρίως Father, and the Son κυρίως Son,"
Orat. i. § 21 ; and in consequence in Their instance alone
is the Father always Father and the Son always Son.
ibid. Sometimes the word is used of us, and opposed to
figuratively, ἐκ μεταφορᾶς, as in Basil. c. Eunom. ii. 23 ;
while Hilary seems to deny that we are sons *propriè*.
Justin says, ὁ μόνος λεγόμενος κυρίως υἱὸς, Apol. ii. 6, but
here κυρίως seems to be used in reference to the word
κύριος, Lord, which he has just been using, κυριολογεῖν
being sometimes used by him as by others in the sense
of "naming as Lord," like θεολογεῖν. vid. Tryph. 56.
There is a passage in Justin's ad Græc. 21, where he
(or the writer), when speaking of ἐγώ εἰμι ὁ ὢν, uses
the word in the same ambiguous sense; οὐδὲν γὰρ
ὄνομα ἐπὶ θεοῦ κυριολογεῖσθαι δυνατὸν; as if κύριος,

the Lord, by which " I am " is translated, were a sort of symbol of that proper name of God which cannot be given.

¶ On κυριολογία, vid. Lumper, Hist. Theol. t. 2, p. 478.

Λόγος,

ἐνδιάθετος καὶ προφορικός.

Vid. art. *Word.*

Μετουσία.

To all creatures in different ways or degrees is it given to participate in the Divine attributes. In these it is that they are able or wise or great or good; in these they have life, health, strength, well-being, as the case may be. And the All-abounding Son is He through whom this exuberance of blessing comes to them severally.

They are partakers in their measure, of what He possesses in fulness. From the Father's οὐσία which is His too, they have through Him a μετουσία. Here lies the cardinal difference of doctrine between the Catholic and Arian: Arians maintain that the Son has only that μετουσία of God, which we too have. Catholics hold Him to be God, and the Source of all divine gifts. The antagonism between Athanasius and Eusebius is the more pointed, by the very strength of the language of the latter. He considers the Son ἐξ αὐτῆς τῆς πατρικῆς [not οὐσίας, but] μετουσίας, ὥσπερ ἀπὸ πηγῆς, ἐπ᾽ [vid. supr. Eusebius] αὐτὸν προχεομένης, πληρούμενον. Eccl. Theol. i. 2. But Athanasius, οὐδὲ κατὰ μετουσίαν αὐτοῦ, ἀλλ᾽ ὅλον ἴδιον αὐτοῦ γέννημα. Orat. iii. § 4.

¶ Athanasius considers this attribute of communication to be one of the prerogatives of the Second Person in the Divine Trinity. He enlarges on this doctrine in many places : e. g. " if, as we have said before, the Son is not such by participation, but, while all things generated have, by participation, the grace of God, He is the Father's Wisdom and Word, of which all things partake, it follows that He, being the deifying and enlightening power of the Father, in which all things are deified and quickened, is not alien in substance from the Father, but one in substance. For by partaking of Him, we partake of the Father; inasmuch as the Word is proper to the Father. Whence, if He was Himself too from participation, and not the substantial Godhead and Image of the Father, He would not deify, being deified Himself. For it is not possible that He, who but possesses from participation, should impart of that portion to others, since what He has is not His own, but the Giver's; as what He has received is barely the grace sufficient for Himself." Syn. § 51.

Μία φύσις,

(of our Lord's godhead and of His manhood.)

Two natures are united in One Christ, but it does
uot follow that their union is like any other union of
which we have cognizance, such, for instance, as the
union of body and soul. Beyond the general fact, that
both the Incarnation and other unions are of substances
not homogeneous, there is no likeness between it and
them.   The characteristics and circumstances of the Incarnation are determined by its history.   The One Self-
existing Personal God created, moulded, assumed, a
manhood truly such.   He, being from eternity, was in
possession and in the fulness of His godhead before mankind had being. Much more was He already in existence,
and in all His attributes, when He became man, and
He lost nothing by becoming.   All that He ever had
continued to be His; what He took on Himself was
only an addition.   There was no change; in His
incarnation, He did but put on a garment.   That
garment was not *He*, or, as Athan. speaks, αὐτὸς, or, as
the next century worded it, "His Person."   That
αὐτὸς was, as it had ever been, one and the same with
His Divinity, οὐσία, or φύσις; it was this φύσις, as one
with His Person, which took to Itself a manhood.   He
had no other Person than He had had from the beginning; His manhood had no Personality of its own;

it was a second φύσις but not a second Person ; it never existed till it was His; for its integrity and completeness it depended on Him, the Divine Word. It was one with Him, and, through and in Him, the Divine Word, it was one with the Divine Nature ; it was but indirectly united to It, for the medium of union was the Person of the Word. And, being thus without personality of its own, His human nature was relatively to Himself really what the Arians falsely said that He was relatively to the Father, a περὶ αὐτὸν, a περιβολὴ, a συμβεβηκὸς, a "something else besides His substance," Orat. ii. § 45, e. g. an ὄργανον. Such was His human nature; it might be called an additional attribute; the Word was "made man," not, was made a man.

Thus Athanasius almost confines the word οὐσία to denote the Word, and seldom speaks of His manhood as a nature; and Cyril, to denote the dependence of the manhood upon His Divine Nature, has even used of the Incarnate Lord the celebrated *dictum*, μία φύσις τοῦ θεοῦ λόγου σεσαρκωμένη. This was Cyril's strong form of protesting against Nestorianism, which maintained that our Lord's humanity had a person as well as the Divine Word, who assumed it.

¶ Athan. says, Orat. ii. § 45, that our Lord is not a creature, though God, in Prov. viii. 22, is said to have created Him, because to be a creature, He ought to have a created substance, which He had not. Does not this imply that he did not consider His manhood an οὐσία ? He says that He who is said to be created, is not at once in His *Nature* and *Substance* a creature ; ἡ λέξις τι ἕτερον δηλοῖ περὶ ἐκεῖνον, καὶ οὐ τὸ λεγόμενον κτίζεσθαι ἤδη τῇ φύσει καὶ τῇ οὐσίᾳ κτίσμα. As the complement of this peculiarity, vid. his constant use of the οὐσία τοῦ λόγου, when we should use the word "Person." Does not this corroborate St. Cyril in his statement that the saying "μία φύσις σεσαρκωμένη" belongs to Athanasius? for whether we say one φύσιν or one οὐσία does not seem to matter. Observe too he speaks of something taking place in Him, περὶ ἐκεῖνον, i. e. some adjunct or accident, (vid. art. περιβολὴ and συμβεβηκὸς), or, as he says Orat. ii. § 8, envelopement or dress. In like manner he presently, ii. § 46, speaks of the creation of the Word as like the new-creation of the soul, which is a creation not in substance but in qualities, &c. And *ibid.* § 51, he contrasts the οὐσία and the ἀνθρώπινον of the Word; as in Orat. i. 41, οὐσία and ἡ ἀνθρωπότης; and φύσις and σάρξ, iii. 34, init.; and λόγος and σάρξ, 38, init. And He speaks of the Son " taking on Him the *economy*," ii. § 76, and of the ὑπόστασις τοῦ λόγου being one with ὁ ἄνθρωπος, iv. 35.

It is plain that this line of teaching might be wrested to the purposes of the Apollinarian and Eutychian heresies; but, considering Athan.'s most emphatic protests against those errors in his later works, as well as his strong statements in Orat. iii., there is no hazard in this admission. We thus understand how Eutyches came to deny the "two natures." He said that such a doctrine was a new one; this is not true, for, not to mention other Fathers, Athan. infr. Orat. iv. fin. speaks of our Lord's "invisible nature *and visible*," (vid. also contr. Apoll. ii. 11, Orat. ii. 70, iii. 43,) and his ordinary use of ἄνθρωπος for the manhood might quite as plausibly be perverted on the other hand into a defence of Nestorianism; but still the above peculiarities in his style may be taken to account for the heresy, though they do not excuse the heretic. Vid. also the Ed. Ben. on S. Hilary (præf. p. xliii.), who uses *natura* absolutely for our Lord's Divinity, as contrasted to the *dispensatio,* and divides His titles into *naturalia* and *assumpta.*

Μοναρχία.

Vid. *Father Almighty.*

Μονογενής.

THE Arians had a difficulty as to the meaning, in their theology, of the word μονογενής. Eunomius decided that it meant, not μόνος γεννηθείς, but γεννηθεὶς παρὰ μόνου. And of the first Arians also Athan. apparently reports that they considered the Son Only-begotten because He μόνος was brought into being by God μόνος. Decr. § 7. The Macrostich Confession in like manner interprets μονογενὴς by μόνος and μόνως, Syn. § 26. (supr. vol. i. p. 107,) i. e. the only one of the creatures who was named "Son," and the Son of ono Father (with Eunomius above), in opposition to the προβολὴ of the Gnostics. (vid. Acacius in Epiph. Hær. p. 839.) Naz., however, explains μόνως by οὐχ ὡς τὰ σώματα. Orat. 25, 16, vid. the Eusebian distinction between ὁμοούσιος and ὁμοιούσιος, Soz. iii. 18, in art. ὁμοούσιος infr. It seems, however, that Basil and Gregory Nyssen, (if I understand Petav. rightly, Trin. vii. 11. § 3,) consider μονογενὴς to include ὑπὸ μόνου, as if in contrast to the Holy Spirit, whose procession is not from the Father only, or again not a gennesis.

¶ If it be asked, what the distinctive words are which are incommunicably the Son's, since so many of His names are given also to the creature, it is obvious to answer, ἴδιος υἱὸς and μονογενὴς, which are in Scripture, and the symbols "of the substance," and "one in substance," used by the Council; and this is the value of the Council's phrases, that, while they guard the Son's divinity, they allow full scope, without risk of trenching on it, to the Catholic doctrine of the fulness of the Christian privileges. vid. art. *Son.* For Ἀγαπητὸς, vid. Matt. iii. in *Scripture Passages.*

The ꞌΟμοιον.

GOD is both One and Three; neither as one nor as the
other can we speak of likeness in connexion with
Him; for likeness, as Athan. says, relates not to
things but to their qualities, and to speak of likeness
between Father, Son, and Spirit, is to imply that
instead of being One and the Same, they are three
distinct beings. Again, so far as they are three, they
do but differ from each other, and are not merely
unlike; they agree in nothing, viewed as Persons;
they have not so much likeness as to admit (in the
ordinary sense) of numbering. Those things, strictly
speaking, alone are like or equal, which are not the
same: the Three Divine Persons are not like Each
Other, whether viewed as Three or One.

However, in the difficulty of finding terms, which
will serve as a common measure of theological thought
for the expression of ideas as to which there is no
experimental knowledge or power of conception, and
in the necessary use of economical language, both
these terms, likeness and equality, have been received
in orthodox teaching concerning the Supreme Being.
The Athanasian Creed declares that the Three Persons
in the Godhead have " æqualis gloria," and are
" co-æquales," and S. Athanasius himself in various
places uses the word "like," though he condemns its

adoption in the mouth of Arians, as being insufficient
to exclude error.

That is, he accepts it as a word of orthodoxy as far
as it goes, while he rejects it as sufficient to serve as
a symbol and test. Sufficient it is not, even with the
strong additions, which the Semi-Arians made, of ὅμοιος
κατὰ πάντα, ὅμοιος κατ᾽ οὐσίαν or ὁμοιούσιος, and
ἀπαράλλακτος εἰκὼν, because what is like, is, by the
very force of the term, not the same. Thus he says,
Syn. § 41 and 53, " Only to say ' *Like* according to substance,' is very far from signifying ' *Of* the substance ' "
(vid. art. *Eusebius*) ; thus tin is only *like* silver, and gilt
brass *like* gold. . . No one disputes that *like* is not
predicated of substances, but of habits and of qualities.
Therefore in speaking of Like in substance, we mean
Like by participation, κατὰ μετουσίαν, and this belongs
to creatures, for they by partaking are made like to
God . . . not in substance, but in sonship, which we
shall partake from Him. . . . If then ye speak of the
Son as being such by participation, then indeed call
Him Like in substance and not in nature God, . . .
but if this be extravagant, He must be, not by participation, but in nature and truth, Son, Light, Wisdom,
God; and being so by nature and not by sharing, therefore He is properly called, not Like in substance with
the Father, but One in substance,"—that is, not
ὁμοιούσιος, but ὁμοούσιος, Consubstantial.

Yet clear and decided as is his language here, nevertheless, for some reason, probably from a feeling of
charity, as judging it best to inculcate first the revealed
truth itself as a mode of introducing to' the faithful

and defending the orthodox symbol, and showing its meaning and its necessity, he uses the phrases ὅμοιος κατὰ πάντα, and ὁμοιούσιος more commonly than ὁμοούσιος :—this I have noted elsewhere.

¶ E. g. ὅμοιος κατὰ πάντα. "He who is in the Father, and like the Father in all things." Orat. i. § 40. "Being the Son of God, He must be like Him." Orat. ii. § 17. "The Word is unlike us, and like the Father." Orat. iii. § 20, also i. § 21, 40, ii. § 18, 22. Ep. Ægypt. 17.

¶ And ὅμοιος κατ' οὐσίαν. ". . Unless indeed they give up shame, and say that 'Image' is not a token of similar substance, but His name only." Orat. i. § 21. vid. also Orat. i. § 20 init. 26. iii. § 11, 26, 67. Syn. § 38. Alex. Enc. § 2.

¶ Also Athan. says that. the Holy Trias is ὅμοια ἑαυτῇ, instead of using the word ὁμοούσια. Serap. i. 17, 20, 38; also Cyril. Catech. vi. 7.

¶ In some of the Arian Creeds we have this almost Catholic formula, ὅμοιον κατὰ πάντα, introduced by the bye, marking the presence of what may be called the new Semi-Arian school. Of course it might admit of evasion, but in its fulness it included "substance." At Sirmium Constantius inserted the above, Epiph. Hær. 73, 22, in the Confession which occurs supr. vol. i. p. 72. On this occasion Basil subscribed in this form. "I, Basil, Bishop of Ancyra, believe and assent to what is aforewritten, confessing that the Son is like the Father in all things; and by 'in all things,' not only that He is like in will, but in subsistence, and existence, and being; as divine Scripture teaches,

spirit from spirit, life from life, light from light, God
from God, true Son from true, Wisdom from the Wise
God and Father; and once for all, like the Father in
all things, as a son is to a father. And if any one
says that He is like in a certain respect, κατά τι, as is
written afore, he is alien from the Catholic Church, as
not confessing the likeness according to divine
Scripture." Epiph. Hær. 73, 22. S. Cyril of Jerusalem
uses the κατὰ πάντα or ἐν πᾶσιν ὅμοιον, Catech. iv. 7.
xi. 4 and 18, and Damasc. F. O. i. 8, p. 135.

¶ S. Athanasius, in saying that like is not used of
substance, implies that the proper Arian senses of the
ὅμοιον are more natural, and therefore the more pro-
bable, if the word came into use. These were, 1. likeness in *will* and *action*, as συμφωνία, of which vid.
Orat. iii. 11. 2. likeness to the *idea* in God's mind in
which the Son was created. Cyril. Thesaur. p. 134.
3. likeness to the divine *act* or *energy* by which
He was created. Basil. contr. Eun. iv. p. 282. Cyril.
in Joan. c. 5. iii. p. 304. 4. like according to the
Scriptures, which of course was but an evasion. 5. like
κατὰ πάντα, which was, as they understood it, an
evasion also.

¶ According to Athanasius, supr. p. 371, the phrase
"unvarying image" was, in truth, self-contradictory,
for every image varies from the original because it is
an image. Yet he himself frequently uses it, as other
Fathers, and Orat. i. § 26, uses ὅμοιος τῆς οὐσίας.

¶ As " of the substance" declared that our Lord
was *uncreate*, so " one in substance" declared that He
was *equal* with the Father; no term derived from

"likeness," even "like in substance," answering for this purpose, for such phrases might all be understood of *resemblance* or *representation*. vid. Decr. § 23. Hyp. Mel. Hil. Syn. 89. Things that are like cannot be the same; whereas Athan. contends for the ταὐτὸν τῇ ὁμοιώσει, the same in likeness, Decr. § 20. " Una substantia religiose prædicabitur, quæ ex nativitatis proprietate et ex naturæ similitudine ita indifferens sit, ut una dicatur." Hil. Syn. § 67.

¶ By "the Son being *equal* to the Father," is but meant that He is His "unvarying image;" it does not imply any distinction of substance. " Perfectæ æqualitatis significantiam habet similitudo." Hil. de Syn. 73. But though He is in all things His Image, this implies some exception, for else He would not be like or equal, but the same. "Non est æqualitas in dissimilibus, nec similitudo est intra unum." ibid. 72. Hence He is the Father's image in all things except in being the Father, εἰκὼν φυσικὴ καὶ ἀπαράλλακτος κατὰ πάντα ὅμοια τῷ πατρὶ, πλὴν τῆς ἀγεννησίας καὶ τῆς πατρότητος. Damasc. de Imag. iii. 18, p. 354. vid. also Basil. contr. Eun. ii. 28. Theod. Inconfus. p. 91. Basil. Ep. 38, 7 fin. For the Son is the Image of the Father, not as Father, but as God. The Arians on the other hand, objecting to the phrase "unvarying image," asked why the Son was not in consequence a Father, and the beginning of a θεογονία. vid. Athan. Orat. i. § 14, 21. Eunom. in Cyril. Thes. pp. 22, 23.

¶ The characteristic of Arianism in all its shapes was the absolute separation of Father from Son. It considered Them as two οὐσίαι, like perhaps, but not

really one; this was their version of the phrase τέλειος
ἐκ τελείου. Semi-Arians here agreed with Arians.
When the Semi-Arians came nearest to orthodoxy in
words, it was the περιχώρησις that was the test whether
they fell short in words alone, or in their theological
view.

Ὁμοούσιος.

THE term ὁμοούσιος, *one in substance* or *consubstantial,* was accepted as a symbol, for securing the doctrine of our Lord's divinity, first by the infallible authority of the Nicene Council, and next by the experimental assent and consent of Christendom, wrought out in its behalf by the events of the prolonged Arian controversy.

It had had the mischance in the previous century of being used by heretics in their own sense, and of incurring more or less of suspicion and dislike from the Fathers in the great Council of Antioch, A.D. 264—272, though already in use in the Alexandrian Church; but, when the momentous point in dispute, the divinity of the Son, was once thoroughly discussed and understood, it was forced upon the mind of theologians that the reception or rejection of this term was the difference between Catholic truth and Arianism.

¶ "We were aware," says Eusebius to his people, "that, even among the ancients, some learned and illustrious Bishops and writers have used the term 'one in substance,' in their theological teaching concerning the Father and Son." And Athanasius in like manner, ad Afros 6, speaks of "testimony of ancient Bishops about 130 years since;" and in de Syn. § 43, of "long before" the Council of Antioch. Tertullian,

Prax. 13 fin., has the translation "unius substantiæ," (vid. Lucifer de non Parc. p. 218,) as he has "de substantia Patris," in Prax. 4, and Origen perhaps used the word, vid. Pamph. Apol. 5, and Theognostus and the two Dionysius's, Decr. § 25, 26. And before them Clement had spoken of the ἔνωσις τῆς μοναδικῆς οὐσίας, "the union of the single substance," vid. Le Quien in Damasc. Fid. Orth. i. 8. Novatian too has "per substantiæ communionem," de Trin. 31. vid. Athan. ad Afros 5, 6. ad Serap. ii. 5. S. Ambrose tells us, that a Letter written by Eusebius of Nicomedia, in which he said, "If we call Him true Son of the Father and uncreate, then are we granting that He is one in substance, ὁμοούσιον," determined the Council on the adoption of the term. de Fid. iii. n. 125. He had disclaimed "of the substance," in his Letter to Paulinus. Theod. Hist. i. 4. Arius, however, had disclaimed ὁμοούσιον already, Epiph. Hær. 69, 7, and again in the Thalia. Gibbon's untenable assertion has been already observed upon, vid. *Nicene Tests*, that the Council was at a loss for a test, and that on Eusebius's "ingenuously confessing that his ὁμοούσιος was incompatible with the principles of [his] theological system, the *fortunate opportunity* was eagerly embraced by the Bishops," as if they were bent at all hazards, and without reference to the real and substantial agreement or disagreement of themselves and the Arians, to find some word which might accidentally serve to exclude the latter from communion.

¶ When the Semi-Arians objected that the Council of Antioch, 264—272, determined that the Son is

not consubstantial with the Father, de Syn. § 43—45,
Athan. answered in explanation that Paul of Samosata took the word in a material sense, as indeed
Arius did, calling it the doctrine of Manes and Hieracas. S. Basil, contr. Eunom. i. 19, agrees with Athan.,
but S. Hilary on the contrary reports that Paul himself accepted it, i.e. in a Sabellian sense, and therefore
the Council rejected it. "Male homoüsion Samo-
satenus confessus est, sed numquid melius Arii nega-
verunt?" de Syn. 86. Doubtless, however, both reasons
told in causing its rejection. But Montfaucon and
Bull consider it a difficulty. Hence, it would seem, the
former in his *Nova Collectio*, t. ii. p. 19, renders οὐκοῦν
by *ergo non;* he had not inserted *non* in his edition of
Athanasius.

¶ The objections made to the word ὁμοούσιον were, 1.
that it was not in Scripture; 2. that it had been disowned by the Antiochene Council against Paul of
Samosata; 3. that it was of a material nature, and belonged to the Manichees; 4. or that it was of a
Sabellian tendency; 5. that it implied that the divine
substance was distinct from God.

¶ The Eusebians tried to establish a distinction between ὁμοούσιον and ὁμοιούσιον, "one in substance"
and "like in substance," of this sort; that the former
belonged to things material, and the latter to immaterial, Soz. iii. 18, a remark which in itself was quite
sufficient to justify the Catholics in insisting on the
former term. For the heretical party, starting with
the notion in which their heresy in all its shades consisted, that the Son was a distinct being from the

Father, and appealing to (what might be plausibly maintained) that spirits are incommensurable with one another, or that each is *sui similis*, concluded that "*like* in substance" was the only term which would express the relation of the Son to the Father. Here then the word " one in substance " did just enable the Catholics to join issue with them, as exactly expressing what Catholics wished to express, viz. that there was no such distinction between Them as made the term "like" necessary, but that Their relation to Each Other was *analogous* to that of a material offspring to a material parent, or that as material parent and off-spring are individuals under one common *species,* so the Eternal Father and Son are Persons under one common *individual substance.*

" The East," says Sozomen, " in spite of its being in dissension after the Antiochene Council " of the De-dication, " and thenceforth openly dissenting from the Nicene faith, in reality, I think, concurred in the sentiment of the majority, and with them con-fessed the Son to be of the Father's substance ; but from contentiousness certain of them fought against the term ' One in substance;' some, as I conjecture, having originally objected to the word . . . others from habit . . . others, aware that the resistance was unsuitable, leaned to this side or that to gratify parties; and many thought it weak to waste themselves in such strife of words, and peaceably held to the Nicene decision." Hist. iii. 13.

Athan. is very reserved in his use of the word ὁμοούσιον in these three Orations. Indeed I do not recollect his using it but once, Orat. i. § 9, and that in what is almost a confession of faith. Instead he uses ὅμοιος κατὰ πάντα, ὅμοιος κατ᾽ οὐσίαν, ὁμοφυὴς, &c.

Ὀνόματα.

THE various titles of the Second Divine Person are at once equivalent and complementary to each other. Son, Word, Image, all imply relation, and suggest and teach that attribute of supereffluence which is one of the perfections of the Divine Being. (vid. *Father Almighty*.)

" The Son of God, as may be learnt from the divine oracles themselves, is Himself the Word of God, and the Wisdom, and the Image, and the Hand, and the Power; for God's Offspring is one, and of the generation from the Father these titles are tokens. For if you say the Son, you have declared what is from the Father by nature; and if you imagine the Word, you are thinking again of what is from Him, and what is inseparable; and, speaking of Wisdom, again you mean nothing less, what is not from without, but from Him and in Him; and if you name the Power and the Hand, again you speak of what is proper to substance; and, speaking of the Image, you signify the Son; for what else is like God but the offspring from Him? Doubtless the things, which came to be through *the Word*, these are *founded in Wisdom;* and what are *laid in Wisdom*, these are all made by the Hand, and came to be through the Son." Decr. § 17.

¶ As Sonship is implied in "Image" (art. *Son*), so it

is implied in "Word" and "Wisdom." For instance,
"Especially is it absurd to name the Word, yet deny
Him to be Son, for, if the Word be not from God,
reasonably might they deny Him to be Son; but if He
is from God, how see they not that what exists from
anything is son of him from whom it is?" Orat. iv.
15. Again, ἀεὶ θεὸς ἦν καὶ υἱός ἐστι, λόγος ὤν. Orat.
iii. 29 init. υἱὸς τίς ἢ ὁ λόγος; de Decr. 17. And still
more pointedly, εἰ μὴ υἱός, οὐδὲ λόγος, Orat. iv. 24 fin.
And so "Image" is implied in Sonship; "being Son
of God, He must be like Him," ii. § 17. It is implied
in "Word;" ἐν τῇ ἰδίᾳ εἰκόνι, ἥτις ἐστὶν ὁ λόγος αὐτοῦ.
§ 82, also 34 fin. On the contrary, the very root
of heretical error was the denial that these titles implied each other.

¶ All the titles of the Son of God are consistent
with each other, and variously represent one and the
same Person. "Son" and "Word" denote His de-
rivation; "Word" and "Image," His Likeness;
"Word" and "Wisdom," His immateriality; "Wisdom" and "Hand," His co-existence. "What else is
Like God, but His offspring from Him?" de Decr. § 17.
"If He is not Son, neither is He Image." Orat. ii.
§ 2. "How is there Word and Wisdom, unless there
be a proper Offspring of His substance?" ii. § 22. vid.
also Orat. i. § 20, 21, and at great length Orat. iv.
§ 20, &c. vid. also Naz. Orat. 30, 20. Basil. contr.
Eunom. i. 18. Hilar. de Trin. vii. 11. August. in
Joann. xlviii. 6, and in Psalm 44, (45,) 5.

¶ It is sometimes erroneously supposed that such
illustrations as these are intended to *explain* how the

Sacred Mystery in question is possible, whereas they are merely intended to show that the words we use concerning it are not *self-contradictory*, which is the objection most commonly brought against them. To say that the doctrine of the Son's generation does not trench upon the Father's perfection and immutability, or negative the Son's eternity, seems at first sight inconsistent with what the words Father and Son mean, till another image is adduced, such as the sun and radiance, in which that alleged inconsistency can be conceived to exist in fact. Here one image corrects another; and the accumulation of images is not, as is often thought, the restless and fruitless effort of the mind to *enter into the Mystery*, but is a *safeguard* against any one image, nay, any collection of images, being supposed *adequate*. If it be said that the language used concerning the sun and its radiance is but popular, not philosophical, so again the Catholic language concerning the Holy Trinity may, nay, must be economical, not exact, conveying the truth, not in the tongues of angels, but under human modes of thought and speech. vid. supr. articles *Illustrations*, p. 174, and *Economical Language*, p. 94.

¶ It is a view familiar to the Fathers, that in this consists our Lord's Sonship, that He is the Word, or as S. Augustine says, " Christum ideo Filium quia Verbum." Aug. Ep. 102, 11. "If God is the Father of a Word, why is not He which is begotten a Son?" de Decr. § 17. "If I speak of Wisdom, I speak of His Offspring." Theoph. ad Autolyc. i. 3. " The Word, the genuine Son of Mind." Clem. Protrept.

p. 78. One or two additional references are given in the article *Word*, p. 337.

¶ It is usual with the Fathers to use the two terms "Son" and "Word" to guard and complete the ordinary sense of each other. Their doctrine is that our Lord is both, in a certain transcendent, prototypical, and singular sense; that in that high sense they are coincident with one another; that they are applied to human things by an accommodation, as far as these are shadows of Him to whom properly they really belong; that, being but partially realized on earth, the ideas gained from the earthly types are but imperfect; that in consequence if any one of them is used exclusively of Him, it tends to introduce wrong ideas respecting Him; but that their respective imperfections, as lying on different sides, when used together correct each other. The term Son, used by itself, was abused into Arianism, and the term Word into Sabellianism; the term Son might be accused of introducing material notions, and the term Word of suggesting imperfection and transitoriness. Each of them corrected the other. "Scripture," says Athan., "joining the two, has said 'Son,' that the natural and true Offspring of the Substance may be preached; but, that no one may understand a human offspring, therefore, signifying His substance a second time, it calls Him Word, and Wisdom, and Radiance." Orat. i. § 28.

Vid. also iv. § 8. Euseb. contr. Marc. ii. 4, p. 54. Isid. Pel. Ep. iv. 141. So S. Cyril says that we learn "from His being called Son that He is from Him, τὸ ἐξ αὐτοῦ; from His being called Wisdom and

Word, that He is in Him," τὸ ἐν αὐτῷ. Thesaur. iv.
p. 31. However, S. Athanasius observes, that properly speaking the one term implies the other, i. e. in
its fulness. "Since the Son's Being is from the Father,
therefore It is in the Father." Orat. iii. § 3. "If
not Son, not Word either; and if not Word, not Son.
For what is from the Father is Son; and what is from
the Father, but the Word? &c." Orat. iv. § 24 fin.
On the other hand the heretics accused Catholics of
inconsistency, or of a union of opposite errors, because
they accepted all the Scripture images together. But
Vigilius of Thapsus says, that "error bears testimony
to truth, and the discordant opinions of misbelievers
blend in concordance in the rule of orthodoxy." contr.
Eutych. ii. init. "Grande miraculum, ut expugnatione
sui veritas confirmetur." ibid. 3. vid. also i. init.
and Eulogius, ap. Phot. 225, p. 759.

¶ Every illustration, as being incomplete on one or
other side of it, taken by itself, tends to heresy. The
title Son by itself suggests a second God, as the title
Word a mere attribute, and the title Minister a creature. All heresies are partial views of the truth, and
are wrong, not so much in what they say, as in what
they deny. The truth, on the other hand, is a positive
and comprehensive doctrine, and in consequence necessarily mysterious and open to misconception. When
Athan. implies that the Eternal Father is in the Son,
though remaining what He is, as a man in his child,
he is intent only upon the point of the Son's con-
naturality and co-equality, which the Arians denied. In
like manner he says in a later Discourse, "In the Son

the Father's godhead is beheld. The Emperor's countenance and form are in His Image, and the countenance of His Image is in the Emperor. For the Emperor's likeness in His Image is a definitive likeness, ἀπαράλλακτος, so that he who looks upon the Image, in it sees the Emperor, and again he who sees the Emperor, recognizes that He is in the Image. The Image then might say, 'I and the Emperor are one.' " Orat. iii. § 5. And thus the Auctor de Trin. refers to "Peter, Paul, and Timothy having three subsistencies and one humanity." i. p. 918. S. Cyril even seems to deny that each individual man may be considered a separate substance, except as the Three Persons are such. Dial. i. p. 409; and S. Gregory Nyssen is led to say that, strictly speaking, the abstract *man*, which is predicated of separate individuals, is still one, and this with a view of illustrating the Divine Unity. ad Ablab. t. 2, p. 449. vid. Petav. de Trin. iv. 9.

¶ The title "Word" implies the ineffable mode of the Son's generation, as distinct from *material* parallels, vid. Gregory Nyssen, contr. Eunom. iii. p. 107. Chrysostom in Joan. Hom. 2. § 4. Cyril Alex. Thesaur. 5, p. 37. Also it implies that there is but *One* Son. vid. Orat. i. § 16. "As the Origin is one substance, so its Word and Wisdom are one, substantial and subsisting." Athan. Orat. iv. 1 fin.

¶ Vid. *passim*. All these titles, "Word, Wisdom, Light," &c. serve to guard the title "Son" from any notions of parts or dimensions, e. g. "He is not composed of parts, but being impassible and single, He is impassibly and indivisibly Father of the Son ...

for ... the Word and Wisdom is neither creature, nor part of Him whose Word He is, nor an offspring passibly begotten." Orat. i. § 28.

¶ As the Arians took the title Son in that part of its earthly sense in which it did not apply to our Lord, so they misinterpreted the title Word also; which denoted the Son's immateriality and indivisible presence in the Father, but did not express His perfection. vid. Orat. ii. § 34—36. "As our word belongs to us and is from us, and not a work external to us, so also the Word of God is proper to Him and from Him, and is not made, *yet not as the word of man,* else one must consider God as man. Men have many words," &c. Orat. ii. § 36. vid. art. *Word.*

¶ The name of Image was of great importance in correcting heterodox opinions as to the words Son and Word, which were propagated in the Ante-Nicene times, and in keeping their economical sense in the right direction. A son who had a beginning, and a word which was spoken and over, were in no sense an " Image " of the Eternal and All-perfect God.

'Οργανον,

Instrument. This word, which is rightly used of our Lord's manhood relatively to His Divine Person (τούτῳ χρώμενος ὀργάνῳ, Orat. iii. § 31, and ὄργανον πρὸς τὴν ἐνέργειαν καὶ τὴν ἔκλαμψιν τῆς θεότητος, 53), is simply heretical if taken to express the relation of His Divine Person towards His Father. In the latter relation the term is inapplicable, unless He " was different from the Father in nature and substance." Decr. § 23. vid. Basil. de Sp. S. 19 fin. In this Arians, Socr. i. 6, Eusebius, Eccl. Theol. i. 8, and Anomœans would agree. At the same time, doubtless, some early writers use it of our Lord's Divine Nature, though not in a heretical sense. vid. art. *Mediation.*

¶ As it was abused by the Arians to mean a servant or ὑπουργὸς, as if our Lord was a mere creature, so it was afterwards used heretically in the doctrine of the Incarnation by the Apollinarians, who looked on our Lord's manhood as merely a *manifestation* of God. vid. καταπέτασμα. Thus σχῆμα ὀργανικὸν in Athan. Apol. i. 2, 15, also a parallel in Euseb. Laud. Const. 13, p. 536. However, it is used freely by Athan., e. g. Orat. iii. 31, 53, as above, and Incarn. 8, 9, 43, 44. And he uses the words πρὸς φανέρωσιν καὶ γνῶσιν, 41 fin., but he also insists upon our Lord's coming being not merely for manifestation, else He might have come in a higher nature. ibid. 8. vid. also 44. It may be added that φανέρωσις is a Nestorian as well as Eutychian idea; vid. Orat. iii. § 30, Facund. Tr. Cap. ix. 2, 3, and the Syrian use of *parsopa*, Asseman. Bibl. Orient. t. 4, p. 219. Thus both parties really denied the Atonement.

'Ορθός.

WHAT is strange to ears accustomed to Protestant modes of arguing, S. Athanasius does not simply expound Scripture, rather he vindicates it from the imputation of its teaching any but true doctrine. It is ever ὀρθὸς, he says, that is, orthodox ; I mean, he takes it for granted that a tradition exists, as a standard, with which Scripture must, and with which it doubtless, does agree, and of which it is the written confirmation and record.

In Orat. ii. § 44, he says, "We have gone through thus much before coming to the passage in the Proverbs, that they may rightly read what admits in truth of a sound (ὀρθὴν) interpretation," as if the authoritative interpretation required to be applied to Scripture, before we could assume that the doctrine conveyed by it was orthodox. And so μετ' εὐσεβείας just below. Such phrases are frequent in Athan., e. g. τὴν διάνοιαν εὐσεβῆ καὶ λίαν ὀρθὴν, de Decr. 13. καλῶς καὶ ὀρθῶς, Orat. iv. 31, γέγραπται μάλα ἀναγκαίως, de Decr. 14. εἰκότως, Orat. ii. 44. iii. 53. τὴν διάνοιαν ἐκκλησιαστικὴν, Orat. i. 44 init. τὸν σκοπὸν τὸν ἐκκλησιαστικὸν, Orat. iii. 58. ἡ διάνοια ἔχει τὴν αἰτίαν εὔλογον, iii. 7 fin. vid. also Orat. i. 37 init. 46. ii. 1, 9 init. 12, 53, iii. 1, 18, 19, 35, 37. iv. 30.

¶ Vid. art. *Rule of Faith.* This illustrates what he

means when he says that certain texts have a " good,"
" pious," "orthodox" sense, i. e. they can be interpreted (in spite, if so be, of appearances) in harmony
with the Regula Fidei.   And so, τὸ ἐν ταῖς παροιμίαις
ῥητὸν, ὀρθὴν ἔχον καὶ αὐτὸ τὴν διάνοιαν. Orat. ii. § 44.
ἤρκει ταῦτα πρὸς ἀπόδειξιν ὀρθὴν εἶναι τὴν τοῦ ῥητοῦ
διάνοιαν. ibid. § 77. τὸ τοίνυν λεγόμενον ὑπὸ τοῦ
μακαρίου Πέτρου ὀρθόν. iv. § 35. vid. also iii. 7, &c. &c.

Οὐσία, ὄν.

Usia, *substance.* The word οὐσία in its Greek or
Aristotelic sense seems to have stood for an individual
substance, numerically one, which is predicable of
nothing but itself. Improperly, it stood for a species or
genus, vid. Petav. de Trin. iv. 1. § 2, but, as Anastasius
observes in many places of his *Viæ dux,* Christian
theology innovated on the sense of Aristotelic terms.
vid. c. 1, p. 20. c. 6, p. 96. c. 9, p. 150. c. 17, p. 308.
There is some difficulty in determining *how* it innovated. Anastasius and Theorian, (Hodeg. 6. Legat. ad
Arm. pp. 441, 2,) say that it takes οὐσία to mean an
universal or species, but this is nothing else than the
second or improper Greek use. Rather, in speaking of
God, it takes the word in a sense of its own, such as we
have no example of in creation, of a Being numerically
one, subsisting in three persons; so that the word is a
predicable, or in one sense *universal,* without ceasing
to be individual ; in which consists the mystery of the
Holy Trinity. However, heretics, who refused the
mystery, objected it to Catholics in its primary philosophical sense; and then, standing simply for an individual
substance, when applied to Father and Son, it either
implied the parts of a *material* subject, or it involved
no *real* distinction of persons, i. e. Sabellianism. The
former of these two alternatives is implied in Athan.'s
text by the "Greek use;" the latter by the same phrase

as used by the conforming Semi-Arians, A.D. 363. " Nor, as if any passion were supposed of the ineffable generation, is the term ' substance' taken by the Fathers, &c. nor *according to any Greek use*," &c. Socr. iii. 25. Hence such charges against Catholicism on the part of Arians as Alexander protests against, of *either* Sabellianism *or* Valentinianism, οὐκ ... ὥσπερ Σαβελλίῳ καὶ Βαλεντίνῳ δοκεῖ, &c. Theod. Hist. i. 3, p. 743. Hence Paul's argument against the Antio-chene Council in Athan.'s and in Hilary's report.

¶ By the substance of God we mean nothing more or less than God Himself. "If God be simple, as He is, it follows that in saying ' God' and naming ' Father,' we name nothing as if about (περὶ) Him, but signify His substance, and that alone." Decr. § 22.

In like manner de Synod. § 34. Also Basil, " The substance is not any one of things which do not attach, but is the very being of God." contr. Eunom. i. 10 fin. " The nature of God is no other than Himself, for He is simple and uncompounded." Cyril Thesaur. p. 59. "When we say the person of the Father, we say nothing else than the substance of the Father." August. de Trin. vii. 6. And so Numenius in Eusebius, " Let no one deride, if I say that the name of the Immaterial is substance and being." Præp. Evang. xi. 10.

¶ In many passages Athan. seems to make *usia* synonymous with *hypostasis*, but this mode of speaking only shows that the two terms had not their respective meanings so definitely settled and so familiarly received as afterwards. Its *direct* meaning is usually substance, though *indirectly* it came to imply sub-

sistence. He speaks of that Divine Essence which,
though also the Almighty Father's, is as simply and
entirely the Word's as if it were only His. Nay, even
when the Substance of the Father is spoken of in a sort
of contrast to that of the Son, as in the phrase οὐσία
ἐξ οὐσίας, (e. g. " His substance is the offspring of the
Father's substance." Syn. § 48, and ἐξ οὐσίας οὐσιώδης
καὶ ἐνούσιος, Orat. iv. 1,) harsh as such expressions are,
it is not accurate to say that οὐσία is used for subsistence or person, or that two οὐσίαι are spoken of
(vid. art. φύσις), except, that is, by Arians, as Eusebius (art. *Eusebius*). We find φύσις τοῦ λόγου, Orat. i.
§ 51 init., meaning His *usia* without including the idea
of His Person. vid. art. εἶδος.

Other passages may be brought, in which *usia* and
hypostasis seem to be synonymous, as Orat. iii. § 65.
"The Apostle proclaims the Son to be the very impress,
not of the Father's will, but of His *usia*, saying, 'the
impress of His *hypostasis ;*' and if the Father's *usia* and
hypostasis is not from will, it is very plain neither is from
will what belongs to the Father's *hypostasis*." And so
Orat. iv. § 1. " As there is one Origin, and therefore
one God, so one is that substance and subsistence
which indeed and truly and really is." And " The
Prophet has long since ascribed the Father's *hypostasis*
to Him." Orat. iv. § 33. And ἡ ὑπόστασις οὐσία ἐστί,
καὶ οὐδὲν ἄλλο σημαινόμενον ἔχει ἢ αὐτὸ τὸ ὄν. . . . .
ἡ γὰρ ὑπόστασις καὶ ἡ οὐσία ὕπαρξίς ἐστι. ad. Afros, 4.

For the meaning in the early Fathers of οὐσία,
ὑπόστασις, φύσις, and εἶδος, vid. " Theological Tracts,"
art. Μία φύσις.

Περιβολή.

ATHAN. seems to say, Decret. § 22, and so de Synod. § 34, which is very much the same passage, that there is nothing of quality (περὶ αὐτὸν) in God. Some Fathers, however, seem to say the reverse. E. g. Nazianzen lays down that " neither the immateriality of God, nor ingenerateness, present to us His substance." Orat. 28, 9. And S. Augustine, arguing on the word *ingenitus*, says, that " not everything which is said to be in God is said according to substance." de Trin. v. 6. And hence, while Athan. in the text denies that there are qualities or the like belonging to Him, περὶ αὐτὸν, it is still common in the Fathers to speak of qualities, as in the passage of S. Gregory just cited, in which the words περὶ θεὸν occur. There is no difficulty in reconciling these statements, though it would require more words than could be given to it here. Petavius has treated the subject fully in his work de Deo, i. 7—11, and especially ii. 3. When the Fathers say that there is no difference between the divine 'proprietates' and essence, they speak of the fact, considering the Almighty as He is; when they affirm a difference, they speak of Him as contemplated by us, who are unable to grasp the idea of Him as one and simple, but view His Divine nature as if *in projection*, (if such a word may be used,) and thus divided into substance and quality as man may be divided into genus and difference.

Πηγή.
Vid. *Father Almighty.*

Προβολή.

WHAT the Valentinian προβολὴ was, is described in Epiph. Hær. 31, 13. The Æons, wishing to show thankfulness to God, contributed together (ἐρανισα-μένους) whatever was most beautiful of each of them, and moulding these several excellencies into one, formed this Issue, προβαλέσθαι πρόβλημα, to the honour and glory of the Profound, βύθος, and they called this star and flower of the Pleroma, Jesus, &c. And so Tertullian, "a joint contribution, ex ære collatitio, to the honour and glory of the Father, ex omnium defloratione constructum," contr. Valent. 12. Accordingly Origen protests against the notion of προβολὴ, Periarch. iv. 28, p. 190, and Athanasius Expos. § 1. The Arian Asterius too considers προβολὴ to introduce the notion of τεκνογονία, Euseb. contr. Marc. i. 4, p. 20. vid. also Epiph. Hær. 72. 7. Yet Eusebius uses the word προβάλλεσθαι, Eccles. Theol. i. 8. On the other hand Tertullian uses it with a protest against the Valentinian sense. Justin has προβληθὲν γέννημα, Tryph. 62. And Nazianzen calls the Almighty Father προβολεὺς of the Holy Spirit. Orat. 29. 2. Arius introduces the word into his creed, Syn. § 14, as an *argumentum ad invidiam.* Hil. de Trin. vi. 9.

Πρωτότοκος.

Primogenitus, " First-born."

¶ Πρωτότοκος and *Primogenitus* are not exact equivalents, though Homer may use τίκτω for *gigno*. Primogenitus is never used in Scripture for Unigenitus. We never read there of the First-born of God, of the Father; but of the First-born of the creation, whether of the original creation or of the new.

¶ First-born, or the beginning, is used as an epithet of our Lord five times in Scripture, and in each case it is distinct in meaning from Only-begotten. It is a word of office, not of nature. 1. St. Paul speaks of His becoming, in His incarnation, the " First-born among many brethren," Rom. viii. 29; and he connects this act of mercy with their being conformed to His Image, and gifted with grace and glory. 2. He is "the First-born of the dead," Apoc. i. 5. 3. As also in Col. i. 18. 4. Col. i. 15. "The First-born of all creation," as *quasi* the efficient and the formal cause whereby the universe is born into a divine adoption. 5. St. Paul speaks of the Father's "bringing the First-born into the world." To these may be added, Apoc. iii. 14, "the beginning of the [new] creation of God." In none of these passages does the phrase "First-born of God" occur.

¶ Our Lord is in three distinct respects πρωτότοκος, First-born or Beginning, as the animating Presence of the Universe, as the Life of the Christian Church, as the first fruit and pledge and earnest of the Resurrection.

The Word never relates in Scripture to His divine nature itself. "It is nowhere written of Him in the Scriptures 'the First-born of God,' nor 'the creation of God,' but it is the words 'the Only begotten,' and 'Son,' and 'Word,' and 'Wisdom,' that signify His relation and His belonging to the Father. But 'First-born' implies descent to the creation. . . . The Same cannot be both Only-begotten and First-born, except in different relations; that is, Only-begotten, because of His generation from the Father, and First-born, because of His condescension to the creation, and to the brotherhood which He has extended to many." Orat. ii. § 62.

In like manner Augustine says that we must distinguish between the two titles "Only-begotten and First-born" that the Son may be with the Father Only-begotten, and First-born towards us. vid. Theol. Tracts, *Arianism*, § 9, circ. fin. And St. Thomas says, "In quantum solus est verus et naturalis Dei Filius, dicitur Unigenitus, . . in quantum vero per assimilationem ad ipsum alii dicuntur filii adoptivi, quasi metaphoricè dicitur esse Primogenitus." Part I. 41, art. 3, (t. 20.)

¶ It would be perhaps better to translate "first-born *to* the creature," to give Athan.'s idea; τῆς κτίσεως not being a partitive genitive, or πρωτότοκος a

superlative, (though he also so considers it,) but a
simple appellative and τῆς κτίσεως a common genitive
of relation, as " the king of a country," " the owner of a
house." " First-born of creation " is like " author,
type, life of creation." As, after calling our Lord in
His own nature " a light," we might proceed to say
that He was also " a light to the creation," or " Arch-
luminary," so He was not only the Eternal Son, but a
" Son to creation," an " archetypal Son." Hence St.
Paul goes on at once to say, " for *in* Him all things
were made," not simply " by and for," as at the end
of the verse; or as Athan. says, Orat. ii. § 63, " because
in Him the creation came to be." On the distinction of
διὰ and ἐν, referring respectively to the first and
second creations, vid. In illud Omn. 2.

¶ " His coming into the world," says Athan., " is
what makes Him called ' First-born ' of all; and thus
the Son is the Father's ' Only-begotten,' because He
alone is from Him, and He is the ' First-born of creation,' because of this adoption of all as sons." Thus
he considers that " first-born " is mainly a title, connected with the Incarnation, and also connected with our
Lord's office at the creation. (vid. parallel of Priesthood, art. *in voc.*) In each economy it has the same
meaning ; it belongs to Him as the type, idea, or
rule on which the creature was made or new-made,
and the life by which it is sustained. Both economies
are mentioned, Incarn. 13, 14. And so εἴκων καὶ τύπος
πρὸς ἀρετήν, Orat. i. 51. (vid. art. *Freedom*, supr. p. 127.)
And τύπον τινὰ λαβόντες and ὑπογραμμόν, iii. 20. vid.
also 21. ἐν αὐτῷ ἦμεν προτετυπωμένοι. ii. 76, init.

He came τύπον εἰκόνος ἐνθεῖναι. 78, init. τὴν τοῦ ἀρχετύπου πλάσιν ἀναστήσασθαι ἑαυτῷ. contr. Apol. ii. 5. Also κατεσφραγίσθημεν εἰς τὸ ἀρχέτυπον τῆς εἰκόνος. Cyr. in Joan. v. 12, p. 91. οἷον ἀπό τινος ἀρχῆς, Nyss. Catech. 16, p. 504, fin. And so again, as to the original creation, the Word is ἰδέα καὶ ἐνέργεια of all material things. Athen. Leg. 10. ἡ ἰδέα . . ὅπερ λόγον εἰρήκασι. Clem. Strom. v. 3. ἰδέαν ἰδεῶν καὶ ἀρχὴν λεκτέον τὸν πρωτότοκον πάσης κτίσεως. Origen. contr. Cels. vi. 64, fin. "Whatever God was about to make in the creature, was already in the Word, nor would be in the things, were it not in the Word." August. in Psalm. 44, 5. He elsewhere calls the Son, "ars quædam omnipotentis atque sapientis Dei, plena omnium rationum viventium incommutabilium." de Trin. vi. 11. And so Athan. says πρωτότοκος εἰς ἀπόδειξιν τῆς τῶν πάντων διὰ τοῦ υἱοῦ δημιουργίας καὶ υἱοποιήσεως. iii. 9, fin. vid. the contrast presented to us by the Semi-Arian Eusebius on the passage which Athan. is discussing, (Prov. viii. 22,) as making the Son, not the ἰδέα, but the external minister of the Father's ἰδέα (in art. *Eusebius*, supra). S. Cyril says on the contrary, "The Father shows the Son what He does Himself, *not* as if setting it before Him drawn out on a tablet, or teaching Him as ignorant; for He knows all things as God; but as depicting Himself whole in the nature of the Offspring," &c. in Joann. v. 20, p. 222.

῾Ρευστός.

VID. Decr. § 11 de Synod. § 51. Orat. i. § 15. 16. vid. also Orat. i. § 28 Bas. in Eun. ii. 23. ῥύσιν. *ibid.* ii. 6. Greg. Naz. Orat. 28. 22. Vid. contr. Gentes, § 41, where Athan., without reference to the Arian controversy, draws out the contrast between the Godhead and human nature. " The nature of things generated," as having its subsistence from nothing, " is of a *transitory* (ῥευστὸς, melting, dissolving, dissoluble) and feeble and mortal sort, considered by itself; seeing then that it was *transitory* and had no stay, lest this should come into effect, and it should be resolved into its original nothing, God governs and sustains it all by His own Word, who is Himself God," and who, he proceeds, § 42, " remaining Himself immovable with the Father, moves all things in His own consistence, as in each case it may seem fit to His Father." vid. Μετουσία, &c.

Συγκατάβασις.

" CONDESCENSION " of the Son. Vid. " Tracts, Theological, &c.," to which, on a subject too large for a Note, the reader is referred.

By this term Athanasius expresses that (so to say) stooping from the height of His Infinite Majesty, which is involved in the act of the Almighty's surrounding Himself with a created universe. This may of course be sometimes spoken of as the act of the Eternal Father, but is commonly and more naturally ascribed to the Only-begotten Son. Creation was the beginning of this condescension; but creation was but an inchoate act if without conservation accompanying it. The universe would have come into being one moment only to have come to nought the next, from its intrinsic impotence, and moreover from the unendurableness on the part of the finite of contrast with the Infinite, had not the Creator come to it also as a conservator.

"The Word," says Athanasius, " when in the beginning He framed the creatures, *condescended* to them, that it might be possible for them to come into being. For they could not have endured His absolute, unmitigated nature, and His splendour from the Father, unless, condescending with the Father's love for man, He had supported them, and brought them into subsistence." Orat. ii. 64. vid. art. ἄκρατος.

This conservation lay in a gift over and above nature, a gift of grace, a presence of God throughout the vast universe, as a principle of life and strength; and that Presence is in truth the indwelling in it of the Divine Word and Son, who thereby took His place permanently as if in the rank of creatures, and as their First-born and Head, thereby drawing up the whole circle of creatures into a divine adoption, whereby they are mere works no longer, but sons of God. He has thus, as it were, stamped His Image, His Sonship, upon all things according to their several measures, and became the archetype of creation and its life and goodness.

As then He is in His nature the Only Son of God, so is He by office First-born of all things and Eldest Son in the world of creatures. Vid. Πρωτότοκος.

Συμβεβηκός,

Or Accident. The point in which Arians and Sabellians agreed was that Wisdom was only an attribute,
not a Person, in the Divine nature, for both denied
the mystery of a Trinity in Unity. Hence St. Athanasius charges them with holding the Divine Nature
to be compounded of substance and quality or accident,
the latter being an envelopement or περιβολὴ or περὶ τὸν
θεόν. vid. as quoted below. Decr. § 22, and so Syn. § 34,
ἕξιν συμβαίνουσαν καὶ ἀποσυμβαίνουσαν. Orat. iii. § 65.
σύμβαμα. Euseb. Eccl. Theol. iii. p. 150. Also Or. ii.
§ 38. Serap. i. 26. Naz. Orat. 31, 15 fin. For περὶ
τὸν θεὸν, vid. Decr. § 22, de Syn. § 34. Orat. i. § 14.
27. ii. 45. iii. § 65.

¶ Thus Eusebius calls our Lord "the light throughout the universe, moving *round* (ἄμφι) the Father."
de Laud. Const. i. p. 501. It was a Platonic idea, which
he gained from Plotinus; whom he quotes speaking of
his second Principle as " radiance around, from Him
indeed, but from one who remains what He was; as
the sun's bright light circling around it, (περιθέον,)
ever generated from it, while the sun itself nevertheless remains." Evang. Præp. xi. 17. vid. Plotin. 4
Ennead. iv. c. 16.

Eusebius could afford to use Platonic language,

because he considered our Lord to be external to the
Divine Nature; hence he can say, (as Marcellus could
not,) by way of accusation against him, σύνθετον
εἰσῆγεν τὸν θεόν, οὐσίαν δίχα λόγου συμβεβηκὸς δὲ τῇ
οὐσίᾳ τὸν λόγον. Eccl. Theol. ii. 14, p. 121. However,
Athan. says the same of the Arians, vid. references,
supr. in this Article; also ad Afros. 8. Basil. Ep. 8, 3.
Cyril. Thes. p. 134. For the Sabellians vid. Ath. Orat.
iv. 2. perhaps Epiph. Hær. 73. p. 852. and Cyril.
Thes. p. 145. Basil. contr. Sabell. 1. Nyssen. App.
contr. Eunom. i. p. 67, &c. Max. Cap. de Carit. t. i.
p. 445. Damasc. F. O. i. 13. p. 151.

"If then any man conceives as if God were compound, so as to have accidents in His substance, or
any external envelopement, and to be encompassed, or
as if there were aught about Him which completes
the substance, so that when we say 'God,' or name
'Father,' we do not signify the invisible and incomprehensible substance, but something about it, then
let them complain of the Council's stating that the
Son was from the substance of God; but let them
reflect, that in thus considering they commit two
blasphemies; for they make God material, and they
falsely say that the Lord is not Son of the very Father,
but of what is about Him. But if God be simple, as
He is, it follows that in saying 'God' and naming
'Father,' we name nothing as if about Him, but
signify His substance itself." Athan. Decr. § 22.

And so elsewhere, he says, when resisting the
Arian and Sabellian notion that the wisdom of God is
only a quality in the Divine nature, "In that case God

will be compounded of substance and quality; for every quality is in a substance. And at this rate, whereas the Divine Unity (μονὰς) is indivisible, it will be considered compound, being separated into substance and accident." Orat. iv. 2. vid. also Orat. i. 36. This is the common doctrine of the Fathers. Athenagoras, however, speaks of God's goodness as an accident, "as colour to the body," "as flame is ruddy and the sky blue," Legat. 24. This, however, is but a verbal difference, for shortly before (23) he speaks of His being, τὸ ὄντως ὄν, and His unity of nature, τὸ μονοφυὲς, as in the number of ἐπισυμβεβηκότα αὐτῷ. Eusebius uses the word συμβεβηκὸς in the same way, Demonstr. Evang. iv. 3. And hence St. Cyril, in controversy with the Arians, is led by the course of their objections to observe, "There are cogent reasons for considering these things *as accidents*, συμβεβηκότα, in God, though they be not." Thesaur. p. 263.

The Τέλειον.

"PERFECT from Perfect" is often found in Catholic Creeds, and also, (with an evasion,) in Arian. "The Word who is perfect from the perfect Father." Orat. iii. § 52. "As radiance from light, so is He perfect Off-spring from perfect." ii. § 35, also iii. § 1 circ. fin. "One from One, Perfect from Perfect," &c. Hil. Trin. ii. 8. τέλειος τέλειον γεγέννηκεν, Epiph. Hær. 76, p. 945.

Not only the Son but the Father was ἀτελὴς, says Athan. 'if the Son were not eternal.' "He is rightly called the eternal Offspring of the Father, for never was the substance of the Father imperfect, that what belongs to it, should be added afterwards.... God's Offspring is eternal, because His nature is ever perfect. Orat. i. 14. A similar passage is found in Cyril. Thesaur. v. p. 42. Dial. ii. fin. This was retorting the objection; the Arians said, "How can God be ever perfect, who added to Himself a Son?" Athan. answers, "How can the Son be a later addition, since God is ever perfect?" vid. Greg. Nyssen. contr. Eunom. Append. p. 142. Cyril. Thesaur. x. p. 78. Also Origen, as quoted by Marcellus in Euseb. c. Marc. p. 22, εἰ γὰρ ἀεὶ τέλειος ὁ θεὸς .... τί ἀναβάλλεται; &c. As to the Son's perfection, Aetius objects, ap. Epiph. Hær. 76. p. 925, 6, that growth and consequent accession from without are essentially involved in the idea of Sonship;

whereas S. Greg. Naz. speaks of the Son as not ἀτελῆ πρότερον, εἶτα τέλειον, ὥσπερ νόμος τῆς ἡμετέρας γενέσεως. Orat. 20, 9 fin. In like manner, S. Basil argues against Eunomius, that the Son is τέλειος, because He is the Image, not as if copied, which is a gradual work, but as a χαρακτήρ, or impression of a seal, or as the knowledge communicated from master to scholar, which comes to the latter and exists in him perfect, without being lost to the former. contr. Eunom. ii. 16 fin.

¶ It need scarcely be said, that "perfect from perfect" is a symbol on which the Catholics laid stress, Athan. Orat. ii. 35. Epiph. Hær. 76, p. 945; but it admitted of an evasion. An especial reason for insisting on it in the previous centuries had been the Sabellian doctrine, which considered the title "Word," when applied to our Lord, to be adequately explained by the ordinary sense of the term, as a word spoken by us. vid. on the λόγος προφορικὸς, art. *Word*, a doctrine which led to the dangerous, often heretical, hypothesis that our Lord was first Word, and then Son. In consequence they insisted on His τὸ τέλειον, perfection, which became almost synonymous with His personality. Thus the Apollinarians e. g. denied that our Lord was *perfect* man, because His *personality* was not human. Athan. contr. Apoll. i. 2. Hence Justin, and Tatian, are earnest in denying that our Lord was a portion divided from the Divine Substance, οὐ κατ' ἀποτομὴν, &c. &c. Just. Tryph. 128. Tatian. contr. Græc. 5. And Athan. condemns the notion of the λόγος ἐν τῷ θεῷ ἀτελὴς, γεννηθεὶς τέλειος. Orat. iv. 11. The Arians then, as being the especial opponents of the Sabellians, insisted on nothing so much as our Lord's being a real, living, substantial, Word, (vid. Eusebius passim,) and they explained τέλειον as they explained away "real," art. *Arian tenets.* "The Father," says Acacius against Marcellus, "begat the Only-begotten, alone alone, and perfect perfect; for there is nothing imperfect in the Father, wherefore neither is there in the Son, but the Son's perfection is the genuine offspring of His perfection, and superperfection." ap. Epiph. Hær. 72, 7. Τέλειος then was a relative word, varying with the subject-matter, vid. Damasc. F. O. i. 8. p. 138.

¶ The Arians considered Father and Son to be two οὐσίαι, ὅμοιαι, but not ὁμοούσιαι. Their characteristic explanation of the word τέλειος was, "distinct," and "independent." When they said that our Lord was perfect God, they meant, "perfect, *in that sense in which* He is God"—i. e. as a secondary divinity.— Nay, in one point of view they would use the term of His divine Nature more freely than the Catholics sometimes used it. Thus Hippolytus e. g. though of course really holding His perfection from eternity as the Son, yet speaks of His *condescension* in coming upon earth as if a kind of completion of His Sonship, He becoming thus a Son a second time; whereas the Arians holding no real condescension or assumption of a really new state, could not hold that our Lord was in any respect essentially other than He had been before the Incarnation. "Nor was the Word," says Hippolytus, "before the flesh and by Himself, perfect Son, though being perfect Word, [as] being Only-begotten ; nor could the flesh subsist by itself without the Word, because that in the Word it has its consistence: thus then He was manifested One perfect Son of God." contr. Noet. 15.

Τριάς,

Vid. *Trinity.*

THE word τριὰς, translated Trinity, is first used by Theophilus ad Autol. ii. 15. Gibbon remarks that the doctrine of " a numerical rather than a generical unity," which has been explicitly put forth by the Latin Church, is "favoured by the Latin language; τριὰς seems to excite the idea of substance, *trinitas* of qualities." ch. 21. note 74. It is certain that the Latin view of the sacred truth, when perverted, becomes Sabellianism; and that the Greek, when perverted, becomes Arianism; and we find Arius arising in the East, Sabellius in the West. It is also certain that the word Trinitas is properly abstract; and expresses τριὰς or " a three," only in an ecclesiastical sense. But Gibbon does not seem to observe that Unitas is abstract as well as Trinitas; and that we might just as well say in consequence, that the Latins held an abstract unity or a unity of qualities, while the Greeks by μονὰς taught the doctrine of " a one " or a numerical unity. "Singularitatem hanc dico, says S. Ambrose, quod Græcè μονότης dicitur; singularitas ad personam pertinet, unitas ad naturam." de Fid. v. 3. It is important, however, to understand, that " Trinity " does not mean the *state* or *condition* of being three, as humanity is the condition of being man, but is synonymous with " three persons." Humanity does not exist and cannot be addressed, but the Holy Trinity is a three, or a unity which exists in three. Apparently from not considering this, Luther and Calvin objected to the word Trinity. "It is a common prayer," says Calvin, " ' Holy Trinity, one God, have mercy on us.' It displeases me, and savours throughout of barbarism." Ep. ad Polon. p. 796. Tract. Theol.

Ὑιοπάτωρ,

THIS word is made the symbol of the Noetians or Sabellians by both Catholics and Arians, as if their doctrine involved or avowed Patripassianism, or that the Father suffered. Without entering upon the controversy raised by Beausobre (Hist. Manich. iii. 6. § 7, &c.), Mosheim (Ant. Constant. sæc. ii. § 68, iii. 32.), and Lardner (Cred. part ii. ch. 41.), on the subject, we may refer to the following passages for the use of the term. It is ascribed to Sabellius, Ammon. in Caten. Joan. i. 1, p. 14; to Sabellius and perhaps Marcellus, Euseb. Eccl. Theol. ii. 5; to Marcellus, Cyr. Hier. Catech. xv. 9, also iv. 8, xi. 16; to Sabellians, Athan. Expos. F. 2, and 7 Can. Constant. and Greg. Nyssen. contr. Eun. xii. p. 305; to certain heretics, Cyril Alex. in Joann. v. 31, p. 243, Epiph. Hær. 73, 11 fin.; to Praxeas and Montanus, Mar. Merc. p. 128; to Sabellius, Cæsar. Dial. i. p. 550; to Noetus, Damasc. Hær. 57.

αὐτὸς ἑαυτοῦ πατὴρ is used by Athan. Orat. iv. § 2. also vid. Hipp. contr. Noet. 7. Euseb. in Marc. pp. 42, 61, 106, 119, υἱὸν ἑαυτοῦ γίνεσθαι. supr. Orat. iii. 4 init. "Ipsum sibi patrem," &c. Auct. Præd. (ap. Sirmond. Opp. t. i. p. 278, ed. Ven.) Mar. Marc. t. 2. p. 128, ed. 1673 as above. Greg. Boet. (ap. Worm. Hist. Sabell. p. 17.) Consult Zach.

et Apoll. ii. 11, (ap. Dach. Spicil. t. i. p. 25.) Porphyry uses αὐτοπάτωρ, but by a strong figure, Cyril. contr. Julian. i. p. 32. vid. Epiphan. in answer to Aetius on this subject, Hær. 76, p. 937. It must be observed that several Catholic fathers seem to countenance such expressions, as Zeno Ver. and Marius Vict., not to say S. Hilary and S. Augustine. vid. Thomassin de Trin. 9. For υἱοπάτωρ, add to the above references, Nestor. Serm. 12. ap. Mar. Merc. t. 2. p. 87. and Ep. ad Martyr. ap. Bevereg. Synod. t. 2. Not. p. 100.

Χριστομάχος,

Vid. θεομάχος.

THE END.

CARDINAL NEWMAN'S WORKS.

1. SERMONS.

1—8. PAROCHIAL AND PLAIN SERMONS. (*Rivingtons.*)
9. SERMONS ON SUBJECTS OF THE DAY. (*Rivingtons.*)
10. UNIVERSITY SERMONS. (*Rivingtons.*)
11. SERMONS TO MIXED CONGREGATIONS. (*Burns and Oates.*)
12. OCCASIONAL SERMONS. (*Burns and Oates.*)

2. TREATISES.

13. ON THE DOCTRINE OF JUSTIFICATION. (*Rivingtons.*)
14. ON THE DEVELOPMENT OF CHRISTIAN DOCTRINE. (*Pickering.*)
15. ON THE IDEA OF A UNIVERSITY. (*Pickering.*)
16. ON THE DOCTRINE OF ASSENT. (*Burns and Oates.*)

3. ESSAYS.

17. TWO ESSAYS ON MIRACLES. 1. Of Scripture. 2. Of Ecclesiastical History. (*Pickering.*)

18. DISCUSSIONS AND ARGUMENTS. 1. How to accomplish it. 2. The Antichrist of the Fathers. 3. Scripture and the Creed. 4. Tamworth Reading-Room. 5. Who's to blame? 6. An Argument for Christianity. (*Pickering.*)

19, 20. ESSAYS CRITICAL AND HISTORICAL. TWO VOLUMES WITH NOTES. 1. Poetry. 2. Rationalism. 3. Apostolical Tradition. 4. De la Mennais. 5. Palmer on Faith and Unity. 6. St. Ignatius. 7. Prospects of the Anglican Church. 8. The Anglo-American Church. 9. Countess of Huntingdon. 10. Catholicity of the Anglican Church. 11. The Antichrist of Protestants. 12. Milman's Christianity. 13. Reformation of the Eleventh Century. 14. Private Judgment. 15. Davison. 16. Keble. (*Pickering.*)

4. HISTORICAL.

21—23. THREE VOLUMES. 1. The Turks. 2. Cicero. 3. Apollonius. 4. Primitive Christianity. 5. Church of the Fathers. 6. St. Chrysostom. 7. Theodoret. 8. St. Benedict. 9. Benedictine Schools. 10. Universities. 11. Northmen and Normans. 12. Medieval Oxford. 13. Convocation of Canterbury. (*Pickering.*)

5. THEOLOGICAL.

24. THE ARIANS OF THE FOURTH CENTURY. (*Pickering.*)

25, 26. ANNOTATED TRANSLATION OF ATHANASIUS. TWO VOLUMES. (*Pickering.*)

27. TRACTS. 1. Dissertatiunculæ. 2. On the Text of the Seven Epistles of St. Ignatius. 3. Doctrinal Causes of Arianism. 4. Apollinarianism. 5. St. Cyril's Formula. 6. Ordo de Tempore. 7. Douay Version of Scripture. (*Pickering.*)

6. POLEMICAL.

28, 29. VIA MEDIA. TWO VOLUMES WITH NOTES. 1. Vol. Prophetical Office of the Church. 2. Vol. Occasional Letters and Tracts. (*Pickering.*)

30, 31. DIFFICULTIES OF ANGLICANS. TWO VOLUMES. 1. Vol. Twelve Lectures. 2. Vol. Letters to Dr. Pusey concerning the Bl. Virgin, and to the Duke of Norfolk in Defence of the Pope and Council. (*Burns and Oates, and Pickering.*)

32. PRESENT POSITION OF CATHOLICS IN ENGLAND. (*Burns and Oates.*)

33. APOLOGIA PRO VITÂ SUÂ. (*Longmans.*)

7. LITERARY.

34. VERSES ON VARIOUS OCCASIONS. (*Burns and Oates.*)

35. LOSS AND GAIN. (*Burns and Oates, and Pickering.*)

36. CALLISTA. (*Burns and Oates.*)

¶ It is scarcely necessary to say that the Author submits all that he has written to the judgment of the Church, whose gift and prerogative it is to determine what is true and what is false in religious teaching.

www.ingramcontent.com/pod-product-compliance
Lightning Source LLC
Chambersburg PA
CBHW052331110726
47901CB00005B/1198